Homo Mysticus

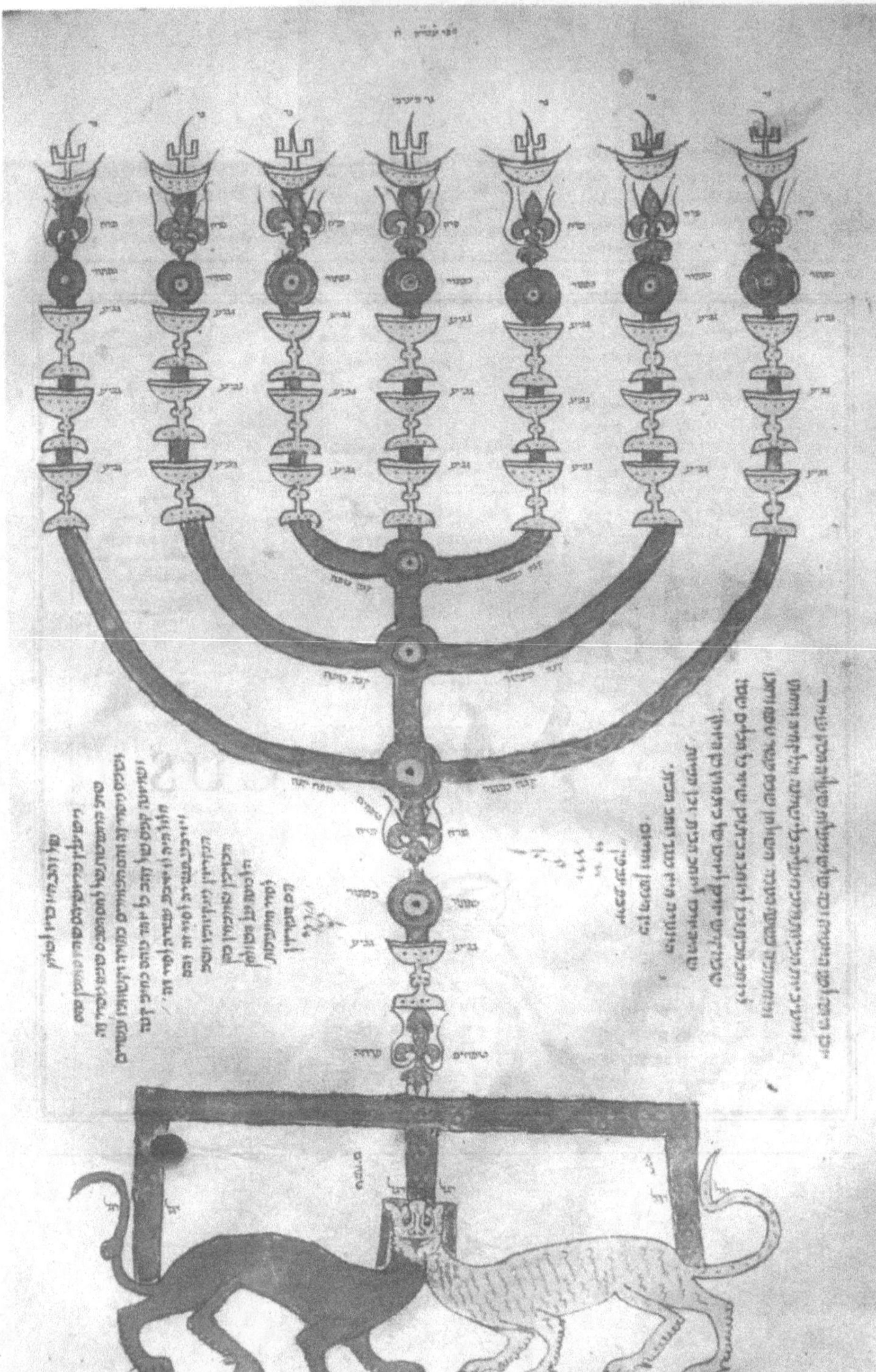

Maimonides, *Misneh Torah* (MS Rab 350, fol. 274). *Courtesy of the Library of the Jewish Theological Seminary of America.*

Homo Mysticus

A Guide to Maimonides's *Guide for the Perplexed*

José Faur

Syracuse University Press

First Edition 1998

99 00 01 02 03 04 6 5 4 3 2 1

Library of Congress Cataloging-in-Publication Data

Faur, José.
Homo mysticus : a guide to Maimonides's Guide for the perplexed / José Faur.
p. cm.
Includes bibliographical references and index.
ISBN 0-8156-2780-7 (cloth :paper).—ISBN 0-8156-2781-5 (pbk. : paper)
1. Maimonides, Moses. 1135–1204. Dalālat al-ḥā'irīn.
2. Mysticism—Judaism. 3. Maimonides, Moses, 1135–1204—Contributions in mysticism. 4. Philosophy, Jewish. 5. Philosophy, Medieval. I. Title.
BM545.D35F38 1998
181'.06—DC21 98-17367

To the memory of my mother,
Aurora Sofia Joli de Faur ז״ל:
Always so sweet, always so wise

José Faur teaches Talmud at Bar-Ilan University and Law at the newly established Law School in Netanya, Israel. He has published numerous studies in the fields of Sephardica, Rabbinic literature and jurisprudence, linguistics, and critical theory. He is author of *In the Shadow of History: Jews and* Conversos *at the Dawn of Modernity* (1992), *Golden Doves with Silver Dots: Semiotics and Textuality in Rabbinic Tradition* (1986), and *Studies in the Mishne Tora* (1978, in Hebrew).

Contents

Preface
ix
Transliterated Characters
xiii
Introduction
1
Part One: Apophasis
The Dialectics of Apophatic Knowledge 20
Apophasis and Paradox 22
The Acquisition of Esoteric Instruction 24
Dissemination of Esoteric Knowledge 27
Hekhalot Literature and Rabbinic Esoterics 29
Subjectivity and Esoteric Insight 33
The Resolution of Unconcluded Subscripts 34
Descending Toward the Inner Sanctuary 35
The Realm of Subjectivity 38
At the Crossroads 42
The Epistle to the Student/Reader 47
The *Guide* in Function of *Meṭaṭron* 48
Part Two: Imagination
Deus Absconditus, Homo Absconditus 53
Apophasis and Imagination 56
Transference of Meaning 58
Imagination and the Loss of Individaul Freedom 62
The Epistemology of Reason and Imagination 65
Prophesy and the Epistemology of the Creative Mind 69
The Prophet's Reflective Consciousness 74
Anthropocentric Theology 79
Joining the Angelical Beings in Chorus and Dance 82

Part Three: Cosmology

Creation Ex Nihilo 89
In Search of the Ultimate Reality 94
The God of Reason 98
The Perimeters of Aristotelian Rationality 102
The Fault with Aristotle 105
At the Cutting Edge of Reason 109
The Realm of the Probable 111
Ma'aśe Bereshit 115
"A Kind of Madness" 119
Tilting on the Side of Creation Ex Nihilo 123

Part Four: Anthropology

Man Before Seth 127
Traces in the Soul 131
Palingenesis at Sinai 137
Annulling the Poison of the Primeval Snake 142
Witnessing Prophecy 147
Overcoming the Pagan Past 150
The Archetypes of Israel 155
The Moment of Mystical Illumination 160
The Demarcation of Cultures 163
Knowing by Virtue of Perfection 168
Training for Intellectual Worship 171
Up and Down Jacob's Ladder 173
At God's Service 178

Notes

183

Bibliography

249

Indexes

Index of Sources 263
Index of Names 266
Index of Principal Concepts and Terms 267

Preface

Quando no es lo que quiero.
Quiera yo lo que es:
Si pesar hé primero,
Plazer avré despues.

—R. Santob de Carrion,
Proverbios Morales

FOR REASONS THAT I CAN ONLY conceive of as providential, my grandfather, Joseph Faur זצ"ל, wanted me to learn Arabic and taught me the rudiments of that language when I was a child. This opened for me the whole field of Judeo-Arabic literature, particularly that of Old Sepharad, which I was able to read in the original. The central figure of that tradition was Maimonides (1135/38–1204). I began reading the *Guide* in Hebrew when I was eighteen. One year later, while browsing in a bookstore, I found a copy of the Arabic original, *Dalalat al Ḥa'irin* (Ed. Isacchar Joel and Solomon Munk, Jerusalem, 1931). Ever since it has been an integral part of my library. The following pages contain ideas upon which I reflected while reading the *Guide* since those early years.

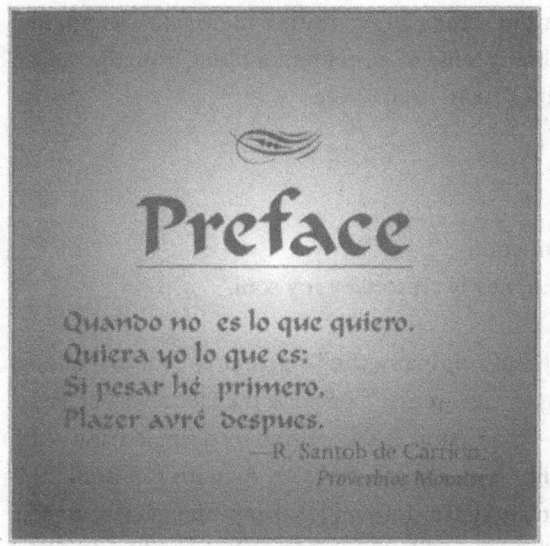

The purpose of this book, as of my preceding *Golden Doves with Silver Dots: Semiotics and Textuality in Rabbinic Tradition* (1986) is to apply to classical Jewish texts some of the ideas, perspectives, and methodologies developed in modern critical theory and poststructural analysis. Western intellectual tradition owes its creation to the splitting of the *logos*. In an inaugural debate between Gorgias and Socrates the logos was formally broken up into two categories, rhetoric and philosophy, each standing in hierarchical opposition to the other.[1] Aristotle, too, proceeded by breaking up *ontology*, "the only form of logic known in Pre-Aristotelian philosophy . . . into the elements Word (*logos*) and Thing (*on*)."[2] Thus, Western intellectual history is punctured by a series of opposing subdivisions, such as logic/metaphysics, physics/theology, and so on. The compartmentalization of knowledge into discrete categories, disjointed from one another, reflects a polytheistic view of reality, whereby every natural phenomenon—a storm, the wind, rain, the blossoming of a tree—is viewed as a disparate event, the direct manifestation of different gods. In modern times the splitting of the logos has led to what José Ortega y Gasset (1883–1955) called the "real disarticulation of knowledge."[3] The splitting of the logos affected the very integrity of speech. In a profound sense the task of the poet is to repair the breach and to restore the *word* to its original state. Referring to the overwhelming sense of alienation resulting from the breach word / thing, Juan Ramón Jiménez (1881–1956) wrote:

Que mi palabra sea
la cosa misma,
creada por mi alma nuevamente.[4]

"Let my word be the thing itself, newly created by my soul."

Vico (1668–1744) noted that originally, the "logos, or word, meant also deed to the Hebrews and thing to the Greeks."[5] Because the Hebrews perceived reality in monotheistic terms—as a cosmic Book written by a single hand—the *logos / dabar* did not split. Reality is essentially holistic. As with the Book, the various semiological elements integrate into an all-comprehensive semantic unit.[6] Thus, all facets of knowledge must be organically connected to the "tree of life" (Prv 3:18): they are either contained in the Book, or they branch off the Book as a *pirush* (commentary) to the Book. One of the designations for sages in rabbinic tradition is *ba'ale asupot* 'the authors of aggregate [knowledge]', that is, a type of wisdom that is *essentially* integrative.[7] Modern Jewish scholarship, inaugurated by *Wissenschaft des Judentums* (1819), grew amid a profound spiritual and intellectual alienation. It is essentially Oedipal and antibook. The methodology shears Jewish texts from their *literary* character, treating them as "documents" void of literary sense, and then applies to them the categories and subdivisions growing in the West as a consequence of the splitting of the logos.[8] A similar methodology affects the "scientific" study of Jewish Philosophy, Maimonidean texts in particular. Maimonides explicitly disclaimed any interest in, or preeminence on, either physics or theology: "The works written about these are sufficient, and if they are wanting in some of their aspects, whatever I would have to say about that particular subject would not be better than what has already been said."[9] Philosophers deal with ideas; Jewish thinkers deal with texts. For a philosopher the text is marginal to the idea. The inverse is true with Jewish thinkers. Yet the *Guide* is treated as if it were a book on philosophy.

The *Guide* is a work *on* critical theory, focusing on the *esoteric* elements of biblical and rabbinic literature. These elements belongs to a genre that the French designate *littérature fantastique.* The intention of this type of literature is to liberate the reader from the constants making up the ordinary world on behalf of a higher class of reality.[10] For Maimonides, too, the esoteric elements of the Scripture and rabbinic texts are to be read as the literature of the fantastic. The *Guide* is to help free the reader from conventional reading. Its purpose is "to elucidate the uncertainties of religion [the Tora] and to expose the truths that lay in her bosom which are above the comprehension of the masses (*jamhur*)."[11]

Naïve readers believe that the *Guide* is a literary unit with a beginning, an end, and a middle. Rather, it is a puzzle that can be resolved in a variety of ways: for every solution there is a countersolution, and for every proof there is a counterproof. The prose is chilling and moody, the wit ice-cold. The style is nonlinear, at times scintillating and exasperating. Abruptly, the road bifurcates, compelling the reader to make a critical decision either to pursue an avenue that may (or may not) lead from a linguistic suggestion to a shrewd, radical political analysis, finding at the end a trapdoor or to explore a perfunctory note, encoding, perhaps, an unresolved message. Following Maimonides's train of thought is like moving at a vertiginous speed along a labyrinth, branching up and down in all directions. Throughout the text are concealed ideas affecting the ebb and flow of moods and thoughts. Stark, primordial emotions insinuate themselves into the reader's consciousness. The *Guide* functions like a multifaceted mirror, reflecting distant, unmapped regions in the readers' psyches. What the reader finds at the conclusion of the road is a jazzy, kaleidoscopic portrait of himself/herself as reflected in the work of the great master. In this type of "reading" the most arduous task comes *afterward*: she/he will spend the rest of her/his life writing a postscript to his/her own *Guide*.

Maimonides forbade the readers of the *Guide* to analyze (*yishraḥ*) and explain (*yubayan*) what they had understood to others.[12] There are several reasons for this prohibition. One is that the *Guide* demands an existential metamorphosis: in the end through their own hermeneutics, successful readers will become the author. (Or, what amounts to the same, the author will live in the reader). Therefore, the aim is not "to prove" or "to demonstrate" or "to establish some ultimate truth," but to point out as a 'signpost,' which is the accurate meaning of *Guide* (Arabic: *Dalala*). Accordingly, the present work is not an elaborated *sharaḥ*, designed to present a scientific analysis of the *Guide*. There are plenty of these around, and there is no point in adding another one to the list. The methodology of the *Guide*, and that which I apply in this work, corresponds to the *derasha* (hermeneutics) methodology, idiosyncratic to rabbinic tradition—the earmark of the Talmudic sage. As with the literature of the fantastic, the objective is not the systematic exposition of the text but to puncture the ordinary and to awaken new levels of consciousness. Mircea Eliade (1907–1986) designates this type of discourse "creative hermeneutics":

> From a certain point of view, one can compare the hermeneutics to a scientific or technological "discovery." Before the discovery, the reality that one came to discover was there, only one did not see it, or did not understand it, or did not know how to use it. In the same way, a creative hermeneutics unveils significations that one did not grasp before, or puts them in relief with such a vigor that after having assimilated this new interpretation the consciousness is no longer the same.[13]

Unless specified all translations are mine.

—JOSÉ FAUR, JERUSALEM, ISRAEL
OCTOBER 1997

Transliterated Characters

HEBREW AND ARAMAIC

א	ʼ	ס	s
ב	b, bh	ע	ʻ
ג	g, gh	פּ, פ	p, f
ד	d, dh	צ, ץ	ṣ
ה	h	ק	q
ו	v, w	ר	r
ז	z	שׁ	sh
ח	ḥ	שׂ	ś
ט	ṭ	ת	t, th
י	y		
כ, ך	k, kh		
ל	l		
מ, ם	m		
נ, ן	n		

ARABIC

ا	ʼ	ط	ṭ
ب	b	ظ	ḏ̣
ت	t	ع	ʻ
ث	ṯ	غ	gh
ج	j	ف	f
ح	ḥ	ق	q
خ	kh	ك	k
د	d	ل	l
ذ	dh	م	m
ر	r	ن	n
ز	z	ه	h
س	s	و	w
ش	sh	ي	y
ص	ṣ		
ض	ṣ̱		

Homo Mysticus

Introduction

THE UNDERLYING THESIS OF this work is that for Maimonides Hebrew mysticism is an anthropological dimension and the very purpose of the human race. For Erich Neumann (1905–1960) this ascertains that mysticism is "a fundamental category of human experience."[1] Unlike Neumann, however, for Maimonides the mystical experience can take place only at the final stage of human development when the individual has reached perfection.[2] Mysticism cannot be experienced through faith or be grounded on rational proof. *Homo mysticus* is, first and foremost, a *post-rational individual*. A serious student of the *Guide* concluded that although "*faith in God is not grounded on the annihilation of rational perception*" and that "rational perception constitutes the very basis for man's relation to God." At the same time, Maimonides maintains that "there is *a perception that is higher than it*, which opens the gates *to a suprarational knowledge*." In fact, for Maimonides, "Through it alone can man reach the ultimate possible closeness to the absolute" [italics in original].[3]

The basic premise of all forms of surrealism is that ordinary reality "does not exists in terms of itself, but as an anteroom of another possible reality."[4] The rabbis, too, taught that "This world resembles an anteroom before the world to come."[5] The superior reality cannot be apprehended in terms of ordinary categories.[6] To become *homo mysticus* the individual must transcend the realms of mythology and rationality and develop a new level of consciousness. A postrational individual knows not by means of ordinary reason but "by virtue of perfection." At a rudimentary level mysticism is the faculty to exercise subjectivity. Humans are conditioned by the ordinary: linguistic, social, and cultural conventionalities. Ordinarily, people are objective. They follow definite patterns of thought and feeling; their behavior and ideas can be categorized and valued according to generally agreed criteria: intellectual, social, political, and so on. The realm of mysticism escapes objectivity. It involves a crisis of choice. The road bifurcates, demanding subjective judgment, thus creating a defining moment, a unique Now. Those having the courage to face it, rather than escape to the realm of conventionalities, would be rewarded by a brilliance piercing the thick darkness—an instant of mystical illumination. It is at this Now that individuals discover—more precisely, forge—their true identities. *Homo mysticus* is one who has forged *his / or her* own individualistic type of perfection, "acquired *his* world" (*qana 'olamo*) in the language of the rabbis.[7]

Perfection is not measured in absolute terms, but according to the specific capacities of the individual.[8] "Every human can be as righteous as Moses," taught Maimonides.[9] A similar view was expressed by Judah Abarbanel (ca. 1460–ca. 1523). In a golden passage he wrote, "And the soul which has achieved such excellence, thus loosed from its fleshy bonds, enjoys without impediment forever its happy union with the Light, even as do the blessed angels and disembodied intelligences, the heavenly bodies and the spirits that move them, each according to the degree of its dignity and perfection forever."[10]

Because at the level of individuation everyone has something absolutely unique to contribute, it is as if God had designed the entire cosmos—launching the chain of events from the inauguration of time—to offer *this* Now for the benefit of *this* individual. Within the infinite concatenation of cause and effect every particular act has cosmological implications. Therefore, advised the rabbis, an individual ought to look at himself and the entire world as if in a state of perennial equilibrium of merits and faults: a single act will suffice to tilt the chain of events affecting his future and that of the world.[11] Similarly, Jorge Luis Borges (1900–1986) wrote, "There is no fact, however insignificant, that does not involve universal history and the infinite concatenation of cause and effect."[12] "No one resembles someone else," taught the rabbis, therefore, "every human must assert, 'For me the universe has been created'!"[13] In the pagan mind human redemption is effected by a backward motion toward a primordial past. The present is insignificant. Human salvation is attained by returning to a mythical beginning. In Judaism the most important time is Now. "If not Now, when?!" asked Hillel (died ca. 20 B.C.E.).[14] The saintly Rabbi of Ger (1789–1866), explained: "This Now, the moment in which we are speaking, has not been from the creation of the world, and it will never be again. Before it there was another Now, and every Now has its sacred duty,"[15] hence, the idea of progress, both collective and personal. Progress takes place when the Now is realized. "There is no human, who does not have a moment (*sha'a*)," taught ben 'Azai (second century).[16] There are common folks, even uneducated heathens and inveterate sinners, who had the courage to seize the Now, gaining eternal salvation. Upon hearing about some such cases, R. Judah the Prince (ca. 160–220), the editor of the Mishna, and one of the most significant figures of the Rabbinic period, wept. Saying: "There are some who acquire their world in a moment (sha'a), and there are some who acquire their world in many years."[17] Concerning this supreme moment, Borges wrote: "Sometimes I have suspected that all human life, regardless of how complex and long it may be, comprises really a [single] moment: the moment in which man knows forever who he is."[18]

The differences between the esoteric views of Maimonides and the Kabbalah developed by the anti-Maimonideans in France and Spain are too complex to be summarized coherently here. They are not, however, merely a matter of content, such as the Theosophy of the Sefirot, and so on. They pertain to different stages of human development, expressing different spiritual and intellectual syntaxes and morphologies. For Maimonides the esoterics of the Tora is theocentric. It concerns postrational human, involving a progressive process of deanthropomorphization.[19] Kabbalah is essentially ethnographic and anthropocentric. Eliade noted that the Kabbalah is akin to the "cosmic religion that disappeared after the triumph of Christianity, surviving only among the European peasants." It presupposes a system of 'cosmic sacrality' that the rabbis tried to suppress and the Kabbalah successfully retrieved "thanks mainly to the tradition embodied in the Kabbalah," a "cosmic sacrality, which seemed to have been irretrievably lost after the rabbinical reform had been successfully recovered."[20] Unlike Kabbalah, for Maimonides the content of a mystic experience is marginal. What defines the experience is the *level* at which it took place: to perceive the most insignificant thing at the postrational level is infinitely more exalting than to listen to the most sublime symphony at the ethnographic stage.

Maimonides's investigations lead to an elemental, conclusive, question: Is the ultimate reality God or Man? The Hebrew Scripture posits God as the Supreme reality preceding and, therefore, categorically independent from anything else. What exists is the result of His will, free and undetermined. Creation ex nihilo postulates a limitless chasm between the Creator and His creatures. Hebrew 'mysticism' is a dimension of this chasm. Because humans abide in a plane of existence other than that of the Creator, the God of the Scripture cannot be discovered.[21] Rather, He *reveals* Himself to humankind. The God of revelation is absolutely unique and omnipotent. A deity fitting a polytheistic system has nothing to do with biblical revelation. This cardinal doctrine is the focus of a verse in Deuteronomy. The Hebrew prosodic mark *atnaḥ* (in function a semicolon) divides the verse into two parallel segments. The first segment reads, "To you it was revealed [at Sinai] that you may know that the Lord (YHWH) is the God." The second part reads, "There is nothing else beside Him" (Dt 4:35). In biblical parallelism each segment comes to complement and further elucidate the other.[22] Accordingly, biblical revelation is not a contact between entities sharing a common realm of existence. There are neither common metaphysical grounds nor ontological links between them. Revelation is a *communicative* act between entities whose existences are irreducible to each other. It posits the principle that God, the Creator, and humans, the created, can transcend their specific realities and *communicate* with one another. Being created in the image of God (Gn 1:26) means, precisely, that God and humans have the faculty to transcend each other's realities and to *reveal* themselves to one another. This type of relation is linguistically (rather than metaphysically) structured. It concerns the dynamic participation of the first and second persons: revelation is the act of speech between God and human. As such, it involves linguistic subjectivity, the faculty to say '*I*' to a *you*. *You* is someone who could address the first person as '*I*.'[23] Structurally, there is no difference between prophecy (where the revelation is initiated by the first person, God, and addressed to the second person, human) and prayer (where the revelation is initiated by the first person, human, and addressed to the second person, God). Prophecy/ prayer is the essence of Hebrew mysticism.

Outside the realm of direct revelation the numinous is the effect of protological projections. Idolatry, whether cultic (in the form of image worship), mythological (in the form of anthropomorphic theology), or intellectual (in the form of philosophical or scientific anthropocentrism), posits man as the ultimate reality. At that level communication is inoperative. There is only 'communion'—a physical or metaphysical contact—allowing the lower entity to be absorbed by the higher entity. Communion is operative only at the mythological level. It excludes dialogue. The 'other' is not a *you* capable of saying '*I*,' but a *thing*, a *force* or an *idea* like the nebulous deity of the deists or the "cosmic force" giving rise to the "cosmic religious feelings" that scientists and mystics experience. The first boundaries that a human recognizes—essential for mental organization and debunking omnipotence of thought—is the second person, *you*. Because anthropocentric thinking posits the ultimate other as void of speech and subjectivity, it could be totally incorporated into the mind of the viewer. Omnipotence of thought is unbound: monodialogue is the only possible form of discourse; interpersonal relations are hierarchical and therefore, necessarily Oedipal.[24] Anthropocentric knowledge, like Platonic hermeneutics, is Greek *a-lethia*, a passive process of 'un-covering'. Regardless of how the ontic-ontological reality is conceived, whether as something transcendental or not, it must be subjected to an anthropomorphic process. A theocentric universe could be meaningful only if the supreme reality is in the image of man. From this perspective the God of Scripture is nothing more than "the image of man magnified to infinite dimension."[25] Truth is total and absolute. In the footsteps of Balaam, the pagan prophet bent on cursing Israel, who claimed to "know the mind of the Most High" (Nm 24:16), the quest of anthropocentric science is to "truly," that is, anthropomorphically, "know the mind of God."[26] At that point human progress stops, inaugurating a platonic paradise, eternally perfect and eternally static.

The theocentric perspective separates creation from nature and the Book from a book.[27] From this perspective truth unfolds within the limitless chasm separating God and human. Because the Creator can never be fully known, revelation and the truly mystical are limitless and never ending. The 'known / unknown' are relative. What may lay beyond the pale of knowledge at a given historical period may be 'self-evident' at a different time and place. 'Mysticism' is the perennial tension between the knowable and the unknowable.

Rather than believing to have unraveled "the mind of God," those privy to revelation are overcome by a pathos of humility before the vast, never-ending mystery of the unknown. Shortly before his death, Isaac Newton (1642–1727) wrote: "I do not know what I may appear to the world; but to myself I seem to have been only like a boy, playing on the seashore, and diverting myself, in now and then finding a smoother pebble or a prettier shell than ordinary, while the great ocean of truth lay undiscovered before me."[28]

The present work has been structured in terms of this question.

In part 1 (Apophasis) I examine Maimonides's doctrine of negative theology, positing that knowledge of God is attained *via negativa*. This knowledge is not gained simply by dismissing positive attributes. It is generated by the dynamics of the paradox 'positive attributes / negative attributes', giving rise to the paradoxes 'knowledge / un-knowledge' and 'praise / silence': each following the other in spiral succession. In the words of Maimonides: "Praise be He who at the moment that the minds glance at His essence, their understanding turns faulty. At the moment of glancing at the necessary correlation between His will and His actions, knowledge turns into ignorance. When the tongues attempt to exalt Him with attributes, all verbosity turns into ineptitude and faultiness."[29] Apophatic knowledge is structurally successive like the flashes of darkness and light emitted by the revolving sword guarding the way to Eden (Gn 3:24).

This knowledge leads to the Maimonidean doctrine of silence. Because apophatic knowledge does not derive from a concept, it is not epistemological. The silence it generates is not absence of words but the discovery of the system by which an expression coheres and is meaningful. In all value systems (such as language, logic, mathematics) the structure of a proposition cannot be *said* by that proposition; it can only be *shown* by it. A sentence can *say* words, but it cannot *say* its own syntax. Invariably, the syntax of a sentence is only made *manifest* by the words, but it is not *located* in them. Arabic-speaking Jews designate with the term *talqin* the instruction of the system showing the logical syntax and structure of Jewish texts. It cannot be imparted in writing.[30] The distinction between what could be *said* and what could only be *indicated* was recognized by Lüdwig Wittgenstein (1889–1951): "There are, indeed, things, that cannot be put into words. They *make themselves manifest*. They are what is mystical."[31] Conversely, "What expresses *itself* in language, we cannot express by means of language."[32] Likewise, Judah Abarbanel maintained, "Human language is inadequate fully to express such experience of our spirit; nor can material sounds reproduce the spiritual purity of things divine."[33] With Maimonides, this ascertains that a description of a mystical experience is a self-contradiction; that which can be *said* does not belong to the realm of the esoteric.

In rabbinic tradition esoteric instruction is imparted through *rashe peraqim* (headings of chapters). These are the *disjecta membra,* what C. G. Jung (1875–1964) described as "beginnings without continuations" disseminated by the teacher that the student must "knead them into a whole."[34] Because total meaning cannot be expressed in positive language, space is an integral element of Jewish writing. Jewish law stipulates that if there is no space between the letters, or if a letter or a word touches another, even at a minuscule point, the scroll of the Tora is *pasul* (liturgically void). The intervals between letters and between words are not absence of space. They represent the hyperspace of the Tora contained between the lines (*shirṭuṭ*) traced on the parchment of the scroll with a blunt instrument. Even when the intervals between the letters are only symbolically filled, that is, when the consonantal text is vocalized and its phormology and syntax definite, the scroll is liturgically void.[35] Accordingly, 'wisdom' (*ḥokhma*) includes two elements: the text, or rashe peraqim, imparted by the teacher and the subtext woven by the student, giving meaning and coherence to the text. Commenting on the verse, "His desire is in God's Tora, and he meditates on his own Tora day and night" (Ps 1:2), the rabbis taught: "At the beginning it [the Tora] is called on God's name, but in the end it is called on his [the student's] name."[36] The tension God's Tora/student's Tora is resolved in a dynamic process of decoding and interpretation designed to weave together the rashe peraqim. In the process the reader becomes the writer and the text becomes the reader. Initially, God's given text is superior to the student. The rabbis observed, "If people stand up [in reverence] for those who study it [the Tora], how much more so [should they stand up] for it [the Tora] itself!"[37] At a later stage a textuological transformation takes place: the student becomes the living text of the Tora. Concerning that stage, the rabbis taught, "Whoever honors the Tora his body will be honored by the people."[38] The living, humanized text embodied in the student is superior to the text written on a scroll. Such a person had become, "a great individual" (*gabra rabba*). Reflecting the belief that the human text is textuologically superior to the text written on a scroll, Raba (d. 352) cried out, "How boorish are those who stand up [in reverence] for the scroll of the Tora, but don't stand up for a great individual (*gabra rabba*)!"[39] In a different context Michael David Levin described the existential metamorphosis whereby the student becomes the text:

> As we perform the prescribed rituals with greater and greater skill, we begin to be inhabited by the powerful living *sense* of the outer texts. With the passage of time continuously repeated in the reading, inner and outer texts begin to coincide. Were there no longer any difference between them, understanding would be complete: thanks to the performance of the rituals prescribed by the outer texts, the *sense* of the inner would be

> fully translated. *We would finally become the one true text.*[40] [italics in original]

There is a further transformation. Miguel de Unamuno (1864–1936) called attention to the process by which "the knower, becomes, in knowing, the known; the lover, in loving, the beloved." Pointing to his own personal experience, he continued:

> I have encountered in some books a man rather than a philosopher or a savant or a thinker, when I encountered a soul rather than a doctrine, I have exclaimed: "But I have been this man myself!" And thus I have lived again with Pascal in his own century and place, and I have lived again with Kierkergaard in Copenhagen, and so with others. And are these phenomena perhaps not the supreme proof of the immortality of the soul? May not these people live in me as I live in them?[41]

Applied to the Tora, this means that in the process of studying the student will encounter the divine Author and realize God's image within. "And they shall build me a Tabernacle," said God, "and I shall dwell within them" (Ex 25:8). The object of the sentence is not the Tabernacle: the Scripture does not say that God will dwell within it (*betokho*), the Tabernacle, but within "them" (*betokham*) in the plural, the *people* who built the Tabernacle.

The preceding considerations underlie the literary strategy of the Tora. Maimonides pointed out that a key characteristic of the Tora is to ascertain its basic doctrines without showing how they are established. To take one obvious example, monotheism is the most fundamental doctrine of the Law. Yet the Scripture does not attempt to demonstrate the validity of such a belief. Maimonides showed that the rabbis distinguished between a scholar having general knowledge of the Tora and a sage (*ḥakham*). The former is one who has mastered the traditional doctrines of the Law on the basis of authority but cannot examine them critically. Wisdom (ḥokhma) is the specific methodology by which the doctrines of the Tora are analyzed and made coherent. Accordingly, special deference is owed to a teacher "who taught him wisdom (ḥokhma) because he is bringing him to the life of the world to come."[42] Maimonides did not explain why the Tora refrained from presenting the bases and steps required to demonstrate its doctrines. One of the reasons is that a method developed on the basis of authority or of some philosophical principles cannot relate to the *specific* appurtenance of the individual. Like all esoteric knowledge, the doctrines of the Tora need to be wedded together and confirmed by each individual separately at the subjective level, each according to his/or her own unique self.[43]

In part 2 (Imagination) I examine the Maimonidean theory of imagination. It is a fundamental theory. Imagination does not interpret reality but substitutes it through a process of mental projections and displacements. It is not a defective rationality but a specific kind of discourse underlying the entire gamut of pagan civilization from the political and religious to the aesthetic and philosophical. This type of discourse characterizes archaic humankind. It is grounded on a semiotical system: identification is made on the basis of certain signs, regardless of context and substance. It is akin to what modern anthropologists designate "mythical thinking." The reality of the world of imagination is myth and illusion. It is man-made, precluding humanity from participating in the real world. At this level of consciousness object and subject are not fully distinguished from one another. Man and his environment are amalgamated into a continuous flow of events with neither past nor future.[44] Reflecting the aesthetics of modern symbolism, Fernando Ossorio, a character in one of Pío Baroja's (1872–1956) novels, declared, "The outside world does not exist; it has the reality that I wish to give to it."[45] Like Adam and Eve hiding "inside" (*betokh*) the tree bearing the forbidden fruit (Gn 2:8), representing the realm of imagination, people sequester themselves deep into their fancy, dwelling perennially in a realm populated by phantoms of their own. Apophasis debunks imagination and lets the light come in.

Imagination is the source of human misery. Referring to human projections, Maimonides remarked: "[A]ll this is the consequence of imagination, which is also the true evil instinct (*yeṣer ha-ra'*) because every intellectual and ethical flaw is either the doing of the imagination or the consequence of its doing."[46] Since reality does not correspond to human fantasies, invariably, the expectations generated by imagination come to an unhappy ending.[47]

Imagination is the source of heathenism. The devotional practices and beliefs of pagan religion are rooted in the peculiar imagination (*al-khayalat*) of these people.[48] The projection of anthropomorphic characteristics onto God, too, is the effect of "the corrupt imagination."[49] It is a most heinous offense, a human assault upon the Creator. In this fashion man displaces God, transforming Him into his own deformed image. This is synonymous with the scriptural prohibition of idol worship. Since no normal individual has ever "imagined" in the past, nor would "imagine in the future, that the image which he had manufactured from metal, stone, or wood" had actually created the heavens and earth, the worship of a fetish "out of love or fear" does not—cannot—constitute idolatry. Fear and love of the fetish represent a preverbal stage of human development when the outside world is made up of internal projections of pleasure and pain.[50] At this stage people could not be ruled by law. Therefore, the Scripture does not condemn pagan humanity for the sin of idolatry. The sin of idolatry is committed at a later stage of mental development when the image is conceived in terms of a theological system "as a symbol of something that is an intermediary between us and God."[51] The preceding leads to the distinction between *religion*—rituals and devotional values based on the notion of a cosmic sacrality—and Tora. "It is unfortunate," wrote Eliade, "that we do not have at our disposal a more precise word than 'religion' to denote the experience of the sacred," adding, "One wonders how it can be indiscriminately applied to the ancient Near East, to Judaism, Christianity, and Islam, or to Hinduism, Buddhism, and Confucianism as well as to the so-called primitive peoples."[52] The term *religion* is essentially Christian and carries on certain connotations that effectively impede an integral concept of Judaism. It is as if one would designate Christianity *halakha* and then try to understand it through its canon law system alone.[53] Properly understood, *religion* is antithetical to the most fundamental principles of Judaism.

The scriptural prohibition of *'aboda zara* wrongly translated 'idolatry', actually is the prohibition of "an alien service," that is, a service "not prescribed" by the Law (see Lv 10:1; cf. Ex 30:9; Dt 17:3). Images are proscribed because they are 'aboda zara, an "unprescribed service," not the other way around. Indeed, Judaism recognizes a legitimate iconology. The cherubim at the Holy of Holies, since they were ordered by the Law, form an integral part of the Temple service.[54] Conversely, not all unprescribed services concern worship images. Talmudic law regards Christianity as 'aboda zara not because it worships images—the worship of images was introduced into Christianity after the Talmudic period—but because it worships with a cult not stipulated by the Law. For the same reason the rabbis taught that even to worship Angel Michael, "Israel's ministering angel," constitutes 'aboda zara.[55] From this point of view it is irrelevant whether a deity is worshiped in the shape of an image or as a pure intellectual concept intended to serve as an intermediary between human and God. In either case 'aboda zara is committed, simply, because such a cult was not stipulated by the Law.

Jewish monotheism is not a concept, philosophical or otherwise, representing, as with the Polynesians and the Ewe, "the speculation of a fraternity of priests who have been consciously selected to be the custodians of certain esoteric knowledge and esoteric rites."[56] Rather, it is the official *faith* of the people in the Supreme Being, absolute Creator of everything, with whom they contracted a *berit* or bilateral "covenant" at Mount Sinai. Thus, the One God, *issues a series of commandments* regulating all aspects of both the spiritual and political life of Israel. In this specific sense Jewish monotheism necessitates monolatry—the worship of God exclusively according to the stipulation of the Sinaitic covenant—just like Jewish monolatry necessitates Jewish monotheism. The whole point of rabbinic tradition and, consequently, of Judaism proper is that worship of God is not a matter of religion—notions and rituals connected with either the experience or the meaning of the sacred—it must involve the fulfillment of a *miṣva* ([divine] commandment) charged by God Himself. The commandments are not general concepts to be fulfilled according to personal endeavor and understanding but definite ordinances to be followed in accordance to the specification of the Law. Hence, halakha, the legal definition of a commandment, is integral to the biblical idea of monolatry. Outside the realm of miṣva all forms of devotion are 'aboda zara, a supreme act of human defiance camouflaged as worship. When performed according to one's fancy, a miṣva is a curse rather than a blessing.[57]

Maimonides regarded the cultural creations and cultural facts of the pagan world and all religious expressions as well, including such notions as sacramental life and the mystery of faith, to be the effect of a sick imagination (*khayal*), distorting reality and camouflaging what is harmful and deviant as beautiful and beneficial. Ethics implies the ability to govern the imagination. An unethical individual cannot know the truth. Conversely, people dominated by imagination cannot be ethical.

The radical distinction between the general ideal of religion and Judaism proper permits a Maimonidean reading of Freud (1856–1939). It is worth noting that the title of Freud's main criticism of religion is *The Future of an Illusion.* (In fact, 'illusion' is a more accurate rendition of the Maimonidean term *khayal*, usually translated as 'imagination'.) More to the point, Maimonides and Freud view culture and religion as the effect of neurotic deformations and pathological deficits, causing humankind to sin (*ḥeṭ*), that is, 'to deviate' from the right path.[58] Both determine that to accept the validity of religion is to reject science and critical knowledge. Both regard this type of thinking as essentially neurotic, precluding the recognition of an objective reality, independent of man. Both consider the deities of such a system a displacement-substitute. Finally, both concur that individuals and societies affected by this type of culture are emotionally troubled and in dire need of mental therapy.

Students of Freud have assumed an un-Maimonidean view of Judaism and, therefore, have concluded that he was in effect *repressing* his Judaism. A typical example is Hans Küng. Projecting his own theology, he assumes that in his criticism of religion Freud was, in fact, rejecting his own Jewish roots. Otherwise, he should have specified that he was only criticizing one form of religion and not the other.[59] Such presumption is disingenuous. It is a well-known fact, verified by no lesser a figure than Jean-Paul Sartre (1905–1980), that the religion attacked by "atheistic" Jews is Christianity, not the faith of the Talmud:

> [A]theistic Jews whom I have questioned admit that their dialogue on the existence of God is carried on against the Christian religion. The religion which they attack and of which they wish to rid themselves is Christianity; their atheism differs in no way from that of Roger Martin du Gard, who says he has disengaged himself from the Catholic faith. *Not for a moment are Jews atheistic against the Talmud; and priest, to all of them, means the vicar, not the rabbi.* [italics added][60]

Indeed, Freud made it quite clear that in his criticism of religion, "we are concerned here with European Christian culture."[61] Küng knows well that within the oppressive society of the time it would have been suicidal for a Jew to be more specific. Freud never disassociated himself from Jews or Judaism. In the "Preface to the Hebrew Translation," of *Totem and Taboo* Freud expressed "the emotional" impact of seeing his work in Hebrew. Although admittedly "completely estranged from the religion of his fathers" he

> feels that he is in his essential nature a Jew and has no desire to alter that nature. If the question were put to him: "Since you

> have abandoned all these common characteristics of your countrymen, what is there left to you that is Jewish?" he would reply: "A very great deal, and probably its very essence." He could not now express that essence clearly in words, but some day, no doubt, it will become accessible to the scientific mind.[62]

Regardless of Freud's thinking on Judaism, a fundamental principle of Maimonides is the rabbinic doctrine that whoever rejects 'aboda zara is as if he had accepted the entire Tora.[63] According to this doctrine, such an "atheist" is closer to the God of the Scripture than someone who worships his own displacement-substitutes.

In part 3 (Cosmology) I examine the Maimonidean doctrine of Creation. In the Maimonidean system knowledge of God as a transcendental Supreme Being means knowledge of God as the absolute Creator. It involves three closely interrelated steps: exiting the realm of imagination, discovering objective reality, and cognizance of the Creator. The first step consists in freeing the mind from the grip of imagination. Because those inhabiting the realm of imagination would process the divine message in mythological terms, at this stage revelation is useless. The antidote to imagination is rationality. Aristotelian logic represents humanity's emergence from the world of imagination into the world of reason. The second step consists of penetrating the realm of reason and perceiving reality as an a objective entity governed by precise and universal laws. Only then can humans begin to realize that the universe in which they reside may be the design of a Creator, Absolute and Supreme. The source for this doctrine is rabbinic. In a lost source cited by Maimonides R. Me'ir (second century) stated, "Scrutinize His creations, for thus you would discern He who had spoken and the World came to be."[64] Observing God's creation is only the first step in a process culminating in love of God and ecstasy.[65]

Only a mythological deity leaves traces of its presence. The God of Israel, even when performing the most astounding miracles, leaves no evidence of His presence. Referring to the splitting of the sea, the rabbis taught that the sea returned to its original condition, bearing no marks of God's intervention. The same is true of all other miracles.[66] Concerning this fundamental principle, the psalmist sang: "Your path is in the sea, your trails are in the many waters. And" in the Hebrew sense of 'yet' "your footprints cannot be known" (Ps 67:20). R. Joseph ibn Abitur (ibn Śatnaś) (tenth to eleventh centuries), the first biblical commentator to emerge from Europe, called attention to the fact that "traces" come as the result of an object resisting a thing "standing" on it. Because God sustains everything (and nothing sustains Him), there can be no *vestigium pedi* to His presence. "A human when walking upon something of substance will invariably leave his footprints. This, however, is not the case with the God of the universe. As it is written, 'And your footprints are not known'."[67] Reiterating the same principle, Newton noted that "bodies find no resistance from the omnipresence of God."[68] Similarly, the rabbis taught, "God is the place of the world, and" in the Hebrew sense of 'therefore' "the world is not His place."[69] The Scripture describes the entire Cosmos as it "hangs from the arms" of the Creator (Dt 33:27).[70] In this fashion God, author of the universe, simultaneously bestows existence to the universe and covers His traces "out of existence."[71]

The Maimonidean doctrine of Creation cannot be demonstrated: it can only be indicated. It is structurally connected with the doctrine of silence discussed previously. If one were to regard Creation as God's speech or writing—as the Scripture and rabbis teach—then a distinction must be established between what the system *says* and what it only *indicates*. To decode God's speech and writing, the hearer/reader must fill in the intervals between the letters and words, discovering the syntax that is *manifested* but not *located* in them, like Bezalel, the builder of the Tabernacle who "knew how to join the letters by which Heavens and earth were created."[72] Thus, "proving" Creation is the same kind of oxymoron as a proposition articulating the syntax of its own syntax.

Theologians have argued that the Aristotelian system rejects the possibility of religion. For the pious masses (*al-'awamm*) religion must be mythological. Rationality, scientific analysis, and objectivity debunk mythological thinking. Accordingly, they are incompatible with revelation.[73] Since things making sense cannot be related to archetypal myths, they are ultimately meaningless. To be meaningful religion must be mythological and irrational. At this level the numinous is the function of a specific syntax and morphology, establishing identity not on the basis of identical subjects but of identical predicates, no matter how trivial. What cannot be processed on the basis of this syntax and morphology does not pertain to the numinous. Accordingly, the pious masses consistently interpret the Scripture in mythical terms.

> Since what the pious masses (ʿawamm) love most and is more pleasurable to their idiocy, is to situate the Law and reason at two opposite poles, claiming that every unusual event is miraculous and outside [the boundaries of] reason. They refuse [to admit] that anything of what was told about past events, or what is currently witnessed in the present, or what it was said that will happen in the future, could follow a natural course. We, however, try to harmonize between the Law and the rational, and maintain that it is possible for all these [events] to proceed according to the natural order of things, with the exception of those [matters] which were clearly expressed to be miracles, and are impossible to explain them [differently]. [Only] then we are obliged to admit that it was a miracle.[74]

Only a postrational human can distinguish between what words *say* and what can only be pointed at but cannot be *said*. The reason that Maimonides dismissed the theological approach to religion and took the Aristotelian road is because theologians do not recognize the objective validity of nature and scientific thought. Hence, their religious notions pertain to the realm of imagination. Maimonides recognized that the Aristotelian concept of the universe does not admit the Creator of the Scripture. He regarded as more fruitful, however, a dialogue about the God of the Scripture with a rational pagan than with a theologian—Jew or gentile—immersed in mythical thinking.

In part 4 (Anthropology) I discuss Maimonides's view of the origin of humankind and its development to ultimate perfection. Humankind's specific appurtenance is the "image of God" (Gn 1:26) with which Adam was created. The image is not biological. It must be transmitted through a sociocultural process. Not all humans have God's image. Adam's children before Seth, were void of this image, hence the pivotal role of learning and education:

> Before learning a human is like a beast since a human differs from all other animal species by virtue of [his] logic because he is a "logical animal." By "logic" I mean the faculty to conceptualize rational matters (*al-maʿqulat*), the loftiest of those

> rational matters being the conceptualization of the Oneness of God and all that pertaining to the Divinity.[75]

Before reaching rationality humans are entrapped in a world of fantasy, like Borges's troglodytes, who are "absorbed in their own thoughts, scarcely perceiving the physical world."[76] Maimonides describes them as brutes having nothing in their "imagination, but eating, drinking, and sex."[77]

Human nature is not a given. There are traces—a particular type of psychic forces originating in the collective psyche of a group or culture (what Jung designates archetypes)—affecting the patterns of thought and feeling of a people. These traces are akin to what Freud refers to as "the impression left behind them by great leading personalities," helping shape the "super-ego" of the community, "under whose influence cultural evolution proceeds."[78] Depending on their character, they may either hinder or promote the psychological well being of both society and the individual. Maimonides believed that pagan civilization has sickened humanity. Like the poison of the primeval snake, their traces paralyze the soul, preventing the rise of human consciousness. Those traces cannot be eliminated through suppression any more than a person can heal himself by ignoring his sickness. The individual and society must undergo a specific therapeutic process. The Israelites were part of pagan humanity.[79] The traces lingering from their pagan past were suspended at Sinai. Accordingly, the purpose of the Tora is twofold: to heal and control the pagan traces and to aid in the attainment of human perfection.

Maimonidean perfection is individual and individualistic. Like the angels in Jacob's vision (Gn 28:12), a human can ascend to heaven. Rationality is the means for climbing up. Upon reaching the summit a metamorphosis takes place whereby the individual realizes a new level of consciousness, knowing "by virtue of perfection." This knowledge is of the same genus as prophecy and is categorically superior to common rationality. Perfection, however, is beyond the reach of 'the general public' (al-jamhur). This is not because the public is stupid or unworthy. Unlike 'the masses' (al-'awamm),[80] the jamhur is not necessarily made up of uneducated, substandard people.[81] The reason that they cannot attain perfection is because collective thinking is the function of imagination. A collective entity, social, political, or religious, can only find unity and psychological wholeness through key-symbols. These symbols are grounded on imagination, not reason. Apophatic knowledge shatters the standard, collective understanding of these symbols. In this fashion the individual becomes independent of the ways of the public, beginning a process of self-assertion and individuation. The uniqueness of the Tora lies in the fact that its key-symbols are significant in both the realms of imagination and reason. Therefore, they contribute to the welfare of both the general public and the individual.

Perfection reaches the general public via individuals coming down Jacob's ladder. A dimension of Hebrew perfection is the urge to share it with others. Thus, a special relation is forged between society and the individual. Those climbing Jacob's ladder must come down and translate their visions into norms and institutions that will directly advance society.[82] According to Maimonides, the prophet is superior to the philosopher simply because the prophet—through the mastery of imagination—starts a chain of events that over time will produce the necessary apparatus to give access to their ideality to the rest of humaniy, through the establishment of proper political and legal institutions. It is in this precise sense, too, that Maimonides points to the failure of the philosophers (not of philosophy!). Unlike the biblical prophets, Greek idealism did not result in the establishment of social and legal institutions that benefited and elevated humanity. Prophetic communication differs from the instruction imparted by the philosopher-king via myths and noble lies because these myths and lies will not unleash a chain of events that will bring about the establishment of legal, social, and political institutions benefiting all. Quite the contrary. As it were, the prophet not only returns to the Platonic cave, but he also sows the seeds that will enable the rest of the people to climb up. The God of the prophets is superior to that of the philosophers because the latter is not a God of kindness and justice. As the rabbis taught, "One who occupies himself only with Tora," without practicing acts of human kindness (*gemilut ḥaṣadim*) "resembles one who has no [true] God."[83] Likewise, "Great is the study of Tora because it leads into [good] action."[84]

The esoteric truth is the truth that individuals discover with their own eyes. It comes to pass at the moment of mystical illumination—"the flash" piercing the darkness of the night. It is subjective because at that specific time and place, society has not designed the intellectual apparatus to express it. Occasionally, the apparatus is realized, and the esoteric truth becomes the patrimony of society or a particular group. When the Patriarch Abraham discovered monotheism, there was no such term in the intellectual lexicon of his contemporaries: monotheism could not yet be enunciated. It was the genius of Abraham accompanied by a series of events marked in the Scripture that made monotheism accessible to all. Likewise, the genius of men like Newton and Einstein is not limited to the conception of a "brilliant idea" but in the formulation of a series of intellectual instruments (calculus, the theory of relativity, etc.) designed to give access to their ideas to the rest of humanity, thus, giving rise to a special kind of technology that could benefit and elevate humanity.

Since a mystical experience lies outside the realm of factual discourse, talk about it cannot be meaningful. The task of the mystic is to translate the vision apprehended at the top of the ladder into expressive actions of human kindness, as did Rabbis 'Aqiba (50–135) and Simon bar Yoḥai (second century).[85] Two examples from the Scripture suffice. The doctrine that humankind was created in the image of God (Gn 1:26) is translated into the sanctity of human life and the sacrilege of murder, "since in God's image was man created" (Gn 8:6). Likewise, the doctrine that the world was created in six days and God rested at the seventh day (Gn 2:2–3), is translated into the prohibition of work on the Sabbath, awarding workers and slaves one day a week of absolute rest (Ex 20:7–10). No legislation in recorded history had done more for the rights of people, in general, and the proletariat, in particular, than the Biblical prohibition against shedding blood and the institution of the Sabbath rest.

Because the key-symbols of pagan civilization operate only at the level of imagination, lacking intellectual significance, they contribute to the disequilibrium of the individual and collective psyche. In his *Civilization and its Discontent,* Freud showed that civilization itself may be the principal source of neurosis and mental illness. Closing with an overwhelming question, "Would not the diagnosis be justified that many systems of civilization or epochs of it—possibly the whole of humanity—have become 'neurotic' under the pressure of the civilizing trends?"[86] He expressed the hope "that one day someone will venture upon this research into the pathology of civilized communities."[87]

I deliberately refrained from examining the Maimonidean view of the *Merkaba* (Chariot)—the most important subject of rabbinic esoterics. The standard interpretations offered by the commentators of the *Guide* stand in such flagrant contradiction with the biblical text that to accept them the reader must presume that Maimonides was scripturally illiterate. Rather, I believe that the Maimonidean *Merkaba* is connected with the doctrine of perfection. There is a specific direction to Cosmology or *Ma'aśe Bereshit*—the other theme of rabbinic esoterics. The "Chariot" represents God's Divine Providence steering the Cosmos, like a rider steering his mount (Dt 33:26). The *Kerubim* (Cherubs, singular: *kerub*) are the holy beings pulling the Chariot.[88] They seem like full-grown humans with children's faces[89] and are identified with "the natural individual forces" in humans effecting human rationality.[90] Probably, *kerub* is a metathesis of *rakhub* (mount).[91] Upon perfection, the individual and community undergo a metamorphosis, becoming God's 'mount', a medium carrying on His will. R. Johanan (ca. 180-279) contrasted the righteous, like Jacob, that "God is standing on him" (Gn 28:13), with the wicked, like Pharaoh who was "standing on the Nile," his deity (Gn 41:2).[92] In the latter the divine becomes an instrument designed to promote the interest of the sinful. In the former the individual becomes the conduit of the divine. In this precise sense the world "stands" on the people of Israel, and they constitute "its vigor."[93] Righteous individuals are not only the kerubim pulling the Merkaba they constitute the Merkaba itself. As the rabbis taught, "The Patriarchs, they themselves are the Merkaba."[94]

THE DIALECTICS OF APOPHATIC KNOWLEDGE

APOPHATICISM, UNDERscoring the limits of human understanding and the absolute transcendence of God, is the master-key to Maimonides's intellectual apparatus. It is a different class of knowledge, superior to common rationality and inferior to prophecy. It is grounded on a special kind of dialectics generated by 'positive attributes / negative attributes'. An adequate understanding of apophaticism is essential to come to grips with Maimonides's negative theology. It has three aspects. First, linguistic considerations prevent the application of positive attributes or any kind of positive knowledge to God.[1] Second, epistemologically, human intelligence is limited: there are subjects transcending human understanding.[2] Third, ontologically, the notion of positive attributes contradicts the doctrine of absolute monotheism.[3] Because the biblical doctrine of Creation posits that there is no ontological relationship between God and His creatures, all attributes referring to God, including those positing His existence, beingness, and omniscience, must be interpreted negatively.[4] "Absolutely, there is no likeness between Him and His creatures in anything. His existence is not like their existence, nor is His life like the life of other living beings, nor is His knowledge like the knowledge of others who know."[5]

Knowledge of God is attained *via negativa*. Concerning the apophatic knowledge resulting from such a methodology, Maimonides raised a fundamental question.

> One may ask: Since there are no means by which His true essence can be comprehended and proofs can only demonstrate that He exists,[6] and as it was demonstrated, positive attributes [of God] are impossible, in which way can there be any distinction among those comprehending Him? According to this [it

> would appear], that whatever was comprehended by our Teacher Moses and by Solomon is the same as what was comprehended by a common student.[7]

Epistemologically, positive attributes are a hindrance to one's knowledge of God. Those applying positive attributes, such as corporeality, which is demonstrably inapplicable to God, are "blind."[8] The more attributes are negated of God, the nearer one comes to Him. Maimonides made the essential point that in the same fashion that positive attributes increase one's knowledge of an object, the negation of positive attributes increases one's knowledge of God:

> The more one increases in a positive description of an object, the more definite the described [object] becomes. Thus, upon describing [an object] one comes closer to comprehending its true essence. In the same fashion the more [positive attributes] one negates of Him, blessed be He, the closer one comprehends. One is closer to Him than one who does not negate [from Him] what had been demonstrated [*tubarhan*] [by] its negation.[9]

Apophatic knowledge is not merely the rejection of a positive attribute or the correction of a mistaken opinion. It involves a dynamic process: apophasis is defined by the very process of negating a positive attribute. This type of negation is not accomplished by removing a contradiction or amending a mistake and accepting the "right" view on the basis of faith. It must be demonstrated by a *burhan* (plural *burahin*) 'proof established on the principle of contradiction'. There are two stages. Initially, there is only negation without a positive proof (burhan). At this level there is no apophatic knowledge, and doubt will linger in the mind of the believer. The second stage requires a positive proof (burhan), demonstrating why such a positive attribute cannot apply to God. Only then apophatic knowledge is realized. At the first level one is yet "intellectually ineffectual." Because the fallacy of the positive attribute was not "demonstrated" (tubarhan) to him, he is in doubt. By contrast, those "who know with a proof (*bi-al-burhan*) that it is impossible to apply such a subject to Him" know with certainty.[10] The second level is attained after arduous work. Occasionally, one "would have to toil for several years, studying a science and the demonstration (tubarhan) of its foundations, until one is assured. The sole objective of such a study would be to negate from God certain subjects that were demonstrated (bi-al-burhan) to be impossible to apply to Him."[11]

Those gaining apophatic knowledge on the basis of demonstrable proofs (burahin),[12] reaching *kamala*, human 'perfection', are designated by the code-term *kamilun* 'perfects'.[13] They are 'men of perfection' (*al-kamalun*), worthy of knowing "the secrets of the Prophetic writings."[14] There are degrees to perfection:

> It has thus been explained to you that whenever the negation of something that does not apply to Him has been proven [tubarhan] to you, you have become more perfect [*akmal*]. Conversely, that when you posit something about Him, you have become confused and distanced yourself further from knowing His true [essence].
>
> In this fashion one comes to understand Him, through scrutiny and investigation, until realizing the impossibility of applying to Him what is impossible to apply to Him: not ascribing to Him something in addition to His essence.[15]

Because apophasis results in a definite knowledge of God, the more attributes are negated of Him, the better understanding one has of His essence,[16] hence the excellence of the educated concept of God over the notions of a "common student."[17]

APOPHASIS AND PARADOX

Structurally, apophasis involves a double paradox whereby 'knowledge / un-knowledge' gives rise to 'praise / silence'. There are two fundamental aspects to apophasis. First, it involves an essential paradox. On the one hand, it is the only means by which humankind can achieve perfection and true knowledge of God. On the other hand, only upon fully developing their intellectual abilities, realizing the inability to comprehend God, can humans fulfill their potential. Apophatic knowledge is *not* to understand Him in a double sense. Understanding Him is attained upon realizing that He cannot be known, and then, upon believing that one has understood Him, realizing that one has failed to understand Him.

> Upon realizing [*sha'ara*] that there is no means to grasp what can be potentially perceived [of God] but negatively and that a negation cannot teach anything about the truth of the subject, it became transparent to all humans, past and future, that God, blessed be He, cannot be comprehended by any mind, that nobody but He can comprehend who He is, that to comprehend Him is the inability to comprehend Him fully.[18]

Second, as a consequence of the first, the perception effected via apophaticism defies linguistic expression. Absolute silence, in the sense of total absence of articulated speech and thought, is essential to the apophatic experience.[19] This perception, too, involves an essential paradox: silence is praise and praise is silence.

> All the philosophers say [*yaqulun*]: "We were illuminated by His Splendor but [He] is hidden from us by the might of His lucidity, like the sun, hiding from the sight because it is too weak to perceive it."[20] This was extensively elaborated [by others] and needs not to be repeated here. The culminating statement on this topic is found in the Psalms (65:2): *Lekha Dumya Tehilla*. Translation: "To You silence is praise." This is a very profound observation! Whatever was intended to have been expressed by way of exaltation and praise of Him will be found to be faulty when applied to Him, sensing that it [the praise] is somehow wanting. Accordingly, silence is fundamental: brevity is proportional to the apprehension of the minds. As it was prescribed by those who are perfect [al-kamilun] (Ps 4:5), "Speak up in your hearts upon your beds and be silent. Selah."[21]

Because of its paradoxical structure, expressed in the dialects 'knowledge ➞ un-knowledge' and its concomitant 'praise ➞ silence', apophatic knowledge may be compared to a succession of light flashes in the darkness. "Sometimes," noted Maimonides, "the truth shines upon us, and we suppose it to be [as clear as] daylight. And behold, it is then concealed by body and habits!"[22] This type of truth may be compared "to the flame of the spinning sword" guarding the road to Eden (Gn 3:24) that "shines and then conceals itself."[23] Therefore, apophatic knowledge cannot be communicated.

> Know that unlike other sciences commonly studied when a person of perfection [*al-kamlin*] in accordance with the level of his perfection [*kamalhu*] wishes to express either orally or in writing something of what he understands about these secrets, he will not be explainable in a thoroughly and orderly fashion even a measure of what he understands. When teaching others, however, he will have the same experience when he had when he [first] comprehended it, namely, that the subject will surface and emit and then conceal itself, as if the nature of this subject would remain unchanged, whether [comprehending] of it little or much.[24]

Esoteric knowledge is not epistemological. It is not grounded on a concept but on apophasis. The entire structure of the *Guide* rests on this principle.

THE ACQUISITION OF ESOTERIC INSTRUCTION

The rabbis taught that one may 'surrender' (*mosrin*),[25] that is, teach authoritatively to the proper student, only the 'headings of chapters' (rashe peraqim). These are the basic doctrines required to develop esoteric knowledge.[26] Unlike in other disciplines a teacher may not fully develop the subject for the student. The student must be "a sage and understand in his own mind."[27] These are two separate qualifications: [1] knowledge of the preliminary disciplines and [2] the ability to grasp a subject in its initial stages and bring it to fruition on his own.[28] The rabbis designated with the term *derasha* (exposition, dissertation) the type of learning that is expected from a sage.[29] Only a ḥakham (sage)—but not an advanced student (*talmid ḥakhamim*)—is authorized to develop a derasha.[30]

Although esoteric knowledge cannot be transmitted, there is a special procedure whereby, after receiving instruction on the headings of the chapters, the student can submit his derasha for approval. Rabbinic literature has preserved one such case. What is particularly revealing about it—and in this one must distinguish between rabbinic esoterics and general mysticism—is that the initiation ceremony does not take place at night or during a magico-religious time. Eliade noted that in the pagan world a particular knowledge is regarded as esoteric "not only because it is secret and is handed on during the course of an initiation but also because the 'knowledge' is accompanied by a magico-religious power."[31] Rabbinic initiation is not magical but pedagogical. The protagonists are R. Eleazar ben 'Arakh (first century) and his teacher Rabban Johanan ben Zakkai. The procedure comprises five steps, each unfolding into two sections. The first step is initiated by the student.[32] It consists of [1] a request to be taught "the headings of the chapters," a reference to the esoteric texts that are not available to the general student body.[33] Protocol requires [2] rejection of the request on the ground that there is no evidence that the student is a "sage, and understands with his own mind." The text reads:

> A story about Rabban Johanan ben Zakkai who was riding on a donkey and R. Eleazar ben 'Arakh who was marching behind him. [1] He [R. Eleazar ben 'Arakh] asked him: "Recite to me [*shene*][34] a chapter of the *Procedure of the Chariot* [*Ma'aśe Merkaba*]." [2] He [Rabban Johanan ben Zakkai] responded: "Haven't I told you that one may not recite [a chapter] on the *Merkaba* [even] to a single person unless he is a sage [ḥakham] [and] understands with his own mind [*mebin meda'to*]?"

Step two demonstrates that the student is qualified. It begins with [1] a declaration by the student expressing his willingness to submit his derasha for inspection. The formula used by the student contains two key terms: *arṣe* (I shall submit for inspection) and *le-fanekha* (before you). The first is a banking term related to *hirṣa* (submit for inspection), a procedure whereby a coin is submitted to a certified banker for inspection. The rabbis used this term to indicate the submission of a tradition or a teaching to the proper authorities for certification and evaluation.[35] In rabbinic literature the second term frequently means 'under the tutelage of'. This step concludes [2] when the teacher authorizes the student to speak, as follows:

> [1] He [R. Eleazar ben 'Arakh] responded: "Now I shall submit [arṣe] before you [le-fanekha]."
> [2] He [the teacher] replied: "Speak up."

In the third step [1] the student "opens" (*pataḥ*)—this is a reference to the 'prologue' (*petiḥa*) preceding rabbinic dissertations.[36] In this case it demonstrates the student's qualification to develop the headings that he is about to receive.[37] Its purpose becomes clear upon realizing that although it was forbidden *formally* to transmit to a student (mosrin) esoteric lore, it was permitted *casually* to point out (*le-ha'ir*) to him esoteric themes.[38] There are two conditions for the transmission of esoteric knowledge. The student [1] must be a "sage" (ḥakham) [2] who "understands with his own mind." These conditions imply that he had previously gained a cursory instruction in esoterics. In particular, such a sage must have been someone capable of decoding the casual remarks made by the teacher. The purpose of the opening prologue (petiḥa) is to avail the teacher of the opportunity to verify that the student does indeed "understand with his own mind." [2] The teacher signals his willingness to transmit the headings and listen to the dissertation by descending from the donkey and wrapping himself in the prayer shawl.[39] The text continues: "[1] R. Eleazar ben 'Arakh opened [pataḥ] and expounded [darash] on the *Proceeding of the Chariot*. [2] Rabban Johanan ben Zakkai descended from the donkey and wrapped himself in his prayer shawl."

The fourth step concerns the selection of an adequate place [1] where the teacher can pass on the headings to the student and [2] hear his dissertation. "[1] And both of them sat on a rock under an olive tree [where he received the headings of the chapters], [2] and [R. Eleazar ben 'Arakh] submitted (hirṣa) [his derasha] before him [*le-fanav*]."

Rabbinic literature reports several cases where the student failed to develop an esoteric dissertation, meeting a tragic end.[40] In this case the procedure ends happily. Although the text does not explicitly state so, it is clear from the context that the headings were transmitted, and the student had the opportunity to develop them fully in the presence of the teacher. Formal approval was expressed [1] by a kiss on the head and [2] by a laudatory oration by the teacher. The text concludes:

> [1] [Rabban Johanan ben Zakkai] stood up, and kissed him on the head, [2] exclaiming: "Blessed be the Lord, the God of Israel, who gave the Patriarch Abraham a son who knows how to understand and expose [*lidrosh*] about his Father in Heaven. There are those who know to expound [*doresh*] properly, but do not know how to certify [*meqayyem*] properly; others who (know how) to certify [meqayyem] properly, but do not (know how) to expound [doresh] properly. Lazar ben 'Arakh [knows how] to expound properly and to certify properly. Fortunate are you, O Patriarch Abraham! who have fathered Eleazar

ben 'Arakh,[41] who knows how to understand and expound [li-drosh] for the glory of his Father in Heaven.[42]

The term *meqayyem* in the text should not be interpreted in its usual sense, 'to fulfill', but in its technical sense, 'to certify', as with the legal procedure of 'certification of the signatures of contracts' (*qiyyum sheṭarot*) by which a document acquires legal tenure.[43] A sage (ḥakham) is defined as one "who can certify [*leqayyem*] his studies," namely, someone who knows how to authenticate the sources of his studies and have them gain acceptability.[44] What was particularly valuable about R. Eleazar ben 'Arakh was that in addition to his ability to expound the esoteric headings he knew the proper procedure by which to validate his dissertation. Other sages went through a similar procedure, each 'submitting' (hirṣa) his dissertation before the teacher.[45]

DISSEMINATION OF ESOTERIC KNOWLEDGE

In Rabbinic tradition a distinction is made between transmission of an esoteric text and the explanation of the text. A teacher was authorized to explain the headings of chapters but not the entire text. Thus, whereas a text containing the esoteric material could be entrusted to a qualified student, it was absolutely forbidden to transmit its actual meaning to anyone. The purpose of the student's dissertation was to have the teacher evaluate his comprehension of the material and to corroborate whether the mind of the teacher 'approved' (*hiskima*) of his exposition.[46] One is told of a "meticulous student" (*talmid vatiq*) who "had expounded a chapter of the *Procedure of the Chariot,*" but the mind of his teacher "did not approve" (hiskima) of it.[47] Some esoteric subjects one may only expound to oneself, in order to explore whether one could adequately express one's own ideas on the subjects and could verify that, indeed, one's own articulation "approves," that is, coincides, with one's inner thoughts. In the words of the rabbis, "You expound and your mind approves" (*maskim*) of what you yourself are saying.[48] Finally, certain esoteric themes transcend articulation, "and you have no authority to speak about them."[49] Such themes, the rabbis counsel, "should remain under your tongue,"[50] that is, inarticulated. Maimonides explained: "There are some significances, traced in the soul of the perfect individual, that if articulated linguistically or expressed in metaphors, would turn coarse and elude one's design."[51]

The limits imposed on the dissemination of esoteric knowledge affected the methodology and aims underlying the teacher-student relationship. In other disciplines knowledge is transmitted vertically. The student recognizes the authority of the teacher: the teacher transmits (*moser*) and the student accepts (*meqabbel*) authoritative knowledge. The vertical process *mesira* → *qabbala* (passing on → accepting) determines the objectivity and authority of the Oral Law.[52] This process, although applicable to the headings, cannot apply to esoteric learning. Because the teacher cannot fully test the student's understanding, the rabbinic authorities never applied the term *qabbala* to the reception of esoteric lore.[53] A major objective of the *Guide* was to discredit the esoteric teachings current in his time. Maimonides maintained that the ancient Jewish esoteric lore had been totally lost. There were two reasons for this, one legal and the other linguistic. The rabbinic authorities have been unequivocal against the dissemination of esoteric material to unqualified students. Concerning this prohibition, Maimonides remarked: "You already know about their opposition to those who would uncover the secrets of the Tora. And they explained that the reward for concealing the secrets of the Tora—which are known and clear to the learned—is very great."[54] This measure prevented the free circulation of Jewish esoteric lore:

> It already has been explained that even the measure [apprehended] by someone to whom [this knowledge] had been opened [*futaḥ*][55] via his own understanding, he is forbidden to teach or explain—a prohibition by the Law—except face to face to a qualified individual. Then he could mention to him only the headings of chapters. This is the reason that this knowledge has totally disappeared from the nation [of Israel]. Nothing could be found of it, whether little or much.[56]

The esoteric teachings of Israel had to be "transmitted from an exceptional individual to an exceptional individual. . . . This is the cause for the disappearance of those awesome fundaments from the nation."[57] A similar position was maintained by R. Hayye Ga'on (939–1038). Concerning the pronunciation and use of the divine name—a key element in Rabbinic esoterics—he wrote, "that it was not transmitted [*nimsar*] to us from a teacher who received it from another teacher to whom it was transmitted to him [*shemesaro*] from another teacher, a triplicate transmission [*mesora meshulleshet*], but we heard it not from tradition [*be-mesira*], but casually from people who differ as to its pronunciation."[58] He further indicated that the esoteric texts in their possession were not "authoritative" [halakha].[59]

The rabbinic prohibition against disseminating esoteric knowledge was accepted by the Ge'onim. "We cannot open (*li-ftoaḥ*) these matters in writing," responded a Geonic authority, "and even not by word of mouth, except to those who are qualified."[60] Compliance with such restrictions precludes the writing of esoteric literature. "If one were to explain all of these matters in a book," argued Maimonides, "is as if he had expounded them to a thousand men."[61] This is why the rabbis opposed "that any of those secrets of the Tora [*sitre tora*] should be composed [in a treatise] and delivered to the people."[62]

Moreover, genuine esoteric insight transcends articulation. The composition of esoteric treatises is impossible because this type of knowledge "no intelligent individual could articulate even to someone face to face. How then could one put it down in writing—lest every ignoramus, thinking to be wise, would use it as a target and aim the arrows of his ignorance toward it."[63]

Since rabbinic authorities were unequivocal about the prohibition against disseminating esoteric lore to the general student body and since such a knowledge transcends articulation, Maimonides concluded that the esoteric views and insights of the rabbis were "never laid down in a book."[64] In this fashion Maimonides was making clear that Jewish Gnostic writings, such as those preserved in the *Hekhalot* literature and *Shi'ur Qoma* are spurious and do not contain the esoteric teachings of the rabbis. It is true that the rabbis had encoded some of these doctrines in their writings, but they had hidden the "pulp" under many layers of peels.[65] In what must be understood as an oblique reference to the mystics of his time Maimonides added, "and people busy themselves with those peels and fancy that underneath there is no pulp at all."[66]

HEKHALOT LITERATURE AND RABBINIC ESOTERICS

Maimonides's view runs contrary to contemporary scholarship. Appealing on intuitive grounds, no lesser a figure than Gershom Scholem (1897–1982) and Saul Lieberman (1898–1982) identified the esoteric teachings of the rabbis with the *Hekhalot* literature and other mystical material such as *Shi'ur Qoma*. To substantiate this view Scholem argued, "There is no reason to assume that the names of great heroes of talmudic learning, such as Ishmael and Akiba, were used by the authors of these writings to cloak unorthodox teachings."[67] One can only ponder at the merits of such argument in view of the fact that the entire corpus of Gnostic literature is pseudographic. Did Scholem mean to say that works attributed to other "folk heroes" such as R. Neḥunya ben Ha-Qana and R. Simon bar Yoḥai, from the tannaitic period, or Enoch, Abraham, and Moses, from the biblical period, could not possibly have been used to "cloak unorthodox teachings"? Scholem's notion of "orthodox" and "halakhic" Judaism merits some attention. To substantiate the thesis that those writings are in "strict conformity . . . to halakhic Judaism" he presented two arguments. The first argument is that one of these writings mentions the theurgic use of a cloth touched by a woman whose immersion was not totally satisfactory to bring down somebody from an ecstatic experience.[68] The second argument is the use of the magical name Yophiel, an angel "who is also responsible for distributing its [the Tora] knowledge among men." The invocation of that name served "in acquiring a perfect knowledge of the Torah and to protect him from its loss through forgetfulness."[69] The arguments are circular. They rest on the highly debatable premise that halakhic Judaism is essentially magical—in which case there would be no need to prove that theurgic material, such as the ones under discussions, are rabbinic. It is only on this basis that one can argue that the magical use of a Jewish motif is in itself halakhic Judaism. Scholem's view on this matter has been prompted by his yearning to authenticate medieval Hasidism and the ensuing French and Spanish mysticism.[70] At the end of the chapter he offered a final argument for his thesis, which should be read tail end first: "As a matter of fact, we have a long chain of such prescriptions, reaching from the Lesser Hekhaloth and the Sar Torah [at the end of the Greater Hekhaloth] through the time of the Geonim and the German Hasidism of the Middle Ages."[71]

The expression "time of the Geonim" is misleading. Scholem was quite aware that not everything coming from the Rabbinic and Geonic periods necessarily represents Geonic tradition and approval. R. Hayye Ga'on mentioned with disapproval the theurgic practices of some of his contemporaries and had strong reservations about the mystical use of divine names.[72] A close reading of his famous *responsum* mentioning the *Hekhalot* literature and practices shows that he refrained from issuing an unequivocal endorsement. Referring to the esoteric texts circulating at the time, he commented: "Certainly, there are many texts [*mishnayot*] that are not authoritative [*she'enan halakha*], and we explain them according to the view of those who transmit them." Explicitly, he advised, "we cannot now guarantee that these matters are authoritative" (halakha). Carefully, approval was mentioned in the third person, "many sages had believed," not in the first person.[73] After expounding the view identifying rabbinic esoterics with the *Hekhalot* literature, he cited the view that these texts are not "authoritative" (halakha).[74] Indeed, in a different responsum he included the *Hekhalot* writings with other theurgic texts that "frighten" those who read them.[75]

The fact that the *Hekhalot* literature is ancient does not necessarily prove that it contains authoritative esoteric teaching. More to the point, one must distinguish between the notion of a 'palace' (or 'Temple', see below, p. 37–38) symbolizing the divine abode, which is found in rabbinic literature and was elaborated by Maimonides himself, and what was included in the *Hekhalot* literature.[76] There is little doubt that there were circles, even in pre-Rabbinic times, that indulged in some of the Gnostic views and practices contained in the *Hekhalot* literature.[77] Some rabbis, too, may have indulged in those views. What needs to be determined is not merely the time of a given text but to what extent it is representative of the views of the rabbinic authorities of the Mishna and Talmud. Obviously, rabbinic legislation restricting the dissemination of esoteric material[78] was designed to discredit certain types of esoteric lore circulating at the time among some rabbis. The same applies to statements such as, "Many have expounded [*darshu*] on the *Merkaba* but have never seen it," and "I looked at the dwellers of the upper chamber, and they are few."[79]

Hence Maimonides's argument: because these writings are in flagrant contradiction with the rabbinic interdiction against writing precisely this type of literature, they cannot represent the esoteric teachings of the rabbis.

Scholem recognized the problem. He raised the question but failed to explore it rigorously. He simply sidestepped it.

> Still, both texts [of the *Hekhalot*] together present us with such an abundance of particulars, in contradistinction to the talmudic material, that we begin to wonder about the relation of these Hekhaloth traditions to the talmudic injunction against precisely this kind of revelation. Tannaitic tradition has it that a pupil who is found worthy to begin a study of mystical lore is given *Rashei Perakim* only. Instead of these "beginnings of chapters," whose function is only to point to the subject matter to be dealt with and leaves to the student the task of proving his understanding, the Hekhaloth texts omit nothing at all that is relevant.

In an uncharacteristic argument he concluded: "We can safely say that such an additional step indicates a post-Tannaitic composition, even though much of the material itself may belong to the Tannaitic period—which of course, was, at the same time, the flowering season of Gnosticism."[80] Whatever that may mean, it would be a bit strenuous to ascertain that that material is "in strict conformity with . . . halakhic Judaism."

There is another, more complex problem. In a different context Erich Neumann noted that "any mysticism that consists in the experience of dogmatically defined or definable content is either low-level mysticism or disguised mysticism." He went on to describe low-level mysticism, "when a personality unable to assimilate the cultural canon and the religious dogma is overpowered by one of the archetypal contents of the canon and experiences it mystically." He illustrated the point, as "when an archetypal content of the Christian cultural canon is mystically experienced by the Negroes in an African mission." This type of mysticism "is not infrequent when a higher cultural canon is imposed on a group whose consciousness is less developed than that of the group to whom the cultural canon belongs." Disguised mysticism is defined as when to escape the "fatal imputation of heresy," mystics "were driven to compromise and who, consciously or unconsciously, redogmatize their authentic mystical experience—i.e., adapted it to the form imposed by the prevailing dogma." One would seldom find "authentic Indian symbolism among Catholic mystics, and vice versa." The only anomaly to this rule is Scholem's Kabbalah: "In this respect the cabala seems to be rather the exception. According to G. Scholem (*Major Trends* . . .), it clearly reveals archetypal Gnostic symbolism strongly at variance with the Jewish system of consciousness. But why from the first apocalypses to Hasidism the Jewish stream of true, antidogmatic mysticism never ran dry is a matter that cannot concern us here."[81] It should be the concern, however, of anyone who is seriously interested in the history and development of Jewish mysticism.

In "La Rosa de Paracelso" by Borges, Paracelso prays "to his God, to his indeterminate God, to any God, that should send him a disciple." Soon, a young man knocks on his door, seeking instruction. Paracelso was reputed to have had the power to annihilate a rose and then resurrect it from the ashes. Before accepting him as a master, the young man demanded to see the miracle. "I am speaking of the Word that the science of the Cabala teaches us," replied Paracelso. "If I would do it," he added, "you would say that this is an appearance imposed upon your eyes by magic. The wonder will not provide you with the faith that you are searching for: Forsake, then, the rose." The young man was not dissuaded. Impulsively, he took the rose and threw it unto the fire. Paracelso remained unperturbed. Eventually, the young man departed. Only then, when alone, Paracelso took the ashes, whispered a word, and "the rose reappeared." The mystical lore discussed by Scholem and the Gnostics can be displayed and portrayed and pertains to magic. It is of no interest to the rabbis. What the rabbis (see *Berakhot* 55a) and Paracelso as well sought is the instrument "which the divinity used to create heavens and earth."[82] In a paradoxical sense Paracelso's prayer was answered. For Maimonides, as with Borges's Paracelso and the rabbis, esoterics is imparted by an initial act of refusal, by *not* teaching.

Authoritative dissemination of esoteric knowledge is not only impossible it is forbidden to attempt—more precisely—to pretend.

SUBJECTIVITY AND THE ESOTERIC INSIGHT

From the preceding a fundamental difference emerges between rabbinic esoterics and Scholem's Gnosticism and mysticism. Gnosticism and mysticism focus on the *content* of the experience. What counts for the rabbis is the *structure* of the esoteric insight. The esoteric insight is not in itself communicable. It does not involve a mysterious, secret knowledge. Rather, it flows from a different level of consciousness. Communication expresses objectivity. The esoteric is subjective: it vanishes as soon as it is translated into the realm of the objective and the ordinary.

Two closely related factors concern the subjective character of an esoteric insight. One is external, pertaining to the mode of transmission. Because esoteric knowledge cannot be transmitted through the regular chain of tradition, it cannot be authenticated on the basis of authority. It cannot be hierarchically transmitted from a "superior" to an "inferior," but, in the words of Maimonides, it can only be "transferred," that is, horizontally.[83] The other factor concerns the uncertainty of the esoteric insight. Maimonides was careful to point out that although he was subjectively convinced of his esoteric views, they were objectively uncertain. To stress the point, when discussing the merits of his esoteric insights, Maimonides was mindful to doubly qualify them with the subjunctive 'might be' (*'aṣa*) and 'for me' (*'indi*), underscoring that "*it might* be that it was revealed, comprehended, and had became clear without any doubt *for me* of what I understood of this."[84] Reflecting on his own understanding of esoterics he admitted, "that what I have ascertained here is the result of conjecture and supposition. I neither had a divine inspiration that taught me what had been intended [by the esoteric texts] nor was I instructed in what I believe by a teacher."[85] In his own style[86] Maimonides was defining the nature of esoteric insight: subjective certainty cannot be attested on objective grounds. On the one hand, he was convinced that he had succeeded in unraveling the true meaning of Jewish esoterics, "that the thing is like this, without a doubt." On the other hand, he recognized "that the thing could be the opposite [*bi-khalafha*], and what was intended may have been something different."[87] Thus, esoteric insight is structurally connected with subjectivity.

Paradoxically, the historical loss of Jewish esoteric tradition served to further strengthen and preserve Jewish esoteric tradition: esoterics must be absolutely subjective, admitting of a (hypothetical) possibility to the contrary. Put another way, objective certainty is objective proof of esoteric inauthenticity. Esoteric insight may develop only within the realm of subjectivity when "the object will surface and emit, and then conceal itself" as with the spinning sword guarding the road to Eden.[88] This is why Maimonides did not view the loss of the ancient esoteric knowledge as tragic. Since the loss of the *content* of Jewish esoterics was the result of the *method* of Jewish esoterics, "it was correct that this had occurred."[89] Anticipating G. E. Lessing (1729–1781), this means that if one would have to choose between the ability to know the truth and the ability to investigate the truth, it would be wiser to choose the latter. From the position of a teacher or outside viewer the content of the student's esoteric insight is irrelevant. As with prophecy, the vision varies according to personal circumstances.[90] What matters is the structure of the insight: the message is in the method.[91]

From this point of view the works of gnosticism and mysticism dealing with the content of esoterics are a self-contradiction.

THE RESOLUTION OF UNCONCLUDED SUBSCRIPTS

Maimonides structured the *Guide* as an intellectual maze designed to "scatter" the headings of chapters. "Don't ask of me here," Maimonides writes in the Introduction to the *Guide*, "for more than the headings of chapters."[92] The task of the teacher is to goad the student to a crossroad, thus generating a crisis of choice. The crisis is brought about by the headings of chapters, underlying the unconcluded subscripts. They involve two types of contradictions.[93]

First are contradictions peculiar to the instruction of any complex subject. At the early stages of instruction, a teacher may have to ignore precision and present the subject in an unconcluded form to help the student grasp the lesson.[94] The "headings" are only "beginnings," requiring further development and refinement as progress is made.[95] The second type of contradiction is peculiar to the instruction of esoterics.[96] The teacher cannot reveal all at once. As with the spinning sword guarding the road to Eden, the teacher must conceal and then reveal.[97] The technique includes the dissemination of contradictions and encoding a subscript that only the qualified student can discover and decode.[98] The model for the tension teacher-student is the metaphor "golden apples in a silver mesh," illustrating the "inner" and "outer" levels of a well-articulated speech.[99] Precisely, because the student has not reached a level to process the "golden apples," the teacher must camouflage the ideas as silver.[100] It would be the specific task of the student to discover and decode the subscript of gold underneath the mesh. The contradictions between the fine-chiseled eyelet themselves and between them and the inner gold bring the student into a state of 'perplexity' (*ḥa'ira*)—a crisis that could only be resolved by shifting from the realm of objectivity to the realm of subjectivity. At this level perplexity cannot be mediated. The resolution requires a breach in the relationship teacher-student whereby knowledge does not proceed from a hierarchical authority but "is transferred"—that is, horizontally—"from one bosom to the other."[101] The crisis is resolved, at the point that the perplexed (*ḥa'iran*) student chooses to probe into his own inwardness rather than to appropriate someone else's truth.[102]

DESCENDING TOWARD THE INNER SANCTUARY

Rabbinic literature has preserved two models illustrating the crisis underlying the esoteric insight. The first model is a royal 'orchard' (*pardes*). The rabbis identified the scriptural expression "they are planted like nails" (Eccl 12:11) with "the words of the Tora," that is, the teachings of the old masters, adding, "just like plants bear fruits and grow, similarly the words of the Tora bear fruits and grow." In a different context Maimonides identified the "words of the Tora" with the esoteric teachings of Israel.[103] There are two distinct qualities to these teachings. Like nails they are deeply instilled and are not easy to remove. At the same time like plants they "bear fruits and grow."

> The words of the Tora were compared to a goad. To teach you: Just like a goad directs the [plowing] cow to its furrow, bringing thus life to the world, in the same manner the words of the Tora direct those who study it away from the paths of death into the paths of life. Lest you might say: Just like a goad could be removed, perhaps, also the words of the Tora could be removed? The text teaches: "nails." Lest you might say: Just like nails decay and do not grow, in the same manner the words of the Tora decay and do not grow? The text teaches: "planted." Just like a plant bears fruits and grows, the words of the Tora, too, bear fruits and grow.[104]

The "orchard" is the grove where the "plants" cultivated by the rabbis grow.

This text centers around the famous four scholars who had "entered into the orchard" (*nikhnesu la-pardes*).[105] The verb *entered* is to be understood in the technical sense of 'to ingress in order to present their respective opening prologue' (petiḥa), under the tutelage of R. Joshua (first and second centuries). Since the foursome were outstanding scholars, one must assume that they had properly decoded the numerous informal references to esoteric material made by their teachers during their education.[106] When R. Joshua wanted to be initiated into the realm of esoterics, he began the prologue (pataḥ) on his own without his teacher's permission. Only later did he present the main lecture (hirṣa) before his teacher.[107] The orchard model pertains to the third step of the procedure mentioned above, before the student had delivered the initial prologue. The task of the student was to present his dissertation for approval.[108] The "orchard" stands for the maze of unconcluded chapters or "plants" that "bear fruits and grow" designed by the teacher.[109] A successful student would find his way through the maze and reach the final destination. An unsuccessful student would be caught up in the maze, failing to complete the dissertation. Approval of the opening prologue is designated 'to enter in peace' (*nikhnas be-shalom*). Approval of the main dissertation is designated 'to exit in peace' (*yaṣa be-shalom*). Only R. 'Aqiba 'entered in peace and exited in peace' (*nikhnas be-shalom ve-yaṣa be-shalom*).[110] This means that he not only counted on his teacher's approval to proceed with the opening prologue but that he had also gained approval for the main dissertation. R. Joshua declined to say *shalom* to one of the students who had lost his way in the orchard.[111] His refusal signaled that the opening prologue was not approved. Instead, he asked him: "Where are you coming from, and where are you going to?" This question is asked of someone who has lost his way. Metaphorically, it addresses someone who has lost his sense of judgment.[112] In disapproval R. Joshua noted, "ben Zoma still is (*'adayin*) outside (*ba-ḥuṣ*).[113] Maimonides took this to mean that ben Zoma was unable to find the entrance into the realm of the esoteric, remaining outside the heavenly city and the heavenly palace.[114] Because ben Zoma had failed in his opening prologue (petiḥa), he could not deliver the main dissertation (see below).

The orchard is the Holy precinct containing the inner Sanctuary (*qodesh ha-qodashim*) at the Temple in Jerusalem. In the Greco-Roman world memorization was effected by imprinting a building in the mind and then proceeding to associate the words of a text with the different parts of the building. The ancient orator is described "as moving in imagination through his memory *whilst* he is making his speech" [italics in original].[115] The rabbis used a different method to memorize the text of the Oral Law.[116] As is evident from the Mishna *Middot*, however, the rabbis had memorized the plan of the Temple at Jerusalem. It served as the model for esoteric discourse. In this fashion the ancient rabbi could "move" in his mind (*le-ṭayyel*) through the different parts of the Temple and reach the inner Sanctuary where the *Shekhina* (Divine Presence) dwells, as did R. Ismael ben Elisha (second century), who, although living after the destruction of the Temple, was able mentally to enter into the inner Sanctuary and to offer the sacraments of the High Priest.[117]

There is a critical clue hinting at the link between the orchard and the inner Sanctuary. The orchard contained an upper chamber (*'aliya*).[118] This detail seems trivial and inconsequential. Elsewhere, however, the Mishna reports that the workers restoring the inner Sanctuary at the Temple in Jerusalem were lowered from a special 'trap' (*lul*) built at the Temple's upper chamber ('aliya). To prevent the workers from peeking (*le-haṣṣiṣ*) at the Divine Glory residing at the inner Sanctuary and "delighting (*lazun*) their eyes from Him," they were lowered inside a box.[119] Generally, "to delight one's eyes" means to look at something and take *mental* pleasure as when opening a window to peek at the outside.[120] When accompanied by the preposition *mi-mennu* (from him or it) it means to peek at someone with unchaste intentions. This expression evokes a passage in Nm 15:39: "Do not deviate after your hearts and after your eyes (*'enekhem*) because you will be whoring (*zonim*) after them." The rabbis interpreted this verse to refer to both 'whoring' and 'heresy'.[121] The connection 'whoring/heresy' rests on the principle that an individual who has not yet learned to control his sexual impulses would end up confusing his own delusions with the divine: the numinous is a function of repression and narcissistic obsessions.[122] Accordingly, heretics are invariably promiscuous and vice versa, thus, the rabbinic doctrine that someone who "delights his eyes" in sexual matters could not possibly behold the divine. Conversely, "Whoever sees a sexual object (*debar 'erva*) and does not delight his eyes from it (*zan 'enav mi-mennu*) will merit to receive the countenance of the Shekhina (Divine Presence)."[123] Moses, taught the rabbis, "did not delight his eyes from the Shekhina. [This is why] he enjoyed the Shekhina."[124] By contrast, Nadab and Abihu "delighted their eyes from Him" and were punished,[125] hence, Maimonides's view that someone who is unable to control his sexual impulses cannot be a prophet.[126]

Since the descent from the upper chamber into the inner Sanctuary is fraught with danger lest the initiate would be lured to peek at the Divine Presence and "delight his eyes from Him," special caution was warranted. Those daring to enter the orchard mentally and to find the Temple through the maze had to climb to the upper chamber and descend to the inner Sanctuary via the trap. The process is referred to as "descending to the Merkaba." The Merkaba or Divine Chariot was pulled by the heavenly cherubs. Although the actual Ark and the cherubs were no longer at the Second Temple, the Shekhina was still present in the inner Sanctuary. Hence, to descend to the Sanctuary was "to descend to the Merkaba."

Maimonides designated the esoteric journey into the Sanctuary 'to parade' (le-ṭayyel)—in the sense of a ceremonial march—'through the orchard'. The same term was used by the rabbis to describe the march of the righteous in Paradise in company of the Almighty.[127]

THE REALM OF SUBJECTIVITY

In the story of the sages entering the orchard only R. 'Aqiba was successful. Rabbinic literature has preserved two statements describing his accomplishment. One states that he "ascended in peace and descended in peace" (*'ala be-shalom ve-yarad be-shalom*).[128] This refers to his ascension to the Temple's upper chamber and descending to the inner Sanctuary via the trap. Since he had taken the necessary precautions (as did the workers at the Temple) not to peek on the way down, he "descended in peace." Another source reports that he "entered in peace and exited in peace" (nikhnas be-shalom ve-yaṣa be-shalom). This means that his prologue (nikhnas) and main dissertation (*ve-yaṣa*) had been approved.[129]

The others failed to take adequate precautions. They "peeked," "delighted" their "eyes from Him," and were unable to exit in peace. One of them died shortly thereafter. Another lost his mind.[130] According to the Babylonian Talmud, it was ben 'Azai who died. R. Hayye Ga'on explained that he died suddenly before he could finish his (erroneous) dissertation.[131] A rabbinic metaphor illustrates that incident.

> To someone who said: "I want to see the Glory of the King!" They told him: "Go to the city and you will see him." He entered [nikhnas] and saw a curtain inlaid with precious stones and pearls stretched over the gate of the city. Unable to delight his eyes from it [*lazun et 'enav mi-mennu*] he collapsed.[132] They told him: "If you were unable to delight your eyes from the curtain stretching over the city's gate, that only has precious stones and pearls, and consequently you collapsed, how much worst would it have been if you had entered the city."[133]

A rabbinic source preserved an important statement that must have been pronounced by one of the participants soon after exiting the orchard: "Do not glance at someone else's vineyard. If you glanced at it, do not come down. If you came down, do not look at it. If you looked at it, do not touch it. And if he [meaning: you] ate [from it], behold this man maimed his soul in this world and in the world to come."[134]

The reference to a "vineyard" rather than to an "orchard" indicates that the statement was pronounced shortly after the event before it was officially formulated by the Academies. The warning not to "glance at the vineyard of another man" brings to mind the biblical prohibition against coveting another man's wife and property. The caution "do not come down," alludes to the descent from the "upper chamber" ('aliya). It is a warning against the temptation to peek at the Divine Presence while descending to the inner Sanctuary, finally tampering with the forbidden fruit. In due course the reason for the failure will be evident.

Ben Zoma succeeded in entering the orchard but failed to find the Temple's gate. The topic of his opening dialogue was the separation between the waters taking place in the second day of creation (Gn 1:6–7). When he was asked by R. Joshua to explicate, he dwelt on the distance between the waters. According to Maimonides, the mistake consisted in believing that the separation between the upper and lower waters was only spatial, both retaining the same original nature. In reality, their separation involved a radical change in their respective natures, just like the separation of light and darkness in the first day (Gn 1:4). Out of the original stuff designated 'water' (Gn 1:2), different substances were created.[135] R. 'Aqiba's warning, "When you reach marble stones, do not say 'Water', 'Water',"[136] came to correct ben Zoma's mistake: the water above heaven was not the same as the water below heaven. A radical change had taken place. The upper water was transformed into a substance designated "marble stone." Therefore, it would be false to designate them by the same name. Hence R. 'Aqiba's warning, "Do not say 'Water', 'Water'."[137] Because the heavenly abode is somehow associated with the upper water, it would be offensive to regard it as of the same substance as the lower water. The point was illustrated with the following metaphor: "To a king who built a palace in a place of sewers, a place of garbage, a place of rubbish. And one comes and says, "This palace is in a place of sewers, in a place of garbage, in a place of rubbish." Isn't he insulting? In the same manner, whoever says that at the beginning the world was water with water, he would be insulting."[138] By "water with water" the similarity of both types of substances was meant. R. 'Aqiba's reference to "marble stones" together with "water, water" acquires precision in light of the rabbinic tradition that the Herodian Temple was built with a marble given the impression of waves.[139] It follows that R. 'Aqiba's warning pertained to the time when ben Zoma was standing *outside* the Temple building, attempting to find the gate to the divine precinct. Thus, his remark was synonymous to R. Joshua's statement, "ben Zoma still is outside" ('adayin ba-huṣ).[140] A final note, in rabbinic literature the expression "water, water" has sexual connotations.[141]

The third member of the group was Elisha ben Abuya (second century). According to the version preserved by Maimonides, the rabbis applied to him the verse, "Have you found honey? Eat only what you can! Lest you are loaded with it and will vomit it" (Prv 26:16). This means that he trespassed the boundaries of his understanding.[142] Thus, he cut some of the plants (*qiṭṭea' ba-neṭi'ot*) to take a further look.[143] The "plants" are the fundamental teachings or "words of the Tora" "planted" by the ancient rabbis.[144] Elisha ben Abuya not only did not further develop these "plants," but cut some of them out. He "delighted his eyes" with the esoteric vision, became lustful, and engaged in sexual promiscuity. After exiting the orchard he propositioned a prostitute. To prove to her that he was not [no longer?] the famous scholar he uprooted a radish on the Sabbath and ate it.[145] The rabbis offered the following illustration: "A model, to what may this be compared? To a royal orchard having an upper chamber built on the top. What a man can do?—to take a glimpse! providing that he would not nourish his eyes [*yazin et 'enav*] from him [the king]."[146] The model conveys the lure present in esoteric discourse. Upon crossing into the orchard one may choose a wrong perspective and fell prey to the temptation of a forbidden insight insinuated by the expression (*yazin et 'enav*).

To illustrate the crossroad structuring this crisis the rabbis offered a second model. Rather than to tread on one of the paths lying ahead, the chartering of a new path is required. In our terms, this means that the only way outside the orchard is through the realm of subjectivity. Since subjectivity cannot be mediated, it cannot be constructed on the basis of someone else's knowledge or authority. By crossing into the orchard and looking at things from within the student places himself outside the realm of objectivity, facing the mystery of God and Creation on his own. The crisis of absolute choice is bound up with the specific subjectivity of each individual. It cannot be processed by a superior authority that would finish the student's unconcluded chapters. Because it cannot be structured on someone else's experience, it involves the final breach of the teacher-student relation. In this manner direct perception—an esoteric insight—is effected. The crisis of subjectivity involves chartering a new road and treading upon a path that no one else has trod before. In this specific way an esoteric insight is necessarily subjective, and subjectivity is necessarily esoteric. The principle is illustrated with a second model: "They further presented another model: to what may this be compared? To a street leading to two paths, one of fire and the other of snow. If he would turn here, he would be consumed by fire, if he would turn there he would be consumed by snow. What is one to do? He must walk in the middle, providing that he would not turn either here or there."[147] A slightly different version was preserved in the Talmud *Yerushalmi*. In it, the "street" leading to the crossroad is explicitly identified with the Tora: "The Tora is analogous to two paths, one [leading] to fire and another to snow. Anyone bearing toward this will perish by fire. Anyone bearing toward that will perish by snow. What is one to do? Let him walk in the middle!"[148]

There are no clues as to what these paths are. In a rabbinic source now lost the rabbis associated this model with the verse, "He who walks perfectly shall be saved, but he who is warped by the paths shall fall in one of them"

(Prv 28:18).[149] Being "warped (*ne'qash*) by the paths" alludes to a trap lying on the way. The plural "ways" indicates that trap involves more than one way.[150] The puzzle is difficult to solve because the rabbis associated these paths with the Tora itself. What could that be?

AT THE CROSSROADS

Maimonides maintained that authentic esoteric material has been encoded in rabbinic literature. One may discover "a few remarks and allusions in the Talmud and Midrashot, containing a small pulp and many peels."[151] In the footsteps of the Scripture the rabbis spoke about esoteric subjects in riddles. Many "wondrous and true subjects attained by the most prominent intellect of the philosophers are scattered throughout the Midrashot."[152] The riddles were only "hinted" at by the rabbis. Since "they are mixed" with the sayings of other scholars and with other types of material, they will not be noticed except by those with the proper background.[153] In his youth Maimonides began to prepare two works designed to decode this material: *Kitab al-Nubu'a* (The book on prophecy) was designed to decode the biblical metaphors and *Kitab al-Muṭabaqat* (The book of correlations) on rabbinic metaphors and homilies (*derashot*) bearing on esoteric subjects.[154] As the title of the second work implies, its purpose was to decode the rabbinic metaphors and homilies by pointing to 'the correlations' (*muṭabaqat*) between the metaphor and the referent object.[155] Since by understanding the proper meaning of biblical metaphors one could decode the words of the rabbis, and vice versa, these works were to complement one another. Because of religious and intellectual scruples, Maimonides was displeased with the results yielded by that methodology and desisted from completing these works.[156] Instead he decided to pursue a different plan: "the significance of prophecy, explanation of its degrees, and the clarification of the metaphors in those writings will be explained in this work [the *Guide*] with a different methodology."[157] This means that the *Guide* will only address the topics of the "Book on Prophecy." The new methodology will enable the qualified reader to accomplish on his own the objectives of the work on rabbinic esoterics interrupted by Maimonides. Indeed, Maimonides associated the use of metaphors and riddles with the methodology used by "every Rabbanite [*rabbani*] theologian [*ilahi*] sage."[158] In this context the term *rabbani* does not mean 'theologian' because then it would be synonymous with *ilahi* and, therefore, meaningless. Rather, here it means 'Rabbanite' in opposition to 'Karaite'. In this sense it was used by Maimonides when he wrote that in the introduction to his commentary to the Mishna he had presented "the principles of prophecy and the principles of the Oral tradition that every rabbani is required to believe in."[159] This is also how it was understood by the early Hebrew translators and is commonly used by Arabic-speaking Jews. The reference to a Rabbanite public is particularly significant in light of the fact that Maimonides believed that he was using the same methodology and pursuing the esoteric tradition of the rabbis.[160]

Therefore, it should not be improper to suggest that Maimonides identified the rabbinic model discussed above and thereby the introductory issue of esoterics with the problem of divine attributes.[161] Concerning the place of attributes, he wrote:

> However, reference to the [divine] attributes, how are they to be negated from Him, and what is the significance of the attributes assigned to Him. . . . Behold all these are very profound subjects and truly belong to the secrets of the Tora [*sitre tora*] and are the mysteries [*al-sodot*] that are always mentioned in the writings of the Prophets and the words of the sages of blessed memory. These are the matters that one ought to speak about only in headings of the chapters [*be-rashe ha-peraqim*], as we have mentioned, and also to a qualified individual.[162]

The problem of attributes in Judaism may be best grasped in terms of the preceding model. The Tora refers to God with positive attributes. At the same time God is described as absolutely one and absolutely different. This could lead to a Gnostic theology, positing two distinct and totally separate aspects of God: a lower one as a creator-demiurge, who revealed himself in the Tora, and a superior *deus absconditus*, transcending the Tora and the concerns of humankind. The first path may be compared to "fire" because it consumes the believer by positing an anthropomorphic deity, too close and too similar to humans. In such a situation one will "delight his eyes from Him" and feed his own narcissistic delusions.[163] The second path may be compared to "snow," a deity disinterested in the affairs of humans. Either of these two paths results in total perdition. In the case of Elisha, who "cut the plants," this doctrine led to immorality, antinomism, and the doctrine of 'two authorities' (*shete rashuyot*) characteristic of the 'heretics' (*minim*).[164]

Concerning this situation the Mishna warned, "Whoever does not care for the honor of his Maker, better for him not to have come to the world."[165] According to Maimonides, this is the opposite of a sage, such as R. Eleazar ben 'Arakh, "who knows how to understand and expound on the Glory of his Father in Heaven."[166] Referring to Elisha ben Abuya, who blundered because he had trespassed the limits of his understanding, Maimonides commented: "It alludes to our explanation, that a man should not charge to speculate with his corrupt imagination. If any misgivings should arise or if a subject is not clear to him, he should not reject it, discard it, and hasten to deny it, but he should be calm 'and care for the honor of his Maker.' He should be fearful and stop."[167] This doctrine was expounded by Rab (second and third centuries). Referring to the above-mentioned Mishna, he applied the following verse:

> "Let the lips of falsehood be mute (which express heinously against the righteous, in pride and scorn)" (Ps 31:19). Let them be hushed, let them be fastened, let them be silent! . . . "Which express heinously [*'ataq*] against the righteous"—which express against the Righteous of the Universe [God], things that He removed from his creatures. "In pride and scorn"—this is one who is arrogant and says, "I expound [doresh] on *Ma'aśe Bereshit*." He thinks that he is exalting [*ki-mga'e*], but he is in fact only insulting.[168]

In this fashion Rab was chastising those who applied to God attributes taken from His creation. Similarly, it was reported in his name, "We have not found the might and strength of the Holy One," meaning that God is beyond human expression. This leads directly to the doctrine of praise ➞ silence discussed above. Addressing the absolute ineffability of God's majesty, R. Abun (third century) elaborated further, "The elixir of everything is silence." He went on to compare this situation, "to a flawless pearl, where all praise is faltering" because it is beyond articulation.[169]

Maimonides developed his negative theology on the basis of these two doctrines. With Rab, he ascertained that "there is no [ontological] affinity between Him and anything of what He created." This is based on the principle that God's existence is categorically different than that of His creation with no point of comparison between Him and anything else.[170] The application of positive attributes to God is the effect of human projections. The attributes are deemed "perfection in Him because you find them to be perfection in us,"[171] thus, the rabbinic warning, "not to delight his eyes from Him."[172] Silence is the highest praise of God.

With the rabbis, Maimonides regarded the Tora (*al-tanzil*), that is, the Tora itself, as the 'path' (*derekh*) leading some people to assign positive attributes to God. To alert the attentive reader that he was alluding to the "path" of rabbinic literature he used the Hebrew *derekh*. This is a code-term used to designate "attributes."[173] Because it can be taken for an Arabic homonym, it was missed by some translators.[174] "Some people followed the course of comparison, and believed Him to be a body with positive attributes. Others have raised above this path [*al-derekh*] negating [from Him] a body but preserving the attributes. All this is the effect of following the overt meaning of the revealed books."[175]

Concerning the inappropriateness of applying to God the attributes of his creatures, a Talmudic authority, R. Yose bar Ḥanina (third century), followed the explanation of Rab. Quoting an old rabbinic text, he taught: "'He who honors himself by putting to shame his fellowman has no portion in the world to come.'"[176] How much more so one who honors himself by [dis]honoring the Eternal one![177] Paraphrasing the above, Maimonides commented, "You should reflect and think: if slander and defamation are awesome sins, how much more so is to speak freely about the essence of God and to describe Him with attributes which He is above." Reflecting on some liturgical poems applying to God all kind of attributes, Maimonides continued:

> I am not saying that these are [mere] sins, but a sacrilege and a blasphemy, inadvertent on the part of the audience and the ignoramus who compose them. Nonetheless, whoever perceives the fault of those sayings and recites them is, in my opinion, one of those about whom it was said, "And the children of Israel attributed things that were not so to the Lord their God" (2Kgs 17:9). [About such a person] it was said, too: "And they spoke unfairness of God" (Is 32:6). If you are one of those who does care "for the Honor of his Maker," it would be unworthy of you to hear them and much more so to utter them.[178]

Hence, assigning positive attributes to God constitutes an affront "to the honor" of the Maker.

A similar attitude was displayed by Maimonides toward those who chose the other 'path' (derekh), leading to antinomism and nihilism. Some rabbis identified the person who "does not care for the honor of his Maker" with someone who "makes a sin in secret"[179]—probably an allusion to antinomian rituals.[180] This is the second "path" negating from God any concern from human affairs. To alert the attentive reader that he was alluding to the "path" of the rabbis Maimonides used the Hebrew *derekh*. As in the preceding case translators mistook it for some Arabic homonym. Commenting on the rabbinic doctrine, "the considerations of sin are harsher than sin,"[181] Maimonides noted:

> As we have explained, if a man sins, he sins because of circumstances related to his substance. Thinking, at any rate, is a human faculty related to his [inner] form. [Therefore,] if he contemplates to sin with his thought, then he sins with the most noble of his being. . . . (This human form and all of the faculties related to it should not be used except for what it [the soul] was designed for—to be connected with what is higher—not to fall to the lowliest path [*lil-derekh*].[182]

The crisis effected by the "two paths" results in bewilderment. It is now clear why the rabbis had established as a condition for esoteric instruction "that his [the student's] heart is troubled in his midst."[183] Only an individual who has been existentially "caught up" in this dilemma could have the sensitivity and stamina for esoteric insight. The constant tension between the "two paths" is resolved in a perennial spinning of darkness and light as with the revolving sword. Apophasis, the positing of a dialectical relationship generated by the tension positive/negative attributes, is resolved in an esoteric insight expressed in the paradox 'knowledge ➞ un-knowledge' 'praise ➞ silence'. It requires constant dialectical evaluation. "Whoever evaluates his footpaths," taught the rabbis, "will have the privilege to behold the salvation of the Holy One."[184]

The rabbis designated a student capable of critical judgment a "crossroad." "What does it mean a crossroad [*parashat derakhim*]," asked the rabbis, "this is an advanced student! [talmid ḥakhamim]."[185] Unlike the common student who is exposed to a single teacher, an advanced student, as its Hebrew designation "student of sages" indicates, had been exposed to many teachers and had acquired a critical knowledge of the Tora. Unlike the sage, however, he has not yet resolved the conflicting views and systems to which he was exposed. A psychological profile distinguishes the sage from the advanced student. The sage (ḥakham) chartered his own path and then moved beyond the crossroad. Having experienced his own subjectivity, he is intellectually autonomous. The advanced student has yet to unravel the subscripts—the text beneath the text—and to resolve the unconcluded chapters structuring his education. At that stage subjectivity is impossible. He is not *at* a crossroad, but, as the rabbis put it, he *is* a crossroad. Maimonides designated such an individual 'perplexed' (ḥa'iran). The *Guide* was composed for him.

THE EPISTLE TO THE STUDENT/READER

Maimonides begins the *Guide* with an epistle addressed to a student. In it he narrates the circumstances that brought to him a student who wanted to know the "secrets of the Prophetic writings." He tells about the student's educational and intellectual background, his stay and eventual departure, and how his parting prompted him to write the *Guide*. It ends with a dedicatory note stating that [1] his absence induced him "to fashion (*li-waḍa'a*) this work which I had fashioned (*waḍa'taha*) for you and those who are like you, although are few"; [2] and that he had "made" the *Guide* into "scattered (*manṭura*) chapters, and all that was written would reach you one by one wherever you are. You (be in) peace."

There are several problems with this epistle. It seems anecdotal and out of character with the *Guide*. The few points of interest about the educational and intellectual background of the student, serving to identify the readership for which the *Guide* was intended, were spelled out in the introduction.[186] The circumstances prompting Maimonides to write the *Guide* seem irrelevant. What could be the significance of the fact that the *Guide* was written after the student left? Or that instead of a complete volume the student would be receiving the *Guide* in installments?

Only upon breaking the umbilical cord with the teacher and deciding to face 'perplexity' on his own can a student be exposed to the technique leading to apophatic knowledge and esoteric insight. In the dedicatory note Maimonides did not refer to the writing of the *Guide* with the more common terms *allafa* (to write, to compose) and *ta'alif* (composition of a book)¹⁸⁷ but with *waḍaʿa* (to fashion, to author). This term also means 'to give birth'. Therefore, the absence of the student was not only a stimulus but a condition sine qua non for composing the *Guide* to him.

The *Guide* is "made" into "scattered (*manṯura*) chapters" that will "reach you one by one wherever you are." Maimonides explained that the "headings of chapters" or basic doctrines contained in the *Guide* are neither "in order nor in succession but mingled and combined" with other matters requiring explanation.¹⁸⁸ Thereby, he was assuring the student and the attentive reader as well that eventually, after a period of maturation, the subtextual order of the *Guide* would "reach" him "one by one" regardless of time and place. Maimonides does not say that the chapters will be sent to the student but that they will "reach" him in due course. A similar point is made later. Addressing the attentive reader, he counsels:

> If you want to attain all that is enclosed [in this work] so that nothing escapes you, apply each chapter on one another. Your aim should not merely be understanding the general significance of a chapter but grasping each word that is mentioned in the development of theme although it does not pertain to the subject of the chapter. Because in this work words are not used haphazardly but with much discrimination, high precision, and care from flaw, in the exposition of a problem. Nothing in it is said out of place but to explain some subject in its place.¹⁸⁹

Proper decoding of the *Guide* requires arduous investigation and careful analysis. The reader should not expect immediate results. In the end, however, the *Guide* will elucidate the most difficult problems of the Law. Maimonides continues: "Do not pursue it with your presumptions because you would be hurting me and not benefit yourself.¹⁹⁰ But you must [first] study whatever you need to study, reflect always on it, and it will explain to you the greatest problems of the Law facing every rational person."¹⁹¹

THE *GUIDE* IN FUNCTION OF *MEṬAṬRON*

There are other aspects to the term *manṯura* (scattered) essential for a proper understanding of the *Guide*. The root *naṯara*, also means 'to write in prose'. The form *naṯr* not only means 'prose' but 'style'. Accordingly, the "scattering" of the material concerns the literary style and structure of the *Guide.* Maimonides could have chosen one of two styles: an expository style, without a dialogue, like the philosophical work of Seʿadya Gaʾon (882–942), or a dialogic form in which he converses with a partner, like the philosophical works of Solomon ibn Gabirol (ca. 1020–ca. 1057) and Judah ha-Levi (ca. 1075–1141). Instead, he developed a special type of expository technique. At the surface the *Guide* contains no dialogues. At the subtextual level, however, a sustained dialogue is initiated not by Maimonides but by a student in search of "the secrets of the Prophetic writings," a student representing the reader for whom the *Guide* was written. Maimonides, a teacher limited by the constraints of the Law and the nature of the subject, is a partner responding to the student/reader. The principal task of the teacher is to develop a technique of indirect communication. The technique is closely related to another aspect of naṭara. The form *naṭri* means both 'prosaic' and 'small fragment'. Maimonides's technique consisted in the naṭr (scattering) of *nuṭar* (small tiny fragments). Essential for the understanding of this technique is the distinction between formal and casual, indirect teaching. As mentioned, although the teacher is restricted from transmitting (mosrin) formally esoteric material, he may, at his discretion, casually enlighten a student on esoteric matters.[192] As Maimonides wrote to his student, when the occasion arose, he 'unsheathed' (*alwaḥ*) and 'insinuated' (*ashir*) to him some of the esoteric teachings in the Scripture.[193] "Whenever we met, and a Scriptural passage or a statement of the rabbis was mentioned, insinuating some unusual concepts, I never refrained from explaining it to you." Similarly, responding to an inquiry, Hayye Gaʾon ascertained that he did not learn about the divine names through tradition, but "casually."[194] Maimonides, however, wanted the student [eventually] to "comprehend the truth methodically, not casually." The system of indirect or casual communication leads into the concept of parergon, or ornamentation of the text.[195] In the *Guide* the function of the parergon is exactly the opposite of that described by Kant. Rather than to expose and to enhance the object that it contains, in the *Guide* the function of the parergon is to conceal the tiny fragments containing the headings of the chapters and to make them appear casual. In turn, because these fragments are scattered in a(n apparently) disorderly fashion, they, too, function as the parergon of the parergon.[196] It would be the task of the student/reader to determine what is ornamental and what is substantive in the *Guide*, or what is the light and what is the darkness concealing the light. As with the Chinese nobleman in Borges's story, "The Garden of Forking Paths," Maimonides was simultaneously writing a book and constructing a maze. Only the student / reader worthy of being initiated into the "secrets of the Prophetic writings" would make the right choices, find his way out of the network of labyrinths, and "exit in peace." An effect of this technique is that the apophatic experience of the student / reader will be absolutely unique and absolutely subjective.

The teacher is not an intermediary shaping, affecting, and controlling the perception of the student / reader. His task is to guide by insinuation rather than by imparting authoritative, objective knowledge. In the language of Maimonides such a teacher functions as a dalala, a 'signpost' pointing externally. It results in bifurcation: by giving direction the dalala branches the path into two. Because in such a situation the truth could be linked with either of the two paths, it appears casual. Thus, a signpost generates, simultaneously, direction and ḥa'ira (perplexity).[197]

The source of Maimonides's signpost pointing externally to the truth is rabbinic. It has been noted that the Rabbinic Angel Meṭaṭron, prominent among the celestial beings, derives his name from *meṭaṭor,* a Latin loanword that in rabbinic literature stands for a 'signpost', or a 'guide', 'scout', "pointing at the way."[198] The specific function of this angel is to herald God's presence. In a dialogue with a heretic, believing in the Gnostic doctrine of "two authorities," a rabbi taught that the name of this angel "is like the name of His master." It means that because his presence announces the presence of God, he is addressed as if he were God. In linguistic terms it means that the angel functions as the *signifier,* not the *signified.* In Maimonidean terminology it is the 'knowledge' preceding the 'un-knowledge', or the 'light' preceding the 'darkness' of the spinning sword.[199] At the existential level the individual must not confuse the angel with God. This is why the esoteric experience involves a first act of nonseeing, of refusing to accept the initial stage of the esoteric experience as revelatory of God, like Moses, who initially "hid his face because he was afraid to glance at the Lord" (Ex 3:6). It was in compensation for this initial act of nonseeing, the rabbis taught, that Moses eventually perceived God (see Nm 12:8).[200] Linguistically, one addresses oneself to the *person* to whom one says *you* rather than to the grammatical *pronoun you.* Similarly, the object of one's address is God himself, not the angel. Only in this fashion, the angel does not displace God. As the rabbi explained to the heretic, one is cautioned not to "worship him" or "substitute him" (the angel) for God. Because unlike the inferior deity of the Gnostics this angel has no authority of its own, it cannot forgive the sins of Israel. "There is a firmly established creed in our hands," continued the rabbi, "that it would not be accepted even as a letter carrier [another version: as an intermediary] [of God]."[201]

The preceding dialogue illustrates Elisha ben Abuya's predicament. The Talmud relates that in his esoteric vision Elisha saw Angel Meṭaṭron "seating and registering the merits of Israel." In rabbinic Hebrew 'seating' implies authority. Since no one may 'seat' in heaven except God, Elisha concluded that Meṭaṭron must be the deity whom the Gnostics claimed has revealed the Tora to Israel and administers their affairs.[202] His error consisted in mistaking the signifier for the signified, or, in the language of the rabbis, the herald for the king. This is why, when Elisha heard a "heavenly voice, coming from behind the veil" announcing that he could not repent, he believed it to be irrevocable.[203] Within this context the following story is highly instructive. R. Sheshat (third and fourth centuries), who was blind, went to a parade honoring the king. A heretic made fun of him. "I could discern more than you," responded the rabbi. When the first battalion marched, there was a tumult. The heretic exclaimned "The king has arrived!" "The king has not arrived!" replied R. Sheshat. The same was repeated when the second battalion marched. Again, R. Sheshat replied, "The king has not arrived!" Finally, when the third battalion marched, there was silence. R. Sheshat told the heretic, "Surely, the king has arrived!" When asked how he knew, he responded, "The earthly kingdom is like the heavenly kingdom." He then illustrated his point from God's revelation to Elijah. The wind, the sound, and the fire were only the heralds of God; His presence was not revealed in them but in the "silent voice" (1Kgs 19:12).[204] R. Sheshat was alluding to the controversy with the Gnostic mentioned before, concerning the distinction between the heavenly herald and God. A similar point had been made by R. Johanan on the basis of the same verse.[205]

Entering into the realm of the esoteric means having to differentiate between the herald and the king, or the parergon and the object of the parergon. The choice will have lasting consequences. The rabbis tell that the students came to visit R. Johanan ben Zakkai, the great master of esoteric knowledge, at his deathbed. When he saw them, he began to cry. Responding to their query, he explained that he was about to face his Maker, and his destiny would be irrevocably determined for all eternity, adding: "Furthermore, two paths lie before me, one toward the Garden of Eden and the other toward Hell, and I do not know through which one I will be taken. And I should not cry?"[206] Addressing this type of situation, Borges wrote: "Hope not that the straightness of your path/ that stubbornly branches off in two, and/ stubbornly branches off in two, will have an end."[207]

The (ḥa'iran) 'perplexed' is an individual facing a crisis of pure choice and pure subjectivity—a crisis effected by the 'signpost', hence, the two terms making up the title of the *Guide* (*Dalalat*) *for the Perplexed* (*al-Ḥa'irin*).[208] It would then be up to the student/reader to establish (or not to establish) a direct relationship with God and to determine (or not to determine) the perception 'knowledge ➞ un-knowledge', 'praise ➞ silence'.

Part 2
Imagination

DEUS ABSCONDITUS, HOMO ABSCONDITUS

REVELATION, IN THE SENSE that God can make Himself known to human, is the cornerstone of Scripture and the Maimonidean intellectual apparatus. Although God as He is to Himself *ad intra* is *deus absconditus* and totally inaccessible, the whole point of the Hebrew Scripture is that God does reveal Himself to humankind.[1] God's essence cannot be known to human, especially in his somatic condition, yet human is privy to discern God through revelation.[2] Following the rabbis, who taught that this world is like "a pitch dark night,"[3] Maimonides compared human's earthly station to someone standing in a pitch dark night. Alluding to the 'palace' symbolizing the divine abode,[4] the rabbis taught that "in the inner chambers" of God's dwelling "luminescence abides with Him," whereas "in the outer chambers" He is surrounded by darkness.[5] The tension "inner/outer chambers" is resolved in a successive series of "flashes/darkness."[6] Referring to the individual grasping the lightning flashing through the night, Maimonides commented:

> He would be illuminated by flashes of lightning rapidly succeeding each other, and, therefore, he would appear to be in continuous light with no interruption. . . . To another the lightning flashes only once during his [entire] night. There are also some, who, from one lightning flash to another [experience] long or short intervals. There are also some that cannot come up to the level of having their night illuminated by lightning but by a radiant body or some type of rock that is iridescent by night.[7]

The "flashes of lightning" represent divine inspiration reaching from above. The "radiant body" or "rock" (like the *lapis philosophorum* of the alchemists) stands for human ability to pierce the night with their own intellectual faculties.[8] The conceptual basis of this model comes from rabbinic literature.

R. Eleazar (d. 279) taught that the primeval light created in the first day (Gn 1:3) was to be a brilliance by which humans could "contemplate the universe from one end to the other." It is inaccessible to the wicked, and it is "reserved for the righteous in the future to come."[9] This light is the culmination of human development. It is not the mystical light known in phenomenology and general religious experience.[10] The primeval light is akin to the Philonic logos and the rabbinic *memra*.[11] Maimonides identified it with "the Glory of God,"[12] which is "the active intellect flowing from God."[13] The motif of a pristine light beamed by God to make Himself manifest is developed at the end of the daily prayer (*'Amida*). Its purpose is to guide humankind: "Because with the light of Your countenance You gave to us Tora and life, love and favor, charity and mercy, blessing and peace." This light, like the Philonic logos and the rabbinic memra is essentially intellectual. Indeed, R. Amme (third century), a colleague of R. Eleazar, taught, "Great is intelligence (*da'at*) that was given between two Signs (*otiyot*) [Names of God]."[14] The expression "given between two Signs" means that intelligence—like the divine light mentioned at the end of the 'Amida—proceeds from God and directs [the individual] to Him, thus establishing a link between them. It parallels the Temple, where the Divine Glory (Shekhina) coming from God dwells, establishing a link between the people and their Maker. Elaborating on this basic theme, the same R. Eleazar taught, "Great is the Temple that was given between two Signs." Since both the Temple and intelligence fulfill parallel functions—the former in the realm of the collective and the latter in the realm of the individual—R. Eleazar concluded, "Whoever has intelligence is as if the Temple had been built in his days."[15] Following up this doctrine, R. Amme eloquently laid out the thesis that "Great is intelligence that was inserted in the first blessing of the daily (prayer)."[16] The blessing reads: "You [God] freely distribute [*ḥonen*] intelligence [da'at] to man and teach discernment to humans. We supplicate from You to distribute freely to us [*ve-ḥonnenu*]: wisdom, discernment, and intelligence. Blessed are You, O Lord! who distributes intelligence freely [ḥonen]."[17]

Ḥonen not only means 'a freely bestowed gift' but also something coming from without. The message is clear. Human intelligence comes from God and is freely bestowed to human—in the sense that it is not generated by inner faculties, hence, the Maimonidean doctrine, that the light beamed by God is the active intellect continuously gushing toward His creations. "One who does not perceive intellectually [*yu'qal*] God at all is like one who is in darkness and has never seen the light."[18] Genuine worship of God must involve the active participation of the human intellect. It can only take place after the individual "has formed an intellectual concept (of God). If you perceived God and His actions according to what the intellect determines, you could thereafter consign yourself to Him, march toward His nearness, and strengthen the link between you and Him, which is the intellect."[19]

By applying their minds, humans can be illuminated and gain access to the divine intellect: "But he who had perceived and directs all of himself according to his understanding is like one who stands by the pure light of the sun."[20] While in the state of intellectual propinquity, the individual "is with God and God is with him."[21] God is ceaselessly projecting His light and does not 'hide' from humans. As mentioned earlier, at the ontological level—outside the perimeters of revelation—*deus absconditus* is human inability to comprehend God. Within revelation, however, this doctrine concerns human attitude toward God. God 'hides' from humans as a result of humans 'hiding' from God. "Only when one departs from Him," by turning off his intellect, then "is hidden from God," and "God becomes hidden from him."[22]

> This doctrine I found corroborated also in the text of the Tora. God, blessed be He, said: "And I shall hide my face from them and it [the people] shall be devoured, and many evils and afflictions will find it [the people]. And in that day it [the people] shall say: because my God is not in my midst these evils have found me" (Dt 31:17). He [God] clarified that (His) "hiding of the face" was caused by us and that we have effected the hiding. As He says, "And I shall surely hide my face in that day because of all the evil that he did" (Dt 31:18).[23]

Deus absconditus is human hiding from God, not God from human (see Is 29:15). Because human refuses to let himself be touched by the light of reason, *homo absconditus* is more dangerous than all the other species in the animal kingdom.[24]

APOPHASIS AND IMAGINATION

To be meaningful negative knowledge must presuppose the *possibility* of gaining some positive notion of the subject at hand. Maimonides's illustration, that through a series of descriptions of what a boat is not it may be possible to come close to the idea of what a boat is,[25] may be applicable to matters that fall within the perimeters of human epistemology, not to God. Furthermore, negative knowledge is effective only a posteriori: *after* gaining a positive knowledge of what a boat is, it would be possible to determine that such a negative description did, in fact, correspond to the actual boat. This process could not apply a priori. Unless one had some prior knowledge that a given vegetable is a banana, its identity could not be determined just by knowing that it is none of the recognizable fruits. More precisely, because God's beingness is hierarchically superior and categorically different than anything else, whatever positive attributes are negated of Him belong to a different genus. Therefore, it would be like negating that a banana has hair and other characteristics peculiar to mammals. Such negative information could not contribute to a meaningful understanding of the object at hand. Similarly, since God transcends the boundaries of human understanding, negative knowledge could not render Him epistemologically knowable.[26]

Apophatic knowledge is structurally connected with the Maimonidean theory of imagination. Imagination is incapable of matching the real, ontological world. The 'proofs' (burhan) designed to bring about apophatic knowledge serve to counteract the effects of imagination, thus, the doctrine "that prophecy cannot descend but upon a sage who is eminent in wisdom."[27] Maimonides opposed the application of positive attributes to God because these attributes are the figments of human imagination. There is nothing, outside human fantasy, corresponding to such a 'God'. People indulging in positive attributes have nothing in their faith except empty words: "But one who applies an attribute to Him knows nothing except an empty word. The thing that he had imagined that this name applies to, however, is a subject that does not exist—a fraudulent illusion. It is as if he had applied that name to a nonexisting subject because there is nothing in reality resembling it."[28]

The situation may be compared to someone who imagines that an elephant is a three-winged beast with a single leg and a transparent body that inhabits the depths of the ocean, that swims like a fish, flies like a bird, and speaks like a man. Obviously, this is nothing but "a design of the imagination to which was applied the name of something that does exist."[29] Although there is such a thing as an elephant, the "elephant" "that he imagined having those attributes is a fraudulent illusion. Nothing in reality corresponds to it. It is a nonexisting thing to which was applied the name of something that does exist."[30] The passion and devotion felt for such a deity has nothing to do with scriptural love. As noted by Judah Abarbanel in a different context, to be real, love must have an actual object outside imagination. Thus, a love "inasmuch as it exists in our imagination" alone is fictitious "for it lacks a real object."[31]

Imagination involves human projection. When applied to God it tells us what *we* "regard as perfection."[32] Maimonides defined 'faith' (*i'tiqad*) as a belief that matches an outer reality, independent of ourselves.[33] The terms of imagination are projections having nothing to do with God but with the human psyche. As a creation of the imagination, positive attributes are not only intrinsically false but they displace God from the mind of the believer: "I am not [merely] saying that one who applies positive attributes to God has a faulty perception or that he is associating [God with something else] or that his perception is different than what He is, but I am saying that he, without being aware, has dislodged God from his faith [*i'tiqadahu*]."[34]

The semantic connotations of people void of rationality are the result of imagination. There are two consequences to this fact. First, unless the semantic connotation of an article of faith is intellectually meaningful—and, in fact, corresponds to an outer reality independent from people—it will be altered by the imagination of the believer. Although creeds accepted on the basis of 'tradition' (taqlid) are valuable at the early stages of human development,[35] they are meaningless when internalized on the basis of 'tradition' (taqlid) alone, regardless of their intrinsic merits. Invariably, the faithful would be interpreting them in terms of their own imaginations. It would be like one admitting that there are "elephants" but insisting that they look like the three winged-beast described above: the same name is applied to two things with no real affinity between them.[36] Maimonides classified those who base their beliefs on 'tradition' (taqlid) together with those who base their 'faith' (i'tiqad) on imagination. In either case the object of faith is internalized in terms of human fantasy. When discussing the people outside the city of the royal palace, representing God's abode, Maimonides remarked:

> One who is always thinking about God and mentions Him repeatedly without knowledge, following only his imagination

> or following a belief [iʿtiqad] that he received as a tradition [qallad] from someone else, he is not only outside the [divine] abode and far from it, but in my opinion, he is not truly mentioning God or thinking of Him because the term in his imagination that he is articulating verbally does not correspond to anything in existence. It is an illusion fabricated by his imagination as we have explained when discussing the attributes [of God].[37]

Second, since the young and the general public (al-jamhur) inhabit the realm of imagination, special care is required not to say something that could prompt them to understand something contrary to our intention. Because, "to them, anything that is not a body or is not found in a body does not exist,"[38] to refer to God in pure abstract terms is tantamount to a denial of His existence. Therefore, when addressing the public, it is important to formulate the basic doctrines and beliefs in terms that will not give rise to misinterpretation and confusion. Commenting on the rabbinic doctrine, "The Tora speaks in the language of man," Maimonides explained that this doctrine comes to instruct that when formulating religious tenets, "the popular imagination" (*al-khayal al-jamhuri*) must be taken into account.[39] It is incumbent upon all "the people of religion" not to say something that the imagination (*tukhayal*) of the public would interpret to mean the opposite of what was intended.[40] Equal caution must be exercised when instructing complex subjects to the uninitiated student.[41] Because the key-symbols that give cohesion to the general public are grounded on imagination,[42] the public is unable to think in terms of reason and will remain totally blind throughout its earthly existence. Consequently, "the truth in its totality is concealed from them, notwithstanding the potency of its radiance, as it was said concerning them, 'And now they have not seen the light, shining brightly in the firmaments' (Jb 37:21). These are the general public [al-jamhur]."[43]

Imagination is a veil shrouding human rationality. Apophatic knowledge does not, cannot, generate understanding of God. Its purpose is to puncture imagination and to let the light come in, thus, allowing humans to be rational.

TRANSFERENCE OF MEANING

In the Maimonidean economy of ideas imagination is not a "concept" to be analyzed by a "rational" methodology but is itself an independent mental discourse standing at the basis of the political, social, religious, and artistic activities of pagan humanity: it is the method by which gentile civilization unfolds.[44] It constitutes a pathological retrogression from Adam's ability to reason. Before sinning, Adam was endowed with the ability to reason—a radically different mental process than imagination. At that stage human language consisted of names (Gn 2:20); it was capable of predication (see Gn 2:23), and it excluded the syntactical apparatus enabling transference of meaning. Adam's sin consisted in suppressing this mental process in favor of imagination. Maimonides called attention to the Hebrew term for snake, *naḥash*—a term that, as the commentators noted, means also 'divination'.[45] This leads directly into the Vichian concept of 'divination/divine'.[46] R. Isaac Abarbanel (1437–1508) incorporated this radical idea in his commentary on Genesis (3:22). Imagination is connected with divination and transference of meaning:

> "And the snake was more cunning than all the animals of the field" (Gn 3:10). It means that Adam's imaginative faculty was more crafty than the imaginative faculty of all the other animals of the field. Because human imagination is capable of making syllogisms and arguments appearing to be true [transference of meaning]—something that the imagination of other animals cannot do. . . . The snake was regarded by them [the rabbis] as [symbolic] of the imaginative faculty because it [the imagination], which is peculiar to diviners [*menaḥashim*], leads to corruption.

Divination is not only the most primitive form of religion but, more importantly, represents transference of meaning whereby a given phenomenon or object is associated with a specific augury and is perceived, not as it is per se, but "as" something else. This is common in schizophrenics. It is also present in the thought development of a child, as when a child plays with a stick and calls it a horse.[47] Borrowing from Eliade, in this realm, things undergo an "imaginative transfiguration" and are perceived in terms transcending sensory perception.[48] In modern philosophy 'seeing as' was discussed by Wittgenstein. Invariably, the *as* is not part of the object itself but is projected onto the object by the viewer. Mythological discourse involves a fundamental process of transformation and displacement: through reflexive associations the object per se is displaced and perceived "as" something other than itself.[49] At the religious level, seeing 'as' constitutes idolatry. Through a process of displacement and projection a sensory object (a totem, a star, an image, etc.) is imaginatively transfigured into a supernatural being. Linguistically, it allows for a syntactical procedure whereby transference of meaning is possible.[50]

Transference of meaning is at the core of the first sin. Eve associated the fact that the "tree is a pleasure to the eyes" with "good for eating," thereby concluding that "it was delightful for understanding" (Gn 3:6).[51] It is no coincidence that thereon, God's presence is grasped through transference of meaning. Before the sin, Adam and Eve heard sound per se, thereafter—borrowing from Wittgenstein—the sound was heard "as." Like the first Vichian giants who associated the "sound" of the thunder with the "voice" of Jove,[52] after the sin Adam and Eve associated the sound of "the daily wind"—a common, natural phenomenon—with the "voice" of God and hide themselves in fear (Gn 3:8, 10).

Adam's acquisition of language permitted him to perceive reality in terms of auditory experience. It has been noted that "Whereas the phantasmatic world is mainly visual and is populated by images and ghosts, the paleologic world is predominantly auditory."[53] A similar transformation took place at the visual level. Immediately after sinning "their eyes were opened and they *knew* [*vayyede'u*] that they were naked" (Gn 3:7). Scripture, Maimonides observed, does not say that "their eyes were opened and they *saw* that they were naked." The change did not take place at the optical or physiological level. Neither was it a case of perceptual alteration as with acute types of schizophrenia. It only affected their *mode* of perception: whereas before the sin they saw, thereafter they 'saw as'. It involved a radical change of orientation. Citing "he changes his face and you expelled him" (Jb 14:20), a verse alluding to Adam's expulsion from Eden, Maimonides noted that in Hebrew 'face' stands for 'direction', 'purpose'. Adam's banishment from Paradise was a direct result of a change in orientation: turning away from the world of reason, Adam transfigured the Garden of Eden into a barren land. This conforms with Maimonides's thesis, whereby *deus absconditus* is the effect of *homo absconditus*.

> Because he [Adam] had changed his direction, striving toward things that he was previously ordered not to aim at, he was expelled from the Garden of Eden. The punishment fits the sin, measure for measure because he had been authorized to eat

> from the best and to delight in leisure and calm. But instead, as mentioned before, he frolicked in the pursuit of his delight and his imagination[54] and ate what had been forbidden to him. . . . He resembled the animals in his eating and in most of his habits.[55]

Maimonides distinguished between the delights that Adam was authorized to indulge in before the sin and "his imaginary pleasures"—newly arisen craving for immediate satisfaction—that caused his perdition.[56] The latter were harmful because they were not motivated by need but by imagination alone.

Before sin, Adam inhabited a world governed by the law of reason. Sinning involved a shift to the realm of conventionality. Reason is expressed in terms of 'truth/falsehood'. Its laws are necessary and universal and are determined by rational principles. Conventionality is governed by a semiological system of binary terms standing in hierarchical opposition to each other. At this juncture it is important to remember that 'conventionality', in the Maimonidean sense, parallels *sensus communis* in Vico.[57] It constitutes the 'normal', including not only socially and politically correct behavior but also association of ideas and transference of meaning. Things are not perceived per se but through a series of key-symbols, beginning with 'good/evil' and leading to 'pleasant/ugly', 'proper/improper', and so on. Because at the realm of the conventional there is no internal criterion by which to distinguish between 'good/evil', the world of conventionality, like its matrix, imagination depends on *authority* and *violence*, that is, on a *political* system with power to enforce 'the normative'. By contrast, truth/falsehood are rational, that is, they do not depend on an *authority*. Contrary to Charles Peirce (1839–1914) and other pragmatists, for Maimonides the truth is not a consensus formed by the community of scholars over time. "Everything that was demonstrated," he declares, "does not increase in validity or become more certain because all the sages agree on it, nor will its validity decrease because the whole world disagrees on it."[58]

At the realm of imagination reality itself is marginal. People don't 'see'. Rather, as with Ossorio, the main character of one of Baroja's novels, man "contemplates with his imagination what he could not perceive with his eyes."[59] Whereas the laws of reason are universal, conventionalities are necessarily local. Hence, they breed division and strife. The realm of imagination/ conventionality can function only within a political system with a hierarchy empowered to support the 'accepted canons' of 'right/wrong' and all such subsequent dichotomies.

IMAGINATION AND THE LOSS OF INDIVIDUAL FREEDOM

Imagination and reason represent two distinct levels of consciousness and, therefore, two distinct thinking processes. Before sinning, Adam was free because he inhabited the realm of reason. Upon sinning, he passed into imagination and conventionality—a specific form of discourse—and henceforth, to the realm of political authority and its concomitant violence. Imagination triggered a sequence of mental processes blocking intellectual perception and distorting reality. It was how Satan enticed Eve.[60] Maimonides called attention to the fact that in Hebrew *saṭan* (lit. 'deceiver') stems from the root *saṭa* (to deviate, to stray from the right path), implying a distorted image of reality produced by the imaginative faculty. This is why the rabbis associate Satan with the yeṣer ha-ra' (evil instinct), moving humankind to sin (ḥeṭ), that is, 'to deviate' from the right path.[61] Accordingly, imagination is symbolized by the fallen woman, in contradistinction to the virtuous woman, who represents the realm of the intellectual.[62]

In Maimonides's intellectual apparatus the real world can be grasped by reason; it can never match the imaged object. Somehow, physical phenomena do not unfold according to patterns that can be grasped by the imaginal consciousness. "There are things that if man were to examine on the basis of his imagination could not possibly be conceptualized."[63] Maimonides substantiated this premise by pointing to some geometrical models impossible according to imagination yet mathematically true.[64] Thus, imagination is excluded from the ontological world. Adam's story concerns the retrogression from the realm of the rational to the realm of imagination. Paleological man had not yet developed a level of consciousness to sense his passing into rationality.[65] Hence, the Scripture only records the retrogression from the realm of the rational to the realm of imagination. It was only *after* retrogressing to the world of imagination that Adam realized what he had lost.[66]

Adam fell prey to "his imaginary desires" sinning and losing [more precisely, sinning *by* losing] his rational grasp of reality. In this fashion Adam shifted directions from the level of rational consciousness governed by the principle of 'truth/falsehood,' to the level of imaginative consciousness governed by a semiological system of 'good/bad', a fictional world defined by the tyranny of the conventional. Adam's punishment matched the sin—banishment to the realm of the imaginary. After explaining how Adam fell prey to "his imaginary desires," Maimonides commented:

> He was punished because that intellectual perception was removed [from him]. Therefore, he transgressed the commandment that he was ordered on account of his intellect, falling prey to the conventionalities that he perceived, and submerging into the [realm] of evil and good. Then, he realized the measure of what he had forfeited and what had been taken away from him. This is why it was said: "You shall be like divinities [*elohim*] who know good and evil" (Gn 3:5). It was not said: "You shall be like divinities who know falsehood and truth" or "who perceive falsehood and truth." There is nothing necessary about good and evil but [only] about falsehood and truth. Note that the text says, "and the eyes of both of them opened and they knew that they were naked" (Gn 3:7). It does not say, "And the eyes of both of them opened and they saw"—because what they saw before [sinning] was what they saw after [sinning]. There was no cover removed from over their eyes. Rather, what had changed, was, his situation whereby [now] he would perceive as evil that which before [sinning] was not perceived as evil.[67]

Imagination processes reality as if it were a pure semiotical system. At this level of human development the mind is incapable of distinguishing between what is felt and objective reality.[68] "Reality" consists of a series of mental projections designed to internalize the world. These projections effectively prevent direct contacts with the outside. Sensory perceptions and natural phenomena are interpreted in terms of human projections. Natural phenomena are not regulated by necessary and universal laws but by an essentially random semiotical system. The order perceived in nature is not the effect of an internal organization regulated by absolute laws, but merely 'incidents of habit' (*jarya 'adat*), much like the habits of human society.[69] In the Arab world the exponents of this view were theologians known as *mutakallimun* who adhered to a philosophy known as *Kalam*.[70] They regarded imagination as the criterion by which to distinguish between 'possible' and 'impossible'. Everything imaginable—namely, whatever could be envisaged jointly such as a centaur or any other mythological figure—is probable and may be found in nature. There are linguistic grounds for such a notion. In Arabic *mumkin* 'possible', comes from the root *k'n/kwn* 'to be', 'to happen', from which the noun *makan* 'place' derives.[71] This is why, anything that can be imagined as spatially contiguous is 'possible' and theoretically probable.[72] Thinking is spatial and related to simultaneous synthesis.[73] In paleologic thinking "ideas associate only by contiguity, because similarity leads only to identification, not association."[74] The mutakallimun concept of nature was formulated on the basis "that whatever may be imagined is rationally possible."[75] Two fundamental corollaries follow. First, the 'rational' must be subordinated to, and determined by, imagination. Because the intellect is hierarchically dependent on the dictates of imagination, "What the mutakallimun designate 'rational'" is, in fact, "imagination and conjecture, not reason."[76] Second, and as a consequence of the first, the laws governing the physical world, like all semiotical systems, may be freely exchanged and substituted for one another. Concerning this last point, the mutakallimun argued that although the physical world appears to be regulated by precise patterns, these patterns are incidental and could have been designed differently. Even size is incidental. There is no reason why there cannot be a man with multiple heads, tall as a mountain; or an elephant minute as a tick, or a tick large as an elephant.[77] Although admitting

> that what exists has a definite structure, precise measurement, and necessary properties that cannot change or be substituted, these are mere incidents of habit. Just like the king's habit is to parade in the boulevards of the city only mounted on a horse and has never been seen otherwise. Yet it is not intellectually impossible [to conceive of the king] walking in the city on foot. Indeed, it is undoubtedly possible, and it may happen. Similarly, the fact that the earth moves toward its center and fire [moves] straight up, or that fire heats and the water chills, are incidents of habit. It is not intellectually impossible [to conceive] that such habit could change whereby the fire would chill and move downward while still [retaining the properties of] fire, and water would heat and move upward, while still [retaining the properties of fluid] water. Their entire thesis rests on this methodology.[78]

The preceding excludes the possibility of a scientific comprehension of nature because "whatever they deem imaginable is possible, regardless of whether or not it may be corroborated by facts; whatever cannot be imagined is impossible."[79] Because theories cannot be corroborated by facts, independent scientific research and experimentation is impossible. Hence the imperative to submit to authority to determine what is 'possible' and what is 'impossible' in the same manner that one is required to submit to authority to determine what is 'good/evil,' 'proper/improper,' and all that which pertains to the realm of conventionality. In this type of science 'truth/falsehood' is a function of the same system of conventionalities determining the content of 'good/evil': it is essentially political.

Following the Aramaic translation of the Pentateuch, Maimonides interpreted the verse "you shall be like divinities [*elohim*] knowing good and evil" (Gn 3:5), to mean not 'gods' but 'political leaders'.[80] Maimonides observed that *elohim* has three meanings. Generally, it is used for 'God' or 'divinity'. It is also used for 'angel'. Because in Hebrew (as in Greek) an 'angel' is a 'messenger', a divine messenger representing God could be designated by the name of the sender.[81] The third connotation 'political leader' reflects the deification of kings common in the ancient world and archaic societies.[82] By specifying that *elohim* here refers to those having the power to regulate good and evil, that is, the realm of the conventional, the snake was ascertaining that by *elohim* 'political authority' was intended. In the same chapter Maimonides cited a biblical passage describing humans as a "little less" than *elohim* (Ps 8:6). Within that context, it means 'angel', 'messenger of God'. Adam had the choice of reason—in which case he would have been a messenger of God. He also had the choice of imagination, leading to political mastery. The subsequent development of humankind would depend on this choice.

THE EPISTEMOLOGY OF REASON AND IMAGINATION

Maimonides held a positivistic view of imagination. To begin with, imagination is not a distinct human faculty.[83] It is related to biological and genetic factors.[84] Psychologically, it is connected with sensory perception, kinetics, conditioned reflexes, and other traits that humankind shares with members of the animal kingdom. *Khayal* (imagination), mental imaging, and *takhayul* (imagining), the forming of new images from the old, are common to the operations of the animal and human mind.[85] There are also basic instincts and urges, such as parental bonding with offspring, that in both humans and animals are related to the imaginative faculty.[86] Imagination is also connected with memory, the combination of discrete images and ideas, transference of meaning, and the formation of dreams.[87] Contrary to Vico's imaginative universals, for Maimonides the imaginative faculty is incapable of abstraction: invariably the imaged object is conceptualized as a body or a bodily force.[88]

Imagination is the source of pagan civilization. Maimonides regarded politics, religion, some forms of philosophical speculations, and poetry (the equivalent of 'secular literature') as the work of imagination. In a chapter dealing with the demarcation of cultures Maimonides classified "political leaders, the legislators of governmental laws (*al-nu'amis*)" or *nomoi*,[89] together with "the sorcerers, diviners, the dreamers of accurate dreams, and also the performers of wonders with unusual tricks, and the performers of magic." All of them form part of a single class, excelling by virtue of their powerful imagination.[90] This applies even to honest and wise politicians who succeeded in establishing good political systems. They are described as "those who excel in the imaginative faculty alone."[91] Pagan myths and rituals, too, are the result of imagination.[92] Some philosophers'—the mutakallimun were the most prominent, but others as well—basic methodology was grounded on imagination.[93] Maimonides's position on poetry is highly significant. "Orators and poets" are censured for their "corrupt imagination."[94] Elsewhere, he distinguishes between poets and jurists (*fuqaha'a*), implying that the former are ignorant of the Law and do not know the basic doctrines of religion.[95] His main objection, however, is not against the content but the *structure* of poetry, particularly the fact that meter and rhyme are used to manipulate ideas. This is evident from the fact that, on the one hand, he consistently opposes the recitation of *piyuṭim* 'liturgical poems' in the services.[96] At the same time, he approves the private recitation of liturgical hymns that are patterned according to biblical psalms and rabbinic liturgy.[97] The only difference between them is that the piyuṭim (in the Sephardic liturgy) contain rhyme and meter, whereas the hymns patterned according to the biblical and rabbinic models, do not.[98] Poetry is manipulative and deceptive because concepts and ideas are developed, approved, or rejected not on substantive grounds but on the trivia of rhyme and meter.[99]

For Maimonides imagination is more or less what anthropologists and philosophers designate 'mythical' thinking,[100] and psychologists call 'paleologic'. Its purpose is not to interpret but to substitute reality. It functions according to the principle formulated by Von Domarus that, whereas in normative thinking, identity is established on the basis of identical subjects, in schizophrenia and paleologic thinking identity is established on the basis of identical predicates with no concern for the subject itself. Since reality is purely semiological, anything could be a 'sign' for anything else. Thus, a schizophrenic believed "that Jesus, cigar boxes, and sex were identical." Investigation revealed that the identifying link was the fact that the three were encircled: the head of Jesus by a halo, the package of cigars by the tax band, and the woman by the sex glance of the man.[101] Because in a semiological system symbols can be freely exchanged, the color of eyes or a piece of clothing may serve as the identifying link with a bird or another object with the same color, ignoring the rest. Silvano Arieti noted that the same type of mental associations affects dreams. Indeed, "this type of thinking occurs not only in schizophrenia; it is at the root of every type of Freudian symbolism."[102] It is also the normative way of mythical and archaic thinking. "A world paleologically interpreted," wrote Arieti, "corresponds in many ways to the mythical world of ancient people and to many cultural repertories of various aboriginal societies today."[103] In the mythical mind names are the most compelling identifying links, functioning, precisely, on the Von Domarus principle whereby dissimilar subjects are equated on the basis of their names regardless of context. Lévi-Strauss described the thinking process peculiar to archaic humans as "bricolage." The totemic logic of classification is grounded on "a logic whose terms consist of odds and ends . . . devoid of necessity." In the same manner that a handyman "detaches the cogwheels of an old alarm clock, and *they can be used again* either for the same purpose or for a different one," archaic thinking can "detach" certain aspects of reality and incorporate them into a myth.[104] Lévi-Strauss did not explain the grounds of such an odd "logic." It can be well understood, however, upon considering that in paleologic thinking identity is established through the predicates regardless of their context. According to this type of thinking, "a = a + b + c because the two terms of the equation have *a* in common."[105]

In this precise sense imagination pertains to semiotics. It is worth repeating: as in all semiotical systems the terms of imagination are context-free. Thus, identifying links may be "extracted" from one context and "inserted"—either in spatial or temporal contiguity—into another, establishing thereby identity between them.[106] This type of logic underlies much of modern advertisement, whereby the object (or fashion item) functions as the identifying link: [1] the object is "inserted" into context A; [2] the viewer psychologically "extracts" it and then "inserts" it into context B [3] thereby establishing an identity with context A. In such as situation the *parergon*—the 'ornamentation' or 'accessory' of an object—identifies the object. As with the idolatrous Israelites at the time of Habakkuk, who regarded images of wood and stone as divine because they were "caged in gold and silver" (see Hb 2:19–20). According to the rabbis, the same thinking process characterized those in their time who regarded someone fit to be appointed as a judge simply because he happened to be wealthy. In both cases something totally peripheral serves as the identifying mark.[107]

Maimonides's theory of imagination forms part of his general theory of epistemology. Maimonides proposed the principle "that the function of imagination is not the function of reason, but its opposite."[108] The function of reason is fourfold: [1] to analyze an object into its constitutive elements, [2] examine the parts, [3] abstract them, and [4] conceptualize them. Borrowing a term from Sartre, for Maimonides, *conceptualization* is "a synthetic unity" of the multiple aspects constituting the object at hand.[109] In accordance with the principle that theory must accommodate to facts, rather than the other way around,[110] this analysis must take into consideration [a] the empirical data—what Maimonides designates "its true reality" (*ḥaqiqatha*). The data [b] must be conceptualized according to a general theory—"its causes" in the language of Maimonides. "Reason (*al-'aql*) [1] analyzes composed [objects], [2] distinguishes their parts, [3] abstracts [4] and conceptualizes them, according to their [a] reality and [b] causes."[111] Second, and as a result of the first, a thing is conceptualized, acquiring logical meaning, thus becoming an object of scientific discourse and investigation. The process consists of [1] the discovery of multiple significances (*ma'ani*) within a single thing,[112] [2] the distinction between the universal and the particular—thus allowing for positive demonstrations; [3] and the differentiation of essential and incidental predicates. Maimonides continued:

> [1] It could also perceive various significances [ma'ani] in a single object; those [significances] appear as clearly to reason as two individuals appear clearly in reality [via sensual perception] to the imagination. [2] Furthermore, through reason, the general from the individual can be differentiated. No proof can be validated but for the general. [3] Through reason can be determined what is an essential predicate and what is accidental.[113]

Since such fundamental categories, as "particular and universal" and "essential and accidental" are the function of reason, reason is at the basis of inductive and deductive thinking. By contrast, imagination is incapable of any of these functions. [1] It is incapable of abstraction. Things are processed globally because they are perceived by the senses not in terms of their constitutive parts. Moreover, [2] it associates and links disparate things without regard to their real nature. Maimonides continued:

> Imagination has none of these functions [1] since imagination can perceive a particular object made up (of various parts) in general terms, [2] and it can combine things that are separate in reality, combining one part with another. All [this type of combinations pertains to] a body or a faculty in a body,[114] as when one imagines a person with the head of a horse and with wings and other such similar things. This is called a "false fabrication" since it does not correspond to anything in reality. Even when abstracting a form to the maximum, imagination can never free its perception from the physical. This is why nothing can be examined on the basis of imagination.[115]

A rational cognitive-construct (*taṣawar*) is different than an imaginative cognitive-construct.[116]

PROPHECY AND THE EPISTEMOLOGY OF THE CREATIVE MIND

On the surface Maimonides's treatment of imagination is puzzling, attributing to it contradictory functions and results. In the preceding chapters imagination was depicted as the cause of Adam's fall, the perdition of humankind, and the medium by which magicians, soothsayers, and politicians perform their craft. Yet Maimonides maintains that God communicates with prophets via imagination. It is through the development of imagination that humankind reaches perfection. Indeed, the biblical prophet is superior to the philosopher because of the former's imaginative powers. At the same time, Moses is the greatest of all prophets precisely because God did not communicate with him through imagination but only through reason! A close reading of these materials shows that Maimonides is weaving, with wit and sophistication, a revolutionary theory, pointing to a fresh view of imagination and the role it plays in the development of human creativity.

Prophecy, or divine inspiration, is regarded by Maimonides as humankind's highest realization. It may come about when an individual has attained a threefold perfection: ethical, intellectual, and imaginative.[117] Ethical excellence, as a precondition for perfection, is well understood in light of the biblical tradition, insisting on moral conduct and individual accountability.[118] Ethics, too, is an essential prerequisite for intellectual excellence. The reasoning of individuals who fail to regulate their passions is flawed.[119] Intellectual perfection, too, conforms with Maimonidean thinking, whereby reason is humankind's quintessential attribute, pertaining to the very "image of God" in which Adam was created.[120]

Concerning the role of imagination in the realization of prophecy, Maimonides explains:

> You ought to know that the reality of prophecy and its essence consists of an emanation flowing from God, blessed be He, through the active intellect, first onto the cognitive faculty and thereafter onto the imaginative faculty [*al-quwat al-mutkhayala*]. It represents the highest human level and the supreme perfection that can be found in this species. This state is the supreme perfection of the imaginative faculty.[121]

The biblical prophet received prophecy through an angel,[122] which Maimonides associated with imagination.[123]

The role of imagination as a factor of human perfection seems highly problematic. As mentioned before, Maimonides held a positivistic view of imagination. It is a faculty that humans share with other members of the animal kingdom. It constitutes a lower level of consciousness, distorting reality, and incapable of providing valid criteria to know the real universe.

A pivotal factor in Maimonides's epistemology is the relation of imagination to reason. In the total equation regulating mental activities there is a radical difference between 'sensory perception → imagination → reason' and 'sensory perception → reason → imagination'. Whereas 'sense → reason' results in an accurate perception, per se, 'sense → imagination' results in a distorted perception 'as'. Since the ultimate criterion for the Maimonidean truth is the real world, reason based on distorted sensory information, that is, on data processed through the imagination, will necessarily result in falsehood. To illustrate this point consider Ptolomean astronomy in which the solar system is seen as moving around the earth, in contrast to Copernican astronomy in which the earth is seen as moving around the sun. In the second case sensory perception is processed through reason. Thus, further astronomical calculations and observations provide an adequate understanding of the solar system. In the first case sensory perception is processed through imagination. Accordingly, all further calculations and scientific observations are skewed. In response to Johann Kepler's (1571–1630) mathematical demonstrations that Ptolomean astronomy was based on "sensory illusion," Francesco Patrizzi (1529–1597) argued that all of Kepler's calculations about the interlocking orbits, cycles, and epicycles of the planes were meaningless because the planets are animate beings endowed with will and freedom.[124] In this type of situation the ultimate basis of reason is imagination. The result is an anthropocentric universe that, like the natural world of the mutakallimun, is shaped to fit certain human projection—the specific conventionalities of the time. As with Adam, imagination first subverts and then subdues and controls the intellectual faculty.

Imagination can be creative and valuable after reason has accurately decoded and processed the data provided by the senses. In the Maimonidean general epistemology not only can imagination not process any of the functions of reason but also reason cannot process any of the functions of imagination. Reason does not have the faculty [1] to perceive things globally and [2] to associate disparate things—the two indispensable ingredients for *creativity.* A creative idea [1] first conceived globally in the mind can be effected only by discovering the proper [2] link between the disparate elements. This cannot be realized by 'inserting' ingredients as with the imaginative world of the mutakallimun and Lévi-Strauss's *bricolage.* To realize a creative idea Maimonidean methodology is indispensable. The link between the components of a creative idea may be discovered by [1] properly differentiating the multiple significances (ma'ani) making up the context of the link one wants to insert, [2] establishing the distinction between the universal and the particular, [3] and the differentiation of essential and incidental predicates. To illustrate, to enable humans to fly it would be necessary to discern [1] the multiple elements making up a "flying bird," such as wings, feathers, color, and so forth; and proceed to discover the [2] 'universal' (the principle of aerodynamics), and [3] the 'essential' (the function of the wings thereon) from the 'particular' (eagle, butterfly) and 'incidental'—(feathers, since some insects fly). Whereas individuals following 'sense ➞ imagination ➞ reason' proceed to fly by putting on wings and jumping from a tall building, those who follow 'sense ➞ reason ➞ imagination' first discover the universal principle of aerodynamics, then determine the essential elements required to realize that principle, and finally proceed to design an airplane. Creative thinking not only requires *reason*—the accurate decoding of natural phenomena—but also *imagination*—the ability to associate hitherto disconnected elements by discovering the link that would effectively transform them into a new entity. In this manner a creative thinker, like the righteous in rabbinic literature, becomes "a partner in the creation of the world."[125] This follows a general principle formulated by R. 'Aqiba whereby "the acts of humans," that is, artificiality, "excel the acts of God."[126]

Reason alone is static and unproductive. The *aletheia* (truth) of the philosopher is contemplative. It is a kind of verbal mimesis of nature and, therefore, incapable of providing humankind with effective direction.[127] Indeed, pagan humanity and civilization have been guided by imagination, not philosophy. But imagination alone is deceiving and destructive. To be creative and nondestructive reason and imagination must complement one another. The epistemology of creativity and the prophetic mind involves three separate steps:[128] the development of the rational faculty, the development of the imaginative faculty, and the conjunction of both of them thereby generating a new form of cognition. The cognition that emerges from this conjunction is not reducible to the sum of its parts. Thus, Maimonides's seminal distinction between ordinary rationality, operating without the aid of imagination, and the rationality emerging from the conjunction reason ➞ imagination.[129] At this level of cognition, the mind bypasses standard epistemological procedures and knows by means transcending ordinary rationality.

The prophet is *intellectually* superior to the philosopher because he has fully developed both his rational and imaginative faculties and learned how to link them:

> [T]his intellectual flow, if flowing solely on the cognitive faculty, spilling nothing from it onto the imaginative faculty either because the flowing substance is scanty or [the person] cannot receive the flow of reason because of some impediment in

> the imaginative [faculty] in its basic biopsychological constitution [*al-jibla*], this is the class of sages, and intellectual men. If the flow flows on both faculties, however, namely, the cognitive and the imaginative, as it was explained by me and other philosophers, and the imaginative [faculty] was flawless in terms of its biopsychological constitution, this is the class of the prophets.[130]

Maimonides was careful to stipulate that the imagination of the prophet is realized *after* the development of the intellectual faculty. The divine intellect, descends first on the "rational faculty and from it the flow reaches onto the imaginative [faculty]."[131] By applying imagination to the realm of reason the prophet transcends the boundaries of pure rationality. In conjunction with reason the imaginative faculty becomes a creative force, enhancing the rational faculties of the individual, generating a new form of cognition, that of dynamic creativity: "You ought to know that true prophets reach rational perceptions [*adrakat naḏariyyat*], which undoubtedly no human can arrive at through reason alone, by examining the causes by which such a knowledge could have been induced."[132]

The prophets' ability to foretell future events is not a matter of conjecture or inference but a class of cognition not available to ordinary humans: the same is true of the prophets' "announcements of matters that no human could foretell through ordinary conjecture and discernment alone."[133] This class of cognition is within the realm of the natural, not the miraculous.[134] The divine emanation reaching the prophet is cosmological, embracing the whole of creation.[135] It comes about when the active intellect not only stimulates reason but also overflows onto the imaginative faculty:

> The cause [for the prophet's extraordinary abilities] is that the emanation itself flowing onto the imaginative faculty caused it to be perfect—enabling it to foretell oncoming events and to behold them as if they were things detected by the senses, as if having perceived the imaged object (*al-mutkhayyala*) through the senses could also activate the intellectual faculty so that it could know real existing things. In this fashion he would come to apprehend that perception as if grasping it by rational propositions.[136]

This special type of intelligence allows the individual to bypass standard epistemological procedures, and to reach new forms of consciousness as well as "the true significance of prophecy and those views that distinguish prophetic wisdom."[137]

A creative mind requires the proper development at both the intellectual and imaginative levels and the ability to link them together. Not all those who develop their intellectual faculties have the ability to develop their imaginative faculties or have the biopsychological energy to link them effectively, hence, the intense preparation in the schooling of the prophet.[138]

THE PROPHET S REFLECTIVE CONSCIOUSNESS

Maimonides distinguished between 'prophecy' and a 'prophet'. 'Prophecy' is a state of consciousness triggered by the divine flow of intelligence embracing the cosmos. Except for Moses, it is effected invariably by an angel.[139] It can reach the common folk indirectly: through an individual who, moved by divine providence, tells or points out something to them; through a prophet who delivers an oracle;[140] or through their own dreams and imagination.[141] In all these cases the medium is designated *mal'akh* (angel), not in the common sense of a celestial being but in the sense of a 'messenger'.[142] Maimonides counted eleven degrees of direct prophetic inspiration. In the first two classes the recipients are the object of divine inspiration, but are not prophets.[143] In the first class divine inspiration moves the recipients solely to *act* superlatively on behalf of a just cause. At this level it does not touch their cognitive faculties, and the recipients are not inspired to articulate the experience verbally.[144] In the second case divine inspiration touches their cognitive faculties, and they are able to verbalize their experiences. It is designated by the rabbis *Ruwaḥ ha-Qodesh* (spirit of the Sanctuary). These individuals are not prophets. In his youth Maimonides counted King Solomon among the prophets.[145] In the *Guide,* however, David, Solomon, Daniel, although privy to divine inspiration, are not prophets. In fact, the Jewish canon does not include their writings with the *Prophets* (*Nebi'im*), but with the *Hagiographa* (*Ketubim*).[146] These two classes pertain to individuals who did not come up to the level of having their "night illuminated by lightning but by a radiant body or some type of rock that is radiant by night."[147] The other nine classes belong to prophets proper.[148] The distinction 'prophecy/prophet' is rabbinic. The rabbis declared that Daniel "was not a prophet."[149] At the same time they counted Daniel among those who had "prophetized" (*nitnabbe'u*), that is, individuals who were the recipients of prophecy.[150] Likewise, although Maimonides stated that Daniel was not a prophet, he illustrated the mechanism of prophecy from the book of Daniel.[151] This distinction leads to the most fundamental aspect of the relation 'reason → imagination'. The prophet must reach a level of reflective consciousness: the prophecy coming from above is to be reflectively interpreted by the rational faculties of the prophet. The point will be better understood upon considering Maimonides's discussion of the Hebrew terms *tabnit* (outline) and *temuna* (image). The first term, from the root *bana* (to build), refers to the outer shape of a thing *outside* the consciousness of the observer, such as a square or a triangle. The Scripture never applies this term to God.[152] The second term refers to the shape of a thing as it is reflected *in* the consciousness of the observer. *Temuna* (from the root *mwn/myn* species, tally) is an 'image' exhibiting the inner nature and structure of a thing. Scripture applies this term to three different types of impressions. First, it applies to the impression produced by "the sensory perception [of an object] outside consciousness."[153] It corresponds to the "sensory impressions" discussed by David Hume (1711–1776). Second, it applies to "the imaginative structure of an entity found in the imagination after discontinuing from the senses."[154] It corresponds to Hume's ideas.[155] Third, it may refer to the image captured by the mind, "the true significance [of an object] perceived by reason."[156] This corresponds to the "synthetic unity" discussed by Sartre.[157] It is in this last sense that it was said of Moses "that he would glance (*yabbiṭ*) at the temuna of God" (Nm 12:8).[158]

Like the Romans, the rabbis conceived of the human mind as a kind of a mirror. They used the Latin *speculum* (in the form *speclaria*) from which *speculation* derives, to explain how Moses was able to glance at the temuna of God. One of the consequences of this simile is that human perception at once reflects and distorts reality. Just like a mirror reduces a three-dimensional object to a two-dimensional image, human perception, too, reflects and distorts the dimensionality of the Divine.[159] The difference between Moses and other prophets is that Moses beheld the Divine Presence from "a *speclaria* that illuminates," whereas all other prophets beheld it, from "a *speclaria* that does not illuminate."[160] The temuna is not the image of God but the *impression* projected by God onto the *speclaria-mirror*.[161] The rabbis meant to say, that whereas all other prophets glanced at the impression of God as reflected in the mirror of their imaginations, Moses glanced at the image of God as reflected in his reason. On the basis of the preceding R.

Ḥanan'el (d. 1055–1056) concluded: "All the prophets perceived His Glory as a dim light from a *speclaria* that does not illuminate, and they imagined [*venidma*] that they had perceived a vision, like an elderly person whose eyesight is weak and sees that which is short as if it were tall, and one as if it were two, and other similar cases although that is not the case [in reality]."[162] Elaborating on the verse, "And in the hand of the prophets I am imagined [*adamme*]" (Hos 12:11)—in the sense that God projects Himself onto the imagination of the prophets—R. Ḥanan'el formulated the doctrine that the prophetic "vision that they [the prophets] behold is imagination, and not the reality."[163] Maimonides accepted this doctrine.[164]

There are two components to prophecy: the vision and the *interpretation* (*pitron*) of the vision.[165] Human imagination is faltering and deceiving. There is a need for a reflective examination—a kind of psychoanalytic investigation—to decode properly the prophetic image. The prophet is to function as his own analyst, carefully decoding the temuna in terms of its linguistic components.[166] The examination must be carried on by the prophet himself.[167] Consequently, prophecy involves a semiotic relationship between the vision reflected in the imagination and the intellect of the prophet: prophecy-imagination is the *interpreted* system; the pirush-reason is the *interpreter* system.[168] Like the revolving sword guarding the way to Eden, this process involves a succession of dark (imagination) and light (reason) flashes. Like Borgesian mirrors, the vision of the prophets is blurred. In the language of the rabbis, it is "a *speclaria* that does not illuminate."[169]

There are two movements to the reflective consciousness of the prophet: a movement *away* from the prophetic vision and then directing the attention *toward* it. A precondition for reflective consciousness and the type of analysis required of the prophet is to shatter the illusion of immanence present in the temuna. As it were, the mirror/mind/imagination reduces the absolute reality of God to a two-dimensional entity. Thus, the prophet must perceive the revelation of the divine as a *reflection*, not as the actual divine. Apophasis is indispensable to distinguish between the object of revelation and the object itself. This type of abstraction is impossible at the imaginative level. For the imaginative consciousness and the paleologic mind the temuna does not stand for a thing: it *is* the thing. As with classical Pavlovian physiology, there is a reflexive condition linking the sign to the thing that the sign represents: the sign of the object cannot be differentiated from the object. Indeed, for Elisha and the Gnostic mentioned earlier the herald *is* the king.[170]

The model for the reflective consciousness of the prophet is the burning bush. Upon realizing that it was a prophetic vision, Moses covered his face and refused to glance (*me-habbiṭ*) *at* the elohim (angel/God) producing the vision (see Ex 3:6). In this fashion Moses ruptured the link between the burning bush, which he "turned to see," and elohim of which the bush was the sign but which he refused to look at. To focus *on* the vision one must first turn *away* from the source of the vision. In the words of the rabbis in reward for "hiding his face" from glancing at (me-habbiṭ) God (Ex 3:6) Moses was privileged to glance at (*le-habbiṭ*) the temuna of God (Nm 12:8).[171]

A reflective consciousness involves passing from the realm of imagination (the interpreted system) to the realm of reason (the interpreter system). It is clear now why Maimonides insisted that only someone who had optimally developed both his imaginative and rational faculties could be a prophet. The prophet's reflective consciousness serves to articulate the prophetic experience and to communicate it to others. By virtue of his interpretation the prophet transforms the prophetic experience into ḥokhma 'wisdom', 'knowledge'—something that both instructs and elevates people. "Accordingly," Maimonides concluded:

> [I]t is necessary to discard someone who has not developed his intellectual faculty to perfection. Only someone who has reached perfect cognition is capable of perceiving other [forms] of knowledge when the divine intellect rests upon him. He is the one who is truly a prophet. This has been clearly expounded. As it is written: "And the prophet is the heart [*lebab*] of wisdom" (Ps 90:12). It means, that the true prophet is the heart of wisdom. This, too, is something that ought to be known.[172]

The distinction between the perception of the image of an object and reflection on that image was explained by Sartre. In the first case consciousness is focused on the object, not on the image. In the second, it is focused on the image, not on the object:

> [I]t is certain that when I produce the image of Peter, it is Peter who is the object of my actual consciousness. As long as that consciousness remains unaltered, I could give a description of the object as it appears to me in the form of an image but not

of the image as such. To determine the properties of the image I must turn to a new act of consciousness: I must *reflect*. Thus the image as image is describable only by an act of the second degree in which attention is turned away from the object and directed to the manner in which the object is given. It is this reflective act which permits the judgment "I have an image."[173]

Certainty is a function of this class of judgment. The prophet has absolute certainty of the temuna he saw: "[W]hatever the prophet is seeing in the prophetic vision is thoroughly certain for the prophet—having absolutely no doubts at all about it. For him, it [the prophecy] belongs to the order of the rest of the real things which are perceived either by the senses or by the intellect."[174]

Through this type of reflection absolute certainty is gained. As noted by Sartre:

> It is necessary to repeat at this point what has been known since Descartes: that a reflective consciousness gives us knowledge of absolute certainty; that he who becomes aware "of having an image" by an act of reflection cannot deceive himself. . . . If this consciousness is immediately distinguishable from all others, it is because it presents itself to reflection with certain traits, certain characteristics, which at once determine the judgment "I have an image." The act of reflection thus has a content of immediate certainty which we shall call the *essence* of the image.[175]

In the first two cases there is no reflective consciousness.[176] The recipient is a passive instrument moved by divine inspiration as with Moses intervening to save the Hebrew from his Egyptian oppressor and David confronting Goliath in battle.[177] In the other nine cases the prophet focuses his consciousness *on* the prophetic vision. Significantly, R. Judah bar Il'ai (second century) maintained that there were nine mirrors where the Divine Presence reflected itself,[178] the original radiation being so potent that a series of nine reflections from one mirror to another may be required to pale it down, the more reflections and mirrors, the more propensity for distortion, and the greater the need for proper decoding. It would be the specific task of the prophet to distinguish between the image and the object of the image. Since the divine transcends direct human experience, the task is difficult. To illustrate, suppose someone is visiting a country where there are no bananas, and the people have never seen a photograph. When a native tells the visitor that he has never seen a banana, the visitor replies, "I happen to have a picture of it," and hands him a photograph of a banana. Since the native never saw a photograph, he may believe that the picture *is* the actual banana and try to eat it. Accordingly, he may either conclude that the previous information about the qualities of the bananas was false or that the visitor has deceived him. A more sophisticated approach, as with the case of the Gnostic mystics, would be to postulate that there are *two* bananas: one transcendental, perennially functioning as *banana absconditus,* and another, accessible to man, but having a funny taste.

Moses's uniqueness rests on the fact that only about him did the Scripture testify that God had spoken to him "mouth to mouth" (Nm 12:8). At the beginning, however, when he was growing up in Egypt, Moses was only moved by divine inspiration.[179] Afterward he received his prophecy through an angel, that is, through his imagination.[180] Subsequently, the Scripture attested that he perceived God's temuna directly reflected *on* his mind rather than *on* his imagination. Therefore, he did not have to decoded the meaning and could perceive it directly without reflective analysis. Although the verbs *ra'a* and *hibbiṭ* mean 'to see', there is a critical difference between them. In the Scripture hibbiṭ is used for a *direct* vision, never for an indirect sight.[181] The verse "and the temuna of God he would *yabbiṭ*" (Nm 12:8), means that he had perceived God's temuna directly, not reflectively: it had been reflected on Moses's intellect, rather than on his imagination, hence Moses's superiority over all prophets, past and future.[182]

ANTHROPOCENTRIC THEOLOGY

There is a fundamental difference between the "speclaria that does not illuminate," identified by Maimonides with imagination and reason, and the "speclaria that illuminates." The former cannot reflect the face of the viewer, the latter does. An early version of the Talmud—later doctored by scribes who could no longer understand its meaning—reads: "speclaria which illuminates the eyes (*'enayyim*),"[183] that is, of the viewer, implying thereby that he could see on it *his* own reflection. Translated into our terminology, this means that the imaginative consciousness can contemplate others but not itself. Unlike rational consciousness, it is incapable of reflection and critical judgment. It operates by focusing the mirror on the 'outside' and on the 'other'.[184] This is why, although *teshuba* (repentance) is one of the pillars of the Hebrew Scripture instituted *before* the actual creation of the world,[185] upon retrogressing to the realm of imagination it was no longer an option for Adam. Within the realm of imagination the only option is atonement—the transference of guilt to 'an-other'. Repentance is possible at the level of rational consciousness. It requires a high level of mental organization to focus on the 'inside' rather than on the 'outside' (and thereby reflect on the 'self' rather than on 'an-other'). When Adam was asked why he ate the forbidden fruit, he blamed Eve; in turn, she blamed the snake (Gn 3:12–13). Retrogressing to the realm of imagination meant that fault lies invariably with the 'other' and the 'outside', never 'inside' the 'self', thus forfeiting the possibility of admitting mea culpa.

The ability to discern 'good/evil' without any concern for 'truth/falsehood' is grounded on the imagination's inability to reflect on itself. This radical self-opacity creates *homo absconditus*. It also cultivates the illusion that the 'outside/other', invariably perceived 'as' 'good/evil', is not a projection. In this fashion imagination creates its own universe, displacing the empirical world outside consciousness. In archaic times nature was not a given, arising bare and in full splendor before humans: "[O]n the contrary, the whole material world appeared shrouded in mythical thinking and mythical fantasy. It was these which gave its objects their form, color, and specific character. Long before the world appeared to consciousness as a totality of empirical things and a complex of empirical attributes it was manifested as an aggregate of mythical powers and effects."[186]

In Borges's story Paracelso asks: "Can you believe that the divinity could have created a place that is not Paradise? Can you believe that the Fall is another thing but ignoring that we are in Paradise?"[187] A consequence of the paleologic mechanism is alienation—"expulsion" in the language of the Scripture (Gn 3:24). "Whereas normal thinking has the purpose of interpreting reality, paleologic thinking becomes a substitute for reality."[188] Before gaining access to the real world, man has to free himself from the tyranny of imagination. The same is true when approaching the realm of the divine. The application of human attributes to God, and the whole gamut of anthropocentric theology, are—like the rest of the realm of imagination—human projections shrouding the divine in terms of mythical fantasy. A prior condition to the realm of the divine is casting off the shackles of imagination. Maimonides warned, "not to charge to speculate" into the realm of the divine, "with the corrupt imagination."[189] When considering matters pertaining to the divine,

> one should not begin by charging with his initial impulse onto this awesome and sublime subject, without [having first] trained his soul in the sciences and knowledge, educated his mores as much as possible, and killed his desires and imaginary passions. Only after attaining true and valid axioms, understanding them, learning the canons of syllogisms and demonstrations, and learning the ways to guard against mental errors can one proceed to investigate this matter. One should not settle on the first view that comes to him, nor should one project one's thoughts from the beginning and put them in command and proceed to march toward the perception of God.[190]

The danger is greater when the individual trespasses the boundaries of his rational powers, attempting to glance at the divine through his imagination. Then, like Elisha

> not only that you would not be perfect, but you will be faultier than the faultiest. You will be overpowered by imagination. A tendency toward faultiness, vice and evil will emerge because of mental disturbances [resulting from] having extinguished its [the mind's] light. In the same manner that when the pressure [on the cornea] of the eye is weakened among the sick, they will see [various] types of false imaginings as do those who force themselves to look at very bright or small items.[191]

This, precisely, was the fault with the "princes of the children of Israel" (Ex 24:10), who "charged" to comprehend these sublime subjects "before they were perfect." Their vision of God "involved corporeality," because "they charged and projected their own thoughts."[192] Other medieval scholars have interpreted the vision of the princes approvingly.[193] Maimonides's authority is Rab, who supported the doctrine "that . . . in the next world there is no eating and no drinking" from the verse stating that these princes "contemplated God and ate and drank" (Ex 24:11).[194] Only by positing that they were sinful could Rab have concluded from the fact that they *have* eaten and drunk that in the world to come there would be none of that.

Anthropocentric theology (like anthropocentric science) is affected by human projections; it pertains to the realm of imagination rather than the divine.[195] Within the Kabbalah system the purpose of *via negativa* is the "demolition of the ego" to reach an "anthropocentric form of mystical experience."[196] In extreme cases, this may lead to a *unio mystica* with God.[197] Ultimately, there is no difference between seeking the dissolution of the ego by claiming that the conscious *I* became absorbed by the divinity or claiming that the divinity was absorbed by the *I*. Both cases are extreme forms of dissolution of the self and unbridled omnipotence of thought: they are two movements of the same narcissistic experience. Addressing himself to this type of experience, Johannes Eckhart (ca. 1220–1327) wrote: "If therefore I am changed into God and He makes me one with Himself, then by the living God there is no distinction between us." As he explained: "By knowing God I take him to myself. By loving God, I penetrate him."[198]

JOINING THE ANGELICAL BEINGS IN CHORUS AND DANCE

In the Maimonidean scheme prophecy and esoterics are different phases of the same process: prophecy is the last attainable phase of esoterics and esoterics is the first step toward prophecy. The initiation into the realm of esoterics ("entering into the pardes") begins a long process of deanthropomorphization whose final phase involves encountering the Ruwaḥ ha-Qodesh (the spirit at the sanctuary). In his legal code, *Mishne Tora* (*Yesode ha-Tora* 7:1), Maimonides begins his dissertation on prophecy by ascertaining the link between esoterics and prophecy. The paragraph comprises three distinct segments. The first segment introduces prophecy as a fundamental doctrine and the essential qualities required for receiving prophecy. Following the rabbis,[199] these qualities are [1] wisdom, identified with the full development of the rational faculties, [2] strength, identified with moral fortitude,[200] and [3] wealth (*'ashir*). At one time, Maimonides followed the standard interpretation and identified it with 'contentment', 'happiness'.[201] Because in this case "wealth" would be an instance of virtue and moral fortitude, it was later discarded. Elsewhere, the rabbis compare a sage capable of "demonstrating his scholarship" to a "wealthy banker" (*shulḥani 'ashir*).[202] Accordingly, Maimonides identifies "wealthy" as a sage who has erudition and critical knowledge. The paragraph begins: "[1] [a] One of the foundations of the Law is that God prophetize humans. [b] Prophecy will not occur but to someone who is [i] great in wisdom; [ii] strong in his mores—who is not overpowered by his impulse on any matter but always controls his impulse with his mind;[203] [iii] and who has wide and highly precise knowledge."[204]

The second segment expands on these qualities and the steps to attain esoteric experience. The purpose is shifting to a higher form of consciousness from the rational to the prophetic. As mentioned earlier, Maimonides maintains that prophecy is within the realm of the natural.[205] Rational consciousness is not the final phase of human development. It is possible to attain a higher class of "rational perceptions"[206] but only after developing ordinary rationality to the fullest. "Only someone who has reached perfect cognition is capable of perceiving other [forms] of knowledge when the divine intellect rests upon him."[207] A barrier excluding the divine light are the sensations, imageries, and ideas resulting from sense ➞ imagination ➞ reason. Therefore, an absolute condition for prophecy is freeing oneself from all types of sensory imagery. This will heighten the level and scope of the conscious mind.[208] Apophasis, or the negation of knowledge processed through imagination ➞ reason, dispells the world of imagination and frees the mind from the fancies of anthropocentric theology. Here, the function of *via negativa* is not demolition of the ego but to divest it from illusory knowledge, thus allowing for the rise of a higher level of rationality and human consciousness. Maimonides continues:

> [2] A man who is total in all these virtues and in perfect health;[209] [i] who enters into the pardes and proceeds [to examine] those great and complex subjects,[210] having a proper knowledge for comprehension and realization;[211] [ii] who sanctifies himself, avoiding the ways of the common people walking in the darkness of time; stirring and teaching himself not to have any thoughts on meaningless subjects or on the vanities and deceptions of time; [iii] having his mind focused always upward, linked under the [divine] throne, [in order] to comprehend those holy

> and immaculate figures,[212] glancing at the entire wisdom of God from the first figure until the core of the earth and knowing from them His greatness:[213] immediately would the Ruwaḥ ha-Qodesh rest upon him.

The Ruwaḥ ha-Qodesh is the lightning flashing through the night. Encounter with it spawns a new class of reflective consciousness. It demands introspection and will emerge upon contrasting the new to the old self. The new self *knows* "that he is not as he was"—that it has surpassed conventional rationality. The knowledge spawned by the new consciousness effects a metamorphosis, resulting in a fundamental change of perspective. To attain it, the individual must *integrate* with the angelic beings and become a link in the big chain of creation, thus, switching from an anthropocentric perspective, to the perspective of a universe orbiting around God. The paragraph concludes:

> [3] At the moment that the Ruwaḥ ha-Qodesh rests on him, [i] his soul integrates with the class of angels called *ishim.*[214] [ii] He is transformed into a different person and would understand with his mind that he is not whom he was but that he had surpassed the class of the rest of human sages. As it was said concerning Saul, "And you shall prophetize with then and be transformed into another man" (1 Sm 10:6).

The ultimate purpose of "entering into the pardes" is dumya—the supreme silence and absolute darkness required for the voice of God to sound and His light to shine.[215] Realization of [i] the limits of reason, [ii] and human subjectivity, [iii] will dispel the realm of imagination, [iv] permitting the Divine Spirit to "rest" on the individual. [v] Then, a transformed consciousness emerges, [vi] linking the individual to the rest of the world, [vii] orbiting around the Creator.

The idea of joining in a chorus dancing around God is rabbinic. The rabbis tell that upon crossing the Red Sea every Israelite

> pointed out with his finger and exclaimed: "This [*ze*] is my God [*Eli*] and I shall make for Him a dwelling" (Ex 15:2). God responded to Israel: "In this world you say to me, 'This is my God' only once. But in the future you shall say it twice." As it

> is written: "And on that day he shall say: 'Behold our God [*Elohenu*] this [ze], we have hoped for Him and He has saved us. This [ze] is the Lord (YHWH) we hoped for Him, we shall dance [*nagila*] and rejoice in His salvation [Is 25:9]."[216]

In Hebrew, *ze* is a deictic pronoun pointing at something 'out here' in space-now. It stands for 'pointing with the finger' at an object *outside* consciousness.[217] The rabbis taught that every Israelite perceived God as is, outside human consciousness. "A maid was able to see in the [Red] Sea, what [Prophets] Isaiah and Ezekiel were unable to see" [in their vision of the Divine Chariot].[218] Elsewhere, Rab declared that during the crossing of the Red Sea, "the bellies of the mothers became like a brilliant speclaria," thus enabling even the embryos to witness the presence of the Lord.[219] Maimonides associated "brilliant speclaria" with rational perception. Accordingly, this would mean that the Israelites were able to transcend imagination and perceive God not in terms of human projection but as a ze. In the second part of the homily God assures the Jewish people that in the future they would be able to say ze twice. It is related to a statement made by R. Eleazar (a pupil of Rab):

> In the future, God would make a dance-chorus (*maḥol*) for the righteous, when He would be seated among them in the Garden of Eden, and each one would point out with his finger. As it is written: "And in that day he shall say: 'Behold our God [Elohenu] this [ze], we have hoped for Him and He had saved us [*vay-yoshi'enu*]. This [ze] is the Lord [YHWH] we have hoped for Him, let us dance [nagila] and rejoice in His salvation (*bi-yshu'ato*) (Is 25:9)."[220]

The root of maḥol is *ḥyl/ḥwl*, which means 'encircling' something or someone. In our context, it means to encircle the *rosh maḥol*, the person leading the public in the 'dance-chorus' (maḥol). The rosh maḥol acts as a precentor. The public respond in antiphonal singing as when Miriam called the women to dance and sing (Ex 15:20–21). In a parallel source found in the Talmud Yerushalmi, describing the dance-chorus of the righteous, God is explicitly identified as the rosh maḥol, that is, the one standing at the center, inviting the public to participate.[221] In the text of the Babylonian Talmud quoted above, maḥol is related to the term nagila from the root *gyl/gwl* 'to revolve', 'to circle', and, therefore, 'to dance around'.[222] Hence, the above passage was interpreted to mean that God would be seated at the center while the righteous would be dancing around pointing at Him, singing His praises ("This is my God").[223] The first ze is related to the earlier deliverance of Israel; the past tense "we hoped for Him and He saved us (vay-yoshi'enu)" warrants such an interpretation. Accordingly, it was associated with the ze sung by the Israelites at the crossing of the Red Sea. Since the second ze appears in a future context ("This [ze] is God. . . . We shall dance [nagila] and rejoice in His salvation (bi-yshu'ato)," it was associated with "the future" stage or "the Garden of Eden." Saying ze for a second time is a function of the perspective acquired by "dancing around God." Whereas the first ze points to a God transcending imagination, the second ze points to a God transcending common rationality. The first ze is anthropocentric. At this level of consciousness God may be apprehended in *positive* terms only, from the perspective of past experience: "We hoped for Him and He saved us [vay-yoshi'enu]" throughout the unfolding of history. His presence is discerned upon realizing that He had fulfilled our individual [Eli, *my* God] and collective [Elohenu, *our* God] expectations.[224] In rabbinic tradition these names are associated with *middat ha-din,* standing not only for 'stern judgment' but also for 'rational logic'. The second ze is spoken from the exocentric perspective of those orbiting the Creator. At this level, God is referred to with the Tetragrammaton (YHWH), which in rabbinic tradition is connected with *middat ha-raḥamim,* standing not only for a God behaving according to the 'measure of mercy' but also implying a God behaving in a manner transcending common rationality. This coincides with a tradition stemming from the Ge'onim and Judah ha-Levi that Elohim (from which Eli/Elohenu derive), is apprehended through common rationality, whereas the Tetragrammaton (YHWH) could only be grasped through revelation.[225]

Liturgy is the means by which common mortals escape anthropocentric claustrophobia and join in the cosmic dance-chorus. One of the four categories of the Jewish liturgy is the *qedusha* (holiness, sanctification; plural: *qedushot*).[226] It is the most solemn theme of the liturgy. It reaches its zenith when, joining hands with the celestial beings, the faithful participate in the cosmic chorus, exclaiming: "Holy! Holy! Holy! God (YHWH) of the Hosts! The Fullness of the whole earth is His Glory" (Is 6:3). The qedusha is recited at three places: in the *Yoṣer,* before the *Shema';* in the *ḥazara,* after the Silent Prayer; and finally in *wu-Ba le-Ṣion.* To bring out its concrete meaning some linguistic remarks are of the essence.

Qedusha is a delocutive expression.[227] It derives from a special class of verb, meaning 'to *say' that* particular word (e.g. 'to welcome', that means: 'to *say*: welcome'!). Similarly, in Hebrew *le-qaddesh* (to sanctify) means: 'to say: *qadosh*! (holy!). Thus, in the *qedusha* of the *ḥazara*, before exclaiming "Holy! Holy! Holy!" it is stated: *Neqaddesh et Shimkha be-'Olamakh, keshem shemeqaddeshim Otakh bi-Shme Marom*. Properly translated it means: "We shall declare that your name is 'Holy', just like it is declared among the heavenly beings." Similarly in the Sephardic liturgy: *Naqdishakh ve-Na'ariṣakh ke-No'am Śiaḥ Sod Śarfe Qodesh*, "We shall declare: 'You are Holy! You are Exalted! as in the reverential chanting of the congregation of holy Seraphim." In turn, *qadosh* (an adjective, plural: *qedoshim*) may be the *object* of a delocutive—the term about which it is said 'qadosh'—or the *subject* saying, qadosh! Thus, in the section of the *'Amida-Ḥazara* where the qedusha is inserted, one reads: "You [God] are Qadosh! and Your Name is Qadosh!"—that is the *object* of our delocutive. It continues: "and *Q(e)doshim* every day praise You. Selah." Literally understood, this means that 'holiness' is not a 'concept' or some 'mysterious force' but the result of a delocutive relationship with God: those capable of declaring Him Qadosh! are indeed Qedoshim.

There are ethical implications in joining in the cosmic dance. Selfishness is overcome upon realizing that the universe is not a part of oneself, but that one is part of the universe. Interpreting the passage those who "beget for themselves" (Gn 6:4), as referring to egocentric, self-centered individuals, Philo wrote:

> We must indeed reject all those who "beget for themselves," that is, all those who pursue only their own profit and think not of others. For they think themselves born for themselves only and not for the innumerable others, for father, for mother, for wife, for children, for country, for the human race, and if we must extend the list, for heaven, for earth, for the universe, for knowledge, for virtues, for the Father and Captain of all; to each of whom we are bound according to our powers to render what is due, not holding all things to be an adjunct of ourselves, but rather ourselves an adjunct of all.[228]

Hence is the radical Jewish concept of acting "for the sake of Heaven."[229]

In Hebrew (in Greek as well) an 'angel' (mal'akh) is a 'messenger', that is, someone *not* acting on *his* own behalf but for the sake of someone else. As such, the essence of an angelic being is pure unselfishness. The ultimate human experience is becoming such an angelic being. It is accomplished by partaking in the cosmic dance-chorus and "rejoicing in His salvation (bi-yshu'ato)," a salvation coming from Him, not us. Because God is infinite, those partaking in the dance-chorus will be "rejoicing," pointing at Him forevermore.

Part 3
Cosmology

CREATION EX NIHILO

IN THE MAIMONIDEAN economy of ideas Creation ex nihilo, negative attributes, and freedom of choice are intimately connected with one another.

Polytheism and monotheism are two distinct ways of apprehending the variety and heterogeneity making up the world. To the pagan mind the multiplicity of existence is the effect of a polytheistic universe. Referring to the Mesopotamian deities, J. J. Finkelstein (1922–1974) noted: "A god's very being was in effect coterminous with the phenomena he 'controlled'. It is, of course, this quality above all that differentiates the 'immanence' that characterizes Mesopotamia deity from the 'transcendence' which characterizes the god of the Bible."[1] In fact, "The single most significant constant through this entire theological history is that speculation never arrives at the notion of the absolute omnipotence of any single deity."[2] The only possible relation between absolute monotheism and a world brimming with diversity is Creation ex nihilo, repudiating an ontological relation between God and the universe. Thus, the story of Creation is the essence of the Hebrew Scripture. God, the ultimate reality, precedes everything and creates everything. He is omnipotent and completely free: there is nothing external or internal to Him that can limit or condition His will. Things are what they are because He willed thus, freely and unrestrictedly. The miracle is testimony that God, author of the laws of universe, can change them at His will. "Belief in the creation of the world," wrote Maimonides, "necessarily requires that all the miracles are possible." Consequently, "Whoever believes in the eternity [of the world] does not belong at all to the congregation of Moses and Abraham."[3]

The Hebrew concept of creation is essentially ex nihilo: there are no ontological links between the Creator and the created. An unbridgeable chasm separates Him from everything else. Therefore, He cannot be compared to anything. Not only such rudimentary concepts as time and space but even the categories of being and existence applied to the universe must be denied of Him.[4] The illusion of similarity between God and man is promoted by language. Necessarily, the realm of the divine is expressed in anthropocentric terminology. At the semantic level, however, there is nothing in common between God and anything else. Analogy could apply to items belonging to the same genus. Man and God are categorically different. Beside the ambiguous expressions generated by linguistic necessities,

> in reality, there is no analogy [*nisba*] at all between Him and any of His creatures, since an absolute analogy can only apply, necessarily, between two items belonging to the same immediate species. When belonging [only] to the same genus, however, there could be no analogy. Therefore, it cannot be said: "This red is darker or lighter than this green" although both belong to the same genus, color. It is evident at first thought, however, that no analogy could be drawn between items belonging to two different genera even when they belong to the same genus. For instance, there could be no analogy between "one hundred cubits" and the "sharpness" of pepper because one belongs to the genus "quantity" and the other to the genus "quality." Likewise, there is no analogy between "knowledge" and "sweetness," or "docility" and "bitterness" although they all belong to the [same] high genus, "quality." Then, how can one draw an analogy between Him and any of His creations, considering the awesome difference in their actual existence—a difference that is impossible to be conceived of as greater.[5]

Negation of anthropocentrism is predicated on the affirmation of two abysmally distant realms, God and creation. Attributes that human language imposes when referring to Him must be understood negatively. When one says that He is "wise," "living," "existing," and so on, one actually means to say that He is not-unwise, not-unliving, not-unexisting. To be exact, the application of a negative attribute to God is differential, nonpredicative. "Likewise, these negations neither function nor apply to Him except in a manner in which, as you know, a negative [proposition] in which a predicate is inappropriately applied to a subject. As when one says about a wall that it does not see."[6]

Maimonides postulated the principle that perfect knowledge is a function of creation. "Therefore, He does not perceive the creations and know them by virtue of themselves, as we know them, but He knows them by virtue of Himself" as a Creator.[7] The modern concept of nature and science began with a metaphor comparing the universe to a clock. It was introduced by Maimonides to explain how God's knowledge of the universe is categorically different from ours. Maimonides conceived of the entire universe as interrelated, whereby everything is interconnected with everything else.[8] To know perfectly a single particle of the universe it would be necessary to know perfectly everything else. The metaphor of the universe as a cosmic clock illustrates the absolute distinctness of God's knowledge. As the cosmic clockmaker, God knows the universe by virtue of having created it, just like a clockmaker knows the different movements of the clock and the relationship between the parts. "There is a great difference between the knowledge that a creator has of what he created and the knowledge that another has of that creation." In the first case the thing created follows from the knowledge in the mind of the creator. In the second case knowledge follows from the thing created. One type of knowledge is creative, the other is contemplative. Depicting a water clock,[9] Maimonides proceeded:

> To illustrate: The artisan who fashioned that box where weights are moved by the movement of water to mark the passage of the hours of day or night—all the flow of water and the change in the position of the flow, every string that is pulled, and every plug that comes down—all these were [previously] known to the artisan who made it. He did not learn about those movements as a result of examining the movements taking place now. On the contrary, those movements taking place now are taking place in accordance with his knowledge. The same is not the case with someone [gaining knowledge about the clock by] examining this apparatus. Someone examining [this apparatus] would be gaining new knowledge through each movement that he observes. As long as he observes, he would continue to increase new knowledge, step by step, until he gained in this manner knowledge of the entire apparatus. If it would be possible for [the variety] of motions in that apparatus to be endless, then it would be impossible through examination [of the pre-

> sent motions] to know about these new motions until they take place, and then he would know what he knows from what had taken place.[10]

On the basis of this principle Francisco Sánchez (1550/51–1623) developed his famous *modus sciendi* (scientific methodology) since only that which is made is truly known, nature could only be known to the extent that it is humanmade, that is, through scientific experimentation.[11] Vico applied the same principle to explain the concept of *verum/factum* among the ancient Italians. This concept means that one can know (perfectly) only that which one has made, and conversely that one cannot know that which one has not made. Vico defined this principle as follows:

> One can thus infer that the ancient philosophers of Italy held the following beliefs about the true: that the true is what is made; that the first truth is therefore in God, because God is the first Maker; that the first truth is infinite, because God is the Maker of all things; and that it is complete, because it makes manifest to God since He contains them, the elements of things, extrinsic and intrinsic alike. Furthermore, to know is to arrange these elements. Thought is therefore proper to the human mind, but understanding proper to the divine mind. For God surveys all the elements of things, extrinsic and intrinsic, because He both contains and arranges them, whereas the human mind, because it is finite and external to everything other than itself, collects only the outermost elements of things, rather than all of them. Consequently, while it can, indeed, think about things, it cannot understand them. It therefore participates in reason, but lacks mastery of it.[12]

Rodolfo Mondolfo (1877–1976) explained the epistemological process underlying the *verum/factum* concept. "Factum" is not a "reality [of an event or a thing] offered to the knowing subject, but it indicates the creative action" of the author of something, who possesses "knowledge (*verum*) of that which he makes [*factum*]" by virtue of being its author.[13]

God has a perfect knowledge of everything because He had created everything. Hence, God's knowledge of the universe is categorically different than human knowledge of the universe. Not only human knowledge is partial, whereas God's knowledge is total, but, more important, God knows the universe as Creator, whereas humans have to acquire knowledge through inference and conjecture.[14] One knowledge is creative, the other is contemplative. Hence, even when knowing the same thing, God and man know it differently. The only thing in common between God's knowledge and human knowledge is "partaking of the same noun: 'knowledge.'"[15]

Denying creation, or postulating an eternal, uncreated substance coeval with God is to deny from God perfect knowledge. It also denies the Hebrew concept of an absolute omnipotent God. Referring to the view that God created the universe from an eternal matter coeval with Him, Maimonides declares:

> To us there is no difference between someone believing that heaven was generated from a necessary thing or that it decays into [another] thing or Aristotle's belief that it [the heaven] was neither generated nor will decay. Since the purpose of all those who follow the Law of Moses and our Patriarch Abraham or those who tread on their paths, however, is that surely there is nothing there [*an laisa ṯamma*] co-eternal with God in any way.[16]

Accordingly, Maimonides formulated the doctrine that a fundamental aspect of Jewish monotheism is that only God is eternal.[17]

At first sight the Hebrew doctrine of freedom of choice and that of God's perfect omniscience and total omnipresence seem irreconcilable.[18] If God knows the future perfectly, then the present has been already determined and man cannot be free; conversely, if man is free, then the future is undetermined and God cannot possibly be perfectly omniscient. Technically, however, each type of knowledge belongs to two mutually exclusive axes, and, therefore, they cannot possibly contradict one another: knowledge of the future pertains to the diachronic axis, whereas freedom of choice is operative only on the synchronic axis.[19] Maimonides's thrust, however, is that one cannot know *how* God 'knows'; to know that one would have to be Him.[20] Since His existence and knowledge are categorically different than that of man, God's omnipresence and omniscience cannot possibly interfere with ours. Isaac Newton further explained this point: "God suffers nothing from the motion of bodies; bodies find no resistance from the omnipresence of God."[21]

Because God created everything out of nothing, His creative knowledge gives sustenance and duration to everything. "If one were to imagine that He is not existent [now], then nothing else could exist." Therefore, His relation to the universe is categorically different from the relation of a creature to Him or to each other, "everything that exists needs Him, whereas He, blessed be! needs not any or all of them."[22] Since man is created, his knowledge and existence have nothing in common with God. Therefore, neither the 'existence' (omnipresence) nor 'knowledge' (omniscience) of God interfere with man's existence and knowledge. To deny Creation ex nihilo it would be necessary to postulate an ontological link between the deity and man, and either deny perfect omniscience and omnipresence from the deity or human freedom of choice.

IN SEARCH OF THE ULTIMATE REALITY

In the realm of imagination man is the ultimate reality: the roots of the numinous lie in the human psyche. The Hebrew Scripture posits God as the ultimate reality. The prohibition of idolatry—a central theme in the Hebrew Scripture—expresses the belief that whereas God could make man in *His* image, man cannot make God in *his* image: the relation Creator → creature is one-directional and irreversible.

Between imagination and prophecy lies reason. Maimonides's central thesis is that it is impossible to pass from the domain of imagination directly to prophecy: the only route is via reason. To ascertain the existence of the scriptural God Christian, Muslim, and Jewish theologians developed a system designed to support the main tenets of revealed religion by rational arguments. The system was designated in Arabic by the term *Kalam* (word) and its spokesmen by *mutakallimun.*[23] To prove the existence of God these theologians sought to demonstrate Creation ex nihilo, concluding that since that which is created must have a creator, there must be a Creator. Maimonides acknowledged that Creation ex nihilo is "necessarily the foundation of the whole Law."[24] It is the only doctrine that Judaism shares in common with Christianity and Islam.[25] One then would have expected that Maimonides would applaud the effort of his correligionists in emulating Christian and Muslim mutakallimun. Yet he rejected the theological approach to religion because of the methodology: it is faulty and grounded on violence.

In a remarkable chapter (part 1, chap. 71), Maimonides traced the methodology of the *Kalam* to the Church Fathers, whom he designated "the Greeks" (because that was the language in which they wrote) and "the Syrians" (from their place of origin) theologians.[26] He further pointed out how the early Muslim theologians first applied and then developed Christian theological methodology. Modern scholars rejected Maimonides's view on two grounds: Muslim historians did not acknowledge Christian influence in this respect, and many of the subjects developed by the *Kalam* are not found in Christian theological writings. The first argument is specious. It seems disingenuous to expect a people to acknowledge freely that one of their major intellectual movements is indebted to another religion. Concerning the second point, Harry A. Wolfson (1887–1974) showed that Christian theological topics have indeed passed to, and were subsequently developed by, Muslim theologians. Finally, lest he should be misunderstood, Maimonides emphasized that what was particularly significant was the *methodology*—not the subjects—inaugurated by Christian theologians and then expanded by their counterparts in Islam.[27]

Maimonides regarded theology as a form of polemics and apologetics. Although using philosophical terminology and argumentation, the aim of the theologian—unlike the philosopher—is not to expose the truth but to defend and promote a set of doctrines. Maimonides traced the origin of this method to early Christendom. Christianity arose in an hostile environment heavily influenced by philosophy. To succeed, Christianity had to defend itself against the objections raised by pagan philosophers. The task of the theologians was to accommodate the truth to Christian doctrine, rather than the other way around. Thus, in framing their arguments and polemics they outlined a series of principles with no regard to the canons of logic and to physical phenomena. Within that system science and truth are subordinated to dogma. Using a rabbinic expression, Maimonides charged that in their zeal to demonstrate creation these "fundamentalists" (*al-uṣuliyun*) had "overturned the universe and transfigured the order of the world."[28] Although pretending to be objective and unprejudiced, their arguments are deceptive. What is purported as nature is pure imagination:

> Generally, in the formulation of their [philosophical] premises, all the early Greek mutakallimin who had converted to Christianity and those from Islam did not first follow what is evident from the subjects at hand. Rather, they first considered how the existent subject must be in order that they could draw

> from it a demonstration [*dalil*] that would either corroborate a given opinion [*ra'i*] or not contradict it.[29] And when this fantasy [*al-tukhayal*] was established, they postulated that the reality is of such a form. Then they proceeded to argue on behalf of those claims on which the premises [needed] to either verify a doctrine or to reject an objection raised against it rest. This is the fashion in which those wise [theologians] first acted to establish this system and presented it in their books. They claimed, however, that they had concluded those [ideas] on the basis of pure thought with no favoritism on behalf of doctrine or preconceptions.[30]

The *Kalam* methodology disregards empirical data and substitutes imagination for reason: "I discovered that all the mutakallimin had adopted a single type of methodology although there are different varieties. The doctrine [espoused] by everyone is to disregard reality as it is because [in their opinion] it is only a habit [*'ada*], which intellectually may be conceived as different."[31] Moreover, in many instances, "they follow imagination [al-khayal] and call it reason."[32] More gravely, they concocted all types of specious 'proofs' (*burahin*) designed to deceive rather than to illuminate. Only those who know not how to distinguish between 'proof', 'dialectics', and 'sophistry' will admit their demonstrations.[33] The method in the *Kalam* to demonstrate the existence of God by 'proving' creation was of strategic significance. The aim was to consolidate the theological-political axis. Since there could not be any apodictic proofs for Creation,[34] the real basis for belief in God and religion must be coercion. Invariably, this type of system is doctrinaire and authoritarian. Underneath the slick, eloquent style of theological discourse lurks violence and the threat of violence. This is why Maimonides pointed out that the *Kalam* originated

> when kings intent upon the defense of religion arose and the learned men of those times among the Greeks and the Syrians saw that their professed belief consisted of assertions exceedingly and patently at odds with philosophical opinions. Thus arose among them this science of *Kalam*. Accordingly, they began to set up propositions that could be useful to them in support of what they themselves believed and by which they

> could also refute those philosophical opinions that could threaten the foundations of their religion.[35]

The mention of "kings intent upon the defense of religion" underscores the close association between this type of discourse and political power. Alluding to religious coercion common in Islam and Christianity, Maimonides pointed out that such 'proofs' could only be maintained by institutionalized violence. Concerning the doctrine of Creation ex nihilo, he asked:

> How can it be used as a proposition to build upon it [belief in] the existence of God, and have the existence of God depending on it with uncertainty, [and argue] if the world is created then there is a God, but if the world is eternal there is no God? It is either that or to proclaim that there is an apodictic proof [burhan] for the creation of the world and impose it by the sword so that we could proclaim that we had taught God apodicticly.[36]

One may now appreciate why Maimonides censured Jewish scholars in the East, both Rabbanites and Karaites, "those of our nation [*millatna*], who mimic them"—Christian and Muslim mutakallimun—"and tread on their paths."[37] The term "our nation" (millatna) is not perfunctory. The chapter opened with a statement that as a result of subjugation "to the ignorant nations" (*al-milal al-jahiliya*) the esoteric subjects that were "in our nation" (millatna) were lost, and now "the great fundamentals of the nation" (*al-milla*) have disappeared completely.[38] Since the methodology in the *Kalam* had been developed by the people who were bent on eradicating Judaism and the Jewish people, it would be wrong to assume that it has some affinity with the faith of Israel. In fact, by using their methodology, Jewish mutakallimun were surrendering the values of Israel to the very system bent on their destruction. Maimonides was particularly concerned with mental assimilation—the adoption of violent ideologies disguised under the cloak of 'religion'. Through conquest and subjugation Jews were bereft of their own culture and value system. Ironically, misguided Jewish mutakallimun endeavored to fill the vacuum by adopting the values and institutions of their persecutors.[39] In an impassioned cry Maimonides denounced the fact that "the evil people from among the ignorant nations [al-milal al-jahiliya] destroyed our wisdom and our works, and annihilated our sages, until we became ignorant like them. . . . We assimilated to them, and their opinions have passed onto us, just like had passed onto us their mores and behavior."[40] In an early work Maimonides had censured "members of our religion who mimic the gentiles—because I am addressing myself particularly to them—" for having adopted ascetic ideologies from their gentile neighbors.[41]

Maimonides regarded the theological approach to religion as faulty and oppressive. Although professing reason and the God of the Scripture, the mutakallimun operated within the realm of imagination and political power. Instead, Maimonides enlisted Aristotelian reason to the aid of prophecy. It seems that it was more meaningful to maintain a dialogue about the God of Scripture with a rational pagan than with a theologian—Jew or gentile—immersed in mythical thinking.

THE GOD OF REASON

Maimonides adapted Aristotle's doctrine of the prime mover to prove the existence of the God of the Scripture. To explain the motion of heavens Aristotle concluded that "there is something which moves without being moved, being eternal, substance, and actuality."[42] Briefly, this doctrine had been interpreted to mean that "the unmoved mover . . . moves the heavens by itself, and through the medium of them, which move themselves, it moves this world of things whose motion is purely external to it."[43]

The Maimonidean strategy seems highly problematic. The relation between the unmoved mover and the heavens, which it is perpetually moving, is based on the law of causality. It is purely mechanical, with no room for intentionality, design, or volition. This doctrine necessitates the eternity of the universe, positing a totally impotent deity with no control over natural and human phenomena.[44] It is a critical point for those who believe in the Scripture. If somehow "they would succeed in proving [burhan] the eternity [of the universe] according to Aristotle's opinion (ra'i)," noted Maimonides, "the Law in its entirety would collapse."[45] Yet Maimonides preferred the prime mover of the Aristotelians to the deity of the theologians. Why?

Maimonides regarded Aristotle as the highest representation of pagan humanity. In a letter addressed to Samuel ibn Tibbon (ca. 1160–ca. 1230), the Hebrew translator of the *Guide*, Maimonides described Aristotle's mind as "the finality of the human mind, with the exception of one on whom the divine flow had poured and reached the state of prophecy, which is the highest state there is."[46] Aristotle's logic in particular, represents human emergence from the realm of imagination, before prophecy.[47] In the pagan world religion is conceived in mythical terms. Consequently, people inhabiting the realm of imagination argue that the Aristotelian system excludes the possibility of scriptural revelation.[48] Maimonides intended to demonstrate that the opposite was the case. Not only are Scripture and myth mutually exclusive but reason—Aristotelian reason in particular—necessitates a prime mover transcending the physical universe. Therefore, "If the world is eternal, then it would be necessary because of such and such a demonstration (dalil), that there is (*an ṭamma*) an existent, who is not the body of the universe, who is neither corporeal nor a corporeal force, who is one, continuously eternal, uncaused and unchangeable, and He is God."[49]

The Arabic adverb *an ṭamma* (that is there) is used as an interjection to point at something *outside* the mind of the speaker. Transcending myth and imagination involves locating a reality that is not a product of the human psyche but is the source of everything that exists. By discovering his absolute dependence on an absolute reality *outside* himself, man succeeds in breaking the grip of imagination and enters the realm of reason. At once, this discovery leads to the recognition of God and the beginning of wisdom (see Ps 111:10; Prv 1:7). Using the same adverb in Hebrew, Maimonides began the first paragraph of the *Mishne Tora:* "The Foundation of [all] Foundations and the Pillar of [all] sciences is to know that is there [*she-yesh sham*] a First Existent. He bestows existence [*mamṣi*] to all that which exists. Whatever exists from heavens to earth and between them, does not exist but from the verity of His existence."[50] The expression "that is there" (*she-yesh sham*) is semantically identical to the Arabic *an ṭamma*. In both languages, it points at something *outside* the psyche, and, therefore, a 'concrete', 'sure' fact, not a fabrication of the mind. In the context here, it stipulates that God is not a human creation, but the other way around. The use of the active participle *mamṣi* (bestows existence) underscores the continuous dependence of all creatures on His transcendental existence and thereby His continuous omnipresence and omniscience.[51]

The Aristotelian prime mover breaks the axis *authoritas*/religion. The strategy of the *Kalam* was to predicate the existence of God and thereby the whole gamut of religion on the doctrine of Creation. Since Creation cannot be proven, religion cannot stand on its own: it requires support from the political authorities, hence, the sanction of institutionalized violence and the dependence of religion on *authoritas*.[52] This is a major point of contention between Judaism and Christianity. Maimonides had postulated as an article of faith to worship God directly without recourse to an intercessor or a hierarchically superior entity as did the Church in Christendom.[53] Now, if humankind cannot discover the existence of God unless 'assisted' by the point of the sword, then it would follow that Creation—the very essence of scriptural religion—implies the establishment of a hierarchically superior authoritas empowered to impose this higher truth,[54] hence, the need to find an alternative to the thesis that the existence of God could (only) be demonstrated on the basis of the doctrine of Creation. Addressing this pivotal point, Maimonides reasoned:

> It is, therefore, clear to you that the demonstrations [*dala'il*] for the existence of God, His oneness, and incorporeality must be drawn, however, from the premise of the eternity (of the world), in order to have a thoroughly apodictic proof [burhan] [of His existence], regardless of whether the world is eternal or created. This is why you will always find that in the legal writings that I compose, when it happens that I must mention a doctrine based on the existence of God, I establish it with statements pointing toward the eternity [of the world]. This is not because I believe in the eternity [of the world] but because I want to establish the existence of God in our beliefs, in an apodictic method that would not be faulted at all. We should not base this true, awesome and exalted opinion [ra'i] [the existence of God], on a doctrine [Creation ex nihilo] which anyone could unsettle and undo, or could venture to propose that it was never created. Specially, since the philosophical demonstrations (dala'il) on these three subjects [existence of God, His oneness, and His incorporeality] are drawn from the nature of things as they are experienced, and they cannot be negated except by someone who is already committed to another opinion.[55]

This is also the position of the Scripture and the rabbis.[56] By contrast, the demonstrations of the mutakallimun "are based on premises contrary to the nature of empirical phenomena so that they were required to posit that there is no nature at all."[57] For the mutakallimun there is no objectivity. Truth is a function of authoritas. Aristotle reasoned that what is moved, that is, the entire universe, "could have been otherwise than it is." In contrast, the prime mover, "which moves while itself unmoved, existing actually, this can in no way be otherwise than as it is." In other words, "The prime mover, then, exists of necessity . . . and it is in this sense a first principle. On such a principle, then, depend the heavens and the world of nature."[58] This had been interpreted to mean that the prime mover is of a "necessary existence," whereas the universe moved by him is only of "possible existence."[59] Things in the realm of creation owe their existence to an external cause,[60] and they are subject to the processes of becoming and decaying. Maimonides concluded that "since, as we can see, are there (an ṭamma) things that are generated and decay, [and] is there (an ṭamma) an Existent who is neither generated nor does He decay, that there is no possibility for His decay at all, but [He] is of necessary existence, not of possible existence."[61]

On this basis Maimonides distinguished two categories of existence: one absolute and autonomous and another contingent and dependent.[62] In the second paragraph of the *Mishne Tora* Maimonides stated: "If it would be imagined that He does not exist, nothing else could exist."[63] There is a *hierarchy* of existence whereby Creation is subordinated to and dependent on God the absolute Existent: "If it would be imagined that nothing except He exists, He alone would exist. He would not vanish when they vanish. Because everything that exists depend on Him, and He blessed be! does not depend on them or on any one of them. His verity, therefore, is unlike the verity of anything else."[64] This doctrine passed from Maimonides to Newton, who in the General Scholium wrote, "that the Supreme God exists necessarily" and is "a Being necessarily existing."[65]

Rationality emerges upon discovering a reality *transcendent* and *independent* of humans. Maimonides's physical theory is pre-Newtonian and, therefore, inadmissible to modern scientific thinking. His methodology, however, is essentially clear: the *scientific* discovery of reality leads to the discovery of God, the *ultimate* reality. Viewed rationally, the whole universe is perceived as a semiological entity that "points out toward Him."[66] The discovery of two categories of reality, one thorough and necessary and another limited and conditional, demarcates the absolute chasm separating the prime mover from the universe that He is constantly generating and preserving. A proper understanding of the abysmal difference between the prime mover and the universe leads to the doctrine of negative attributes and apophasis. Since antiquity, the Aristotelian doctrine of the unmoved mover was plagued with serious textual and conceptual difficulties.[67] Maimonides exploited these problems to demonstrate either that Aristotle never believed that the world is uncreated, or that such a view could never be proven.[68]

THE PERIMETERS OF ARISTOTELIAN RATIONALITY

Maimonides regarded Aristotelian logic as the basis of human rationality. The special esteem for Aristotle concerned his monumental contributions in the field of logic. Aristotle had "taught humankind the method of apodictic proof [al-burhan], its canons and stipulations."[69] In an early work Maimonides commented on the importance of the works contained in Aristotle's *Organon* and his contribution to the development of a methodology of investigation based on objective, verifiable data: "And because this art, originated and developed in eight parts [the *Organon*] by Aristotle, it imparts to the rational faculty rules for the attainment of ideas, which are the inner speech, guarding it against error and leading it in the right path until it acquires the truth insofar as it is in human power to attain truth, and it also impart those rules, common to all languages, which lead external speech in the right path, guarding it against error."[70]

On the basis of Aristotelian logic Arab philosophers distinguished between an apodictic, deductive proof [burhan], and an inductive inference (*istidlal*). The latter, is related to *dalala* 'a sign-post'. The verb *dalla* means 'to show', 'to point out', 'to denote'. *Dalil* (indicator, inference) translates the Stoic term *semeion* (Hebrew: *simman* sign). In opposition to *burhan*, establishing necessary relations on the basis of causality and universal principles, *dalil* establishes connections on the basis of external factors without stipulating any causal or necessary relation between them. For example, the fact that a woman's breasts have milk is a dalil that she has given birth. Knowledge gained from burhan is deductive. Istidlal is inferential. Although it may be critical and sophisticated, because it is not apodictic it is not absolutely necessary.[71] Therefore, it is inferior to burhan.[72] A third term, 'opinion' (ra'i), stands for a thesis that is not proven apodictically but only supported by *ḥijaj* (argument) or at best *istidlal*. Although some of these opinions may be highly probable, they should not be regarded as certain; hence, the fundamental distinction between something confirmed by a scientific demonstration, which one must accept, and an approximation, which is 'like the truth' (verisimilitude) where there is room for disagreement.[73]

Scientific knowledge is not perfect knowledge. Scientific knowledge is a function of reason; perfect knowledge is a function of creation. Moreover, since the whole universe is interrelated and everything is interconnected with everything else, perfect knowledge is humanly impossible. Finally, there are both absolute and relative boundaries to the human mind. The rabbis taught that some concepts and subjects transcend, absolutely, the boundaries of human reason and will never be understood by any mortal at any time in history.[74] Likewise, Maimonides maintained that there are areas of knowledge transcending human understanding. There are other subjects that could be understood only partially by some members of the species at certain periods of human development.[75] The historical boundaries of human understanding are not necessarily rigid and fixed for all time. Today's unknown may well fall within the grasp of tomorrow's scientific horizon. At the same time an individual cannot transcend the perimeters of his period. If somehow one could travel back in history and confront Aristotle with the astronomy prevalent at the time of Maimonides, "he would reject it totally." Simply, such a knowledge would have caused havoc in his mind. "If he would have accepted it, [then] he would have become totally perplexed (*ḥa'iran*)."[76]

It follows that scientific knowledge must be structurally connected to a fundamental skepticism. Scientific knowledge is restricted to areas that can be submitted to direct analysis (*baḥat*). Thus 'certainty', which is a function of scientific knowledge, is not operative in areas such as metaphysics and astronomy where only inference (istidlal) is possible, but no direct proofs (burahin). In such areas there is only opinion (ra'i). This leads to a classification of human knowledge. Not all 'knowledge' is equivalent. There are areas where scientific investigation is possible, and the subjects can be demonstrated on the basis of 'proof' (burhan). In areas where no adequate tools of investigations are available, nothing can be known scientifically, and, therefore, knowledge is not certain. In such a situation one can only form an 'opinion' (ra'i). Since it cannot be deduced but only inferred (istidlal), such an opinion falls into the realm of the 'possible'. On this basis Maimonides distinguished three areas of human endeavor: mathematics, where knowledge is positive,[77] physics, where knowledge is partial, and matters pertaining to theology where "proof [burhan] transcends the human faculty." Since apodictic proof in those matters is impossible, "opinions proliferate, disagreements between investigators prevail, and there are always doubts." Generally, each party is thoroughly convinced it has "discovered the way by which the truth of the subject can be determined." In reality, however, "it is not within the faculty of the human mind to bring proofs [burahin] on these matters." Evidence to this, are the numerous controversies on these subjects, whereas, in reality "anything whose truth was learned with a proof [burahin], there is no controversy about it." Perplexity (ḥa'ira) pertains, exclusively, to areas transcending apodictic proofs. This is why perplexity is "very numerous in theological subjects, infrequent in subjects of physics, and nonexistent in mathematical subjects."[78]

The discovery of a scientific methodology splits reality into two: what can be known by means of burhan and what transcends scientific methodology and is, therefore, scientifically unknown. Since real things transcend the aspect that has been scientifically grasped, it follows that they cannot be perfectly known. Different sciences have different aims, areas of interest, and methodologies. The following is a fruitful analogy. An astronomical charter may appear to be certain from a mathematician's point of view. Yet to an astronomer dealing with concrete bodies and motions it may only be a conjecture. "If someone who is only a mathematician," remarked Maimonides, would examine an astronomical charter, "he would think that it is an absolute proof [burhan], concerning the shape and numbers of spheres. This, however, is neither the case nor purpose of the science of astronomy." The purpose of astronomy is to postulate the fewest orbits at a uniform velocity.[79] Accordingly, when making astronomical computations and proposing hypotheses about the shape of heavenly bodies, their trajectories and orbits, the knowledge of the astronomer is fragmentary and conjectural. There can be no certainty that those hypotheses are actually true. The aim of the astronomer is to appraise—rather than to instruct—about the possible movements between two points. Because such a view on science could have a negative impact on the unlearned public, Maimonides alerted the *reader* that he had communicated this doctrine to his student only *orally*. After discussing the different trajectories and orbits of the celestial bodies, Maimonides remarked: "I have explained to you face to face that what astronomers maintain is not necessarily [factual], since their intention is not to estimate for us what the real shape and existence of the spheres are. Rather, their sole intention is to propose to us an astronomical system according to which there can be uniform orbital motions, corresponding to what we perceive visually—irrelevantly whether that is the case or not."[80]

All scientific systems, Aristotelian rationalism included, must acknowledge their limits and delineate the areas transcending their particular methodology. In this precise sense a scientific methodology must be structurally linked to a formal skepticism. Only the specific aspect that was properly examined by a scientific method could actually be known. The rest belongs to the realm of the unknown.

THE FAULT WITH ARISTOTLE

As mentioned before, Maimonides regarded Aristotle as the highest representation of pagan humanity. This perception passed from Maimonides to other philosophers in the Middle Ages, including the Scholastics. Modern scholars have confused esteem with subservience, surmising that Maimonides had invested Aristotle with authoritas. This is not the case. In sharp contrast with the Scholastics Maimonides rejected the notion of authoritas.[81] Concerning physical phenomena, Maimonides formulated the principle that "facts do not follow opinions, but true opinions ought to follow the facts."[82] He could have cited Aristotle. Instead, he cited Themistius, a minor philosopher. The message is clear: rejection of authoritas is not the effect of authoritas.[83] Explicitly, Maimonides dismissed the notion of authoritas in the realm of physics and metaphysics. Although Maimonides regarded Aristotelian physics as sound, this was because he believed that Aristotle's physics was usually demonstrable. He pointed out, however, that when contradicted by "factual datum," Aristotelian physics is to be rejected. "I shall not contradict at all that which he had actually proven," he declared.[84] What counts is the proof (al-burhan), not who proved it. This principle applies even to Jewish law. Concerning the application of Greek astronomy for the computation of the Jewish calendar, Maimonides taught:

> The proofs for every item are [to be found] in the science of astronomy and geometry about which Greek scholars wrote plentifully, and they [their writings] are now found in the hands of scholars. The books [on astronomy written] by Jewish scholars from the children of Issachar at the time of the prophets, however, have not reached us. Nonetheless, since all these matters are [based on] clear and unambiguous proofs, which no one can doubt, it is unimportant who the author is, whether a prophet or a gentile. Because every item whose reason is exposed and its truth is discerned with unambiguous proofs

> [burahin], we may rely on the person who said it or taught the proof that was exposed and the reason which was discerned.[85]

Since the Aristotelian views on metaphysics and the trajectory of celestial bodies above the lunar orbit cannot be verified, they must be regarded as pure fabrication. Aristotelian astronomy, "does not conform with the real order of things."[86] In general, Maimonides believed "that the sciences at his [Aristotle's] time were inadequate and were not yet properly developed."[87] After examining the Aristotelian views in light of contemporaneous astronomy, Maimonides concluded: "The truth is that he [Aristotle] did not understand or hear about it [contemporary astronomy] at all because the mathematical sciences were not adequately developed at his time. And if he would have heard about it [contemporary astronomy] he would have rejected it totally. And if he would have accepted it, he would have been totally perplexed [ḥa'iran] about all that which he had proposed on this subject."[88]

Maimonides censured those philosophers who invested Aristotle with authoritas, claiming "that whatever [Aristotle] mentioned is categorically proven (burhan) with no doubt whatsoever. For them, it is hideous to either disagree with him or to attribute to him ignorance of something or an error on any subject."[89] Some Aristotelian views were plainly unscientific and a leading cause of the dissemination of harmful misconceptions. Carefully distinguishing Aristotelian metaphysics and astronomy from Aristotelian physics, Maimonides introduced the following critical principle:

> Let me formulate a general principle. Although I am quite aware that many of the [Aristotelian] zealots would attribute this to my lack of understanding or to being deliberately misleading, I will not refrain on this account from expressing what I perceived and understood, my limitations notwithstanding. The general principle is: Whatever Aristotle said about all that which exists below the moon's sphere up to the center of the earth is undoubtedly true. No one would differ from him unless he has either misunderstood him, or has already formed an opinion that he now wants to defend or because those [Aristotelian] views lead him to deny a factual datum. Aristotle's discussions on [subjects] from the moon's sphere and above, however, are a kind of conjecture and fancy, except for a few

> items. This is all the more true in his discussions about the order of the [disembodied] intellects and some of those theological opinions that he happened to believe in, containing many absurdities and resulting in palpable harm that is evident among all the nations and the [cause for the] propagation of injuries. And there is no proof [burhan] on them.[90]

The last sentence—that Aristotle had conducted his investigation without the benefit of apodict proof (burḥan)—is particularly important. It is the critical principle by which to differentiate Aristotelian astronomy and metaphysics from his physics. On the one hand, "Whatever Aristotle mentioned about the sublunary [world] was carried on according to the rule of logic [*qiyas*]." On the other hand, "What lies in heaven, the human mind cannot apprehend except for the little measure acquired through mathematics"[91]—a science, which, as noted by Maimonides, had not been sufficiently developed during Aristotle's time. Within the Aristotelian system, however, physics and metaphysics are interlinked.[92] Therefore, by challenging Aristotelian metaphysics, Maimonides was, in fact, questioning the authority of Aristotelian physics. It is no wonder, then, that the twenty-six propositions to demonstrate the creation of the world, based on Aristotelian physics, were formulated in the introduction to part 2 and, thus, were excluded from the main body of the *Guide.*

Maimonides's first reference to Aristotle is in the fifth chapter of the first part of the *Guide.* The chapter opens with [1] a brief introductory remark about Aristotle, and [2] a reference to a passage in *De Caelo* (ii. 12, 291b). It reads:

> [i] As the leader [*rayyis*] of the philosophers proceeded in the investigation [*al-baḥat*] and demonstration [*wal-istidlal*] of very profound subjects; [ii] he said by way of apology, something to the effect, that those examining his writings should not regard his investigation [*yubḥat*] [of this type of subject] as an affront or audacity and impulsiveness for speaking on what he has no knowledge. It should be ascribed, rather, to his yearning and struggle to find and acquire true beliefs [*i'tiqadat*] as much as is humanly possible.[93]

Aristotle was not introduced by name, but by the title rayyis 'prince', in the sense of 'political leader'.[94] At first sight this seems to be a sign of rank and deference. Upon consideration, the title is confusing. In the same chapter Maimonides examined the story of "*aṣile* of the children of Israel" (Ex 24:10). Maimonides did not give a translation of that term. The educated reader, however, already knows that it is the exact translation of rayyis, the title used by Maimonides to introduce Aristotle. This is how it was rendered by the Aramaic Targum. The same Aramaic term, *rabrebaya,* was used by the Targum to translate *elohim* in Gn 3:5.[95] More poignant is the fact that Maimonides used the term rayyis in the sense of a 'political leader', a 'political boss', and *ri'asa* in the sense of 'authoritarian', 'domineering'.[96] This is particularly disturbing in light of the fact that Maimonides associates political leadership with imagination, not reason.[97] Finally, according to Maimonides, the 'princes/political leaders' of the children of Israel were guilty of charging impulsively into the field of esoterics and were punished for their affront.[98] Generally, it is presumed that Aristotle was mentioned here as an authority by which to evaluate the "princes of the children of Israel." It will be obvious in this discussion that the opposite was the case: the purpose was to assess Aristotle in light of the Scripture.

The other two terms, 'analysis' (baḥat) and 'inference' (istidlal), are germane to the Aristotelian methodology. 'Analysis' (baḥat) is the direct examination of a subject without recourse to authoritas. Significantly, in his introduction of Aristotle Maimonides omitted any reference to apodictic proof (burhan). Thus, at the same time that Maimonides was acknowledging Aristotle's preeminence because of his investigative methodology, he was faulting him for not always adhering to it. Aristotle's admission that he was now investigating [yubḥat] without recourse (even) to istidlal, but solely moved by the "yearning and struggle to find and acquire true beliefs [*i'tiqadat*]" must indeed be construed as "an affront or audacity and impulsiveness" because now he is "speaking on what" admittedly, he "has no knowledge." Aristotle's defense that he should be excused to proceed in this manner because he desires to "acquire true beliefs [i'tiqadat]" is senseless in light of the Maimonidean definition of 'faith' [i'tiqad] as a belief corresponding to an outer reality independent of human projections.[99] After citing Aristotle's apology, Maimonides added, "And so say we!" thereafter proceeding to list the requirements necessary for esoteric investigation on the bases of biblical and rabbinic sources and "the authentic tradition" (*al-naqal al-ṣaḥiḥ*) of Israel.[100] The hasty reader will presume that Maimonides intended to draw support to the rabbis from Aristotle. This is not the case. The remark, "And so say we!" is addressed to Aristotle; meaning, "And so say we *to you!*" *We* comprises the Community of Israel.[101] Thus, Maimonides was censuring Aristotle for discarding his own methodology and "investigating" such "profound subjects" on the basis of conjecture and supposition. After pointing out what happened to the princes of Israel for their impudence, Maimonides offered an afterword: "If this has taken place with them, how much more would the case be with us who are beneath them and with those who are beneath us?"[102] Since in the first clause "us" refers to members of the Community of Israel, the second clause, "those who are beneath us," must allude to those who do not belong to the same group.[103]

The title "rayyis of the philosophers" is a sarcasm.[104] In his metaphysical investigations Aristotle behaved like the aṣile of Israel, expecting special latitude of his authoritas. Explicitly, Maimonides stipulated as a condition for perfection that the individual should have already "canceled his design, and annulled his passion for false leadership [*al-ri'asat*], I mean, wanting to triumph or the admiration of the public or gaining their respect and obedience for its own sake."[105] Spiritual adventurism, like that of Elisha, invariably leads to disaster.[106] It will be seen that the antipode of "Aristotle, rayyis of the philosophers," is "Moses, *sid* [sir, lord] of the sages."[107] Rayyis represents a hierarchical relationship effected by power. Sid is an individual recognized by his peers for his excellence.

AT THE CUTTING EDGE OF REASON

The Tora does not contradict rationality: it transcends it. Rationality pertains to the second stage of human development. Prophecy, as represented by the Law of Moses, concerns the final unfolding of humankind. In his praise of Aristotle Maimonides was mindful to point out that his achievements do not represent the highest peak of humanity. The authority for this distinction is rabbinic. The rabbis taught: "If you are told that there is wisdom among the nations, you may believe it. But if they tell you that there is Tora among the nations, do not believe it."[108] Thus, in a very exact language Maimonides described Aristotle as "the finality of the human mind, *with the exception of one . . . [who] had reached the state of prophecy, which is the highest state there is.*"[109] In terms of Maimonides's famous parable Aristotle had only entered level six:[110] he had emerged from the realm of imagination but had not been privy to prophecy. Nonchalantly, Maimonides dismissed the Aristotelian view concerning the eternity of the world with a rabbinic quotation: "Our perfect Tora shall not be like their worthless babble."[111] The distance between rationality and prophecy is greater than the distance between imagination and reason. Apodictic proof, which constitutes the very essence of human rationality, is totally inoperative at the 'meta-physical' realm, represented by the Hebrew shamayim. Playing on the motifs of the verse, "The heaven is heaven for the Lord, and the earth He gave to the children of man" (Ps 115:16), Maimonides proposed a fundamental distinction between the realm where scientific methodology is applicable and the 'yonder' (shamayim). Matters pertaining to the realm of reason may be analyzed (baḥat), demonstrated (istidlal) and confirmed with conclusive proof (burhan). Beyond the cutting edge of reason, however, lies another realm where scientific understanding and methodology are inoperative. Shamayim, generally translated 'heaven', is related to the particle *sham* (there), meaning 'that which is there', 'the yonder', 'the beyond'.[112] Accordingly, it may be interpreted as 'what lies beyond human boundaries', what can be intuited from afar but cannot be adequately examined because of lack of proper scientific tools. Rather than scientific knowledge and objectivity, at the shamayim level only opinion (ra'i) and inference (istidlal) are possible. Concerning this pivotal point, Maimonides noted:

> Permit me to tell you in the manner of poetic oddities [*nawadir*]: "The heavens are heavens of the Lord, and the earth He gave to the children of Adam" (Ps 115:16), meaning, God alone knows perfectly well the truth about the heavens, their natures, substances, shapes, motions, and causes. For man, however, it is possible to know only that which is below heavens, since he can study it,[113] because it is the habitat in which he was placed and he forms a part of it. This is the truth. Since in what applies to the heavens we lack the grounds for inference [al-istidlal] since they are far above us in space and category, the general inference [istidlal] that can be gathered from them (the heavens), which is that they point out to their mover [God], is a subject that the human mind cannot study. To exhaust the thoughts trying to reach that which cannot be apprehended and which [human] has no instruments to reach is the effect of either some biological weakness or a kind of madness.[114]

Beyond the cutting edge of reason lies a higher reality that rational humanity can intuitively grasp but cannot articulate. To enter the *shamayim*—that is, pass from the realm of reason to the realm of prophecy—the individual must switch from an anthropocentric to a cosmic perspective.[115] At the cutting edge of reason, before crossing into the threshold of prophecy, a human faces a crisis of knowledge. He must choose between renouncing the realm of prophecy by turning to the realm of the rational or abandoning the realm of objectivity and apodictic proof on behalf of a new universe enshrouded in darkness. Louis Vax designates the borderline between two orders "the pure fantastic" where there is a "rupture of the constants of the daily world, which is the point of departure of the organization of a new universe ruled by new laws."[116] Since at this juncture neither rationality nor prophecy are operative, there is ḥa'ira (perplexity). Borrowing a rabbinic expression, the individual "has one leg on the ferry and one leg on the dock"—he is neither here nor there. Common language cannot articulate the fantastic, hence, the need for metaphor. As with Borges, for Maimonides, too, the function of metaphor is "to penetrate the mysterious relations between the different orders of things."[117]

One can now appreciate why Maimonides, who consistently disparaged poetry as an expression of imagination,[118] referred here to "the manner of poetic oddities [nawadir]." Since at this juncture the terms of imagination have lost their original connotation, they can be used as empty indicators to denote the relation between the realm of rationality and prophecy.[119] To serve this purpose the relation imagination ➞ reason must be inverted to reason ➞ imagination.[120]

THE REALM OF THE PROBABLE

Maimonides recognized two distinct systems of thought: one rabbinic and the other Aristotelian. To the Aristotelian system he dedicated a small handbook, *The Treatise on Logic*, written in his youth. His mature efforts were dedicated to the rabbinic system, resulting in three monumental works: the *Pirush ha-Mishnayot*, *Sefer ha-Miṣvot*, and *Mishne Tora*. None of these works was ever duplicated. They constitute the most authoritative works on rabbinics. Aristotelian logic, which is mainly deductive, is based on universal principles and categories and the classification and development of syllogisms. The aim is nothing less than perfect knowledge. Since for the rabbis knowledge is a function of creation, the Aristotelian definition, "science is the perfect cognition of a thing," is humanly impossible.[121] The rabbinic system is inductive rather than deductive. It focuses on the probable, not the absolute. The rabbis deal with probability, analogical inference, discrete sets, equiprobable and nonequiprobable logical alternatives, and subjects pertaining to statistical knowledge and indeterminacy, conceptual analogs and analog constructs.[122] If the prophets are the conduits of a perfect truth revealed by God, then, borrowing two expressions from Maimonides, the aim of the rabbis is "what is approximate to the truth," or 'by way of frequency' (*'al derekh ha-rob*).[123] The most important categories governing rabbinic jurisprudence are based on statistical inference. Unlike Aristotelian categories, rabbinic categories are quantitative, not qualitative. Similarly, Philo distinguished between the "truth" and "opinion." The latter "is based on likelihoods and plausibilities."[124] The rational and the probable represent two distinct systems of thought and reality. Within the realm of probability, necessity, causality and, therefore, burhan are inoperative; it only operates within the boundaries of istidlal. The function of burhan is to establish necessary relationships; istidlal establishes a possible, that is, statistical, relationship. Rationality deals with *qualitative* differences. These differences are categorical: something could either be true or false. Probability establishes *quantitative* differences: things are more or less close to a given model. Regarding probability, Maimonides noted: "Concerning probable things, some of them are highly probable and some of them highly improbable. The probability of some of them ranges between these [two extremes]. The probable has a very wide range."[125] Within the category of the rational, things are determined by a necessary chain of cause and effect. The 'probable' is only apparent ignorance of the specific causes that have determined it. The opposite is within the realm of the possible: 'necessary' relationships pertain to a contingent system. Thus, the Aristotelian and rabbinic systems are grounded on two irreconcilable concept of God and the universe.

Aristotle conceived of the universe as an uncreated system governed by the law of causality. This law embraces everything, including the relation between the prime mover and the universe. From this perspective it is senseless to speak of the prime mover in terms of intentionality (*qaṣda*), will (*radiya*), or volition (*sha'a*).[126] The doctrine of Creation teaches that 'necessity' and 'causality' are not intersystematic but were freely instituted by God. Contrary to Aristotle, "since there cannot be any analogy [nisba] between matter and that which is not matter," Creation is not the necessary effect of a sublime prime mover.[127] It is a spontaneous act of pure volition, free and undetermined. The universe is contingent, not necessary. Causality is the effect, not the grounds, of creation.[128] One might argue that since Aristotle rejected the Epicurean notion that the universe is the result of chance, the Aristotelian prime mover may be somehow analogous to the Creator of the Scripture. Maimonides rejected this view.[129] An integral dimension of creation is 'will'—a dynamic process having 'intentionality' (qaṣda) and 'determination' (*takhṣiṣ*), neither of which is conditioned by causality. Like the ideality in the mind of the first person, represented in Hebrew tradition by the "golden doves," intentionality and determination precede the "silver dots," or pragmatic realization of a thing.[130] Intentionality comprises a series of alternative models. It involves 'will' (*rias)*—in the sense of consent on the part of the Creator—and 'selection' (*ikhtar*). Determination is the implementation of a model, for example, determining that a particular plant should have white flowers rather than red or sweet fruits rather than bitter. Therefore, any given model is a 'probability' that theoretically could have been made differently. Selections and determinations are not random: God's volition (*mashiya*) is synonymous with His wisdom. Thus, the probable, too, is contained within the limits imposed by the very nature of the possible.[131] As a statistical possibility, the actual universe represents the deliberate selection of one model over another.[132]

Although Aristotle conceived of the first cause as a pure and sublime intellect that 'wants'—in the sense of being 'pleased'—what was effected by it, "it is impossible for it to will something else." "This," Maimonides noted, "can neither be called 'intentionality' nor has the sense of 'purpose'."[133] Above all, the scriptural Creator is willful and deliberate:

> To argue, however, that since it [the universe] is not self-generated, it was purposely and willfully [made by God]—I don't think that Aristotle believes such a thing. Indeed, to try to merge the [notion] of existence by way of necessity with [the doctrine of] Creation by way of intentionality and will and to reduce them to a single concept is, in my opinion, close to one wanting to merge two opposites. Because the concept of 'necessity'—as believed by Aristotle—is that everything in this world that was not artificially made is the inexorable result

> of a cause, which determines necessarily that a thing be what is. To this cause, there is another cause. To that cause another, until reaching the first cause, which to him [Aristotle] is the cause of everything—since it is impossible to have an infinite regression [of cause and effect].[134]

Will and necessity are two mutually exclusive concepts. Intentionality and selection are synonymous with purposiveness and creation. Necessity is a mechanical function determined by an inexorable principle controlling the chain of cause and event.[135] Since Aristotle's prime mover lacks intentionality and determination, it has nothing in common with the Hebrew Creator.

Scriptural Creation is willful.[136] Thus it is declared in the *Qaddish: "Di bera khir'uteh"* (that [He] created according to His will). It is also acausal. The question 'why?'—presupposing causality—does not apply to 'will'. "The verity of will and its essence," wrote Maimonides, "has the following meaning: to will and not to will."[137] This is akin to the principle of probability. The possible is a function of God's dynamic willing: "[He] does not will but what is probable, and nothing is probable unless His wisdom intended that it be so."[138] There are three major implications to this principle. First, the probable is not erratic, but a function of God's wisdom.[139] Second, the occurrence of one contingency over the other is acausal: "The nature of the probable is unattainable unless one of the probabilities is realized. It is improper to ask, 'What for was this probability and not another probability?' since the same question would apply if the other probability instead of this one would have occurred. Know this concept and understand it!"[140] Finally, since probability does not fall within the realm of causality, it cannot be 'determined'. Indeed, if it were possible to forecast a particular outcome, it would still retain all the characteristics of a probability. Therefore, although God knows the future, it remains indeterminate. "From the verses of Scripture it became clear to me that God's knowledge that a given probability will come to be does not affect in any way the nature of the probable: it will still retain the nature of the probable. Knowledge of the outcome of probabilities does not necessitate any of these probabilities. This is one of the fundamental doctrines of the Law of Moses. There is no doubt about it or disagreement."[141] "This," Maimonides concedes, "is very difficult to be conceptualize, according to our diminutive minds."[142] Our thinking habits are Aristotelian. One would need to overcome "conventional thinking" before accessing the realm of rabbinic probability and esoterics.[143]

Causality is not a primary law but was itself established by an acausal act of creation. Indeed, although governed by the principle of causality, the laws of physics are only statistical. The statistical character of nature was indicated by Maimonides in an early work. It is on the basis of a probabilistic concept of the laws of physics that there can be a distinction between essential and accidental. Frequent (*'ala al-akṯar*) phenomena are designated 'essential', and what is infrequent, for example, a man with six fingers, is 'accidental'.[144] Elsewhere, Maimonides wrote that "the major subjects of nature are, however, [a matter of] frequency [*akṯariya*]."[145] Indeed, "What happens frequently, this is something 'natural' . . . [and] what ensues rarely, that is the 'miraculous'."[146] The source of this concept is rabbinic. Commenting on the verse, "and the sea returned in the first light of morning to its course [*le-'etano*]" (Ex 14:27), the rabbis explained: "le-'etano—to the first condition [*le-tena'o*] that I had stipulated from the beginning." Note that the 'course' (*'etano*) or primary state of the sea, is described as a 'condition' (*tena'o*).[147] Thus, the rabbis were teaching that the physical laws themselves are contingent. Anticipating Joshiah Willard Gibbs (1839–1903), this means that the universe is a contingent entity, predictable only within statistical limits.

MA'AŚE BERESHIT

In accordance with rabbinic tradition Maimonides maintained that there is a general cosmological organization. *Ma'aśe Bereshit* is the conceptual model that permits the explanation of the basic principles of such an organization, and, as it were, surveys the entire cosmological system in a single ray of light.[148] Since the very concept of 'organization' implies the integration of disparate systems into a 'whole,' before their final integration phenomena lacked (present) structural uniformity. Therefore, a basic premise of the Maimonidean general theory of cosmology is that "what is found in the state of completion and full development" (i.e., presently, after being integrated into a system and total organization) "that state does not indicate [what] its state [was] before it was completed."[149] The referent of *bereshit* (in the beginning), the first word of the Hebrew Scripture (Gn 1:1), is not time, but the verb *bara* (created), meaning, "at the principal [stage] of creating the heaven and earth."[150] The authority for this doctrine is rabbinic. Maimonides called attention to a metaphor offered by the rabbis, comparing the first act of creation to the sowing of different seeds. The strewing is done simultaneously—at a single moment. The growth and development unfolds successively: each cosmic seed grows and unfolds separately, according to its own timing and makeup. In the translation of this metaphor Maimonides used *najama* (to raise)—a verb connected to the noun *najm* (star)—to describe the sprouting of these cosmic seeds, rather than the common verb *nabata* (to grow, to sprout), thus suggesting that the metaphor was referring to the spawning and growth of the celestial bodies disseminated throughout the universe.[151] This means that the cosmos as it is now was not made in a single instant but that it went through, or is presently undergoing, a process of growth and organization. *Ma'aśe Bereshit*—the rabbinic term for cosmology—probes into the "six days of creation," a period during which "there was no stable nature."[152] Translated into our own terminology, this means that phenomena were yet to be systematically structured and integrated. Elsewhere, the rabbis taught that what was made during *Ma'aśe Bereshit*, or initial stages of Creation, "*for* their size they were created, *for* their intelligence they were created, *for* their excellence they were created" (*le-qomatan nibre'u, le-da'tan nibre'u, le-ṣibyonam nibre'u*). The Hebrew preposition *le-* in the sense of 'toward', indicates purposefulness and finality, not a fixed state. Indeed, the term *Ma'aśe* (process), involving successivity, presupposes that the universe went through a "stage of becoming" (*fi-ḥal takunha*).[153] The early stages of cosmology comprised the phases of "creation, development, and stability" of the universe.[154] In the initial stage even such a fundamental concept as time was not operational.[155] Time is a magnitude pertaining to the present realm of things. Its application to the initial stages of the universe is a fallacious extrapolation of the imagination.[156] At the initial stages of the cosmos there were no statistical patterns; phenomena did not proceed according to (more-or-less) structured order. Since there was no 'frequency', physical phenomena were not yet structured into 'law'.[157]

The difference between cosmology and physical sciences is huge. Cosmology pertains to a another realm of reality. Physical sciences focus on the *structured* order, interpreting natural phenomena in terms of causality. Cosmology focuses on the *process* of becoming, prior to become *structured* into law (and integrated with other systems into a general organization). It unfolds within the realm of the possible, not the necessary. To explore the question of cosmology on the basis of present physical condition is to premise the inquiry by negating cosmology altogether. Expanding further on the metaphor of cosmic seeds mentioned earlier, Maimonides regarded the efforts to deduce cosmology from physics, as trying to infer embryology from the physiology of a mature specimen. It is fallacious "to infer [istidlal]" the early stages of the universe "from any phase" of the physical world, just as "one cannot infer [*yustaddal*]" from the state of a fully developed child "the state of that thing [the embryo] before it moved to be born or infer [yustad-dal] from its state when it began to move [labor], its state before it began to move." It is deceitful to "draw an inference [al-istidlal] from the nature of things that have realized their actuality and infer their nature when they were in potential." Aristotelian 'cosmology' is deceptive. Its methodology consists in extrapolating ideas derived from structured physical phenomena and applying them to prestructured phenomena in which case there is no cosmology. Such a procedure is analogous to drawing "al-burhan from all those true facts" known from the physiology of a mature person and concluding that human embryology is impossible, insisting that since: "Every living person, if he stops breathing, would die and his movements would deteriorate after a moment. Then, how can it be conceived that someone could subsist in a hermetically closed container, enveloped in it within another body for months, and that it could live and move?"[158] Similarly, Aristotle "opposes us and infers [wa-yustaddal] against us from the nature of stable and fully developed existence that has reached its potential." Maimonides agrees with Aristotle "with respect to the state [of the world] after it became stable and fully developed. [The point here, is however, that the present state] is not at all analogous to what it was when at the process of becoming, since it came to exist from absolute nothingness."[159]

Since cosmology cannot be based on scientific observation, Maimonides maintained that neither creation nor eternity of the world can be proven (burhan)[160] or inferred (istidlal).[161] One can pronounce an opinion (ra'i), present an argument (ḥijaj) and an educated conjecture (*naḍr*), but cannot prove (burhana) either creation or eternity of the world, hence, the criticism against both, the mutakallimun and Aristotelians, who claimed that they could prove their respective views.[162] Only through deception could either position be 'proven'.[163] Indeed, a scientifically based theory of cosmology is an oxymoron. To "prove" a theory of cosmology one would have to presuppose that the present state of the universe is analogous to its initial stages, in which case, cosmology would be indistinguishable from physics and not a topic on its own. This notion runs contrary to the concept of *Ma'aśe Bereshit*, postulating a *process* of becoming. More significantly, with their facile theories and fallacious shortcuts both creationists and anticreationists circumvent—more precisely, eliminate—cosmology. The worst effect of this methodology is depriving humankind of asking fully comprehensive questions about the world's greatest enigma, locking it up within the solipsistic delusions of false rationalism.

From the preceding it follows that it would be wrong to regard Aristotle or the pre-Socratic philosophers as cosmologists. Their methodology of extrapolating notions derived from structured phenomena and applying them to the initial stages of the universe is skewed and deceitful; it is grounded on the axiom that there is no cosmology, in which case, all investigation in this area would be nonsensical. According to Maimonides, *Ma'aśe Bereshit* of the rabbis is a middle point between the skeptic view that nothing can be known about the origins of the world and the naïve theorization of cosmology on the basis of fallacious inferences. Since neither Creation nor non-Creation can be scientifically demonstrated, it is a 'possible' (*mumkanat*) theory either way.[164] When confronting the problem, it is important to bear in mind that since belief in Creation means that there was absolutely nothing before, it cannot be examined as if it were a statistical probability. Statistical probabilities can only function within the realm of the pragmatic and apply to a definite item within *structured* particulars.[165] Thus, to examine the possibility of Creation ex nihilo one must shift away from the realm of the pragmatic into the purely abstract.[166] The question to be asked is not whether Creation is *statistically* probable but whether it is *logically* possible. Could a Creator/prime mover have devised this world out of nothing?[167] The Aristotelian view that Creation is "impossible" is the effect of imagination, projecting the inherent boundaries of (Aristotelian) rationality onto God.[168]

Maimonides's analysis of the problem of Creation is twofold. The first step consists in showing that Creation is not a logical absurdity[169] and, second, 'tipping the balance' (*tarjiḥ*) in favor of Creation ex nihilo. These could be accomplished by means of naḍr (educated conjecture, speculation): "After showing that our claim is possible, I will proceed to tip the balance on its behalf. On the basis, also, of speculative inference [*dalil naḍri*], I mean to tip the balance [*tarjiḥha*] of Creation over the eternity [of the world]. I shall explain that just as there are some reproofs against belief in Creation, there are stronger reproofs against belief in the eternity [of the world]."[170]

Speculative inference (dalil naḍri)[171]—the methodology proposed by Maimonides—was initially applied by Patriarch Abraham to ascertain that the world had a Creator.[172]

A KIND OF MADNESS

The Hebrew Scripture begins with the story of Creation, precisely at the point where rationalism ends. Cosmology and the problem of Creation expose the boundaries of Aristotelian rationalism. If the discovery of God as the ultimate reality opens the gates of reason, freeing the people from the grip of imagination, then Creation is the scale by which to soar above reason and enter the realm of esoterics and prophecy. Creation and cosmology cannot be properly investigated until first the boundaries of rationalism are acknowledged. Were one to accept the concepts of causality, necessity, and the prime mover as *first* principles, then there is nothing more to investigate. Thus, recognition of the limits of Aristotelian rationalism is a sine qua non for cosmology. It is now clear why Maimonides insisted that it must be acknowledged that there are areas of investigation where the burhan methodology is inoperative. As a condition for mental sanity, Maimonides offered a threefold advice: "not to fool oneself in believing that it was proven, that which cannot be proven," or "to dash, reject, and conclude that it is a lie, that of which its opposite is unproved," or "to attempt to understand that which you cannot understand."[173] "To exhaust the thoughts trying to reach that which cannot be apprehended," he observed, "is the effect of either some biological deficiency or a kind of madness."[174] Since an abstract possibility cannot be demonstrated on the basis of causality, the possible—the outcome of one possibility over the other—is not demonstrable. By pretending to prove that which belongs to the realm of the "possible," something that "approaches the truth" but cannot be determined on the basis of reason, both the mutakallimun and the Aristotelians exposed their inability to acknowledge the limits of their own methodology. After showing the futility of trying to prove either thesis, Maimonides pronounced a statement that is both a challenge and a confession: "It is possible that someone else has a proof [burhan] to demonstrate the truth of that which I do not know. The greatest homage that I can pay to the truth is that I elucidated and communicated my own perplexity [*ḥa'irati*] on those matters, and that I have not heard any proofs [burhana] on any of them and do not know it."[175]

It is now clear why the rabbis assigned cosmology to the realm of esoterics. Since it cannot be demonstrated, it is a source of perplexity. There are two aspects to this crisis, each requiring a different methodology. First, creation or eternity of the world can only be resolved on the basis of authority (taqlid). Second, creation ex nihilo or from a primeval substance can only be resolved by an existential 'tipping the balance' (tarjiḥ) on behalf of one position and against the other. Tarjiḥ involves subjectivity, the essence of rabbinic esoterics. It can only be exercised at the crossroad when confronting two equiprobable alternatives.[176] It is not open to all, but only to those worthy of esoteric knowledge. A prerequisite for "tipping the balance" is impartiality: "when either of the two opposing extremes appear to him equiprobable." Someone predisposed to one of these two possibilities, either because of education or profit, has already "tipped" the scale, and his judgment would be skewed. To exercise tarjiḥ an impartial individual must meet three conditions. First, he must arrive at a sound evaluation of his natural and intellectual faculties. To meet this condition an adequate knowledge of mathematics and logic is necessary. Second, it is necessary to have a scientific knowledge of physics. To avoid self-deception and authoritarianism scientific knowledge entails the identification of those areas of investigations that are assumed to be accurate but, in fact, are scientifically uncertain. Third, correct ethical conduct is of the essence. People unable to control their morals are prone to embrace ideologies that support their personal flaws.[177]

The problem of creation/eternity of the world cannot be subject to tarjiḥ. Those espousing belief in the eternity of the world—that is, Aristotle and his followers—are not impartial and cannot exercise tarjiḥ on this subject. Similarly, those who believe in the Law are committed to the doctrine of Creation. The only option available for either position is taqlid: uncritical acceptance of some authoritas. One may opt to uncritically accept (*qallad*) the view that the world is uncreated[178] or that the world is created.[179] For those believing in the Scripture the choice is simple. "Since this issue, I mean eternity of the world or its creation, is possible [*mumkana*]," Maimonides writes, "I accept it on the authority of prophecy, which elucidates matters that one cannot conclude by means of speculation [al-naḍr]."[180] Usually, taqlid is intellectually meaningless.[181] In this case it leads to two diametrically opposing positions. Choosing eternity of the world is to revert to the realm of imagination. Those choosing Creation would step into the threshold of prophecy.

Accepting eternity of the world on the basis of authority postulates, simultaneously, [i/ii] the infallibility of human reason, and [ii/i] a vertical view of humanity. [i/ii] 'Proof' of eternity of the world rests on the assumption that human and divine rationality are qualitatively the same. It is on this assumption alone that Creation ex nihilo is deemed impossible and the eternity of the universe 'proven'. There is consistency to this reasoning. Eternity of the universe posits a Platonic kind of knowledge, essentially contemplative—not a function of creation.[182] Therefore, there is no real difference between the knowledge in the mind of the prime mover and in the mind of a human. There are serious implications to this position. Once one postulates that divine and human knowledge are homogeneous—and that humans are capable of 'knowing the mind of God'—it would be impossible for the deity to know the affairs of humankind or to exercise particular providence, since any of these activities would imply changes in the mind of the divine.[183] From a theocentric perspective to presume that human reason can partake in the divine reason is the supreme expression of arrogance. Accordingly, the rabbis taught, "whoever has a haughty spirit is as he is worshipping idols," and "as if he had denied the existence of God," and "as if he had built (for himself) a sacrificial table," and he will not be resurrected from the dead[184] and will go down to hell.[185] Because arrogance (anthropocentrism) is intrinsic to idolatry, upon seeing a pagan temple one must recite the verse, "the house of the arrogant may the Lord obliterate" (Prv 15:25).[186]

The identification of human and divine knowledge is the effect of protological thought whereby identity is established semiotically on the basis of similar predicates, in this case, by confusing words with reality. The only common element between the knowledge of the Creator and that of a human is the word *knowledge*.

> There is no correlation between His knowledge and human knowledge, just as there is no correlation between His beingness and human beingness. The error here [of the Aristotelians] lies in the correlation made between [God and human] on the basis of the word *knowledge*. The correlation, however, is only verbal; the difference is in His reality. It is on this basis [alone] that all reproofs [against Creation] are inferred—because it was imagined that matters affecting human knowledge would also affect His knowledge.[187]

Maimonides refers to anthropocentrism as "that imagination."[188] Pointing at the amazing vastness of the universe, Maimonides wondered how can it be presumed that it was made for the sake of humans:

> Consider the existence of these [astral] bodies: how awesome their seize, how huge their numbers! In comparison to the sphere of the stars, the entire earth does not amount to even a [single] component. What then could the position of humankind be in comparison to all these creatures? How can any of us imagine [yutkhayal] that these exist for his behalf and because of him and that these [astral bodies] are his paraphernalia? This is only in consideration of the magnitude of their bodies. What then if you would consider the existence of intelligence [of celestial beings]?[189]

This argument, Maimonides concludes, supports "our belief in the creation of the world."[190]

Furthermore, belief in the eternity of the world and the supremacy of Aristotelian reasoning is connected with the belief that [ii/i] Aristotle is to be accepted vertically by virtue of his status as rayyis. It is critical to note that it was precisely in the chapter dealing with tarjiḥ when exhorting the reader to reject eternity of the world that Aristotle was referred to for the second and last time as a rayyis: "Aristotle, the rayyis of the philosophers, had already expressed in his principal works words of exhortation intended to promote his view on the eternity of the world."[191] In so doing, Aristotle was reverting to the world of mythology and imagination.

Like the rest of his contemporaries, Maimonides had no access to the works of classical mythology. He knew, however, the literature of the Sabeans—a pagan enclave that managed to survive in the Arab world. Correctly, Maimonides surmised that their views stemmed from and in certain fundamental aspects represented the mind of pagan humanity *before* the revelation of the Tora. Their religion was idolatrous, involving barbaric and repulsive cults. He regarded the Sabeans as a people wrapped in fantasy and imagination, confined to the most primitive stages of civilization. Their most fundamental belief was the eternity of the world.[192] It is in this passage that Maimonides refers to Aristotle as a rayyis, exhorting his followers to believe in the eternity of the world. Maimonides asked. "Since he [Aristotle] supports his opinion with the fantasies of the Sabeans, why should we refrain from supporting [our opinion] with the words of Moses and Abraham in all what concerns this matter?"[193]

The association Aristotle / Sabeans dispels any pretense to some sort of Aristotelian tarjiḥ. It also points out the ultimate, existential links between pagan rationalism and myth. Invariably, the pagan world resolves its rational crises by reverting to the world of myth and imagination under the leadership of a rayyis. Such a rayyis functions as a Cosmocrator to be accepted by virtue of his hierarchical superiority.[194] Because the very concept of a Cosmocrator is a product of myth and imagination, rationality must be suspended in reference to the rayyis.

Maimonides exhorted the reader not to be persuaded by the Aristotelian view. Instead, he should accept the taqlid of Abraham and Moses because they "are the pillars for the prosperity of the human race in our beliefs and in our social lives. Do not depart from the belief in creation of the world unless there is a proof. This, however, is not to be found in nature."[195] Accepting Creation on the basis of taqlid is an acknowledgment of the limitations of reason: "Therefore we shall stop at the boundaries of our faculties and acquiesce those matters which cannot be apprehended through judgment [*qiyas*] to him [Moses] who was the recipient of that divine and awesome flow, and who was worthy of the statement: 'Mouth to mouth I am speaking in him' (Nm 12:8). This is all that I have to say on this problem."[196]

TILTING ON THE SIDE OF CREATION EX NIHILO

Choosing Creation over non-Creation results in a quandary that cannot be resolved by taqlid. When examining the different theories of creation, Maimonides discussed the Platonic view of a primeval substance, coeval with God, from which the universe was created.[197] This view is appealing on several grounds. It does not flagrantly contradict the Scriptural text. Both grammatically and conceptually, Hebrew Creation could be interpreted to mean "from a primeval substance."[198] Moreover, there are rabbinic texts that seem to indicate that the universe was created from a preexistent substance.[199] Finally, unlike the Aristotelian view denying the possibility of miracles, this thesis "neither demolishes the basic doctrines of the Scripture nor results in the repudiation of miracles, but in their feasibility."[200] Since there is no taqlid on this item, both Creation ex nihilo or from a preexistent matter are equiprobable. Maimonides, chose to "tip the balance" against the Platonic view. Since it cannot be proven, this is not an opinion that we shall tilt on its behalf." Therefore, Maimonides declared, "we shall explain the texts [of Scripture] according to their obvious meaning," that is, Creation ex nihilo. He offered two reasons for this decision: [1] "the Law had informed us on a subject that our faculties cannot fully comprehend," and [2] "the miracles are evidence to the validity of our claim."[201]

Maimonides rejected the Aristotelian view on the eternity of the world for two reasons: [1] "it implies demolition [*had*] of the foundations [*uṣul*] of the Law" [2] "and is an affront [*aftiyat*] to the truth of God."[202] The first reason concerns the fact that this view denies the possibility of miracles, of reward and punishment, and of any hope for future redemption. Thus "demolishing [had] the Law in its foundations."[203] The second reason reflects the rabbinic doctrine concerning those having "a haughty spirit" mentioned in the preceding section of this volume. To the Hebrew ethos there could be no greater affront than pretending to know the mind of God.[204] The affront is an outcome of the Aristotelian presumption that human and divine knowledge are qualitatively the same. "The philosophers had affronted [*ifta'at*]," in the sense of being slighting and contemptuous, "against God, His knowledge of others—a most preposterous affront [*iftiyatan*]—and they had committed a blunder for which there will be no redemption either to them or those following their view."[205]

In assessing the Platonic doctrine Maimonides only said that it "does not demolish [had] the basic doctrines of the Scripture" since "it does not result in the repudiation of miracles, but their feasibility." He refrained, however, from acquitting Plato from affronting God. The message is clear: although allowing for the possibility of miracles, nonetheless, the Platonic primeval matter is an affront to God. Because for the rabbis perfect knowledge is a function of creation, by postulating that the primeval matter was uncreated, the Platonic thesis implies that divine and human knowledge are homogeneous, thus, committing the same affront as the Aristotelians.[206] Writing in the first person, Maimonides explained why he rejected the Aristotelian view and did not tilt in favor of the Platonic primeval matter. Although it would be possible to explain the text of the Scripture according to the Platonic view, "there is no need requiring us to do that unless that opinion would be proven." Referring first to the Platonic and then to the Aristotelian view, he continued: "Since it will not be proven, however, *this* [my italics] is not the opinion toward which we will tilt [*nijnaḥ*]. We shall not let ourselves be persuaded by the other opinion, but we will explain the texts [of Scripture] according to their plain meaning." Maimonides concluded with two arguments. The first is directed against both the Platonic and Aristotelian theses, which constitute an affront to God. The second only addresses the Aristotelian thesis that rejects the possibility of miracles. [1] "And we shall say that the Law had informed us about a subject that our faculty cannot reach. [2] And the miracles are evidence to the truth of our claim."[207] In no equivocal terms he identified belief in Creation ex nihilo as a basic fundament: "the foundation of the entire Tora consists in the doctrine that God produced the world out of nothing."[208] After writing the *Guide*, Maimonides included it among the thirteen fundamental doctrines of Judaism: "You must know that a principal doctrine of the Law of Moses our Teacher is that this world is created and that God brought it to be and created it from absolute nothingness." [209]

There is a major consequence between tilting on behalf of Creation ex nihilo or tilting on behalf of the Platonic primeval substance. The doctrine that the world is created involves "belief that there is nothing there [an laisa ṭamma] that in any way is coeternal with God. And that to have an existent come to exist from nothing, it is not impossible for God, nay according to some experts in speculation [al-naḍr] it is also necessary." It also permits the believer "to follow the Law of Moses and the Patriarch Abraham."[210] "To follow"—rather than to merely accept—implies the possibility of pursuing the matter further. This leads to *Ma'aśe Merkaba*, the second and final topic of rabbinic esoterics. Unless regressing to myth and imagination, Merkaba, (Chariot) implying cosmological direction, is inconceivable in terms of Platonic creation. Thus, whereas the Platonic view is the end of the road, Creation ex nihilo involves the bifurcation of the road and the possibility of tarjiḥ.

Cosmology results in a crisis of reason that could be resolved either by regressing to mythology or by entering the world of esoterics and prophecy. Either choice entails its own particular thought processes: imagination ➞ reason or reason ➞ imagination. Choosing Creation is to enter the world of esoterics: a world bifurcating into perfectly balanced alternatives that an individual must tilt either way. In their trajectory away from the realm of imagination both the people of the Scripture and pagan humanity can share the rationalistic belief in a deity moving ceaselessly the cosmos. This stage does not include humankind final development. Upon reaching its full rationalistic potential, the people find themselves at a crossroad. At this critical point some will choose the world of esoterics and prophecy under the guide of the Creator leading the Cosmological Chariot. Others, will revert to the world of myth under the direction of a rayyis/Cosmocrator. Mythical ideology will affect and finally dominate and subvert scientific progress. As modern thinkers are beginning to acknowledge, "Our scientific notions are not independent of our ideologies."[211]

Part 4
Anthropology

MAN BEFORE SETH

THE UNIQUENESS OF ADAM, his specific appurtenance, is the "image of God" with which he was created (Gn 1:27). The primary function of this image is 'intellectual perception' (*al-'adrak al-'aqli*).[1] Its ultimate purpose is to establish contact with the intellect flowing from God. It "resembles" God not only because it could seize the flow of the divine intellect "without the use of senses, or the aid of 'a hand or an arm',"[2]—that is, without a specific organ designed for this purpose—but more significantly, because it ultimately can "make contact" with the divine flow and thereby establish a communicative link with God.[3] "It is on account of the divine intellect that is connecting with him that he is in 'the image of God and in His likeness'."[4] Without fulfilling this image, a human forfeits his rank and is not intrinsically different than other animals. The people who do not partake in "the flow of the divine intellect"[5] are described as "the wicked ignorant people who, because they abandoned that flow, have low rank. They have deteriorated to the level of other members of the animal kingdom."[6]

Only Seth was said to be in Adam's image (see Gn 5:3). The rabbis taught that before Seth Adam was begetting 'phantoms'. R. Nissim Ga'on (ca. 990–1062) reported in the name of Sherira Ga'on (ca. 906–1006) that these were misfits "like women who give birth to deformed creatures." Prior to the birth of Seth, Adam was engendering "freaks of nature" who, because of their deformed faces and bodies, were regarded as monsters (*shedim*), "and it is the habit of people to call those with forbidding countenance and evil men *shedim!*"[7] Likewise, Maimonides identified these phantoms with the shedim 'monsters'—creatures similar to Vico's *grossi bestioni* and Borges's troglodytes. These shedim were humanoids void of the image of God: "And all the children preceding him [Seth] lacked the true human image, which is Adam's image and likeness, on account of which it was said, 'in the image of God and in His likeness' (see Gn 1:27, 5:1)."[8]

Although connected to human—a biological organism—Adam's image is not a biological entity. This leads to a radical concept of humanity. Unlike other species, humanity cannot transmit its fundamental characteristics by means of biological procreation. Maimonides called attention to a rabbinic doctrine interpreting, "And the Lord God took man," to mean, 'He had raised him' "and put him in the Garden of Eden" (Gn 2:15), 'He had established him'.[9] Commenting: "They [the rabbis] did not interpret the verse to mean that He had removed him from one place and placed him in another, but that He had raised the level of his existence over the existence of those things that generate and decay and put him in a special situation."[10]

Adam represents a quantum jump above the rest of the animal kingdom. The method of reproduction and the preservation and development of humanity are different from other species. A fundamental premise of Maimonides's anthropology is that Adam's image is transmitted and developed by means of guidance and instruction. The difference between the shedim and Seth is not biological. To develop Adam's image in a human, the mind must be properly stimulated and guided. The dissimilarity between the shedim and Seth stems from the fact that Adam imparted instruction to the latter but not to the former: "On the other hand, however, because he [Adam] had taught him and explained to him, he [Seth] attained human perfection. Therefore, it was said: 'And [Adam] engendered in his likeness like his image' (Gn 5:3)."[11]

The propagation of Adam's image involves a sociocultural rather than a biological process. The main characteristics of humanity are developed through education. Deprived from instruction, the children of men develop as shedim, humanoids void of humanity's quintessential quality. They become a source of violence and affliction:

> You already know that whoever fails to have this image whose significance we have explained,[12] he is not a human but a beast with the appearance and shape of humans. More than any other beast, however, he has power to do a variety of injuries and to invent evils because the sagacity and insight that were designed to help him reach a perfection that he did not reach, he would now apply to different types of cunning. [This] led to evils and the proliferation of injuries. He is like a thing that resembles and imitates man. These were Adam's children before Seth.[13]

The shedim and Seth share a common ancestry. Their differences are neither biological nor racial. Pre-Seth humanoids applied their intellectual capacities to harmful enterprises.

In the metaphor comparing the divine abode to a royal palace, Maimonides described the people outside the royal city as "all types of people who do not have a guiding doctrine, either cognitive or traditional."[14] Since they are hidden away from the intelligence flowing from God, they are not fully human. "In my opinion," wrote Maimonides, "these are not in the class of man, but in a class below man and above apes, since they have the appearance and shape of man, and [their] discernment is above the discernment of apes."[15]

An effect of this concept of humanity is that the biological parents are not the true progenitor of an individual, but those who gave him instruction or conceived the ideas, values, and institutions that helped shaped his mind and character, thus, the rabbinic doctrine that one must first aid his teacher and then his father, "because his father brought him to this world, but his teacher who taught him wisdom brings him to the life of the world to come."[16] The Hebrew *yalad* (to engender, to give birth) can also apply to ideas and value systems: "In this sense, whoever taught something to an individual and benefited him with an opinion is as if he had given birth to that individual because he is the author of that opinion. It is in this sense that the disciples of the prophets were called 'the sons of the prophets'" (2 Kg 2:3).[17]

This is consistent with the rabbinic doctrine that "The Scripture regards someone who had taught [even] a single chapter to another as if he had fashioned [him], embroidered [his body], and brought him out into the world. . . . His [mouth] is equal to that mouth [God's] which had placed the soul in the first man."[18] The rabbis explained the verse, "and the souls that they made in Haran" (Gn 12:5) to mean the men and women that Abraham and Sarah instructed.[19] On this basis the rabbis formulated the doctrine that "Whoever brings forth a single creature under the wings of the Divine Presence [Shekhina] is regarded by the Scripture as if he had fashioned, embroidered, and brought him out into the world."[20] In an epistle addressed to Obadiah, a Moslem who converted to Judaism, Maimonides wrote

> that our Patriarch Abraham is the one who taught the entire humanity. He made them thoughtful and informed them about the path of truth and oneness of God. He rejected idol-

> atry and assembled many under the wings of the Divine Presence. He taught and instructed them. And he commanded his children and the members of his household to keep the way of the Lord. As it is written in the Tora: "For I discern him [Abraham] in order that he should keep the way of the Lord" (Gn 18:19). Therefore, all who convert [to Judaism], until the end of all generations, and whoever declares the oneness of God, as prescribed in the Tora, are the disciples of the Patriarch Abraham and members of his household. Since he has turned all of them to goodness just like he turned [to goodness] the people of his generation with his words and his teachings. It follows, that our Patriarch Abraham is the father of his upright posterity who walk in his ways and the father of his disciples, who are all the proselytes. Accordingly, you may say [in the daily prayer], "Our God and the God of our Fathers" since the Patriarch Abraham is your father.[21]

The ideas generated by humans may be true or false, beneficial or harmful. They can be used to awaken and stimulate Adam's image, or to oppress and prevent its development in themselves and in others. As when a wasp injects her eggs in a caterpillar, some ideas are inseminated in minds empty of reason. Eventually, these ideas incubate breeding concepts destined to destroy the host organism: like the wasps' larva, they would devour it from within. Thus, an oppressive sociocultural environment shapes the mind and character of its subjects. Once inseminated with falsehood, the mind will generate, nurture, and develop ideas believed to be its own but that were, in fact, injected onto it by its oppressors. These ideas and values constitute the basic mental apparatus, setting the mental habits determining the possible and impossible, the real and the unreal. Thus, the mental constitution of humans is dominated by factors escaping the control of the individual. As an illustrative example, Maimonides cited the verse, "in the children [*yalde*] of aliens, they find pleasure" (Is 2:6)—a reference to the mental assimilation assailing Jews in biblical times. Remarkably, the Aramaic translation renders it: "in the nomoi"—that is, the basic sociopolitical canons—"of the nations they walk."[22] The "children" born under mental captivity, whom the enslaved rejoice, believing to be their own, are, in fact, the brood of their masters. As these children grow, they devour their host organism from within.

According to the Scripture (Jos 24:2; cf. Ez 16:1–7) and the rabbis, the Hebrews before the Exodus were part and parcel of pagan humanity. During their bondage in Egypt, the children of Israel had retrogressed into the ways of Egypt. The rabbis tell that upon crossing the Red Sea the angels asked God why was He saving the Israelites and drowning the Egyptians, arguing: "Just like these worship idols, so these worship idols?"[23] The Exodus from Egypt, the Theophany at Sinai, and the Forty Years of Wandering through the Desert, took place against this background.

TRACES IN THE SOUL

Two general principles govern Maimonides's anthropology. First, God does not change directly the nature of humans. Miracles are performed in the realm of the physical world, not in human nature. It is not that God could not but He would not. The very idea of revelation and promulgation of divine commandments rests on this principle:

> God, however, will not change the nature of people in any way by means of miracles. . . . We do not ascertain this because we believe that it would be cumbersome for Him to change the nature of a particular individual. This is feasible and within His power—but because He never willed to do that and never will, in accordance to the basic doctrines of the religious Law. If His will would have been to change the nature of all the people, whenever He wanted something from somebody, then it would have been pointless for Him to send prophets and promulgate the Law.[24]

Second, the mental constitution of human beings is not a given.[25] A determining factor shaping human nature is habit (*al-ma'luf*),—the values and patterns ingrained in the individual by society. A second factor is custom (*'ada*), the individually adopted patterns characterizing a culturally accepted behavior.[26] These include habits and methods of thinking,[27] conventionalities,[28] standards of religious beliefs,[29] opinions,[30] and general patterns of behavior.[31] It is not possible within the confines of human psychology to immediately relinquish all sociocultural habits. Borrowing psychoanalytical terminology, the ego does not have total control over the id. "[E]ven in so-called normal people the power of controlling the id cannot be increased beyond certain limits. If one asks more of them, one produces revolt or neurosis in individuals or makes them unhappy."[32]

Under the pressure of such "civilizing trends" humanity may become neurotic.[33] Maimonides recognized that there are matters contradicting the standard of normalcy, "which are inconceivable to be accepted, because of human nature, which is always fond of the habitual."[34] The human psyche is incapable of sudden, drastic transformations. Extreme changes invariably degenerate into social negativism and moral masochism. When forced to abandon cults and concepts that were ingrained in it by the sociocultural environment, the human psyche is 'repelled' (*tunfar*).[35] Indeed, it is psychologically "impossible to move from one extreme to the other at once. Therefore, it is not possible, on account of human nature, to abandon at once every ingrained habit."[36]

Support for this thesis may be found in the fact that the Israelites leaving Egypt did not proceed directly to the land of Israel. Since they were not psychologically ready to face war, they were ordered to proceed via the Desert (Ex 13:17–18).[37] In spite of the numerous wonders wrought on their behalf, God did not miraculously transform the Israelites into instant warriors. Just as they were not expected to suddenly shed the habits acquired during their bondage in Egypt and go forth to battle—because it is psychologically impossible—they were not expected to suddenly shed their standards of normalcy. Those habits made up their mental constitution and functioned like primary notions:

> Just like it is not within human nature to have been brought up as a slave, toiling in mud, bricks, and the like, and then quickly wash the filth off the hands and go forth at once and fight giants, similarly, it is not natural to have been raised up in a large variety of cults and practices—that were ingrained in their psyche, of which they were fond, and had become [for them] like a primary notion—and [then be expected to] abandon everything at once.[38]

These two principles are functionally linked to the idea of 'traces' (*āṯār*, singular: *aṯar*)—a key concept in Maimonidean psychology. Traces are different than 'the imprint of the senses', an impression left by sensory perception in the conscious memory.[39] They are psychic forces that escape verbal articulation.[40] Maimonides refers to key concepts only in passing. Traces are mentioned in a remarkable passage in which he examines the role of imagination in false prophets. Maimonides recognized that not all false prophets are willful impostors. Some, although not authentic prophets, genuinely believed they had experienced a revelation originating outside themselves. This phenomenon is characterized as an exteriorization of an unconscious process involving traces of suppressed thoughts. The traces themselves originate in suppressed notions whose imprints are concealed by and in the imagination. Referring to the type of revelation experienced by this class of false prophets, Maimonides commented: "It may also be possible, that what they perceive are, however, their own opinions,[41] whose traces remained imprinted in their imagination, together with all the other [items embedded] in their imaginative faculties. After annulling and suppressing many imaginations, only the traces of those opinions remain, and [then] they become manifest to them. They presume that is something fresh and a phenomenon coming [to them] from the outside."

In a most effective and lucid metaphor the traces embedded in the imagination are compared to animals roaming through the mind. "In my view this may be compared to a person who had in his house thousands of different beasts, and all [the beasts] that were in that house exited except for a single one that had been together [with the other beasts] in the house. When that person finds himself alone with that particular [beast], he presumes that it had come to the house now. This is not the case, but it is part of the horde [of beasts] that have not left."[42]

The comparison of traces to beasts indicate their unique characteristics. Although embedded in his own psyche, the individual has no control over them. They only appear later after a psychic process whereby the "beasts" leave the conscious mind. Maimonides used the Arabic root *Kh-R-J* to describe the beasts "exiting" from the "house." It is commonly read *kharaja* 'leaving'. According to this reading, the subject of the verb is the beasts. Both syntactically and morphologically, however, it can be read as the stem form 2, *kharraja* 'expelled' them. In that case the subject is the person expelling the beasts. In either case—whether by an unconscious process of 'forgetting' (kharaja) or by an act of psychological suppression (kharraja)—it is only after the beasts leave the conscious mind that their traces are exteriorized as something new as if coming from the outside. Because the original ideas are encoded as traces, the individual can no longer recognize them as his own.

Traces play a significant role in human mental health. Discussing certain rabbinic norms, Maimonides wrote that their purpose was "that there should not linger in the soul a trace for arrogance."[43] The human soul is capable of sickness.[44] An important factor in mental health is imagination. Because of harmful traces embedded in it, it may become defective and malfunction.[45] A wicked person is not someone who acts wickedly, but someone who *craves* wickedness. Through his sick imagination (khayal) he perceives that which is ugly and harmful as beautiful and beneficial, and vice versa: "[T]hose who are psychologically ill, I mean, the wicked and the vicious, imagine what is harmful to be beneficial and what is beneficial to be harmful. The wicked always covet that which is really harmful, which as a consequence of his sickness he imagines to be beneficial."[46]

Maimonides regarded social negativism as a psychological illness.[47] In this type of psychotic disorder a crime is only the *means* by which antisocial impulses are expressed. There are two stages to psychotic disorders: one, when the subject is aware of the problem and seeks help, and another, when the subject cannot or refuses to recognize the problem. These disorders need to be treated with the same care due a sick organ. When psychological imbalances are neglected, the patients will malfunction and perish, exactly as with sick organs. Imagination plays a decisive role.

> In the same manner that upon realizing his sickness a patient who knows not the art of medicine should consult physicians that would instruct him what he must do and warn him against things that he imagined to be pleasurable. . . . Likewise, he who is psychologically ill must consult the sages, who are the physicians of the soul. They will alert him about the injuries involved in what he fantasizes to be beneficial, and they will heal him with the art that heals the [harmful] habits of the soul that we will explain in the following chapter. Those who are psychologically ill, however, and refuse to acknowledge their ailments, imagining [them] to be healthy, or who do acknowledge them but do not wish to be cured, their prognosis is the same prognosis [as] of a patient [who] pursues what is pleasurable and does not wish to be healed—that he will surely perish.[48]

Traces do not originate only in the individual but also in the collective psyche of a people.[49] They can linger from the remote past and affect the individual psyche and the collective ethos of a people. If suppressed, they will resurge as with the idol worshippers in biblical times.[50] More subtly, feelings such as "guilt" or sudden "illuminations" may be psychological stratagems designed to keep the same old habits camouflaged under the cover of innovative cults and values. This was, precisely, the ground for Judah ha-Levi's criticism of Christianity and Islam.[51] It explains why, generally, religious reforms and political revolutions tend to replace one corrupt system with another. Freud, too, maintained that "the primitive mind is, in the fullest sense of the word, imperishable."[52] Accordingly, "Every historical man carries on, within himself, a great deal of prehistoric humanity."[53]

Some traces originate in the conscious mind of the individual, but others are embedded in the ethos of a people and are ingrained in the individual by the sociocultural environment. As noted by a distinguished ethnopsychiatrist:

> The unconscious is composed of two elements: that which never was conscious—i.e., the psychic equivalent of the id—coming of the psychic representatives or counterparts of instinctual forces, and that which was conscious once upon a time but was subsequently repressed. The *repressed* material is made up partly of memory traces of both outer (objective) experiences and certain internal (subjective) experiences, such as emotions, fantasies, and former bodily states, and includes also the defense mechanisms and a substantial portion of the superego.[54]

C. G. Jung, too, recognized two distinct elements directly affecting the unconscious:

> First, fantasies (including dreams) of a personal character, which go back unquestionably to personal experiences, things forgotten or repressed, and can thus be completely explained by individual anamnesis. Second, fantasies (including dreams) of an impersonal character, which cannot be reduced to experiences in the individual's past, and thus cannot be explained as something individually acquired. These fantasy-images undoubtedly have their closest analogues in mythological types. We must therefore assume that they correspond to cer-

> tain *collective* (and not personal) structural elements of the human psyche in general, and, like the morphological elements of the human body, are *inherited.* Although tradition and transmission by migration certainly play a part, there are, as we have said, very many cases that cannot be accounted for in this way and drive us to the hypothesis of "authochtonous revival." These cases are so numerous that we are obliged to assume the existence of a collective psychic substratum. I have called this the *collective unconscious.*[55]

The collective unconscious is the source of archetypes. These are the "Link with the Past," between the "conscious mind" and "certain instinctive data of the dark, primitive psyche, the real but invisible roots of consciousness."[56] Reality is not experienced as it is, but as it is processed and transformed by a variety of archetypes. Archetypes do not emerge from physical facts. They are psychological structures dominating the "involuntary manifestations of the unconscious process."[57] Therefore, they are impervious to tangible reality. Quoting Jung again: "The archetype does not proceed from physical facts, but describes how the psyche experiences the physical fact, and in so doing the psyche often behaves so autocratically that it denies tangible reality or makes statements that fly in the face of it."[58]

From this perspective myth antecedes the hero. The latter is a consequence, not the source, of myth.[59] Archetypes dominated, to a degree unfathomed by modern humans, the mind of the ancients. Eliade demonstrated that in pagan society "reality" is the deliberate imitations of archetypes. For the primitive human

> reality is acquired solely through repetition or participation; everything which lacks an exemplary model is "meaningless", i.e., it lacks reality. Men would have a tendency to become archetypal and paradigmatic. This tendency may well appear paradoxical, in the sense that the man of the traditional culture sees himself real only to the extent that he ceases to be himself (for a modern observer) and is satisfied with imitating and repeating the gestures of another. In other words, he sees himself as real, i.e., as "truly himself", only, and precisely, insofar as he ceases to be so. Hence it could be said that this "primi-

> tive" ontology has a Platonic structure; and in that case Plato could be regarded as the outstanding philosopher of "primitive mentality", that is, as the thinker who succeeded in giving philosophic currency and validity to the modes of life and behavior of archaic humanity.[60]

The myths and symbols of archaic society have persisted to modern days: "We have seen that myths decay and symbols become secularized, but that they never disappear, even in the most positivist of civilizations, that of the nineteenth century. Symbols and myths come from such depths: they are part and parcel of the human being, and it is impossible that they should not be found again in any and every existential situation of man in the Cosmos."[61]

The preceding considerations lead up to a most radical question. Since traces and archetypes make up the very structure of the human psyche, and the collective unconscious cannot be affected either by personal consciousness or by will power, how was it possible to effect such a drastic change as from the archaic society of pagan Egypt to the Tora-society of Israel?

PALINGENESIS AT SINAI

Concerning the impact of the sin on Eve, the rabbis taught that upon witnessing the Theophany at Sinai the Israelites were cleansed of the "slime of the snake": "When the snake came upon Eve it injected [*hiṭṭil*] in her slime. Israel who stood at Mount Sinai, their slime was discontinued. The gentiles who did not stand at Mount Sinai, their slime was not discontinued."[62] Maimonides regarded this doctrine as "marvelous." He alerted the reader that if one were to consider it superficially, it would seem "hideous." If one had "properly understood the chapters of this work," however, then he "would marvel at the wisdom of such a metaphor and its correspondence to reality." After citing the rabbis, he challenged the reader, "Resolve this too!"[63]

On the basis of rabbinic sources Maimonides identified the snake with Satan and Satan with the "evil impulse" (yeṣer ha-ra').[64] The source of the evil impulse is the imaginative faculty, "which is also the true evil instinct [yeṣer ha-ra']." Indeed, "every intellectual and ethical flaw is either the doing of the imagination or the consequence of its doing."[65] The tree of knowledge was a figment of Adam's imagination. A close reading of the text (Gn 2:9) shows that whereas the Scripture says that the "tree of life was inside the

Garden," it does not specify the place of the "tree of knowledge of good and evil." Addressing this quandary, the rabbis taught: "[Concerning] the tree of knowledge. God did not reveal that tree to Adam and will not reveal it in the future."[66] This doctrine is puzzling, since both Eve and the snake seemed to have known where the tree was. After citing the rabbis' comment, Maimonides added, "This is true, since the nature of existence had decided thus."[67] In fact, "the tree of knowledge of good and evil" is nothing but a distortion of "the tree of life" caused by human imagination. Since everything "that God made was very good" (Gn 1:31), the notion of evil in the world is a projection of human egocentrism, the imagination distorting the facts of the tree of life.[68] The yeṣer ha-ra'–imagination pertains to the somatic aspect of humans and begins to develop at birth.[69] In contrast, the 'good impulse' (*yeṣer ha-ṭob*), or special rational faculty will develop at a later stage. Since imagination pertains to the flesh, the yeṣer ha-ra' is identified with death.[70] Adam, representing the image of God, and Eve, representing corporeality-imagination, join to form a single structure: human. "[F]rom a certain aspect they are two, but they are [also] one," sharing one flesh.[71] Accordingly, although they can affect each other at a certain level, they remain independent. As with Job, the Satan-death-yeṣer ha-ra' has no control over the human soul.[72] This is why the snake was unable to approach Adam but only Eve, and why the rabbis ascertained that Adam did not know, nor would it ever be known, where the tree of knowledge is. Since the higher human soul cannot directly become affected by imagination-yeṣer ha-ra', the enmity was established not between Adam and the serpent but between Eve and the serpent. The Scripture (Gn 3:15), connects "its [the snake's] seeds with her [Eve's] seeds, the head with the heel. She would be capable of overpowering it with the head, and it [the snake] would be capable of overpowering her with the heel."[73]

"Heel" is the lowest part of the body, directly touching the ground and symbolizes the most carnal aspects of the human.[74] Like poison, the "slime of the snake"—or ills of mythical thinking and imagination—reaches the mind of the victim through the body and paralyzes it. The situation can be corrected by inverting sense → imagination → reason, to sense → reason → imagination, thus accessing the realm of prophecy.[75] In the case of the Israelites, the liberation of the mind from imagination was accomplished by their collective experience at Sinai when they rationally grasped the existence and oneness of God.

The rise and development of human consciousness is an oddity. There is nothing in nature that can explain the quantum jump from collective unconsciousness to individual consciousness. Indeed, the very notion of 'consciousness' *is* the struggle against the 'natural', like Jacob challenging the 'natural' right of Essau, the firstborn, daring to wrestle an angel. "The ascent toward consciousness is the unnatural thing in nature; it is the specific of the species Man, who on that account has justly styled himself Homo sapiens. The struggle between the specifically human and the universally natural constitutes the history of man's conscious development."[76]

The genesis of the consciousness of Israel—the matrix of what may be properly designated the Jewish archetype—originated at the Theophany at Sinai. It was at this pivotal moment in human history that the children of Israel overcame the traces and archetypes of pagan humanity by jumping a quantum leap from the realm of myth to the realm of reason. A further stage, to be examined in the following chapter of this book, involved the realm of prophecy, the final unfolding of the human spirit. Both stages began at Sinai.

Raising from mythical to rational thinking came at the moment that the people discerned an absolutely external reality, categorically irreducible to man—God. Mythical man is wrapped in his own imagination. Not only is he incapable of perceiving anything outside his own projections, but, consequently, he cannot come to grips with himself. At that stage, "Man is not yet thrown back upon himself, against nature, nor the ego against the unconscious; being oneself is still a wearisome and painful experience, still the exception that has to be overcome."[77] Consequently, he is incapable of discerning a nonanthropomorphic deity. It is by virtue of divine revelation that the people of Israel grasped God as an absolute nonanthropomorphic Reality, thus, breaking the grip of imagination. The people did not, could not, ascend to God. At that stage of human consciousness God, as an absolute nonanthropomorphic Supreme Reality, is nonexistent, as color to the blind and sound to the deaf. Rather, He "came down" to Mount Sinai before "the eyes of all the people" (Ex 19:11, 20).[78] The true miracle was not the awesome "voices and lightning" at Sinai but the fact that the people perceived them as indices of a nonanthropomorphic Supreme Reality, thus, effecting a quantum jump from mythical to rational thinking.

The concept of God in Jewish tradition elucidates the function of the Theophany at Sinai. The Scripture and rabbis distinguish between the concept of God as Elohim and the concept of God as represented by the

Tetragrammaton YHWH. The Scripture uses Elohim when referring to God as relating to a specific physical or social order. It may be inferred through reasoning upon realizing the harmony and arrangement prevalent in the universe. YHWH designates God in reference to something unique and individual, transcending the general order of things.[79] It cannot be inferred by means of analytical reasoning, but only through revelation. Because Elohim is only inferred, knowledge of His existence is not free from uncertainty. The only possibility of 'certainty' (*yaqin*) is when God is perceived directly by means of revelation. In such a case He would be perceived as YHWH, as with Job. At the beginning he knew God only through tradition (taqlid). Later, upon experiencing the majesty of YHWH directly, he gained certainty (yaqin), recanted his previous criticism, and confessed.[80] The Rabbanites (in opposition to the Karaites) maintained that knowledge of YHWH is "intuitive" to the Jewish people. This intuition is not an anthropological development but the effect of a specific historical event—the Theophany at Sinai. Thus, it is the exclusive patrimony of the people of Israel. From this perspective the difference between Elohim/YHWH is methodological: one is inferred indirectly by analytical means; the other is apprehended directly by revelation. The methodology will determine whether God appears as engaged in the general and universal or in the personal and individual. There is a radical difference between the perception of Elohim and YHYH: perception of Elohim cannot be free of doubts, he who is privy to YHWH is absolutely certain (yaqin).[81]

The purpose of the Sinaitic revelation was to have the Jewish people 'reach certainty' (*al-yaqin*) of YHWH's existence and His oneness through 'direct experience' (*bi-al- mushahada*).[82] Some rabbis maintained that the people heard all the ten commandments directly from God, others that they only heard the first two. Maimonides regarded the second view as more authoritative.[83] On this basis he distinguished between the first two commandments, which are described as "rational" since they could be fully grasped by reason, and the other commandments, which are "conventional." The sequence rational commandments → conventional commandments is essential for the prophetic process. Otherwise, the relation imagination → reason, peculiar to pagan thinking, would prevail.[84] Because of their essential rationality, only the first two commandments were directly heard by every Israelite. In this manner the existence and oneness of YHWH were directly grasped by all.[85] Although they are two different commandments, they were issued in a single voice.

> [W]hat ensues from the Scripture and the words of the sages is the following: the congregation of Israel did not hear at that standing [at Sinai] except one single voice, only once. From that voice Moses and all Israel perceived, "I am [the Lord who took you from Egypt]" and "There should not be [for you any other deities before me"] (Ex 20:2-3). . . . And they [the rabbis] explained that they [the people at Sinai] did not hear another voice from God.[86]

These commandments are intimately related to one another. The second commandment constitutes a repudiation of polytheism and the very foundations of mythical thinking. For the Scriptures and the rabbis mythical thinking is not peripheral to polytheism: it is the method by which polytheism is established.[87] As was brilliantly expressed by Cassirer:

> In the multiplicity of his gods man does not merely behold the outward diversity of natural objects and forces but also perceives himself in the concrete diversity and distinction of his functions. The countless gods he makes for himself guide him not only through the sphere of objective reality and change but above all through the sphere of his own will and accomplishment, which they illuminate from within. He becomes aware of the trend peculiar to each concrete activity only by viewing it objectively in the image of the special god belonging to it. Action is differentiated into distinct independent functions not through abstracts, discursive concept formation but by the contrary process, wherein each of these functions is apprehended as an intuitive whole and embodied in an independent mythical figure.[88]

Polytheism and monotheism do not represent different modalities striving to express the same Supreme Being. Rather they constitute two different patterns of mental perception: the second commandment is a repudiation of both polytheism and mythical thinking.

To apprehend the existence of YHWH is necessary to cast off mythical thinking: to cast off mystical thinking it is necessary to apprehend the existence of YHWH. Hence, the first and second commandments were proclaimed in a single voice. The experience was so awesome that upon hearing the voice the souls of the Israelites "exited [*yaṣe'a*] from them." They were later resurrected with a special dew that will be used again on the Day of Resurrection.[89] Death, resurrection, and the apprehension of the first two commandments were simultaneously experienced.[90] The verb 'exited' (*yaṣe'a*) is used by the Scripture and the rabbis to designate the Exodus from Egypt (*yeṣi'at miṣrayim*). It implies 'exiting' a state of bondage (e.g., Ex 21:1–5). The discovery of an absolute God, fully transcending human existence, liberated the Israelites from the prongs of imagination—"the iron furnace" (Dt 4:20) imprisoning pagan humanity. In this manner unfolded an event unparalleled in human history: the collective palingenesis or rebirth of an entire nation, soaring to a higher level of existence and consciousness. Greek palingenesis is a return to a primordial mythical beginning. For the Jew palingenesis is a "birth" into a higher, further develop state.[91] The Theophany at Sinai was the means by which God extracted the Israelites from "the belly" of Egypt (Dt 4:34), halting the "slime of the snake" and opening a new chapter in the history of human consciousness.

At first sight the death and resurrection at Sinai seem to parallel the ritual death and resurrection found in the initiation rites and ordeals of many ancient religions.[92] There is, however, a fundamental difference. Unlike pagan rituals of death and resurrection, the Sinaitic experience cannot be repeated, ceremonially or otherwise. Judaism does not have a ritual of *renovatio* whereby the community or individual pass through a cycle of mythical death and spiritual rebirth as when Christians celebrate the Eucharist. Whatever the experience at Sinai was, its ultimate effect was not existential but legal: the establishment of a bilateral berit (covenant) between God and Israel. Finally, the Sinaitic experience unfolded in historical time.

ANNULLING THE POISON OF THE PRIMEVAL SNAKE

The Theophany at Sinai was, first and foremost, a *historical* event. Four features distinguish the Sinaitic experience from mythology. The first two features pertain to the space-time continuum essential to the Jewish mind. This continuum establishes a structural relation between its components: space becomes locality and time chronology. In Judaism it constitutes the basic structure for human discourse: those unable to organize their thoughts within that structure cannot serve as witnesses. Before examining (*derishot*) the content of a testimony, a prospective witness must answer a series of seven question (*ḥaqirot*). The first question deals with the *location* where the alleged event took place. The other six questions deal with *chronological* time: the week of the Jubilee cycle, the year of the week, the month of the year, the day of the month, the day of the week, and the hour of the day. Failure to answer to any of these questions renders the testimony void and inadmissible.[93] Those unable to structure their thoughts in a space-time continuum apparatus can be objects but not subjects of the dialectical process of Israel.

The Sinaitic Theophany took place, first and foremost, in a *geographical* local, not a mythical space. Sinai is devoid of sanctity.[94] Second, it unfolded in a *chronological*, not a mythical, time: in the third month, exactly fifty days from the Exodus from Egypt. Chronological time was possible because before the Exodus, Moses and Aaron were charged with the establishment of a calendar. Rabbinic tradition identifies the beginning of the Jewish calendar with the commandment, "This New Moon [*ha-ḥodesh*] constitutes for you the head of the months. It constitutes for you the first of the months of the year" (Ex 12 :2).[95] The date of arrival at Sinai and the eventual Theophany was based on this calendar: "In the third month to the exodus of the children of Israel from the land of Egypt; in that very day, they arrived at the Desert of Sinai" (Ex 19:1). Chronological time is man-made. The most important principle regulating the Jewish calendar ascertains that whether the calendar computations approved by the Jewish court happen to be correct or faulty, the holiday will take place, precisely, at the time that "you"—that is, the Supreme Court of the Jewish people—have determined. In the language of the rabbis: "*You* even when erring [in the computation]. *You* even if [the error was] willful."[96]

In the pagan world revelations take place in extratemporal time at a cosmogonic, primordial beginning. Mythological time is cyclical and reversible. Through the proper ceremony and the imitation of the right gesture it is possible to reverse time and return to a primordial moment. Pagan revelations do not concern the present but an event that took place in a primordial time:

> The myth relates a sacred history, that is, a primordial event that took place at the beginning of time, *ab initio*. But to relate a sacred history is equivalent to revealing a mystery. For

> the persons of the myth are not human beings; they are gods or culture heroes, and for this reason their *gesta* constitute mysteries; man could not know their acts if they were not revealed to him. The myth, then, is the history of what took place *in illo tempore,* the recital of what the gods or semidivine beings did at the beginning of time. To tell a myth is to proclaim what happened *ab origine.*[97]

The Jewish Sabbath does not mark a primordial cosmological moment but the beginning of historical time. The Christian and Moslem Sabbaths, celebrate, respectively, the first (Sunday) and last (Friday) day of Creation. The Jewish Sabbath is the "seventh day," a post-Creation date in which God "rested," that is, when there was *no* Creation (Ex 20:10).[98] In the Friday night services (*Me'en Sheba'* and *Qiddush*) and in the Sabbath morning (*'Amida and Musaf*), the faithful proclaim the Sabbath as a "commemoration" (*zekher*)—not a return—to the atemporal "procedures of Creation." Within this context it would be helpful to remember that the first day included in the Jewish calendar is not Sunday, the first day of Creation, but the Sabbath (*Shabbat Bereshit*), the first day after Creation. The Sabbath was first proclaimed by Adam *after* exiting the Garden of Eden.[99] Thus, the Jewish Sabbath marks not only sacred time but, as proclaimed in the *Habdala* prayers, the beginning of desacralyzed time.[100] Historical time is linear and one-directional. The Jewish calendar does not mark the return to an original "sacred" moment. Holidays are not the reactualization of an original event: past and present do not coalesce. The Exodus from Egypt, marking the commencement of the Jewish Festivals, is not reenacted. A holiday is not a retrogression in time. Rather, as emphasized in the liturgy (Qiddush and 'Amida), the holidays are a "commemoration" (zekher) of the Exodus (cf. Ex 12:14; 13:3; Dt 16:3, etc.). The whole concept of 'remembering'—so fundamental to the Hebrew Scripture and rabbinic tradition—is a repudiation of the pagan belief in circular time: it rejects the notion of a ritual regression to an atemporal event, occurring "at the beginning." The dates marked by the calendar are sanctified by the people, not by a mythical or cosmic mechanism.

Because events unfolding in historical time are unique, the Sinaitic experience is not repeatable. "There was nothing like it before," wrote Maimonides, "and it will not be repeated."[101] The mind is terrified at history—an experience demanding response and personal participation—particularly, when it cannot be made to fit into the standard models. The Theophany at Sinai was "an awesome experience, more awesome than any prophetic vision, transcending any reasoning."[102] Historical time pertains to successive synthesis. It is dynamic and unfolds in a series of events. Mythology transpires in a static, atemporal situation. It pertains to simultaneous synthesis.[103]

Third, the protagonists of mythological events are nonhumans. At Sinai, Moses and the people of Israel are active participants. Finally, for the archaic mind present time and present existence are meaningless. In itself, present time is not significant; common mortals cannot participate in meaningful events. They acquire meaning, not by being themselves but by fitting into a mythological model and becoming something or someone else. To a mythological society historical time is meaningless. To be meaningful the present must be assimilated into mythical models, pertaining—not to a past, in a contemporary sense—but to a different realm; that of extratemporal time. "[P]roperly speaking," writes Eliade, "it is a primordial mythical time made present."[104] Outside these models reality and personal experience are worthless.[105]

The Theophany at Sinai is addressed to the people. It is the people, not some extra human beings, who experienced the presence of God and exclaimed, "We shall do and we shall hearken" (Ex 24:7). The berit (alliance) with God, stipulating the laws and institutions of Israel, was contracted by the people, not by mythological beings. The Theophany at Sinai was validated not in a mythological ceremony but by the direct testimony of the people. Moses's apostleship was not confirmed in a mythical scenario, inaccessible to common experience, but *in the presence and with the consent* of all Israel:

> On what grounds did they [the people of Israel] believe in him [Moses]? On the basis of the Theophany at Sinai! Because their eyes had witnessed not a stranger, and their ears heard not someone else—the fire, the voices, and the flames. He [Moses] approached the darkness as the voice was speaking to him. And we heard: "Moses, Moses, go and tell them [to the people of Israel] so and so." . . . How is it known that the only proof that his prophecy is genuine, without any doubt, is the Theophany at Sinai?[106] Because it is written: "Behold I come to you in the thickness of the cloud, in order that the people

> should hear when I am speaking to you, and also in you they will believe forever" (Ex 19:9). From this is evident that prior to this event they did not believe in him with a faith that could last forever, but only with a faith that allowed skepticism and second thoughts.[107]

The Theophany at Sinai inaugurated a new chapter in humankind: historical time (and geographical space). Henceforth, reference to God's wondrous manifestation must be made in concrete terms. In the language of the rabbis: "in those days, at this time," or, "in this place, at this time."[108] Unlike pagan deities the God of Israel makes His presence manifest in concrete situations. On this fundamental point Eliade penned a golden passage.

> This God of the Jewish people is no longer an Oriental divinity, creator of archetypal gestures, but a personality that ceaselessly intervenes in history, who reveals his will through events (invasions, sieges, battles, and so on). Historical facts thus become "situations" of man in respect to God, and as such they acquire a religious value that nothing had previously been able to confer on them.[109]

Thus was the development of historical rationality by the Jewish people.[110] The people of Israel have historical characters because *they* had discovered historical time, not the other way around. Only *after* and as a *consequence* of Sinai has Israel a pre-Sinaitic history.[111] Otherwise, "historical" events and personalities would have been subjected to a process of mythicization.[112] This type of phenomenon lingered to modern days. Simple incidents, witnessed by common folks, are transfigured into mythological phenomena. When folklorists draw the attention of the people to what actually transpired, they reply that "the real story was already only a falsification."[113] Eliade has so astutely pointed out that

> This reduction of events to categories and of individuals to archetypes, carried out by the consciousness of the popular strata in Europe almost down to our day, is performed in conformity with archaic ontology. We might say that popular memory restores to the historical personage of modern times its

> meaning as imitator of the archetype and reproducer of archetypal gestures—a meaning of which the members of the archaic societies have always been, and continue to be, conscious.[114]

Historical traces and historical archetypes alone can effectively resist and displace their mythological counterparts. Because Israel's values and laws are structured on historical experience and were spawned from Sinai henceforth, they countered and eventually superseded the mythological traces and archetypes of pagan humanities. Thus, in the language of the rabbis, was the poison of the snake nullified.

WITNESSING PROPHECY

Moses played a pivotal role in the Theophany at Sinai. At Sinai the children of Israel reached the confines of the realm of rationality. Personally and directly they heard the first two commandments, ascertaining the existence and oneness of the Creator. Vicariously, through Moses, they "witnessed"—without actually participating in—prophecy. The ultimate goal of the Sinaitic experience was for the children of Israel to become "a kingdom of priests and a holy nation" (Ex 19:6).[115] Passing to this stage is much more difficult and complex than passing from imagination to reason. The first stage affected their mode of perception and thinking. Becoming a kingdom of priests and a holy nation involves personal behavior. It could only be effected through a psychological metamorphosis. The process began at Sinai.

Maimonides grouped the rest of the commandments of the Tora into two. One group comprised conventional obligations, pertaining to the sociopolitical order. This type of obligation is not extra psychic rules to live by; the rules must be internalized, constituting the standards of cultural and psychological normalcy. Those failing to internalize this type of commandment, having to struggle against contrary impulses, are psychologically ill. They must be taught to control and redirect those impulses.[116] The commandments contained in the second group are designated ceremonial. They comprise rituals and religious acts. Some of these commandments were intended to counteract instinctual forces lingering from pagan humanity. They are idiosyncratic to Israel and do not establish a standard of normalcy. Quite the contrary. Maimonides quoted a rabbinic doctrine stating that these commandments are to control, rather than to eradicate, these impulses.

"A person should not say: 'I have no desire to eat meat and milk'. 'I have no desire to wear a mixture of wool and linen'. 'I have no desire to have illicit sexual intercourse.' But [he should say] 'I desire! But what can I do, and my Father in Heaven had forbidden [them] to me'?"[117] This posture must be taken only in relation to ritual prohibitions, but not with the conventional commandments.[118] Ritual prohibitions must be internalized not because of their intrinsic rationality but because they were specifically commanded to Israel. This leads to a cogent distinction between sociopolitical values, regarded as universally human and what is specifically Jewish. By internalizing a series of basic sociopolitical norms, acknowledging at the same time the particularity of its own rituals and ceremonies, Judaism at once defined the standards regulating its relation to the rest of humanity and asserted its own distinctive character.

Conventional and ceremonial commandments can neither be inferred from nor be fully comprehended on the basis of pure reason. They pertain to prophecy.[119] Prophecy hinges on individuation and personal growth. Therefore, these commandments could not be grasped directly and equally by all. Rather, the people grasped them each according to their individual capacities:

> Concerning the standing [of the Israelites] at Sinai. Although everyone witnessed the awesome fire and heard the terrifying voices that produced dread in a miraculous manner, no one reached the state of prophecy unless he was worthy of it in accordance to [his or her] own rank. Do you not see that it was said, "Ascend to God, you and Aaron, Nadab, and Abihu and the seventy elders of Israel" (Ex 24:1). He [Moses] was at the highest rank, as it was said, "And Moses alone approached God, but they did not approach" (Ex 24:2). Aaron was beneath him. Nadab, and Abihu were beneath Aaron. And the rest of the people were beneath them [each] according to his [respective] perfection. A quotation from the rabbis: "Moses was in a panel by itself, and Aaron was in a panel by itself."[120]

The general public was not privy to prophecy. Yet every one at Sinai witnessed prophecy. There were two components to the Sinaitic experience: the divine voice and the articulation of the commandments. On the basis of Scripture and rabbinic authority Maimonides concluded that in its pristine state the divine voice by which the first two commandments were apprehended was inarticulate. It was Moses who articulated these commandments into words.[121] Because the rest of the commandments pertain to prophecy, the general public did not perceive them directly. They were heard first by Moses and then were transmitted to the people:

> It became clear to me that during the Theophany at Sinai all that had reached Moses did not [fully] reach the rest of Israel. The speech [of God] was addressed to Moses alone. This is why the entire speech containing the ten commandments was addressed in the singular. And he [Moses]—peace be upon him!—would descend to the foot of the mountain, and inform [*waykhabbar*] the people what he had heard. The text of the Tora: "I am standing between the Lord [YHWH] and you to relate [*le-haggid*] to you the words of the Lord [YHWH]" (Dt 5:5). . . . It is plainly stated in the *Mekhilta* that he [Moses] would repeat to them what he had heard. The text of the Tora also [supports this view]. "So that the people would hear as I am speaking to you" (Ex 19:9) indicates that the speech was addressed to him [Moses] and that they [the people] only heard that awesome voice, not articulated words. [Referring] to that awesome voice, it was said: "As you hear the voice [*qol*]" (Dt 5:20). And it was [also] said: "You have heard the sound [qol] of words, but you have not seen any shape, except for a sound [qol]" (Dt 4:12). It was not said, "words you have heard!" Whenever it is mentioned about "hearing words," it was meant "hearing the sound." Moses made them hear the words and delivered them [the words] to them [the people]. This is evident from the text of the Tora and from most of the words of the sages of blessed memory.[122]

A key term in Maimonides's analysis is *higgid* (Arabic: *khabara*) 'to inform'. It refers to an utterance delivered by the speaker in his own words rather than the repetition of a definite text or formula.[123] Accordingly, "standing . . . to relate" (le-haggid) means, precisely, "in Moses's own words."

Moses' apostleship was at the center of the Sinaitic experience. At that event amid thunderous sounds and lightning Moses was confirmed by God as His sole apostle in the presence of all Israel. Moses's specific mission was to articulate God's commandments to the people. Because the people had realized that they could not hear directly the words of God (see Ex 20:19), it was necessary for Moses to deliver the commandments to the people. This realization was a testimony to their intellectual sobriety. Only a people who have transcended mythological thinking can realize their own boundaries. Because Moses's apostleship had been witnessed and corroborated by the people at Sinai, it is known intuitively; belief in Moses and the Law are integral to the very structure of the Jewish ethos. To deny his apostleship is to ascertain that one has not participated in the Sinaitic experience.

Linguistics can help us understand the distinction between prophecy, from which the general public were excluded, and hearing God speak to Moses, which was witnessed by the entire people. The category of person is the function of speech. It could only apply to the first two grammatical persons while in the act of speech, that is, during discourse. *I* may be said only to a *you*, who in turn could address the speaker, and say *I*. Because the third person is excluded from the act of speech, it is the grammatical nonperson.[124] Prophecy designates the act of speech by the first person, God, addressed to the second person, the prophet, who in turn could say *I* to the second person, God. The general public at Sinai was the third person "witnessing" the discourse between God and Moses.[125] Hence, they could only hear the *sound* of words but not the words themselves.

The Sinaitic experience was so overwhelming that it constitutes a phylogenetic trace of the people: whoever doubts Moses's mission cannot possibly be a descendant of the Israelites standing at the foot of Mount Sinai. Upon their rebirth at Sinai the "nature" of the Israelite acquired its own specific texture. Belief in the existence of God, His oneness, and Moses's apostleship became permanently imprinted in the Jewish ethos.[126]

OVERCOMING THE PAGAN PAST

The Arabic term *luṭf* 'kindness', 'benevolence', is used in a variety of ways as 'subtlety' or 'surreptitiousness' when one is acting in a seemingly cruel way but actually having 'kind' and 'benevolent' intentions, for example, a parent or teacher disciplining a youngster.[127] Since it may camouflage a hidden intention, luṭf may stand for 'cunning'. In an analogous sense it could denote the craftiness and strategy deployed by an artisan to overcome hindrances and to achieve his design. This term may occasionally refer to a strategy designed to outsmart an adversary, achieve a mental objective, or gain an intellectual or moral virtue. It can be applied for either a good or an evil purpose.[128] A fundamental doctrine of Maimonides is that God acts in nature with benevolent luṭf.[129] This is evident in the design of living bodies, human bodies in particular, which are contrived to perform most efficiently and to overcome hindrances impeding their full development.[130]

Luṭf describes God's twofold strategy in helping the Israelites rise to "a kingdom of priests and a holy nation" (Ex 19:6).[131]

In general, the commandments were designed to bring fulfillment in this and the next world.[132] For purpose of classification their immediate objectives are threefold: excellence of political life, and the attainment of proper opinions and behavior.[133] As mentioned earlier, the ultimate purpose of the Sinaitic covenant was to guide the people into becoming "a kingdom of priests and a holy nation" (Ex 19:6).[134] To reach their final destination the people first had to shed their habits and overcome the traces of pagan humanity. These habits constituted an effective barrier, impeding human development. Invariably, the divine message will be processed according to pagan norms and, thus, distorted and rejected. In this precise sense idolatry—representing the archetypes and religious apparatus of pagan humanity—is the antithesis of the Tora, and vice versa. Maimonides cited a rabbinic doctrine that, "Whoever admits idolatry is rejecting the whole Tora, and whoever rejects idolatry is admitting the whole Tora," adding, "Understand that![135] At the same time the Patriarch Abraham and the early Hebrews originated in and were affected by the values, ideas, and practices of the pagan world.[136] That period is described as "those dark days."[137] It was the spread of biblical monotheism that brought a measure of enlightenment and progress to the pagan world. Unlike Judah ha-Levi, Maimonides regarded the spread of both Christianity and Islam as a positive advancement for pagan humanity. Alluding to the spread of these religions among pagans, Maimonides commented, "And were it not because of the extent to which the existence of God is now propagated among the nations, our days now would be darker than then, but in a different form."[138]

Because pagan habits had shaped the mental apparatus of man, they could not be eradicated "at once" by a magic formula. It required an intricate and painful process performed with luṭf, "cunning benevolence." With exquisite care and kindness the Law proceeded to help the children of Israel to surmount the obstacles standing in their way: "And through this divine guidance (*tullaṭuf*) the memory of idolatry was successfully eradicated [in order] to establish in our beliefs the true monumental doctrine, which is the existence of God and His oneness."[139] Eradication of the "memory of idolatry" included the traces embedded in the soul.[140]

Luṭf was the means by which the traces and habits lingering from the pagan past were eradicated. To protect the people from adverse impulses and temptations idolatrous rituals and mores were prohibited.[141] When viable, religious concepts were "transferred" to the service of God, that is, the Temple and sacramental sacrifices.[142] Because of the pagan past and the bondage in Egypt, the soul had been in distress.[143] Occasionally, to overcome a newly acquired habit a change in the environment sufficed.[144] Generally, the traces linger for generations. Maimonides regarded the biblical doctrine of atonement as a kind of divine therapy. As a manifestation of divine luṭf, the Tora provided sacramental atonements—in the Hebrew sense of "cleansing"—designed to eliminate traces of the pagan past. In this "manner the evil opinions—which are the diseases of the human soul" are healed.[145] Left unattended, the traces would resurge and affect the people for generations to come.[146] Some of the rituals prescribed by the Law, particularly the sacramental sacrifices, function as antidotes, perennially controlling the traces affecting the soul.

The rituals and sacramental sacrifices were not included in the ten commandments.[147] It was after the children of Israel had worshipped the golden calf and retrogressed to idolatry that special commandments and injunctions designed to control the effect of the pagan traces were issued. An important rabbinic passage sheds light on this doctrine:

> A gentile asked Rabban Johanan ben Zakkai: "These things that *you* perform seem like witchcraft! They bring a [red] heifer; they burn it and mash it and [then] take its ashes. When one of yours is defiled by a corpse, they sprinkle on him two or three drops [of water in which those ashes are mixed], and someone tells him: 'You are pure'!" He [Rabban Johanan ben Zakkai] asked him: "Have you ever been possessed by an evil spirit?" He answered: "No!" He [Rabban Johanan ben Zakkai] asked him, "Perhaps you have seen someone who has been possessed by an evil spirit?" He answered, "Yes!" He [Rabban Johanan ben

Zakkai] asked him, "And what did *you* do to him?" He answered, "They bring roots, burn them, cause the smoke to come up from underneath him, and pour water on it, and it flees." He [Rabban Johanan ben Zakkai] replied to him: "Let your ears listen to the utterance of your mouth! The same is the case with this spirit [of impurity]." After he [the pagan] left, his disciples told him: "You dismissed him with a straw [i.e., lightly]. What can you reply to us?" He told them: "By your lives! Neither does the corpse impurify nor does the water purify. God had said, 'I have promulgated a law for you; I have issued a decree. You have no authority to transgress my decree.' As it is written, 'This is the promulgation of the Law'" (Nm 19:2).

How come every sacrifice is a male, and this one is a female? R. Aybu said, [I will offer] a parable: "The son of a maid polluted the palace of the king. The king said: 'Let [his] mother come and clean the filth.' In the same manner God said, 'Let the heifer come and atone for what happened with the [golden] calf'." [italics added][148]

For our purposes here, we must consider three major points. First, Rabban Johanan ben Zakkai did not explain to the gentile the rational of the ritual. As he had cleverly demonstrated with the question about exorcism, the gentile thought in mythical terms. It would be pointless to try to explain to such an individual the rationale of a biblical ritual. Second, the basis of Jewish ritual is acceptance of God's Law. From the perspective of a system positing an *omnipotent Creator* a ritual is *ethically* meaningful because He thus commanded it; it acquires *ethical* connotation by the fact that it was prescribed by the Law, not the other way around.[149] Third, the Law, like all value systems, can be examined both synchronically and diachronically. The synchronic axis functions by the fiat of law. For example, the French word *garage* is meaningful in English solely by the fiat that the English-speaking community uses it. Once the synchronic principle is accepted, a diachronic "explanation", that is, the fact that the early history of automobiles was French, may be meaningful.[150] One can now appreciate the textual strategy of the editor. R. Aybu's explanation was appended to elucidate a *detail* of the ritual—"How come every sacrifice is a male, and this one is a female?"—not to explain the principal rationality of the ritual. A diachronic explanation may be acceptable only *after* the synchronic basis of the ritual is properly established. R. Aybu must have had a tradition connecting the golden calf with the Egyptian goddess Hathor. It is depicted as a cow and in the Hellenistic world was identified with Aphrodite. The reason for the peculiar color of the heifer will be clear, upon realizing that *aduma* here does not mean red (just as Jacob's lentil pottage was not "red"; see Gn 25:30). Rather, as it was properly translated by Se'adya Ga'on, it means *ṣafra* the color 'gold' in Arabic, hence the symbolism of the 'mother' 'cleansing'—in the specific sense of biblical 'atonement'—the filth caused by the 'golden' calf, whose color she bears.

It is important to note that Maimonides distinguished between the general purpose of a commandment, about which he was willing to theorize, and its specific details, which he refused to rationalize. He based this thesis on a rabbinic doctrine establishing "that the commandments" (*miṣvot*) have no other purpose "than to refine (*leṣaref*) the people." Maimonides interpreted this to mean that the details of the ceremonial commandments escape rationalization. To try to rationalize these details is madness and folly. "You must know," wrote Maimonides, "that wisdom required—if you wish, you may say that necessity determined—that there should be details for which no reason could be given. It would be something impossible within the context of the Law not to have contained this type [of detail]." Maimonides linked this view to the theory of probability where it is senseless to ask, "What for came to pass this probability and not another probability?" because the same question could be asked if the other probability instead of this one had occurred. The implementation of any given model will contain details, such as the color of a particular flower, that theoretically could have been different. It is pointless to ask why detail *a* rather than *b* was selected because the same question could be asked if detail *b* had been selected instead, for example, why a particular ceremony is made with a lamb rather than a goat.[151]

The precision of this view is realized upon considering that the term leṣaref mentioned above, refers to a metallurgic process by which fine metals like gold and silver are purified from alloys. The sense is particularly poignant in light of the Maimonidean thesis that the ceremonial commandments of the Law serve to erase the pagan traces embedded in the collective subconscious of the people. These traces are not erased by a magical ritual or a mythological process but, as taught by Rabban Johanan ben Zakkai, by submitting to the decrees of the Law. Submission to the Law is expressed by complying with the details and minutia of the commandments. Since they cannot be reduced to human canons of thought, their fulfillment constitutes recognition of God and the supreme authority of His Law in contrast to idolatry where the divine is a function of human projections.

Maimonides distinguished between the secondary objective of the Law designed to remove the traces of pagan humanity and the primary objective of the Law pertaining to the full development of the individual and society on the basis of correct teachings and practices.[152] Maimonides's source is rabbinic. God taught the rabbis, instructed Moses to tell the people of Israel: "The words of the Tora that I gave you, [i] are medicine to you, [ii] are life to you." By "medicine," the therapeutic purpose of the Tora is meant;[153] *Life,* as common in rabbinic literature, stands for immortality, the primary design of the Law.[154]

THE ARCHETYPES OF ISRAEL

There is another dimension to luṭf. It was manifested in the forty years of wandering. Hebrews associate the Desert with "perplexity."[155] Deliberately, God "perplexed (*ḥayyar*) them away from the right path" leading to the Promised land.[156] The Desert has cathartic, therapeutic properties. The rabbis compared the Israelites wandering through the Desert, "to a king whose son was sick, [and] had taken his son to heal him.[157] Through a process of luṭf the mind of the children of Israel expanded, rising to new levels of consciousness. Because of their own personal growth and evolution, the traces of the pagan past became more and more marginal. To achieve this feat they had to develop a unique psychological quality:

> God guided them with cunning benevolence throughout their perplexity in the Desert until their soul became brave [*tushajja'at*]. As is known, dwelling in the desert and austerity of body, engenders brazenness [*al-shaja'a*], whereas its opposite engenders timidity. Thus was born a nation who knows no abasement or slavery. And all this was by God's commands through Moses: "At the commandment of God they encamped and at the commandment of God they departed, the ordinance

> of God they obeyed, at the commandment of God by the hand of Moses" (Nm 9:23).[158]

Two points require comment. *Shaja'a* is a middle course between two equally harmful failings, cowardice and heroism.[159] Like its Hebrew equivalent *gebura*, *shaja'a* is not merely a physical quality.[160] Unlike the pagan hero, acting impulsively and without understanding the situation at hand, or the coward, paralyzed by irrational fear, *shaja'a / gebura* denotes psychological 'determination' and 'collected reckoning' manifested in a daring, striking realization of the plan in mind. The Desert was the setting for carefully designed tests. The resolution of these tests depended, exclusively, on shaja'a / gebura. If one were to measure Israel's history on the basis of the pagan concept of heroism / cowardice, the Maimonidean view that Israel is "a nation who knows no abasement or slavery" makes little sense. From the prism of shaja'a / gebura, however, Jewish survival is a testimony to the unique determination of a people for self-assertion. The realization that this aspiration was yet unfulfilled rendered the people free even in the midst of captivity. It requires supreme shaja'a / gebura to admit *Galut* 'Exile' with all the sociopolitical and psychological opprobrium that it entails rather than to proclaim to be free because they were too afraid or too dense to admit being slaves. Whereas heroism / cowardice takes place in a mythological time and geography, shaja'a / gebura unfolds in historical time and geographic local.

Israel developed shaja'a / gebura during the forty years of meandering through the Desert, a rising generation that would serve as the archetype of the future Israel. Maimonides discussed this point in conjunction with the rabbinic doctrine of "testing of the just" (*nissayon*). Briefly, this doctrine teaches that occasionally, the tribulations of the righteous are a testing rather than a punishment. There are three aspects to this doctrine. First, because God is omniscient, the testing is to show the people "what is required of them to do or to believe in."[161] Unlike the pagan archetypes forged by gods and demigods, the archetypes of Israel are made of human traces. The shaja'a / gebura exhibited by the righteous in the pursuit of a mission leaves a trace challenging future generations.

> You must know that the purpose and meaning of every testing [nissayon] mentioned in the Tora is to educate the people what is required to do or to believe in. Accordingly, the meaning

> of testing [nissayon] is "performance of an act whose (final) objective is not the particular act itself, but to become a paradigm to be emulated and an imprint (*aṭarha*) that must be followed."[162]

Rabbinic tradition teaches that Abraham was the subject of "ten testings."[163] He also was the first archetype of the Jewish people. God, taught the rabbis, had commanded Abraham to leave his country and family and come to the Holy Land in order that "your seal (*ṭib'akha*) should be made public throughout the world,"[164] that is, he should become the paradigm of humanity. Isaiah exhorted the Jewish people to look up to Abraham as their ancestral foundation and to emulate his exemple (Is 51:2). By this he meant, "to follow in his [Abraham's] footsteps (*aṭarhu*), to adopt his religion and demeanor, because the nature of the source is necessarily to be found in that which was extracted from it."[165]

There is a huge difference between Hebrew and pagan archetypes. Pagan archetypes are mythological figures to be imitated. Mythical humans duplicate these archetypes by returning to an atemporal beginning and commencing a new cycle of regeneration. As in all mythical systems, identity is established on the basis of predicative similarities.[166] By reproducing a gesture of the mythical archetype, a human *becomes* the archetype. Hence, the life of the archaic human, "is the ceaseless repetition of gestures initiated by others."[167] Since historical time is linear, historical archetypes cannot be duplicated; they only leave footprints (*ãṭãr*) pointing toward a direction. The objective is not to *imitate* somebody but to *march forward*. It is opportune to note that the root of *nissayon* is *nes*, 'ensign', 'banner', indicating a forward direction. Pointedly, the Hebrew *shana* stands for both 'transmission' and 'change'.[168] Mythological archetypes repeat themselves in ahistorical and, therefore, essentially static, realm. The Hebrews conceived of transmission as unfolding in historical time, at once implying 'repetition' and 'change'. Jewish cults do not imitate the gestures of the patriarchs. Rather, they subject the original event, circumcision, the paschal meal, and so forth, to a transformational process. If performed exactly, according to its original model, the ritual is invalid.[169] Some of the paradigms established in the Tora were intended "for the nations" as a standard that they, too, may follow.[170] The second aspect of nissayon is related to *nissa* 'direct, personal experience'. From this perspective, the purpose of nissayon is to 'train', 'to instruct' someone. In this respect the most important nissayon was the Theophany at Sinai. Its purpose was *le-nassot* (Ex 20:20): to afford the people a direct, historical experience (*bi-al mushahada*), resulting in (yaqin), intuitive knowledge of God.[171] The experience gained through nissayon/history will be embedded in the ethos of Israel and become "eternalized" (*takhlid*) in and through the people.[172] Maimonides applied this sense of nissayon to the verse, "In order to torment you, and in order to train you (*le-nassotekha*), to benefit you in your end" (Dt 8:16). The torment experienced by Israel in the Desert led to the necessary shaja'a/ gebura to conquer and appreciate the land of Israel: "It is known that if it were not because of their tribulations and toil in the Desert, they would not have been able to conquer the land or to battle. . . .Because complacency dislodges shaja'a, whereas little bread and toil brings about shaja'a. This is the benefit that in this episode was realized at the end."[173] As with its Arabic counterpart, 'your end' (*aḥaritekha*) suggests the 'hereafter'. Without the shaja'a/gebura to face the tribulations of life neither Tora, the land of Israel, nor the World to Come, can be properly secured.[174]

There is a third aspect to nissayon. It designates the perimeters of the Hebrew concept of faith and love of God. The paradigm is Abraham's sacrifice of Isaac. It is the first time that testing (nissayon) is mentioned in Scripture. Remarkably, Maimonides examined it last. Why?

History begins at Sinai. Prior to Sinai, the Hebrews, like the rest of the pagan world, lacked historical consciousness. At that stage the Hebrews could relate to the past only in mythological terms. It was after escaping the realm of myth that the Israelites were capable of perceiving their past in historical terms. In this precise sense pre-Sinaitic history is post-Sinaitic.[175] To properly grasp the sense of Abraham's ordeal one must first gain shaja'a/gebura. It is paradigmatic of a new type of spiritual experience—love of God and faith in the absolute validity of the prophetic message.[176] Otherwise, Isaac's sacrifice would have been viewed as another instance of human sacrifice. This idea was beautifully expressed by Eliade:

> His [Isaac's] sacrifice by Abraham, although in form it resembles all the sacrifices of newborn infants in the Paleo-Semitic world, such a sacrifice, despite its religious function, was only a custom, a rite whose meaning was perfectly intelligible, in Abraham's case it is an act of faith. He does not understand

> why the sacrifice is demanded of him; nevertheless he performs it because it was the Lord who demanded it. By this act, which is apparently absurd, Abraham initiates a new religious experience, faith. All others (the whole Oriental world) continue to move in an economy of the sacred that will be transcended by Abraham and his successors. To employ Kierkegaard's terminology, their sacrifices belonged to the "general"; that is, they were based upon archaic theophanies that were concerned only with the circulation of sacred energy in the cosmos (from the divinity to man and nature, then from man—through sacrifice—back to the divinity, and so on). These were acts whose justification lay in themselves; they entered into a logical and coherent system: what had belonged to God must be returned to him. For Abraham, Isaac was a *gift* from the Lord and not the product of a direct and material conception. Between God and Abraham yawned an abyss; there was a fundamental break in continuity. Abraham's religious act inaugurates a new religious dimension: God reveals himself as personal, as a "totally distinct" existence that ordains, bestows, demands, without any rational (i.e., general and foreseeable) justification, and for which all is possible.[177]

The first stage of Israel's regeneration into a "kingdom of priests and a holy nation" (Ex 19:19) consisted of passing from the realm of imagination to that of reason. It was *accomplished* at Sinai upon grasping the first two commandments. The second stage, consisted not of intellectual perception but in the actual implementation of the rest of the commandments. To realize this goal the people of Israel had to displace the pagan traces and archetypes by embedding onto their ethos new traces and archetypes. The process only *began* at Sinai. The rabbis taught that by the end of the Babylonian Exile, the yeṣer ha-ra' (evil inclination) of idolatry was eradicated from the Jewish psyche.[178] Eventually, sometime during the rabbinic period, the entire Tora became part of the Jewish ethos. Maimonides adopted this doctrine when explaining the theory of coercion in rabbinic law. Rabbinic jusisprudence decreed that when required by law, the court may coerce a husband until he declares that he is willing to divorce his wife. At first sight, this statute seems to contradict the principle that a divorce must be executed with the full consent of the husband. Maimonides explained that coercion is invalid (and illicit) only when compelling an individual to do something not required by the Law. Since the Law is an intrinsic part of the Jewish ethos, to refuse to abide by the dictates of the court is to succumb to passion. In psychoanalytical terminology the authentic will of an individual is represented by the ego not the id. In *halakhic* terminology the authentic will of a Jew, as dictated by the collective consciousness of Israel, is to abide by the Law.[179]

THE MOMENT OF MYSTICAL ILLUMINATION

Generally, Western man copes with suffering in three ways: by transforming suffering into hatred, by escaping through licentious and other forms of gratification, and by showing contempt for suffering.[180] For Maimonides the suffering endured by the righteous has a specific function: dispelling human imagination about "the ways of the Lord." In this manner, like the Israelites in the Desert, an individual can develop the necessary shaja'a/gebura to realize and appreciate divine illumination. Maimonides discussed this theme in conjunction with the book of Job. Suffering is the result of imagination. Not that suffering is illusory, as generally in mystical thinking, but the tribulations of the righteous are *caused* by their own imagination; the stress is more psychological than physical. What was particularly distressing about Job was not the actual loss of property, family, and health, but that God had not behaved with him according to the canons of human imagination. The illusion that there is a similitude between the ways of the Lord and a human's is linguistic. Human language uses the same terminology to designate both: "The meaning of His providence is unlike the meaning of our providence. Neither is the meaning of His guidance of His creatures like the meaning of the guidance that we employ. Unlike what every perplexed person assumes, no common definition includes them both: except for the name, there is nothing in common between them [the Lord's way and a human's]."[181]

The preceding is a consequence of the Maimonidean epistemology whereby perfect knowledge is a function of creation.[182] Since a human cannot have perfect knowledge of God's creations, he is incapable of understanding the courses and procedures by which God guides and provides His creations. Maimonides identified the biblical *leviathan* as a universal biological force—something akin to Bergson's (1859–1941) *élan vital*, "which is the agglomeration of all the biological characteristics distributed in the animals, fish, and fowl." Referring to this biological force, Maimonides argued that

> Because our mind is unable to grasp how those natural things found in the world of generation and corruption were created and cannot conceptualize how the existence of that natural force [i.e., *leviathan*] began, since it resembles nothing of what we can do, how, then, can we pretend that His guidance and providence of them should resemble the way we guide and provide [others].[183]

In conclusion, "In the same fashion that natural ways differ from artificial ways so the divine guidance, the divine providence, and the divine purpose of natural phenomena differ from human guidance, providence, and intent of what we guide, provide, and intend"[184] The lesson to be learned from the book of Job is that one "should not blunder and fancy that His knowledge ought to be like our knowledge, or that His purpose, His providence, and His guidance, ought to be like our purpose, our providence, and our guidance."[185]

Happiness is achieved upon the realization that God's ways are not reducible to human imagination. It requires a shift from an anthropocentric to a theocentric perspective, thus allowing the individual to participate in the cosmological chorus dance.[186] The source of Job's tribulations was that he "imagined fictitious happiness, like health, wealth, and children, to be the goal."[187] He was able to entertain such notions because he knew God only through "tradition [*taqlidan*] like the masses of the believers."[188] At this level 'God' is a projection of human imagination. The faulty perception lasted "as long as [Job] knew God through narrative [*khubran*], not through intellectual ways. This is why he was overcome by these perplexities and said what he said."[189] Through suffering Job overcame imagination, gaining shaja'a / gebura. Thus, he came to know God by personal experience. Acquiring "certainty [*yaqinan*], he confessed that true happiness, which is knowledge of God, is spared to all those who know Him. None of these tribulations could spoil it for man."[190] As mentioned before, absolute certainty is the effect of intuitive knowledge gained through revelation, like the nissayon at Sinai. The mystic mood resulting from such an experience has been beautifully captured by Bertrand Russell (1872–1970). In a memorable passage he described the moment of mystical illumination.

> The first and most direct outcome of the moment of illumination is the belief in the possibility of a way of knowledge which may be called revelation or insight or intuition, as contrasted with sense, reason, and analysis, which are regarded as blind guides leading to the morass of illusion. Closely connected with this belief is the conception of a Reality behind the world of appearance and utterly different from it. This Reality is regarded with an admiration often amounting to worship; it is felt to be always and everywhere close at hand, thinly veiled by the shows of sense, ready, for the receptive mind, to shine its glory even through the apparent folly and wickedness of Man. The poet, the artist, and the lover are seekers after that glory: the haunting beauty that they pursue is the faint of its sun. But the mystic lives in the full light of the vision: what others dimly seek he knows, with a knowledge beside which all other knowledge is ignorance.[191]

Suffering, in its traumatic, psychological anguish, is the result of imagination. Once Job ceased to project his imagination onto God and recognized that God's ways are unlike humans', his misgivings vanished. Maimonides paraphrased Job 42:6 as a confession: "Therefore, I am repulsed by all that which I had desired, and I am consoled for the dust and the ashes."[192] Because tribulations are designed to shatter the illusions about 'the ways of the Lord' and to help the individual reach a higher realm of existence, those privy to mystical illumination are no longer mindful of their past hardships. From the new perspective the agonies endured in the previous stage are meaningless. Job is never told why he had suffered: upon witnessing God in the whirlwind (Job 38:1), the reason for his past injuries became inconsequential as with Borges's Tzinican, the Aztec priest. During his torturous imprisonment he longed for the moment of divine illumination when he could decode the secret script and, thus, crush his torturer, fulminate the Spaniards, and rule over all the lands of Moctezuma. But alas! Reading the secret script entailed ascending to a higher level of consciousness. That is why, upon gaining this moment of mystical illumination, Tzinican no longer wishes to crush his enemies. "Whoever has seen the universe," confesses Tzinican, "whoever has beheld the fiery designs of the universe," he explained, "cannot think in terms of one man, of that man's trivial fortunes or misfortunes, though he may be that very man," adding, "This is why I do not pronounce the formula, why, lying in the darkness, I let the days obliterate me."[193] A similar view was expressed by Russell: "What is, in all cases, ethically characteristic of mysticism is absence of indignation or protest, acceptance with joy, disbelief in the ultimate truth of the division into two hostile camps, the good and the bad."[194] Noticeably, Maimonides closed the chapter on Job with a quotation from the rabbis, characterizing the righteous as those who "Act out of love, and rejoice in [their] tribulations."[195]

For Maimonides imagination constitutes the basic psychological apparatus of protological human.[196] In pagan humanity it is a dynamic faculty outlining the key structures and associations fundamental to all forms of religious, political, social, and artistic activity. Shedding the pagan habits involves breaking the grip of imagination.[197] The Israelites achieved this with a twofold luṭf: the promulgation of laws and rituals designed to inhibit and heal the traces of pagan bondage and the journey through the Desert that would forge new archetypes based on shajaʿa / gebura. Luṭf in the Desert was manifested in a series of labyrinths exquisitely designed to free the mind from the traces of pagan imagination, and rise onto a new level of consciousness. The "torment" endured by the Israelites in the Desert is the psychological process designed to debunk imagination. Thus, from the "belly" of Egypt (see Dt 4:34) a society of slaves rose to be a kingdom of priests and a holy nation. The verse "You shall remember all the journey that the Lord your God led you, now forty years through the Desert" (Dt 8:2) is God's assurance that the experience at the Desert will be embedded in Israel's ethos till the end of time, even throughout the Diaspora.

At the eve of the destruction of the Kingdom of Judah, shortly before the Exile, Jeremiah proclaimed: "Thus spoke the Lord: 'I remember for you the grace of your youth, the love of your nuptials, journeying after Me through the Desert, in an uncultivated land'" (Jer 2:2).

THE DEMARCATION OF CULTURES

Maimonides divided the people into three groups: the general public, the philosophers, and the prophets.[198] "The general public" (al-jamhur) is not an amorphous mob but a social entity constituting a psychological unit. The members of the group are bound together by a system of values and institutions stemming from a series of psychobiological processes peculiar to the human species. These values and institutions concern the very strategy for survival.[199] Since for its biological survival the human species depends on the ability of its members to communicate and collaborate with one another, human is, fundamentally, a sociopolitical entity.[200] Accordingly, the human species has the ability to generate political leaders. The task of the political leader is to establish and apply laws designed to produce equilibrium and stability in the state.

> Because his [human] nature resolved that among its members there should be such a variety and [at the same time] his nature demands social intercourse, it would have been impossible to maintain a full social life without a political leader regulating their actions, complementing what is wanting, curbing what is excessive, and establishing actions and mores for all to practice, always consistently according to the same norms. In this fashion the natural variety [peculiar to the human species] could be supplanted by the amplitude of organized agreement. Thus, is society established.[201]

This is why, political leadership is essential for the human strategy of survival: "God's wisdom instituted in nature that for the survival of this [the human] species, which He wanted to endure, that some individuals should have the faculty to lead."[202]

Although individuals can communicate with one another rationally, imagination is the means by which humankind communicates and develops the key-symbols and institutions needed to forge and promote political and social cohesion. A corollary of the preceding is that imagination is not something peripheral. It is the structure allowing for communication and human intercourse: without imagination, human society is impossible. Imagination is also the method by which a crowd thinks without any recourse to rational discourse.[203] There is a peculiar mode of discourse, the "popular imagination" (*khayal al-jamhur*), by which the public apprehends and processes reality.[204] "The conceptions of the general public," are the key symbols governing the collective mind of society.[205] The general public does not think rationally not because it is composed of mentally impaired individuals, but because imagination is the only means by which humans can think collectively. Maimonides emphasized that it is not "within the nature of the general public" to grasp intellectual matters pertaining to the full development of the human mind.[206] Thus, it is irrelevant whether the public is composed of superb philosophers or common folk: collective communication can only function via imagination. This type of imagination is a biopsychological factor. It affects everyone, including prophets and—somehow—even Moses, representing (individual) human perfection.[207]

Second are the philosophers. These are individuals capable of rational thinking and creativity. They lack, however, a well-developed imagination either because of their own psychobiological constitution (al-jibla) or their intellectual orientation. Philosophers, although affected by imagination like the rest of society, are incapable of relating to the imagination of the general public.[208] This is why they are inept political leaders.[209] Political leadership is the exclusive patrimony of people with powerful imaginations. Even the constitutional laws of the philosophers and wise political leaders (known as *nu'amis*, an Arabization of the Greek *nomoi*), which are designed on rational principles, are, in fact, grounded on imagination.[210] Referring to those who think exclusively in terms of imagination, Maimonides included "political leaders, the legislators of constitutional laws" (al-nu'amis), together with "the sorcerers, diviners, the dreamers of correct dreams, and also the performers of wonders with unusual tricks, and the performers of magic." All these are people who succeed by virtue of their powerful imaginations.[211] The political leaders who had succeeded in establishing good governmental systems are described as "those who excel in the imaginative faculty alone."[212]

Third are the prophets. Prophecy comes to resolve a specific human quandary. The survival of society depends on establishing a measure of homogeneity and accord between its members. One way to accomplish this is by excluding rationality and individuation. Within this context polytheism and rejection of rational thinking constitute a strategy designed to assure political and social stability.[213] The perennial cycle of repetition peculiar to archaic societies and mythical thinking fills this need. 'Philosophy'—in the general sense of rational thinking—allows not only for creativity but also for individuation, threatening the very fiber of society. Thus, the tension 'rationality / imagination' and 'philosopher/ general public'. The prophet is the ideal political leader precisely because he communicates simultaneously at both the imaginative and rational levels thus bridging between the general public and the individual. Prophets are described as individuals upon whom the divine emanation flows over "the intellectual and imaginative [faculties]."[214] Maimonides and Judah ha-Levi and the Geonic authorities as well, regarded the Tora as a two-dimensional system. One dimension may be described as 'spiritual' and is intended to provide guidance and information to the individual and to the public. The other is 'political'. Its purpose is the promotion of social harmony and stability.[215]

> In general, the Tora has a two-fold purpose. These are: prosperity of the soul and prosperity of the body. Prosperity of the soul is when true opinions reach the public, according to their own faculties. Consequently, some [of these opinions] are explicit and others are in metaphors because it is not within the nature of the general public that their faculties could encompass and grasp these matters as they [actually] are. Material well being, however, consists of the prosperity of their daily lives with one another. The accomplishment of this task involves two things. One is the elimination of oppression. This means that no individual person can be permitted to act as he wishes, according to his might, but he must be curbed for the benefit of the public. The second is to provide every person with mores beneficial to the society in order that the matters of state be orderly. You must know that of these two goals, surely one, that is, the prosperity of the soul, is more sublime than the other, I mean, providing true opinions. The second, relating to the prosperity of the body, is prior in nature and time. It consists in the organization of the state and the prosperity of all the inhabitants, according to what is possible. The second is the more urgent. It has been thoroughly examined, including all of its details, because it is only after achieving this aim that the first aim can be achieved.[216]

These aims are interdependent. The systems created by pagan culture are concerned with only a single dimension of humanity, either the political or the spiritual. The uniqueness of the Law of Moses is that it alone provides guidance to attain this two-fold perfection.[217]

The preceding considerations permit an adequate understanding of the literary strategy of the Tora. Because it addresses the general public as well as the individual, focusing on both the political and spiritual aspects of humankind, the language of the Tora must be significant at both the imaginative and intellectual levels. Maimonides interpreted the rabbinic principle, "The Tora has spoken in the language of humankind," to mean that the Tora was designed to suit "the imagination of the general public,"[218] hence the paramount distinction between the exoteric and the esoteric sense of the Scripture. On the one hand, the esoteric aspects of the Tora are highly sophisticated and complex and cannot be reduced to the imagination of the general public. Had the Tora exposed these matters in a clear and forthcoming fashion, they would have been processed by the public in a manner resulting in "great damage to the imagination": breeding confusion, and promoting false doctrines about God and His Law.[219] To expose the *sodot* (secrets) and *sitre tora* (enigmas of the Tora)[220] to the general public is as harmful as feeding a baby "wheat-bread, meat, and wine."[221] The ultimate aim of the Tora is to help individuals attain full spiritual growth. To this end it uses metaphors and cryptograms that the general public comprehends in an innocuous way, but the intellectual and moral individual would properly grasp and decode.[222] Thus, the Tora is meaningful both according to the imagination of the public and the minds of rational individuals.[223]

The above leads to what may be properly described as a demarcation of cultures dominated by distinct modes of thinking: one rational and the other imaginative, Hebrew thought being a third type, including, but not reducible to, either of the two others. Although these cultures are characteristic of certain people and civilizations, for Maimonides they represent social rather than anthropological groups: the general public and the philosopher on either extreme of society with the prophet realizing a vision that includes, but is irreducible to, either the purely rational or the imaginative.

Outside the Tora are two forms of government. Although outwardly different, one unfolding in mythical terms and the other purporting rational aims and methodology, both are grounded on mythical concepts and ideology. In either case time is cyclical. Salvation is achieved by retrogressing to a primeval moment.[224] Because the sociopolitical structures and institutions were established either by extra-human (mythological societies) or superior humans (rational societies), both types of society depend on hierarchical authority and, therefore, are grounded on institutionalized violence.[225] The aim of pagan political leadership is to preserve the established order and to ward off the elements that can disturb the hierarchical relationship between the governed and the governing. In the Tora time is linear, continuously branching in a forward direction. The Hebrew *teshuba* (repentance) is not a return to a mythical moment, but to God; more precisely, to the path leading to His luṭf. The root of the term *Tora* is *yara* 'to point ' the way, a cognate of the Arabic *dalala* 'guidepost', making up the first word of Maimonides's *Guide for the Perplexed.*[226] Salvation is effected by a forward march, choosing the appropriate path, and climbing new heights of consciousness. The purpose of political leadership is *not* to maintain the status quo, but, as the divine luṭf, to exploit the *āṯār* of previous generations for climbing new heights. To effect this progress the political leader must fuse the imagination of the public with the insight of the philosopher. Hence, the prophet is the ideal political leader. Maimonides explained the excellence of the Tora in contrast to other political systems, such "as the constitutional laws [nu'amis] of the Greeks [rational law], the fantasies of the Sabeans [mythical thinking], and others," on the basis that those systems are the product of "political leaders, not prophets."[227]

KNOWING BY VIRTUE OF PERFECTION

Maimonides maintained that human perfection is possible. Perfection is not to be conceived in absolute terms, Platonic or Aristotelian. There are different classes of perfection.[228] The twofold purpose of the Tora discussed in the preceding chapter corresponds to two different classes of human perfection, one material and another spiritual. Maimonides distinguished between "human perfection" in general, connected with the individual's somatic and social situation, and "true human perfection."[229] Only the latter permits "the individual to achieve a true perfection" as himself is *ad intra.*[230] Within each class there are gradations.[231]

Individual perfection is not an end but a preparation for further development. For example, it could serve as the groundwork for understanding "the secrets of prophecy" or even reaching prophecy itself.[232] Perfection is "relative to what their [individual] capacities are."[233] Individual perfection is "final" only in the sense that it cannot be achieved without having first attained material perfection.[234] Maimonides characterizes someone reaching final perfection as a person "being intellectual in actuality, by this I mean, that he has actual intellect. It consists of knowing by virtue of his final perfection whatever it is possible to know of everything that exists, according to human capacity."[235]

The key term of this passage is "by virtue of his final perfection."

Because there are different classes of knowledge, Maimonides emphasized that the final goal is reached by understanding "by virtue of his final perfection." In Maimonidean terminology it means to have actualized "the image of God" within and, thus, been privy to divine illumination and guidance.[236] Accordingly, one must distinguish between two forms of human understanding: one before, leading up to, and another after, deriving from, individual perfection. The main question of this chapter is: What constitutes knowledge "by virtue of his final perfection"?

Maimonides distinguished between intellectual worship (*al-'abadat al-'aqliya*),[237] which is "the goal of humanity,[238] and individual perfection. Intellectual worship, is the seventh category of Maimonides's parable of the royal palace[239]—after successfully cruising the labyrinths leading to the royal chamber and arriving at the presence of the King.[240] Only then can an individual worship God, qua individual, in a specific manner.[241] It is the ultimate form of worship and a human's furthest fulfillment.[242] Individual perfection is the sixth category of Maimonides's royal palace.[243] At that stage the individual is still conditioned by the social and psychobiological terms of the species. He could not yet worship God intellectually but only develop the type of rational concept that will serve as the *basis* for intellectual worship.[244] It corresponds to Maimonides's "fourth type" of perfection described as "the true human perfection" because it *generates* concepts that will "award"—in the sense of helping to realize—"correct opinions about the divinity." The "final goal" of these concepts is to help the individual advance further and to attain a "true perfection." This type of perfection, however, cannot be passed onto others. "It is for him alone and will award him lasting existence. By virtue of it is the human a human."[245] To reach the seventh category, however, he would have to "march a final *sa'y*"—a quick, prolonged stride toward a target: "then he would be in the presence of the King. He [God] would appear to him either from afar or from near, and he [the individual] could either hear the words of the King or speak to him."[246]

There are three aspects to intellectual worship: specific concepts ensuing "after understanding what is He"; the technique to achieve it, and the final outcome.[247] Intellectual worship is accomplished when "after reaching [intellectual] perfection," the individual "focuses his mind"

> on [matters pertaining to] the divinity, shifting all of his being toward God.[248] casting off everything that is not Him; focusing

> all his mental activities in the analysis of [all] that exist, and deriving from them an impression about Him, learning thereby what constitutes the realm of the possible, according to the way in which He governs them.[249]

By insisting that intellectual worship ought to be based on the ways that God actually rules the universe as they are empirically perceived, rather than anthropomorphically, according to the ways that one supposes He ought to behave, imagination and theological anthropocentrism are excluded.[250]

The bases for intellectual worship are the commandments to love and to fear God. The last stage of human perfection is effected by fulfilling the commandment to "Love the Lord, your God, with all your heart, and with all your soul, and with all your might" (Dt 6:5).[251] Loving God is a function of knowing God. It includes the comprehension of a cluster of fundamental concepts about the way He is and guides His creatures. The more genuine the knowledge of God, the more genuine the love for God.[252] Although purely intellectual, the Scripture stipulates that love of God must be "with all your heart." This means, "with all the forces of the body, since the beginning of everything is the heart. The intention [of this commandment] is that the aim of all your actions should be to perceive Him."[253] Fear of God (Dt 6:13) is not dread of retribution but awareness of His omnipresence. It could only come after and as a consequence of love of God. Because to love God is to be in His presence, those privileged to enter the royal chamber are required to behave with proper demeanor. Thus, whereas the commandment to love God is realized mentally,[254] the commandment to fear God is realized in the meticulous observance of the Law, including both positive and negative commandments, as befitting a guest in the divine chamber.[255] "These two objectives, to love and fear [God], are accomplished in two ways. Love is realized through the opinions of the Law, which are included in the perception of His existence according to what He is. Fear [of God] is realized through all of the fulfillment of the Law, as we have explained. Understand this summary."[256]

In general, intellectual worship may be described as "focusing the mind on the First Idea."[257] It comes after perceiving "God and His actions, according to what reason dictates."[258] It consists of "focusing the mind on God alone after knowledge of Him, as we have explained. This is the specific worship for those who have perceived the truths. The more that [these individuals] increase their thoughts on Him and are before Him, the more their worship gains."[259] This view is based on the thesis that "all the rituals (*'abadat*) [prescribed by the Law], like studying the Tora, the prayers, and the fulfillment of the rest of the commandments, have as their goal training [the individual] to be engaged in His commandments, rather than to be [exclusively] engaged in mundane matters. [Being engaged in the Tora, etc., is] as if you are engaged in Him, rather than in someone else."[260]

TRAINING FOR INTELLECTUAL WORSHIP

The model for the Maimonidean intellectual service is the 'Amida (Silent Prayer) described by the rabbis as "the service (*'aboda*) of the heart."[261] The term 'amida (standing up) comes from the root *'amad* (to stand up). One of the principal features of this term is "to stand in a posture of submission before the king or a superior" (Gn 18:8, 41:46; Dt 1:38; 1 Kgs 1:2), "ready to execute his command" (see Nm 16:9; Dn 1:19; 2:2; 2 Chr 10:6). The Hebrew prayer consists, precisely, in standing before God in a posture of obedience (cf. Gn 18:22; Dt 10:8; 18:7; 1 Chr 23:30; 2 Chr 5:14; 7:6; 20:13; 29:11). In this fashion individuals present themselves before Him, ready to obey His commandments. Similarly, "the intellectual worship" is described as "drawing near God, and presenting oneself (*al-maṯul*) before Him."[262] The Arabic maṯul (appearing, presenting oneself) is semantically equivalent to *'amida.* An essential feature of this prayer is for the individual "to empty his heart from all thoughts and to see himself standing (*'omed*) before the Shekhina (Divine Presence)"[263] in a submissive posture.[264] Keenly, Maimonides illustrated the different connotations of 'amad with three groups of verses. The first contains three verses, each implying, respectively, standing before a superior in submission, supplication, and servitude. The second contains two verses: one implying interruption of speech and the other interruption of a bodily function. The last group has three verses, implying, respectively, permanency, endurance, and continuation.[265] They represent the principal features of the 'amida: appearing before God in submission, interruption mundane and corporeal activity, and the attaining eternity.

Understanding by "virtue of perfection" is essentially liturgical—an "intellectual service" in the language of Maimonides. It requires a liturgical posture. As with the 'amida, the individual submits to God and is willing to serve Him according to His rules. By perceiving reality from the realm of the divine and admitting reality as it is, the individual joins the rest of creation and becomes fully human. Thus, learning how to comply with the facts of nature and discovering the splendor of God as manifested in His creations, "The learned virtuous, however, already knows the wisdom of this reality and understands it. . . . Those complying with the nature of reality and the commandments of the Law—understanding the purposes of both of them—know clearly the manner in which [the divine] munificence and the truth [are manifest] in everything. This is why they set as their aim [fulfillment of] what was intended of them in quality of humans, which is understanding."[266]

The rabbis expressed the same idea in poetic language. God, they taught, "will place a crown on the head . . . of those who do His will and glance at His splendor." The prize is awarded only to an individual "who places himself at the borderline,"[267] that is, as something marginal and peripheral—shifting from an anthropocentric to a theocentric perspective. In this fashion an individual transcend the mundane, establishing a direct and, therefore, lasting relationship with God. Establishing this relationship *before* death affords the individual "continued permanency" *after* death.[268] With old age as bodily pressures intruding between the individual and God begin to wane and ultimately through death itself, [269] "understanding" attains "continued permanency in a singular manner. Because the impediments occasionally hampering [the individual] vanish, his permanency will continue [after death] in that majestic pleasure that does not belong to the class of bodily pleasures, as we have explained in our works, and others have explained before me."[270]

Maimonides designed a program to train for intellectual worship. It consists of three phases: "consecrating (*al-inqiṭa'*) oneself to Him, marching toward His nearness, and strengthening the link between you and Him, which is the mind."[271] Maimonides offered "instruction" (*irshad*) about "the form of training" required "to reach this awesome goal." The first phase al-inqiṭa' (to consecrate) translates the Hebrew *le-yaḥed 'aṣmo,* which means "to set oneself exclusively" for a particular task.[272] It consists of three steps: focusing on God through the prayers (shema' and 'amida), through the study of Tora, and through the rest of the Scripture and liturgy. The individual is instructed to empty his "thoughts from everything [extraneous]" when reciting the shema' and the 'amida.[273] Indeed, the rabbis reported a tradition, "Before praying, the devout men of yore would wait for an hour to be able to focus their hearts toward their Father in Heaven."[274] Before proceeding to the next step, it is necessary to train for several years. In the following step the individual trains to focus on the text of the Tora. He is instructed whenever studying or hearing a passage from the Tora, "to turn [the mind] toward the comprehension of what you are reading or hearing," concentrating "with all of yourself and the totality of your mind." The third step is an expansion of the same routine in scope and intensity: it must be applied to the rest of the Scripture and the liturgy as well, and the mind must be "pure," in the sense of absolute concentration. The purpose is "to reflect on everything that you articulate and [actually] to comprehend its significance."[275] In this fashion through liturgy, study, and fulfillment of the Tora, an individual is expected to puncture the mundane habits and to think about God. "At the times of fulfilling the Law," Maimonides instructs, "do not occupy your mind with anything except what you are doing, as we have explained." To realize those special moments and to let the light in, the mind must be "clean from thinking about anything mundane." The second phase seeks to invert the situation. The individual must be in constant mental contact with God except for certain moments reserved for mundane affairs when "you are eating and drinking, or when you are in the bath, or when you are speaking to your wife, to your young children, or to the general public."

> At the time that you are all alone, however, and at the time that you wake from sleep be extremely careful in those precious moments, and do not engage in anything else except that intellectual worship, which is to draw near God and to come before His presence in the true fashion that I taught you—not in the fashion of unruly imagination. In my opinion this is the limit of what a member of the scholarly community can reach upon deciding to undertake this type of training.[276]

Because God will invariably appear from a distance,[277] there is a perennial need to "march closer toward His presence.[278] The third phase involves a circular movement (like the *maḥol* dance of the righteous) whereby understanding generates worship and worship generates understanding: "a march in His understanding and a march toward his worship after His understanding."[279]

UP AND DOWN JACOB S LADDER

Jacob's vision of God's angels going up and down the ladder that joins earth and heaven (Gn 28:12) is the biblical model for prophecy—the ultimate mystical experience. Solomon ibn Gabirol noted that because these angels first ascend and then descend heaven, they could not be celestial beings. Rather, they are humans ascending with their minds to heaven and then proceeding to bring their vision down to earth.[280] The source of this idea is the Talmudic doctrine identifying the rabbinic scholar with the ministering angels.[281] Significantly, the ladder is first "established on earth" wherefore it reaches heaven, not the other way around. Reflecting the original sense of the term, these angels are God's messengers: people serving as the conduit effecting His designs on earth. Maimonides identified these angels with the prophets.[282] This leads to the fundamental distinction between the personal perfection of "a member of the scholarly community" (*ahl-u-l-naḍr*) and that of a prophet. The former is an individual in whom the divine flow touches his intellect but not his imagination.[283] Therefore, he cannot pour it over others. His perfection "is for him alone."[284] Translated in terms of the preceding metaphor, the aim of this individual is to reach the highest possible point of the ladder and to linger up there. As God's messengers, the ultimate goal of the prophets is to bring their vision down to earth. The divine flow gushes over their intellects, overflowing from it onto their imaginations, in such a bounty that it would help them attain not only their own perfection but also that of others.[285] The prophet's final objective is not heaven but taking the heavenly vision down to earth. Thus, the prophetic vision is integral to the community of Israel. The rabbis compared the people of Israel to a vine in which the cluster and the leaves, tendrils, roots, and branches cannot subsist without joint participation and support. Similarly, the different elements of Israel (the uneducated, the common folk, the townspeople, and the sages) interact, forming a single organic unit.[286] In this specific sense prophecy is essentially political. Commenting on the angels "ascending and descending" the heavenly ladder, Maimonides remarked: "How wise was saying . . . 'ascending' before 'descending'! Because after ascending and reaching a definite echelon in the ladder, what was perceived [must be] brought down to lead (*tadbir*) and teach the inhabitants of the earth."[287] Tadbir implies political 'guidance' and 'organization.'[288] The purpose is not to 'hang around heaven' but to bring down a message that will enhance the condition on earth. When the prophet fails to translate his vision into sociopolitical facts, functioning instead as "a member of the scholarly community," his ministry is terminated. A close reading of a passage ascribed to R. Joseph ibn Judah (twelfth and thirteenth centuries)—Maimonides's famous disciple—shows that this was the case with Elijah. Elijah is described as the embodiment of (the Maimonidean concept of) individual perfection. At the same time he proposed that Elijah had been summoned back to heaven because he failed to give the jamhur (general public) leadership. Elijah himself was (partially) responsible for the sins that he was blaming on Israel. In response to the charge that the people had forsaken God he was told that the fault lay with Ahab and his ministry. To correct the situation he not only had to replace Ahab but must also appoint a new prophet: "God's response [to Elijah's charge against Israel] was as follows: Concerning what you have mentioned that Israel removed itself from the worship [of God], this is because of the king. Therefore, you must remove him and appoint another in his place. . . . But you, too, are incapable of civilizing and educating the public [*lil-tamdin wal-ta'lim al-jamhur*]. Therefore, you must appoint a prophet in your stead to teach them." The term *tamdin* (civilizing) from *madaniya* (civilization) implies 'civic sophistication and culture'—in its political connotation. The thesis reflects the Maimonidean doctrine that the prophet represents the ideal political leader.[289] Note that Elijah is replaced by Elisha, a family man and a farmer with deep roots in society. The request, that before departing to heaven Elijah should bestow on him "two- portions" of his spirit (2 Kgs 2:10), reflects his awareness that although practical in earthly ways, he may be intellectually wanting, and, therefore, unqualified to furnish proper political guidance.[290]

The distinction between the final perfection of the individual and that of the prophet concerns the essence of the Hebrew concept of 'aboda (worship). 'Aboda from *'ebed* (slave, servant) involves a 'service', 'a specific labor done by a subordinate on behalf of a superior'. In Hebrew an 'ebed is considered an extension of his master. This relationship is embodied in the legal principle, "the hand of an 'ebed is like the hand of his master" (*yad 'ebed ke-yad rabbo*).[291] The term 'ebed also describes the relationship of an officer to his superior (see 1 Sm 18:23, 30; 25:10, 40) and a political subject to the king (see Gn 50:71; 1 Sm 17:8; 1 Chr 18:2, 6, 13; 2 Chr 10:7). Because God is "the King of the Universe," the term 'ebed is applied to the righteous who carry on God's commandments, such as Abraham (Gn 26:24), Moses (Nm 12:7; Dt 34:5; Jos 1:2,7; 12:6; 2 Chr 24:6,9), Joshua (Jos 24:29; Jgs 2:8), David (Ps 18:1; 36:1; 89:4, 21), the prophets (2 Kgs 10:23; 2 Kgs 9:7; 17:3; Jer 7:25; 26:55; 44:4; Ez 38:17), and the people of Israel in particular (Lv 25:42,55; 26:13; Is 41:8-9, 48:20, 52:13; Ez 28:25; 37:25).

How does the Hebrew sense of 'aboda apply to the intellectual worship of God? In the last chapter of the *Guide,* Maimonides went into great lengths to demonstrate that the Scripture and rabbis coincide with the philosophical view that the ultimate perfection is intellectual. The scriptural text proof is a passage in Jeremiah (9:22–23) in which God declares that neither the wise (*ḥakham*), strong (*gibbor*), nor wealthy (*'ashir*) should be praised but only someone, "who understands and knows me." To demonstrate that the ultimate perfection is intellectual Maimonides explained that in the passage, "wise" (ḥakham) is one "who has acquired ethical virtues"—not a sage! Usually, gibbor (strong) refers to a person with strong moral character. This sense cannot apply here, since then ḥakham-virtuous would be a tautology. To avert this problem Maimonides resolved that here gibbor is a physically strong person. The explanation is awkward on several grounds. At the beginning of the chapter Maimonides pointed out that the primary sense of ḥokhma (wisdom) and ḥakham (wise) in the Scripture and rabbinic literature is intellectual. Furthermore, these three terms are mentioned by the rabbis as a precondition for prophecy.[292] Within that context ḥakham, gibbor, and 'ashir must be interpreted as someone who had acquired wisdom, moral fortitude, and contentment. This is how Maimonides himself had explained these terms in several places, including the *Guide.*[293] According to rabbinic tradition this was how the Jewish sages interpreted these terms to Alexander.[294] Eventually, this interpretation was incorporated in *Pirqe Abot* (4:1). What makes the rabbinic interpretation of these terms particularly poignant is that it alludes to the passage in Jeremiah (hence, the terms ḥakham, gibbor, and 'ashir in the precise order of the verse). Finally, in the same chapter Maimonides pointed out that the end of the verse ("that I am the Lord who performs munificence, justice and charity on earth, since these are my desire, said the Lord") is inconsistent with the explanation that he had offered.[295] If the ultimate goal is pure intellectual contemplation, then the verse should have said that praise is due someone "who understands me" or "who understands that I am One" or "that I have no shape" or that "there is none like me," and so on.

> It said, however, that praise is due to [those having] perception and knowledge of my attributes, meaning, His actions; as we have explained concerning his [Moses'] request, "Let me know your ways" (Ex 33:13). This verse [in Jer] explains to us that the actions [of God] that must be known and emulated are "munif-

> icence, justice, and charity," adding a pivotal point, "on earth," that is the axis of the Law. Unlike the delusions of those who affront [God] presuming that His providence ends at the moon's sphere, and that the earth and all that it contains are neglected, "The Lord had abandoned the earth!" (Ez 9:9).[296] But as [He had] explained to us through the head [sid] of the sages, "that the earth is the Lord's!" (Ex 9:29). It is saying that His providence reaches also earth, according to what it warrants, just like His providence reaches heaven according to what it warrants. This is [the meaning of] what was said: "that I am the Lord who performs munificence, justice, and charity on earth." Having concluded the subject, he proceeded further, declaring: "Since these are my desire, says the Lord." It means that my objective is that among you there should be munificence, charity, and justice on earth. We have already explained in connection with the thirteen attributes that the purpose [of ascribing these characteristics to God] was that we should emulate them. [Similarly,] the purpose of mentioning [these three attributes] in this verse is to explain that human perfection warranting praise is that of someone who perceived God according to his capacities and knows how His providence is manifested in His creatures, giving to them existence and guidance. As a result of this perception, the individual will always be aiming his ways at munificence, charity, and justice, emulating the actions of God, in the fashion that I have explained in this work several times.[297]

Maimonides's explanation of the second half of the verse was carefully planned. He had devoted the preceding chapter to an explanation of the terms munificence, charity, and justice. The contradiction is deliberate. It belongs to the seventh class—a class that it is peculiar to the *Guide* and excluded from philosophical works.[298] As mentioned earlier, there are two classes of ultimate perfection: the philosophers', acquired by *ascending* Jacob's ladder, and that of the prophets acquired by *descending* the ladder. The first is perennially locked in the paradox 'knowledge ➞ un-knowledge', 'praise ➞ silence', 'light ➞ darkness', generated by the two paths stemming from anthropocentrism: one leading to anthropomorphism and the other to gnosticism. The second class resolves the paradox existentially[299] by opting to come down the ladder and to serve God, imitating His ways on earth, that is, by practicing munificence, justice, and charity.[300] Such an option ought to be kept secret. Because of their sociopolitical implications, some biblical doctrines are to be concealed from everyone: the political authorities, the general public, and the philosophers in particular,[301] hence, Maimonides's use of the seventh type of contradiction.

The two interpretations of the triad "wise, strong, wealthy" are the result of two different perspectives, a philosophical (first part of the verse) and a prophetic (second part). From the philosopher's perspective, where the ultimate contact with God is contemplative, the ḥakham criticized by Jeremiah could not possibly be a sage but only someone "who has acquired ethical virtues." To avoid ending in a tautology the philosopher would then be required to explain the following two terms as "physically strong" and "wealthy." Thus, despite his rhetoric, the philosopher ends up sharing the anthropomorphic scale of values of the general public (al-jamhur).[302]

AT GOD S SERVICE

The intellectual ʿaboda consists in enlisting into the service of God. It is performed on the way down the ladder, furthering God's work on earth. In the Scripture the world created by God is not definitive but "to be made" (*la-ʿaśot*) (Gn 2:3).[303] What the world is or would turn out to be depends solely on what humans make of it. The rabbis taught that a judge "who rendered a true judgment, even for a moment . . . is as if he were a partner with God in the creation of the world.[304] Such an individual, "causes the Divine Presence to abide in Israel."[305] In a meticulous sense, when humans fashion the world in the way of "munificence, charity, and justice," it is God Himself who is acting through them as a master acts through his ʿebed and a lord through his *mal'ak*: they are the kerubim pulling the divine Merkaba.[306]

Maimonides devoted the last chapter of the second part of the *Guide* to development of the doctrine that the Scripture occasionally attributes something that was made or that had occurred according to "God's will and His choice," as if it were made by God Himself. "This," Maimonides added, "is the opinion of the entire community of our Law."[307] From the foregoing it is clear why Maimonides exhorted the reader "to reflect on the particulars" of the chapter dealing with the service of the Lord "more than you reflect on any of the other chapters of this work."[308] Similarly, Isaac Cardoso (1604–1681) maintained that the art and sciences are the means by which God manifests His Providence on earth "in order that the creatures could attain and reach the goal which God has assigned to them."[309]

The model of a ladder on which God's angels ascend in order to descend and practice "munificence, charity, and justice" on earth, permits an adequate understanding of R. Simon bar Yoḥai. To escape Roman persecution he hid with his son in a cave. Together they studied Tora uninterruptedly. Twelve years later, when they were no longer sought by the authorities, they left the cave. Noting that people were tilling the land and going on with their daily business, they protested, "They abandon eternal life and busy themselves with temporal life!" Thereupon, a heavenly voice replied: "You came out to destroy my world. Return to your cave!" It took them twelve months (one month each year) to deprogram themselves and adjust to civilization. After recuperating from his travails, R. Simon bar Yoḥai said, "Since a miracle happened to me, I will go and fix something." He then proceeded to investigate, "Is there anything that needs to be fixed?" This involves a purely *civic* responsibility. He found something to contribute to his fellow citizens. The rabbis noted that the model for R. Simon bar Yoḥai's was the Patriarch Jacob. Rabbinic tradition teaches that after wrestling with the angel and reconciling with his brother Essau, Jacob wanted to express his own fulfillment by "engracing" the first city that he encountered. There are different views concerning the specific way in which Jacob assisted the citizens of that place. Some maintain that he established for them a monetary system, another, that he organized for them a market system. A third opinion maintains that he set up for them public baths.[310] All of these things were designed to improve the material well being of strangers, helping them to promote "munificence, charity, and justice" on earth. The message is particularly poignant if one interprets Jacob's return to the Promised Land as the last step on his way down from the celestial ladder. In which case, the purpose of the angel—like the angels standing in Moses way—was to prevent a mere human bringing down the Tora to earth.[311] The angel's plea, "Send me out because the morning has risen!" (Gn 32:27), reflects the rabbinic doctrine that the just "causes the Divine Presence to abide in Israel."[312] As it were, Essau's angel could not suffer God's light to be reflected on earth.

The immediate model for R. Simon bar Yoḥai was his famous mentor, R. 'Aqiba. It has not been noticed hitherto that the problem with the pardes of rabbinic esoterics is not in the entrance but in the exit. All four students had indeed "entered" the pardes. Their failure was in their exits. Only R. 'Aqiba entered and exited successfully (nikhnas be-shalom ve-yaṣa be-shalom).[313] In our own terms, this means that only R. 'Aqiba knew how to descend Jacob's ladder and apply his vision on earth. The outcome of this vision was the Bar Kochba's revolution. It resulted in the greatest genocide suffered by the Jewish people. Yet he is recognized as the greatest leader of rabbinic Judaism. His vision taught the people that to preserve the ways of the Tora they had to stand up and fight Roman oppression. Otherwise, like Christianity, they would succumb to the ways of the persecutor and lose their soul.[314]

Notes
Bibliography
Indexes

Notes

All references to Maimonides's *Guide* are to the Arabic original, Moses Maimonides, *Dalalat al-Ḥa'irin*. The references are to section, chapter, page, and line of the Arabic original.

PREFACE

1. See José Faur, *Golden Doves with Silver Dots: Semiotics and Textuality in Rabbinic Tradition* (Bloomington,: Indiana Univ. Press, 1986), xxvi, 63–64.

2. Werner Jaeger, *Aristotle* (Oxford: Oxford Univ. Press, 1962), 370.

3. José Ortega y Gasset, *The Revolt of the Masses*, trans. anonymous (New York: W. W. Norton, 1957), 111.

4. Juan Ramón Jiménez, "Inteligencia," in *Segunda Antología Poética* (Madrid: Espasa Calpe, 1920).

5. Giambattista Vico, *New Science,* tran. Thomas Goddard Bergin and Max Harold Fisch (Ithaca, N.Y.: Cornell Univ. Press, 1968), par. 401.

6. See Faur, *Golden Doves,* 23–27.

7. *Sifre,* ed. Louis Finkelstein (New York: Jewish Theological Seminary of America, 1969), par. 41, 86; the expression comes from Eccl 12:11. See Faur, "The Splitting of the *Logos:* Some Remarks on Vico and Rabbinic Tradition," *New Vico Studies* 3 (1985): 83–103.

8. The intellectual value of such a methodology is analogous to someone applying to Shakespeare's *Julius Caesar* the canons of early nineteenth century German historiography. For some further insights see José Faur, "Monolingualism and Judaism," *Cardozo Law Review* 14 (May 1993): 1713–44.

9. Maimonides *Guide* sect. 2, chap. 2, p. 176 (lines 13–16).

10. On this type of literature see Roger Caillois, *Anthologie du fantastique* (Paris: Editions Gallimard, 1955); André Breton, *Manifestation du surréalisme* (Paris: J.-J. Pauvert, 1962); Marcel Schneider, *La Littérature fantastique en France* (Paris: Librairie Arthème Fayard, 1964). Cf. below, p. 111.

11. Maimonides *Guide,* part 2, chap. 2, p. 176 (lines 9–10).

12. Ibid., Introduction, 10 (lines 4–8).

13. Mircea Eliade, *The Quest: History and Meaning in Religion* (Chicago: Univ. of Chicago Press, 1984), 61–62.

INTRODUCTION

1. Erich Neumann, "Mystical Man," in Joseph Campbell ed., *The Mystic Vision: Papers from the Eranos Yearbooks,* ed. Joseph Campbell (6) (Princeton, N.J.: Princeton Univ. Press, 1982), 377. On Maimonides's "philosophical mysticism" see the very valuable studies of David R. Blumenthal, "Maimonides: Prayer, Worship and Mysticism," in *Priére, Mystique et Judaisme* (Strasbourg: Collection Strasbourg, 1984), 89–106; idem, "Maimonides's Intellectualist Mysticism and the Superiority of the Prophecy of Moses," *Medieval Culture* 10 (1978): 51–67. On Maimonides and the Kabbalah in general see the very erudite and illuminating work of Moshe Idel, *Maimonide et la mystique juive* (Paris: Editions du Cerf, 1991).

2. The Maimonidean concept of perfection has been the subject of a succinct, eminently useful monograph by Menachem Kellner, *Maimonides on Human Perfection* (Atlanta, Ga.: Scholars Press, 1989).

3. Yehudah Evenshmuel, *More Nebukhim*, pt. 2, vol. 1 (Jerusalem: Mossad Harav Kook, 5718/1958), Introduction, 126.

4. R. M. Albérès, *Histoire du roman modern* (Paris: Editions Albin Michel, 1962), 436. See André Breton, *Manifestes du surrealism* (Paris: J.-J. Pauvert, 1962), 40.

5. *Pirqe Abot* 4:21.

6. See Maimonides, *Mishne Tora, Teshuba* 8:7. It is as if a blind or deaf person would attempt to apprehend color or sound, see idem, *Pirush ha-Mishnayot,* ed. and trans. Joseph Qafiḥ, 7 vols. (Jerusalem: Mossad Harav Kook, 1967), 4: 203–4. The source is rabbinic; see *Sifre,* no. 356, p. 424. Cf. *Berakhot* 34b.

7. See *'Aboda Zara* 10b, 17a, 18a.

8. See *Ketubot* 66b, *'Aboda Zara* 17b; *Ta'aniyot* 29a (the story with Rabban Gamli'el); the extraordinary story about Elijah and the jail keeper, *Ta'aniyot* 22a and in Nissim ben Jacob ibn Shahin, *An Elegant Composition Concerning Relief and Adversity*, trans. William M. Brinner (New Haven, Conn.: Yale Univ. Press, 1977), 4–5; the story of the two clowns, *Ta'aniyot* 22a; and the story with Abba Ummana, ibid. 21b. Cf. *'Azarya de Fijo, Bina le-'Ittim,* vol. 1

(Jerusalem: Ch. Wagschel, 5749/1989), 5b; Moses Ḥayyim Luzzato, *The Path of the Upright*, trans. Mordecai M. Kaplan (Philadelphia: Jewish Publication Society, 1936), end of chap. 26.

9. Maimonides, *Mishne Tora, Teshuba* 5:2.

10. Leone Ebreo (R. Judah Abarbanel), *Dialoghi d'Amore*, English translation, *The Philosophy of Love*, by F. Friedberg-Seeley and Jean H. Barnes (London: Soncino Press, 1937), sect. 1, 51.

11. *Tosefta Qiddushin* 1:13, cited in *Qiddushin* 40a–b.

12. Jorge Luis Borges, "The Zahir," trans. Dudley Fitts, in *Labyrinths* (New York: New Directions, 1964), 163.

13. Mishna *Sanhedrin* 4:5.

14. *Pirqe Abot* 1:14.

15. Quoted in Neumann, "Mystical Man," 409.

16. *Pirqe Abot* 4:3.

17. *'Aboda Zara* 10b, 17a, 18a.

18. Jorge Luis Borges, "Prólogo," in *Evaristo Carriego*, by Evaristo Carriego (Buenos Aires: Emecé Editores, 1955), 139.

19. A similar process takes place in the formulation of modern scientific theory; see Ludwig von Bertalanffy, *General System Theory* (New York: George Braziller, 1993), 239–48.

20. Eliade, *The Quest*, preface (no pagination). See *Maimonide et la mystique juive*, 14 ff. Cf. below, p. 237 n. 114. It is similar to the "cosmic force" and "cosmic religious feeling" of the scientists; see Albert Einstein, "Religion and Science," in *Ideas and Opinions*, trans. Sonja Bargmann (New York: Crown Trade Paperbacks, 1982), 36–40. I have further developed this subject in Faur, "A Crisis of Categories: Kabbalah and the Rise of Apostasy in Spain," in *The Jews of Spain and the Expulsion of 1492*, ed. Moshe Lazar, (Lancaster, California: Labyrinthos, 1997), 41–63.

21. See below, Introduction, pp. 13–15.

22. The same idea is more succinctly stated in the first half of Dt 32:39.

23. See Faur, *Golden Doves*, 41–48.

24. On the "cosmic force", and so on, see above, Introduction, n. 20. Linguistically, it stands for the third person, formally excluded from the act of speech; see Faur, "The Third Person in Semitic Grammatical Theory and General Linguistics," *Linguistica Biblica Bonn* 46 (1979): 106–13. On the Oedipal structure of anthropocentric thought see Faur, "De-authorization of the Law: Paul

and the Oedipal Model," in *Psychoanalysis and Religion*, ed. Joseph H. Smith and Susan Handelman (Baltimore, Md.: Johns Hopkins Univ. Press, 1990), 222–43.

25. See J. J. Finkelstein, *The Ox That Gored* (Philadelphia: American Philosophical Society, 1981), 12.

26. Stephen Hawking, *A Brief History of Time* (New York: Bantam, 1990), 175. Concerning Balaam's claim, the Rabbis (*Berakhot* 7a) noted in humor, "Now, the mind of his beast he did not know, the mind of the Most High, how would he know?!"

27. See Faur, *Golden Doves*, chap. 2–3.

28. Cited in Faur, "Newton, Maimonides, and Esoteric Knowledge," *Cross Currents: Religious and Intellectual Life* 8 (1990): 536.

29. Mamonides *Guide*, sec. 1, chap. 58, p. 93 (lines 23–26).

30. See Faur, "Some General Observations on the Character of Classical Jewish Literature," *Journal of Jewish Studies* 28 (1977): 36. This corresponds to the distinction between the semantic and the semiotic; see Faur, *Golden Doves*, 76–79, and below, Introduction, n. 31.

31. Wittgenstein, *Tractatus Logico-Philosophicus*, trans. D. F. Pears and B. F. McGuinness (London: Routledge and Kegan Paul, 1961), 6.522. Cf. Faur, *Golden Doves*, 126–27. Similarly, at the linguistic level one must distinguish between an interpreter system (Oral Law), which cannot be interpreted by any other system, and an interpreted system (Written Law), which must be interpreted by the interpreter system; see Faur, *Golden Doves*, 111–12, and below, Introduction, n. 32.

32. Wittgenstein, *Tractatus Logico-Philosophicus*, 4.121. Similarly, in the introduction of his *Wörterbuch für Volkesschulen* (Vienna: Holder-Picher-Tempsky, 1977), xvii, he wrote: "My work consists of two parts, the one present here plus all that I have *not* written. And it is precisely this second part that is the important one." Cf. Faur, *Golden Doves*, 117.

33. Leone Ebreo, *Dialoghi d'amore*, sec. 1, 46.

34. See Jung's foreword to Erich Neumann, *The Origins and History of Consciousness*, trans. R. F. C. Hull (Princeton, N. J.: Princeton Univ. Press, 1993), xiii. Like the "golden doves" in the mind of the first person, that invariably appear to the second person as "silver dots," see Faur, *Golden Doves*, 114–18.

35. See Faur, *Golden Doves*, 116, and ibid., 10–12. On the *shirṭuṭ* see ibid. 105. In my view, a vocalized scroll cannot be used for liturgical purposes because under this condition there is no "reading" but a "recitation from memory" instead. According to this theory, even authorities such as Maimonides, who

permit reading from a "void scroll" (see Faur, *Studies in the Mishne Tora* (in Hebrew) [Jerusalem: Mossad Harav Kook, 1978], 180–181), would disqualify reading from a vocalized scroll. Similarly, those who had read the *Megilla* from a vocalized text would not have fulfilled their obligation because they had only "recited the text from memory" rather than "read" it. The same applies to a *geṭ* (bill of divorce) and other documentation requiring "reading" from a "written text." Conversely, because there is no requirement to "read" a *mezuza* or a *tefillin*, a vocalized text is not void. Maimonides distinguished between the calligraphic requirements of the mezuza and the tefillin because they were not designed for reading and the scroll of the Tora, which is designed for reading; see Maimonides, *Mishne Tora*, *Tefillin* 1:2. The standard view on this matter overlooks a fundamental dimension of Hebrew reading; cf. R. Joseph Refael 'Uzziel, in R. Ben-Ṣion Uzziel, *Mishpaṭe 'Uzziel* (Tel-Aviv, 5695/1935), 1:165b.

36. *'Aboda Zara* 19a.

37. *Qiddushin* 33b.

38. *Pirqe Abot* 4:8. Cf. Maimonides, *Pirush ha-Mishnayot*, 4:446.

39. *Makkot* 22b. On the meaning of *gabra rabba* cf. *Baba Qamma* 59b. See Faur, *Golden doves*, 23–32, 167 n. 1.

40. David Michael Levin, "The Loving Body of Tradition," *Religious Traditions* (Univ. of Sidney) 5 (1983): 54.

41. Miguel de Unamuno, "What is Christianity?" in *The Agony of Christianity*, trans. Anthony Kerrigan, (Princeton, N. J.: Princeton Univ. Press, 1974), 16.

42. Mishna *Baba Meṣi'a* 2:11. See Maimonides, *Guide*, sec. 3, chap. 54, p. 467 (lines 2–27), and below, pp. 4, 129–30.

43. See below, pp. 33–34; and the rabbinic quotation in Faur, *Golden Doves*, 119.

44. See Alfred Ribi, *Demons of the Inner World*, trans. Michael H. Kohn (Boston: Shambala, 1990), chap. 9.

45. Pío Baroja, *Camino de Perfección* (New York: Las Américas Publishing, n.d.), chap. XX, p. 91. For an in-depth analysis of this work see C. A. Longhurst, "*Camino de perfección* and the Modernist Aesthetic," in *Hispanic Studies in Honour of Geffrey Ribbans*, ed. Ann L. Mackenzie and Dorothy S. Severin (Liverpool: Liverpool Univ. Press, 1992), 191–203. See below, p. 61.

46. Maimonides, *Guide, sec.* 2, chap. 12, p. 195 (lines 15–17). Cf. below, pp. 137–38.

47. See Maimonides, *Guide*, sec. 3, chap. 12, pp. 320 (line 24)–22 (line 4).

48. See ibid., sec. 3, chap. 29, p. 377 (line 3).

49. Ibid., sec. 1, chap. 32, p. 47 (lines 8–9).

50. See above, Introduction, n. 57; and Julia Kristeva, *Powers of Horror,* trans. Leon S. Roudiez (New York: Columbia Univ. Press, 1982), 61–63.

51. Maimonides, *Guide,* sec. 1, chap. 36, p. 56 (lines 19–24); idem, *Mishne Tora, 'Aboda Zara* 2:1. The rabbis did not regard the worship of idols by the uneducated masses of Babel as *'aboda zara* because they were merely "following the practices of their ancestors." For a full examination of this subject see Faur, *Studies in the Mishne Tora,* 219–230.

52. Eliade, *Quest,* Preface (no pagination).

53. On its precise etymology and meaning see Émile Benveniste, *Indo-European Language and Society,* trans. Elizabeth Palmer (Coral Gables, Fl.: Univ. of Miami Press, 1973), 516–28. It was only recently introduced to Judaism as a result of mental assimilation. It came to Judeo-Spanish about one hundred years ago as a direct influence of French.

54. See Faur, "Idolatry," *Encyclopaedia Judaica,* vol. 8, cols. 1227–32. Reprinted in *Jewish Values* (Israel Pocket Library, 1974), 52–60; and idem, "The Biblical Idea of Idolatry," *Jewish Quarterly Review,* 69 (1978): 1–26. Of particular significance is the Septuagint version noted by the rabbis in *Megilla* 9b.

55. See Faur, *Studies in the Mishne Tora,* 230–37.

56. Paul Radin, *Primitive Religion* (New York: Dover Publications, 1957), 259.

57. On the rabbinic doctrine of monolatry see R. Ila, *Yerushalmi Shabbat* 13, 3, 14a. For a further examination of this subject see Faur, "Understanding the Covenant," *Tradition* 9 (1968): 44–48; and idem, "Two Forms of Jewish Spirituality," *Shofar* 10 (1992): 7–10.

58. See Maimonides, *Guide,* sec. 3, chap. 22; and Sigmund Freud, *The Future of an Illusion,* trans. W. D. Robson-Scott (New York; Doubleday Anchor Books, 1957). See below, p. 62.

59. See Hans Küng, *Freud and the Problem of God,* trans. Edward Quinn (New Haven, Conn.: Yale Univ. Press, 1990).

60. Jean-Paul Sartre, *Anti-Semite and Jew,* trans. George J. Becker (New York: Schocken Books, 1976), 66.

61. Freud, *Future of an Illusion,* 68. Similarly, ibid., 31; "I have singled out one such phase of development, which more or less corresponds to the final form of our contemporary Christian culture in the west." In Freud, *Group Psychology and the Analysis of the Ego,* trans. James Strachey (New York: Bantam Books, 1965), chap. 5, Freud compared the morphology of the Catholic Church to the morphology of an army.

62. Printed in Sigmund Freud, *Standard Edition of the Complete Psychological Works of Sigmund Freud (S.E.)*, ed. and trans. James Strachey (London: Hogarts Press, 1953–74) 13: XV. Austrio-German literature of the time written by assimilated Jews must be read as the literature of *conversos.* In which case, Freud's *Moses and Monotheism,* is a code-term for *"Christ" and "Christians."* The principal thesis is that the Roman, that is, proto-Christian murder of Jesus was the ground for his eventual deification. See Faur, *In the Shadow of History: Jews and Conversos at the Dawn of Modernity* (New York: SUNY, 1992), 260 n. 130. Accordingly, the Oedipus complex is the matrix not of universal culture and religion but of the specific process of displacement and substitution peculiar to Christianity and Western culture. In Freud, "An Autobiographical Study," *S.E.*, 20: 68, Freud wrote:

> The son's rebelliousness and his affection for his father struggled against each other through a constant succession of compromises, which sought on the one hand to atone for the act of parricide and on the other to consolidate the advantage it had brought. *This view of religion throws a particular clear light upon the psychological basis of Christianity,* [italics added] in which, as we know, the ceremony of the totem meal still survives, with but little distortion, in the form of the *Communion.*

See Faur, "De-authorization of the Law," 222–43. Freud's characterization of religion as "the enemy" of science, *New Introductory Lectures, S.E.*, 22: 160, is perfectly understood to every individual who had to camouflage his or her thoughts as a converso. Küng's reproach to Freud, "Is it possible, however, to provide historical evidence of such a parricide?" (*Freud and the Problem of God,* 38), and his criticism that ethnological research shows that the Oedipus complex cannot be the source of religion, (138); or his point that both the Oedipus complex and the castration complex in woman, "have not been shown clinically, ontogenetically, or phylogentically to be *universal phenomena,"* [italics added] (107), and so on, fail to take into account that in the overheated, finger-pointing atmosphere characterizing the cultural and religious discourse of the time "universal phenomena," may have been the most prudent (and appropriate) way to refer to "Catholic"—that is, universal—Christianity. The same applies to the criticism raised by Mircea Eliade, *Images and Symbols,* trans. Philip Mairet (Princeton, N.J.: Princeton Univ. Press, 1991), 23 n. 8.

63. *Qiddushin* 40a; *Horayot* 8a–b; cf. *Megilla* 13a.

64. Cited by Maimonides in his *Teshubot ha-Rambam*, ed. and trans. J. Blau, 3 vols. (Jerusalem: Mekize Nirdamim, 1975), no. 150, 1: 280; see editor's note ad loc. Similarly, in the *Sifre* no. 355, p. 422, Moses teaches: "from the measure of the lower heaven you may know what is the measure of the Glory above." On the lower and higher heaven see *Bereshit Rabba*, ed. J. Theodor and C. Albeck, 3 vols. (Jerusalem: Wahrmann Books, 1965), sec. 4, chap. 2, vol. 1, p. 26. According to the same R. Me'ir, there is a higher form of knowledge of God that is attained through knowledge of the Tora; see *Sifre* no. 33, p. 59; cf. no. 49, p. 115, and Introduction, n. 65, below.

65. Maimonides, *Sefer ha-Miṣvot*, ed. and trans. R. Joseph Qafiḥ (Jerusalem: Mossad Harav Kook, 1971), positive commandment no. 3, p. 59.

66. See Maimonides, *Guide*, sec. 2, chap. pp. 242 (line 15)–43 (line 5). Cf. Joseph Heller, "Maimonides's Theory of Miracle," in *Between East and West*, ed. Alexander Altmann (London: East and West Library, 1958), 112–27.

67. In *Ḥadashim Gam Yeshanim*, ed. Abraham E. Harkavi, (Jerusalem: Carmiel, 5730/1970), 4. For some interesting insights on the "tracks of the miraculous" see Mircea Eliade, *Autobiography*, vol. 2, trans. Mac Linscott Ricketts (Chicago: Univ. of Chicago Press, 1988), 22–25.

68. Isaac Newton, *Principia* (Berkeley and Los Angeles: Univ. of California Press, 1934), 2: 545. See "Newton, Maimonides and Esoteric Knowledge," 526–38.

69. *Bereshit Rabba* 68, 28 (11), vol. 2, 777–78; cf. *Nedarim* 25a; *Shebu'ot* 29a; *'Aboda Zara* 40b; and *Diqduqe Soferim* ad loc. Similarly, Philo, *The Migration of Abraham*, 32, 183 (Loeb Classical Library), 4: 237–39, writes that "the existent Being can contain. But he cannot be contained." And see ibid. 35, 193, p. 245: "God, has not His abiding-place outside all material nature, containing, not contained." Cf. ibid. 33 131, p. 207. This doctrine teaches that the relationship between God and the universe is to be understood in the sense proposed by ibn Abitur; cf. Maimonides, *Guide*, sec. 1, chap. 8, p. 70. Maimonides began the *Mishne Tora, Yesode ha-Tora* 1:1, by reformulating this doctrine into the famous principle that God's relation to creation is that of *mamṣi/nimṣa* (Creator/created). The elementary sense of this doctrine escaped later Jewish thinkers; cf. Harry A. Wolfson, *Crescas' Critique of Aristotle* (Cambridge, Mass.: Harvard Univ. Press, 1929), 123–24. The hyperspace of the rabbis cannot be measured in terms of ordinary geometry. Thus, the area of the Ark of the Covenant at the Holy of Holies did not displace ordinary space; see *Megilla* 10b. On hyperspace in general see Michio Kaku, *Hyperspace* (New York: Anchor Books, 1994).

This critical point has been overlooked by Max Jammer, *Concepts of Space* (New York: Dover, 1993), in his treatment of space in Judeo-Christian tradition.

70. See Abraham ibn ʿEzra's Commentary ad loc., *Bereshit Rabba* 48, 10, vol. 2, p. 778; Maimonides, *Guide*, sec. 1, chap. 70, pp. 118 (line 26)–20 (line 12).

71. See Faur, "God as a Writer: Omnipresence and the Art of Dissimulation," *Cross Currents: Religion and Intellectual Life* 6 (1989): 37–38.

72. *Berakhot* 55a. See Faur, *Golden Doves*, 18–27; and Faur, "God as a Writer," 31–43.

73. This is also the perspective of the secularist. In spite of all the rhetoric, secularism expresses the same archetypes and value system dominating the mythological realm; see Introduction, n. 74, below. Both the secular and the mythical mind conceive of biblical revelation as mythical and, therefore, mutually exclusive with rationality. The Tora, however, marks not only the realm of the sacred but also of the profane, establishing a dialectical relationship between them. This is the theme of the *habdala* prayer recited at the end of the Sabbath; see Faur, *Golden Doves*, xxiv. It is worthy of note that *Qadashim* (The Sacred), forming the fifth order of the Mishna, includes not only the tractates dealing with the sacramental but also Tractatus *Ḥolin* 'Profane'.

74. Maimonides, *Treatise on Resurrection*, ed. Joshua Finkel (New York: American Academy for Jewish Research, 1939), 22. See below, p. 109ff. At the mythological level words function like graffiti and have only a semiotic function free from semantic connotations; see Faur, *Golden Doves*, 1–4. Therefore, they are context-free (see idem, *Golden Doves*, 27–29) and establish identity regardless of their specific context, as in the medieval romance *Tristan and Iselut* where the hero weds a woman just because she bears the same name as his beloved princess.

75. Maimonides, *Pirush ha-Mishnayot*, Introduction, 1: 41–42.

76. "The Immortal," in *Labyrinths* (New York: New Directions, 1964), 113. My translation.

77.Maimonides, *Pirush ha-Mishnayot*, Introduction, vol. 1: 42.

78. Sigmund Freud, *Civilization and Its Discontents*, trans. Joan Riviere (New York: Doubleday Anchor Books, 1958), 100. See below, pp. 131–37.

79. See Jos 24:2; and Kellner, *Maimonides on Human Perfection*, 21. Legally, however, "from the moment that Abraham was consecrated" [to the service of God], his children are no longer regarded as "the descendants of Noah" but as "the descendants of Abraham," Maimonides, *Mishne Tora, Nedarim* 9:20–21; see *Nedarim* 31a; *Pesaḥim* 67a; *Mishne Tora, Bi'at ha-Miqdash* 3:4.

Therefore, contrary to common practice the graves of the Patriarchs and other pre-Sinaitic figures of Israel have the same legal status as those of the Israelites after Sinai; see Jacob Ḥai Zrehen, *Bikkure Ya'aqob* (Tiberias: 5666/1906), *Yore De'a* no. 20, 85a–89c.

80. Maimonides used this term in the pejorative, both in the singular, *Pirush ha-Mishnayot*, 2: 177, and the plural, ibid. 360; vol. 4: 201, 449. Cf. *Teshubot ha-Rambam* no. 1, vol. 1, p. 1.

81. See Mainmonides, *Pirush ha-Mishnayot*, Introduction, vol. 1: 22, 23, 34, 36; vol. 4: 200.

82. The *Mishne Tora* begins with the fundamental doctrines pertaining to the Hebrew concept of God (*Hilkhot Yesode ha-Tora*), and concludes with the basic political principles of Jewish Government (*Hilkhot Melakhim*). Likewise, Maimonides's famous thirteen doctrines of Judaism begin by postulating (1) the existence of God, and (2) His Oneness, concluding with the credo in (12) the political redemption of Israel, established by the Messiah, and (13) eventual resurrection, in its bodily dimension, of the people of Israel.

83. *'Aboda Zara* 17b.

84. *Qiddushin* 40b. See Maimonides, *Pirush ha-Mishnayot*, Introduction, 1: 43.

85. See below, pp. 179–80.

86. Freud, *The Future of an Illusion*, 103.

87. Ibid., 104.

88. See Maimonides, *Guide*, sec. 1, chap. 70; sec. 2, chap. 2.

89. See ibid., sec. 2, 1.

90. Ibid., sec. 2, chap. 6, 184 (lines 3–19).

91. Cf. ibid. chap. 43, 278 (line 22)–279 (line 14). See S. D. Luzzato, *Commentary to the Pentateuch* (in Hebrew), (Jerusalem: Horev, 1993), 367.

92. *Bereshit Rabba*, 69, 28, (13), vol. 2, 791.

93. See *Sifre*, no. 356, 423; *Midrash ha-Gadol*, *Debarim*, ed. Solomon Fisch (Jerusalem: Mossad Harav Kook, 1972), 477.

94. *Bereshit Rabba* 82, 13, vol. 2, 983.

PART ONE: APOPHASIS

1. See Faur, *Golden Doves*, 70–83.

2. See Maimonides, *Guide*, sec. 1, 31–32.

3. Ibid., 51.

4. See Faur, *Golden Doves*, 79, 175 n. 47.

5. Maimonides, *Guide*, sec. 1, chap. 35, 54 (lines 8–10).

6. But nothing more; see ibid., chap. 58.

7. Ibid., chap. 59, pp. 93 (line 29)–94 (line 3).

8. Ibid., p. 94 (line 13). Cf. ibid., Introduction, 4 (lines 8–12).

9. Ibid., sec. 1, chap. 59, p. 94 (lines 5–8).

10. Ibid., (lines 4–13).

11. Ibid., (lines 8–11).

12. See ibid., (lines 8–13). The term *pophasis* appears in rabbinic literature; see Saul Lieberman's note in *Pesikta de-Rav Kahana,* ed. Bernard Mandelbaum, 2 vols. (New York: Jewish Theological Seminary of America, 1962), 2: 476.

13. This was one of the qualities of the disciple to whom Maimonides dedicated the *Guide,* see "Introductory Epistle"; see p. 1 (lines 6–7); and ibid., Introduction, pp. 4 (line 12), 5 (line 2), 6 (line 1). See below, pp. 168–71.

14. For a definition of such individuals see ibid., "Introductory Epistle," 1, especially lines 14–15; Introduction, p. 4 (lines 7–8).

15. Ibid., chap. 59, p. 94 (lines 23–27). See below, p. 168.

16. See Maimonides, *Guide,* sec. 1, chap. 59, 94 (lines 5–8), quoted above, p. 21.

17. See ibid., Introduction, p. 4 (lines 7–8).

18. Ibid., sec. 1, chap. 59, p. 95 (lines 1–5).

19. Concerning the function of silence see Faur, *Golden Doves,* 116–17.

20. This paragraph was misunderstood by commentators and translators because they took the form *yaqulun* as a perfect (said), when, in fact, it is the present continuum (they say). Maimonides could not possibly have written that *all* philosophers have *made* such a statement. What he was saying, which somehow escaped the grasp of translators and commentators, is that all (*genuine*) philosophers, that is, those who have attained apophatic knowledge, do acknowledge the above. The acknowledgment serves to identify the "(genuine) philosopher."

21. Maimonides, *Guide,* sec. 1, chap. 59, p. 95 (lines 5–13). Cf. ibid., chap. 50, p. 75 (lines 21–22). The source of this doctrine is rabbinic; see below, p. 44.

22. Maimonides, *Guide,* Introduction, p. 3 (lines 25–26). The model of a truth that glows and then conceals itself is suggested in a Talmudic passage comparing the light of the heavenly beings to the flashing of lightning. See *Ḥagiga* 13b and R. Ḥanan'el ad loc.

23. Maimonides, *Guide,* Introduction, p. 3 (lines 6–7). The Hebrew *mithappekhet,* commonly translated as 'revolving', 'spinning', stems from

hafakh 'to turn around', 'to change and become its opposite'; see Ex 14:5. Rather than 'the spinning sword', the exact translation is 'the sword which it is constantly becoming its opposite'.

24. Maimonides, *Guide,* Introduction, p. 4 (lines 12–17). See ibid., sec. 2, chap. 39, pp. 243 (line 29)–44 (line 11).

25. This is the standard version. Maimonides, *Pirush ha-Mishnayot* on *Ḥagiga* 2:1, vol. 2, 377, however, reads; *shonin lo rashe peraqim* (they recite to him the heads of chapters), which coincides with the *Tosefta Ḥagiga* 2:1 (cited below, p. 25) "recite to me" (*shene*). Similarly, in the standard editions of the Talmud *Ḥagiga* 13a one finds: *sabe de-pumbedita havu tanu be-ma'a'se bereshit.* Cf. Saul Lieberman, in Gershom G. Scholem, *Jewish Gnosticism, Merkabah Mysticism and Talmudic Tradition* (New York: Jewish Theological Seminary of America, 1960), 118 n. 3. The Aramaic verb *gamir, agmerakh, agmerun,* and so on, (to teach), ibid., corresponds to *shinun* rather than to *mosrin.* In Maimonides, *Mishne Tora, Yesode ha-Tora* 2:12, however, and in the idem, *Guide,* Introduction, p. 3 (line 10), the text is mosrin. This term involves the transference of authority, (see Faur, *Golden Doves,* 14, 88, 123–24) and delegation of responsibility (see, e.g., the *barraita* cited in *Baba Qamma* 9b). Most probably, the reading *shinun* was the version of the Talmud with which Maimonides was familiar in his youth. Upon arriving in Egypt and discovering the ancient versions of the Talmud preserved in the Orient, Maimonides changed it to *mosrin.* Cf. Faur, "Maimonides's Discovery of a Saboraitic Version of Tractate *Nidda*" (in Hebrew), *Tarbiz* 65 (1996), 721–28.

26. In general, this expression refers to the basic axioms upon which the entire education of the student is structured. Therefore, they are the last matters that a student will forget; see *Abot de R. Natan,* ed. Salomon Schechter (Vienna, 5647/1887), 24, p. 78. Cf. Faur, *Golden Doves,* 90. These are equivalent to the "plants" quoted below, p. 36.

27. Mishna *Ḥagiga* 2:1, *Tosefta Ḥagiga* 2:1. This is the version preserved by Maimonides, *Guide,* sec. 1 chap. 33, 48 (line 20); and the Ge'onim; see *Oṣar ha-Ge'onim,* ed. B. M. Lewin vol. 4 (Jerusalem, 5691/1931), *Ḥagiga,* 12.

28. See Maimonides, *Guide,* sec. 1, chap. 33, p. 48 (lines 22–25).

29. See *Ḥagiga* 15b and the sources cited above, n. 27. For a further analysis see Faur, *Golden Doves,* 126.

30. See Faur, *Golden Doves,* xviii. The reason is examined below, pp. 46–47.

31. Mircea Eliade, *Myth and Reality,* trans. Willard R. Trask (New York: Harper and Row, 1963), 15.

32. See below, p. 27ff.

33. Such as the texts mentioned above, p. 24.

34. See above, p. 194 n. 25.

35. See Faur, *Golden Doves,* 142.

36. See Mishna *Sheqalim* 5:1; *Yerushalmi Ḥagiga* 2, 1, 77b. The same term was used to introduce esoteric material; see quotation below, n. 37. It was used by the Ge'onim; see *responsum* in *Oṣar ha-Ge'onim,* vol. 4, *Ḥagiga,* 12, and Maimonides to allude to esoteric openings, for example, Maimonides, *Guide,* sec. 1, chap. 33, p. 48 (line 21); cf. sec. 3, chap. 7, and below, nn. 37, 46, 55, 60, 103, 107. A close reading of the end of the last paragraph of the introduction to the *Guide* reveals that Maimonides regarded the explanation of ambiguous biblical terminology dealt with in part 1 as the opening prologue to esoteric discourse. The choice of verse, "Open (*pitḥu*) the gates, and let a righteous people pass" (Is 26:2), as the introduction of the first chapter of the *Guide,* is precise and to the point.

37. According to another tradition preserved in *Yerushalmi Ḥagiga* 2, 1, 77a, the prologue is said by the teacher. The task of the student is to develop it: *keṣad hu 'ośe? be-teḥilla rabbo poteaḥ lo rashe peraqim, wu-maskim.* Within this context *maskim* must be understood in the sense of 'to supplement'.

38. See Maimonides, *Guide,* sec. 2, chap. 29, p. 244 (lines 3–11), and below, nn. 58, 192, 193.

39. According to other versions, he descended from the donkey before the opening prologue; see Saul Lieberman, *Tosefta Ki-Fshuṭa, Mo'ed* (New York: Jewish Theological Seminary of America, 1962–90), 1287. The version here is confirmed by *Yerushalmi Ḥagiga* 2, 1, 77a. Cf. above, n. 37.

40. As was the case with three students of R. Joshua, see *Tosefta Ḥagiga* 2:3; *Ḥagiga* 15a; and *Yerushalmi Ḥagiga* 2, 1, 77b. A somehow similar story is told about a disciple of R. Judah the Prince, ibid., 2, 1, 77a.

41. For a similar expression see *Qiddushin* 66b and cf. *'Erubin* 53b.

42. *Tosfeta Ḥagiga* 2:1. For parallel sources see editor's notes ad loc.

43. See *Ketubot* 21b, in *Yebamot* 63b and *Tosefta Yebamot* 8:7. This expression was used as a wordplay to ridicule the fact that ben Zoma was praising the virtues of marriage while he himself remained unmarried. See, however, Lieberman, *Tosefta ki-Fshuṭa Mo'ed,* 1288.

44. See Faur, *Golden Doves,* 142–43. Therefore, it is used in contrast to 'forget' as in *Yerushalmi Ḥagiga* 2, 1, 77b: *le-adam shelamad tora be-na'aruto wu-shkhaḥah, wub-ziqnuto ve-qiyemah.* Cf. *Pirqe Abot* 4:18.

45. *Tosefta Ḥagiga* 2:2; see *Yerushalmi Ḥagiga* 2, 1, 77b.

46. *Yerushalmi Ḥagiga* 2, 1, 76a: *rabbo poteaḥ lo rashe peraqim wu-maskim.* See the note of Z. W. Rabinovitz, *Sha'are Torath Eretz Israel* (Jerusalem: I. Rabinovitz, 5700/1940), 320.

47. *Yerushalmi Ḥagiga* 2, 1, 76a. For a definition of such a student see Maimonides, *Mishne Tora, Gezela* 14:13.

48. *Yerushalmi Ḥagiga* 2, 1, 77c.

49. *Ḥagiga* 13a.

50. Ibid.

51. Mainmonides, *Pirush ha-Mishnayot,* 2: 376. Cf. Introduction to idem, *Pirush ha-Mishnayot,* 1: 35–36; idem, *Guide,* sec. 2, chap. 29, pp. 243 (line 29)–44 (line 3).

52. On the precise meaning and function of these terms see Faur, *Golden Doves,* 14, 123–24.

53. The usual sense of this term among post-Talmudic authorities, is 'tradition'. Occasionally, it was used in the sense of 'trustworthy lore', probably translating the Arabic *taqlid;* see R. Ḥanan'el on *Sukka* 45b and *Ḥagiga* 12b, 13a; cf. *Oṣar ha-Ge'onim, Ḥagiga,* pp. 11 n. 5, 15. The usage of this term by the anti-Maimonideans as a synonym of mysticism was intended to vacate and thus to displace, the chain of rabbinic tradition; cf. Faur, "A Crisis of Categories," 46.

54. Mainmonides, *Guide,* sec. 3, Introduction, p. 297 (lines 8–10).

55. This term is analogous to the Hebrew *pataḥ* and *petiḥa,* the 'opening' prologue preceding the induction into esoteric matters. See above, p. 195 n. 36.

56. Maimonides, *Guide,* sec. 3, Introduction, 297 (lines 15–18).

57. Ibid., sec. 1, chap. 71, p. 121 (lines 22–24).

58. In *Newly Discovered Geonic Responsa,* (in Hebrew), ed. Simcha Emanuel (Jerusalem: Ofeq Institute, 5755/1995), no. 115, p. 135. My son, R. Abraham Faur, pointed out to me that the source for "a triplicate transmission" is the passage in *Ḥagiga* 14b: *shalosh harṣa'ot hen . . . de-'arṣe ve-'arṣu qamme qa-ḥashib, de-'arṣe ve-lo 'arṣu qamme, la qa-ḥashib.* See *Tosafot* ad loc. According to this interpretation, the "third group" (*kat ha-shelishit*) in *Ḥagiga* 14b, refers to those who had the privilege to triplicate their transmission, hence the expression, "You and your disciples and the disciples of your disciples are invited to the third group"; see *Gaonic Responsa,* ed. Simcha Assaf (Jerusalem: Darom, 1928), 77 n. 2. Cf. *Baba Meṣi'a* 85a.

59. See below, p. 197 nn. 73–74.

60. *Newly Discovered Geonic Responsa,* no. 115, p. 218.

61. Maimonides, *Guide,* Introduction, 3 (lines 19–20).

62. Ibid., sec. 1, chap. 71, 121 (lines 21–22).

63. Ibid., Introduction, p. 3 (lines 5–7). Similarly, in the introduction to Maimonides, *Pirush ha-Mishnayot,* 1: 35: "If one were to expose the truth to them they would reject it . . . because their mind was not (sufficiently) developed to accept the truth as it is."

64. Maimonides, *Guide,* sec. 3, Introduction, p. 297 (lines 19–20).

65. Quoted below, p. 42.

66. Maimonides, *Guide,* sec. 1, chap. 71, p. 121 (lines 27–28).

67. Scholem, *Jewish Gnosticism,* 10.

68. Ibid., 10–12. The same "proof" is found in Gershom Scholem, *Major Trends in Jewish Mysticism* (New York: Schocken, 1961), 359 n. 359.

69. Scholem, *Jewish Gnosticism,* 12–13.

70. Cf. Moshe Idel, *Kabbalah: New Perspectives* (New Haven, Conn.: Yale Univ. Press, 1988), 91.

71. Ibid., 13. A similar claim is found in Scholem, *Major Trends in Jewish Mysticism,* 52.

72. *Oṣar ha-Ge'onim, Ḥagiga,* 14–27; cf. *Newly Discovered Geonic Responsa,* no. 115, pp. 124–25, 127–35, 145. See Idel, *Kabbalah,* 90–91.

73. *Oṣar ha-Ge'onim, Ḥagiga,* 14; *Newly Discovered Geonic Responsa,* no. 115, p. 132. See Idel, *Kabbalah,* 90–91.

74. *Oṣar ha-Ge'onim, Ḥagiga,* 15 (2).

75. Ibid., 21; *Newly Discovered Geonic Responsa,* no. 115, p. 132.

76. The heavenly *teraqlin* (tricliniam) in *Pirqe Abot* 4:21 (which in rabbinic literature is associated with the marriage chamber; see *Yerushalmi Sanhedrin* 10, 8, 30c) is translated by Maimonides *al-qaṣar* 'palace', 'castle'; see Maimonides, *Pirush ha-Mishnayot,* 4: 448, and ibid., 96. This is the term that he used to designate his famous castle; see Maimonides, *Guide,* sec. 3, chap. 51. There is a highly informative and accurate analysis of this metaphor in Kellner, *Maimonides on Human Perfection,* chap. 3. For other such mystical palaces or castles in rabbinic literature see *Yerushalmi Ḥagiga* 2, 1, 77c, cited below, p. 40; cf. below, p. 208, n. 4.

77. See Morton Smith, "Ascent to the Heavens and the Beginnings of Christianity," *Eranosjahrbuch* 50 (1981): 403–29. See below, pt. 1, n. 119.

78. Mishna *Ḥagiga* 2:1, and so on.

79. *Tosefta Megilla* 3 (4):28; *Sukka* 45b.

80. Scholem, *Jewish Gnosticism,* 13. See the valuable remarks of Ephraim

E. Urbach, *The World of the Sages* (in Hebrew) (Jerusalem: Magness Press, 1988), 486–513.

81. Neumann, "Mystical Man," 386–87, and n. 8. For a glimpse at this problem in Spain, see Faur, "Crisis of Categories," 45–46.

82. Jorge Luis Borges, "La Rosa de Paracelso," in *Obras Completas* (Madrid: Ultramar, 1977), 389–92.

83. See below, n. 101.

84. Maimonides, *Guide,* sec. 3, Introduction, p. 297 (lines 20–21).

85. Ibid., (lines 26–28).

86. See below, pp. 47–50.

87. Maimonides, *Guide,* sec. 3, Introduction, pp. 297 (line 29)–98 (line 1).

88. See above, p. 193 n. 23.

89. Maimonides, *Guide,* sec. 3, Introduction, p. 297 (lines 18–19). Cf. ibid. sec. 1, chap. 71, p. 121 (lines 24–25).

90. See Maimonides, *Mishne Tora, Yesode ha-Tora* 1:9.

91. To illustrate, what was consequential for the foursome entering the "orchard" mentioned below on pp. 36–42 was not the "what" but the "how" of their experience; namely, that one "went up," and so on. A teacher confronts one of the faltering students with the question, "From where to where?" See below, p. 200 n. 112.

92. Maimonides, *Guide,* Introduction, p. 3 (line 11).

93. The fifth and seventh type, ibid., p. 13 (lines 13–15). See ibid., 11–13.

94. See ibid., "Fifth Contradiction," p. 11 (lines 19–26).

95. See ibid., p. 13 (lines 8–9). Cf. below, p. 210 n. 41.

96. The "Seventh Contradiction." See ibid., p. 12 (lines 7–12).

97. Not the inverse. Cf. Maimonides, *Guide,* sec. 1, chap. 33.

98. Ibid., Introduction, p. 12 (lines 7–12); sec. 2, chap. 29, p. 244 (lines 10–11).

99. Ibid., Introduction, p. 7 (lines 15–28). See Faur, *Golden Doves,* 115.

100. Cf. Maimonides, *Guide,* sec. 1, chap. 33.

101. Ibid., sec. 3, Introduction, p. 297 (line 19).

102. See Faur, *Golden Doves,* 75–76.

103. Maimonides, *Guide,* Introduction, p. 7 (lines 2–6). In this precise sense it was said (*Ḥagiga* 14a), "When he *opens* (*poteaḥ*) with 'the words of the Tora,' all become speechless before him." And "He is one worthy of surrendering to him 'the words of the Tora' which were given in silence." Similarly, ibid.,

13a, "not to surrender 'the words of the Tora' to an alien"; see Faur, *Golden Doves,* 124. On the expression "open" in reference to esoteric exposition see above, p. 195 n. 36. On the expression "before him," see above, p. 25. The "Tora given in silence" refers to the creative silence intrinsic to apophatic knowledge; see *Ḥagiga* 13b, about the celestial beings keeping silent when God speaks. For the same reason "all are speechless" when "before," that is, under the tutelage of, an individual who expounds esoteric teaching.

104. *Ḥagiga* 3b; see *Tosefta Soṭa* 7:11. For parallel sources see *Tosefta Ki-Fshuṭa* ad loc.

105. *Tosefta Ḥagiga* 2:3. There is a fine discussion of the standard views and the variants and further developments of the sources in Urbach, *World of the Sages,* 486–513. Much of the pertinent bibliography may be found in Yehuda Liebes, *Heṭ'o shel Elisha'* (Jerusalem: Academon, 1990).

106. On ben Zoma and ben 'Azai see *Sanhedrin* 17b; *Horayot* 2b; and Maimonides's remark on ben Zoma, Introduction to *Pirush ha-Mishnayot,* vol. 1: 45. Cf. above, p. 195 n. 43.

107. *Ḥagiga* 14b. Cf. *Tosefta Ḥagiga* 2:2. Thus, he was required to obtain divine approval; see *Ḥagiga* 14b.

108. See above, p. 25. Evidence for this is the order in which the paragraph appears. It is the third in a series of seven paragraphs in *Tosefta Ḥagiga* chap. 2, dealing with esoteric instruction. Paragraph 1 stipulates that *Merkaba* studies cannot be taught except to a single qualified student. The principle is substantiated by the story of R. Eleazar ben 'Arakh and his teacher examined above, pp. 24–27. Paragraph 2 contains a list of scholars who, like R. Eleazar ben 'Arakh, submitted (*hirṣa*) their expositions successfully under the tutelage (*lifne*) of their teacher. Paragraph 3 contains the story of the four who entered the orchard and the failure of three of them. Paragraph 4 reports that unlike the others R. 'Aqiba was successful in his exposition of both the prologue and the main dissertation; see below, p. 38ff. Paragraph 5 presents two models that illustrate the specific predicament facing the four. Paragraph 6 describes what happened to one of the three failing scholars. Paragraph 7 establishes the perimeters of esoteric material that could be investigated. Then, it stands to reason that the story in paragraph 3 is the continuation of the initiation process developed in the first paragraph. Specifically, this paragraph deals with the very beginning of the initiation procedure when the student develops the petiḥa. The next four paragraphs explain what happened to each of them. See below, pp. 39–41.

109. Cf. Maimonides, *Mishne Tora, Yesode ha-Tora* 4:13, 7:1.

110. See below, p. 203 n. 129.

111. *Tosefta Ḥagiga* 2:6. In Hebrew the senior first greets the junior with "peace"; see Mishna *Berakhot* 2:1. Concerning whether it is permissible for a disciple to greet the teacher first with "peace", see *Berakhot* 27b; *Yerushalmi Berakhot* 2, 1, 4b; Maran Joseph Caro, *Bet Yosef, Yore De'a* 242 (16); s.v. *ve-lo-yiten shalom;* and the remarks of R. Meir Eisenshmat, *Panim Me'irot*, vol. 1 (Lemberg, 5649/1889), Introduction (n.p.) s.v. *ve-ha-yerushalmi.*

112. *Tosefta Ḥagiga* 2:6. The two senses of the expression *me-'ayin le-'ayin* were preserved in the Arabic of the Jews of Damascus, *min-wen la-wen.* In its primary sense it is addressed to a traveler who has lost his sense of direction and is commonly applied to someone who has lost his sense of judgment. In the *Seder* night this expression is used in its primary sense to show that, contrary to what Pharaoh thought (Ex 14:3), the Israelites had not lost their way in the desert. When reenacting the Exodus from Egypt, each one takes turns to carry the *maṣṣot* while the other participants, pretending to be passersby, ask, *"Min wen ja'e?"* (Where are you coming from?), and he or she responds, *"Mi-Miṣrayim!"* (From Egypt!). This is followed by a second question, *"La-wen rayeḥ?"* (Where are you going to?), and the response, *"Li-Yrushalayim!"* (To Jerusalem!). In this double sense R. Joshua applied the question to ben Zoma. See, however, Lieberman, *Tosefta Ki-Fshuṭa, Mo'ed,* 1292.

113. *Tosefta Ḥagiga* 2:6. Cf. below, p. 204 n. 140.

114. Maimonides, *Guide,* sec. 3, chap. 51, 456 (line 1).

115. Frances Yates, *The Art of Memory* (Chicago: Univ. of Chicago Press, 1966), 3; see Faur, *Golden Doves,* 32–33.

116. See Faur, "Signon ha-Mishna ve-ha-Shinnun be-'al-Pe," *Asupot* 4 (1990): 12–31.

117. *Berakhot* 7a. Likewise, when praying alone, one should face a window opened toward Jerusalem and "imagine" that one is actually standing in that city; see Maimonides, *Teshubot ha-Rambam* 2, no. 216: 381. A mystical vision does not unfold in objective reality but as told in *Megilla* 24b, *be-'ubenta de-libba* (in the intellection of the heart)—something like Robert A. Johnson's "Active Imagination." See Johnson, *Inner Work* (San Francisco, Calif.: Harper, 1986), chap. 3. According to Geonic tradition, the vision of Ismael ben Elisha took place "in the intellection of his heart;" see the *responsum* printed in Faur, *Rabbi Yiśrael Moshe Ḥazzan: The Man and His Works* (in Hebrew) (Haifa: Academic Publishers, 1978), 128. Cf. *Oṣar ha-Ge'onim, Ḥagiga, Ha-Teshubot,* 14. The same applies to the sacramental offering that he is supposed to have presented

at the Temple. *Ruwaḥ ha-Qodesh* does not mean 'holy spirit', but 'the spirit *at* the Sanctuary'. Indeed, the whole notion of "Holy Spirit," "Holy Ghost," and so on, is another instance of Christian influence on Jewish thought and lack of regard for elemental Hebrew Grammar. There is a basic difference between *qodesh* and *qadosh*. *Qadosh* is an adjective, 'holy'. *Qodesh* is a noun. It does *not* mean 'holy' (*qadosh*) but 'Sanctuary'. It refers to the spirit residing at the Sanctuary reaching the faithful *outside* the Sanctuary. See Ps 20:3, the Aramaic version and the commentaries of Rashi and ibn 'Ezra ad loc.; cf. ibid. 51:13; 93:5. God's light, too, comes from the Temple at Jerusalem; see *Bereshit Rabba* 3, 4, vol. 1, p. 20; *Vayyiqra Rabba* 31, 7, vol. 4:726. Accordingly, *ruwaḥ ha-qodesh* parallels the expression *leshon ha-qodesh*, meaning 'the language spoken at the Sanctuary'; see Faur, *Golden Doves*, xx. Therefore, as indicated by Maimonides, *Mishne Tora, Yesode ha-Tora* 7:1, upon entering the "orchard" the *Ruwaḥ ha-Qodesh* will immediately descend on him." The *Hekhalot* in Jewish Gnostic literature, too, refer to the Temple. On the relation between the *Hekhalot* and *Merkaba* literature and the tradition of the Temple in Jerusalem see the very erudite and illuminating article by Rachel Elior, "From Earthly Temple to Heavenly Shrine" (in Hebrew), *Tarbiz* 64 (1995): 341–80. R. Judah ha-Levi was privy to this tradition. The following poem in *Selected Poems of Jehudah Halevi*, ed. Heinrich Brody and trans. Nina Salaman (Philadelphia: Jewish Publication Society, 1924), no. 4, p. 9, alludes to this type of experience, [occasionally, when the original warranted or for the sake of clarity I departed from the English translation]:

> "My God, Thy dwelling-places are lovesome! / Your nearness is lucid, not in riddles.
>
> My dream brought me into the sanctuaries of God, / and [there] I did sing His exquisite services:
>
> The burnt-offering, the meal-offering, and the drink offering. / Round-about there were heavy clouds of smoke.
>
> I was in ecstasy upon hearing the Levites' songs, / being in their midst, in the array of their services.
>
> I awoke. I am still with You, O God! / I thanked, and to You it is fitting to thank!"

118. About the Temple's upper chamber it was said, "I saw those who inhabit the upper chamber" (*bene 'aliya*), and they are few," *Sukka* 45b. Its

function is similar to the "crack in the rock" (Ex 33:22) protecting Moses; see Maimonides, *Guide,* sec. 1, chap. 21; and *Pesaḥim* 54a; the cave protecting Elijah, see 1 Kgs 19:9; and the cave of R. Simon bar Yoḥai, *Shabbat* 33b; cf. *Sanhedrin* 98a. Hence, the warning against those who expound about "what is above," see Mishna *Ḥagiga* 2:1 and *Tosefta Ḥagiga* 2:7. Maimonides associated this expression with someone who goes "above" the boundaries of his own intellectual capacities; see *Guide,* sec. 1, chap. 32.

119. Mishna *Middot* 4:5. On the connection between the *lul* and the *'aliya* see *Tosefta Baba Batra* 1:4, *Tosefta Neziqin,* 130; and Lieberman, *Tosefta Ki-Fshuṭa,* ad loc., vol. 2:333. The verb *le-haṣṣiṣ* 'to peek' may be used to mean 'from above.' Cf. *Tosefta Baba Batra* 1:5, *Tosefta Neziqin,* 130; Lieberman, *Tosefta Ki-Fshuṭa,* ad loc., vol. 2:334; and *Baba Batra* 3a. In this sense it is used in the context here to denote "glancing on the way down." There is a reference to the Temple's upper chamber in Mt 4:5 and Lk 4:9 where it is said that Satan took Jesus to the upper chamber at the Temple (*tò pertúgion tou hieron*) and tempted him to cast himself down. Because the specific function of this upper chamber was not adequately understood, the translators and commentators failed to grasp the precise meaning of this passage and rendered it "pinnacle of the temple." Its precise sense was preserved in *The Polemic of Nestor the Priest,* ed. Daniel J. Lasker and Sarah Stroumsa, 2 vols. (Jerusalem: Ben-Zvi Institute, 1996). In the Arabic version, vol. 2, no. 143, p. 76, the above passage was rendered *ajaãr il-haikhal* 'the roof of the Temple'. The term *ajaãr* is an Arabization of the Aramaic *agara* 'roof'. Like the Greek *pertúgion, ajaãr* may also stand for 'a structure built on the roof,' that is, an 'aliya or upper chamber. The second term, *haikhal,* is an Arabization of the Hebrew *hekhal.* Unlike its Arabic cognate, however, the Hebrew means not only 'palace' but also 'Temple', particularly the Temple in Jerusalem. Accordingly, *hieron* must be understood in its usual sense of 'temple', 'sanctuary', rather than as 'the outer wall of the precinct of the Temple' as proposed by the commentators, ad loc. The incident refers to Jesus's attempt mentally to enter the inner Sanctuary and to gain access to Jewish esoteric knowledge. The usual interpretation, that Satan challenged Jesus to throw himself down the roof, makes little sense. Rather, Satan was challenging him to *descend* from the upper chamber down the trap to the Sanctuary. The temptation (his supreme temptation according to Lk 4:9) is the temptation luring all those daring to come down to the inner Sanctuary via the trap at the Temple's upper chamber to take a peek at the Divine Presence and to "delight (*lazun*) their eyes from Him." Properly, Jesus refused to descend. Thus, unlike the other three

scholars, Jesus did not meet a tragic end on his way down. See below, pp. 38–41.

120. See Mishna *Ohalot* 13:4; *Tosefta Ohelot* 14:4.

121. *Sifre* (*Bamidbar*), ed. M. Friedman (Vienna, 1864), no. 115, p. 126. On the association *zenut* (whoring)/ *minut* (heresy), see *Berakhot* 12b. The Hebrew noun *min* means both 'heretic' and 'sex'. The sexual pleasure indicated by this expression is purely mental, involving no action, see *Yebamot* 61a. Thus, it affects the soul *directly* and requires *kappara* 'expiation', in the Hebrew sense of 'cleansing' (cf. below, p. 239 n. 145); see *Shabbat* 64a–b; Maimonides, *Guide*, sec. 3, chap. 8.

122. See Kristeva, *Powers of Horror*, 45; Faur, *In the Shadow of History*, 6–7.

123. *Vayyiqra Rabba* 23, 13, vol. 3, p. 548.

124. Ibid., xx, 10, vol. 2, p. 466.

125. Ibid., 466–67. They did not marry; see below, p. 204 n. 141, and p. 218 n. 194. Since those who maintain proper sexual conduct become the location of the *Shekhina*, they are designated *mal'akhe ha-sharet* (ministering angels); see *Nedarim* 20b. Cf. below, p. 174.

126. Maimonides, *Guide*, sec. 2, chap. 40, p. 272 (lines 1–15); *Mishne Tora*, *De'ot* 7:1. The source indicated by Maimonides is *Sanhedrin* 89a. This was the reason why Judaism rejected the view that Jesus (and Mohammed) had been privy to divine revelation; see the uncensored editions, *Sanhedrin* 107b. See, however, the analysis of R. Travers Herford, *Christianity in Talmud and Midrash* (London: William and Norgate, 1903), 50–54, showing that this passage is chronologically impossible. Maimonides used the expression *laḏḏathu* (*his* delights), *Guide*, sec. 1, chap. 2, p. 17 (line 16), to indicate narcissistic pleasure in contradistinction with *laḏḏat* (pleasure); ibid. (line 15).

127. *Mishne Tora, De'ot* 4:14. This term refers to a mental kind of parading, as in *Sanhedrin* 102a, where David is said to be marching by the side of God in paradise, see above, p. 200 n. 117. In accordance with Geonic tradition Maimonides associated *pardes* with paradise; see *Oṣar ha-Ge'onim*, *Ḥagiga*, 61; R. Ḥanan'el on *Ḥagiga* 14b. Cf. however, Urbach, *World of the Sages*, 498.

128. *Tosefta Ḥagiga* 2:4.

129. See above, p. 36. This reading was preserved in *Yerushalmi Ḥagiga* 1, 2, 77b ; in the margin of the Erfut ms., critical apparatus, line 21, *Tosefta Ḥagiga* 2:4; and in Maionides, *Guide*, sec. 1, chap. 32, p. 46 (line 10). The standard reading *'ala* in the *Tosefta* is a transposition from paragraph 3, line 17, where it is said that R. 'Aqiba "went up" ('ala). There it means that "he went up" to the "upper chamber" (*'aliya*) mentioned in paragraph 5; see preceding n. 128. The copyist

mistook it as a reference to the orchard and, therefore, corrected paragraph 5 in the standard editions to read *'ala* instead of *nikhnas.* Concerning the actual topic of R. 'Aqiba's dissertation, *Ḥagiga* 15b–16q, has preserved four traditions. Possibly, it comprised all these topics, but each rabbi reported a single aspect.

130. There is disagreement as to who died and who lost his mind; see Lieberman, *Tosefta Ki-Fshuṭa*, 1289. On the meaning of 'losing the mind' see the brilliant note of Lieberman, *"Yaṣa le-'Olamo," Ginze Kedem* 5 (1934): 177–79.

131. *Ḥagiga* 14b; *Oṣar ha-Ge'onim, Ḥagiga, Ha-Teshubot,* 14. A similar view was held by Maimonides; see *Guide,* sec. 1, chap. 34, p. 50 (lines 26–27).

132. This is the correct reading; see critical apparatus ad loc., and Lieberman, *Tosefta Kifshuṭa, Mo'ed,* 1291.

133. *Sifre* no. 355, pp. 422–23.

134. *Abot de-R. Natan,* 33, B, p. 72. See Lieberman, *Tosefta Ki-Fshuṭa,* 1291.

135. See Maimonides, *Guide,* sec. 2, chap. 30, pp. 247 (line 4)–48 (line 7).

136. *Ḥagiga* 14b.

137. See Maimonides, *Guide,* sec. 2, chap. 30, pp. 247 (line 4)–48 (line 7).

138. *Yerushalmi Ḥagiga* 2, 1, 77c. Cf. *Ta'aniyot* 10a; *Bereshit Rabba* 4, 2, vol. 1, p. 27.

139. *Baba Batra* 4a.

140. *Tosefta Ḥagiga* 2:6. This is Maimonides's reading; see *Guide,* sec. 3, chap. 51, p. 456 (line 1), and the standard version in *Ḥagiga* 15a. In the *Tosefta* and in a *responsum* by Hayye Ga'on, *Oṣar ha–Ge'onim, Ḥagiga,* p. 15, the reading is *kebar* 'he is already', implying that before he had been inside and that only now he went outside. The expression *ba-huṣ* comes from the Greek; see David Daube, "Ecstasy in a Statement by Rabbi Joshua ben Hanina," in *Collected Works of David Daube,* ed. Calum M. Carmichael, vol. 1 (Berkeley and Los Angeles: Univ. of California Press, 1992), 455–58. It may have been intended as a criticism, implying that his demeanor did not conform to Jewish mystical practice; cf. above, pp. 36–37.

141. See *Vayyiqra Rabba* 23, 3, vol. 2, p. 530. It is worth recalling that ben Zoma never married; see above, p. 195 n. 43, and p. 203 n. 125.

142. Maimonides, *Guide,* sec. 1, chap. 32, p. 46 (lines 18–19). Cf. below, p. 48

143. *Tosefta Ḥagiga* 2:3. On the fault of Elisha see below, p. 51.

144. See above, p. 36. On the conceptual relation of 'planting' to 'text' and 'studying' see Faur, *Golden Doves,* 183 n. 58.

145. See *Ḥagiga* 15a. Cf. below, p. 43.

146. *Tosefta Ḥagiga* 2:5.

147. Ibid.

148. *Ḥagiga* 2, 1, 77a.

149. Cited in R. Menaḥem Me'iri, *Pirush ha-Me'iri le-Sefer Mishle* (*Commentary to Proverbs*) (Jerusalem: Hoṣa'at ha-Posqim, 5729/1969), ad loc., 267. This passage further elaborates but, contrary to the editor's note ad loc., does not come from the *Yerushalmi Ḥagiga* cited above but, as indicated by R. Me'iri, from a *derash*.

150. R. Menaḥem Me'iri identified the "right" and "left" roads with "faulty perception" (*shibbush ha-haśaga*) caused by either too much or too little knowledge. See his *Pirush ha-Me'iri le-Sefer Mishle,* (Commentary to Proverbs), ad loc.

151. Maimonides, *Guide,* sec. 1, chap. 71, p. 121 (lines 25–27); cf. sec. 1, chap. 70, 120 (lines 4–8); sec. 2, chap. 29, p. 244 (lines 7–9). See Faur, *Studies in the Mishne Tora,* 191–93.

152. Maimonides, *Guide,* sec. 1, chap. 70, p. 120 (lines 4–8).

153. Ibid. sec. 2, chap. 29, p. 244 (lines 7–10).

154. Maimonides, *Pirush ha-Mishnayot, Sanhedrin* 10:1, vol. 4, 209.

155. See Maimonides, *Guide,* Introduction, p. 9 (lines 15–16) and p. 4 (lines 21–22).

156. See ibid., p. 5 (line 18)–6 (line 7).

157. Ibid., p. 6 (lines 5–6).

158. Ibid., p. 4 (lines 17–18).

159. Maimonides, *Treatise on Resurrection,* Arabic text, 4.

160. See Maimonides, *Guide,* sec. 2, chap. 29, p. 244 (lines 10–11).

161. See Maimonides, *Pirush ha-Mishnayot, Ḥagiga* 2:1, vol. 2, p. 377, where the problem of attributes is related to *Merkaba* studies, cf. Maimonides, *Guide,* sec. 1, chap. 70.

162. Maimonides, *Guide,* sec. 1, chap. 35, 54 (lines 20–28).

163. So it was with much of the mystical experience narrated by the *alumbrados* in the sixteenth and seventeenth centuries, both Jewish and non-Jewish. See above, pp. 37–38.

164. See *Yerushalmi Ḥagiga* 2, 1, 77b–c; cf. *Ḥagiga* 15a–b. In *Ḥagiga* 15a belief in "two authorities" is explicitly attributed to Elisha ben Abuya. As with Paul, this type of antinomism is a theological strategy designed to "cut the plants" and to gain direct access to the king. Cf. Morton Smith, "The Reason for the Persecution of Paul and the Obscurity of Acts," in *Studies in Mysticism and Religion Presented in Honor of Gershom G. Scholem* (Jerusalem: Magnes Press, 1967), 261–68. Cf. above, p. 204 n. 145.

165. Mishna *Ḥagiga* 2:1.

166. *Tosefta Ḥagiga* 2:1, quoted above, pp. 26–27.

167. Maimonides, *Guide,* sec. 1, chap. 32, p. 47 (lines 8–11). Here Maimonides was alluding to Elisha, whom Maimonides regarded as a sage who had attempted to understand more than he could; see above, p. 204 n. 142.

168. *Yerushlami Ḥagiga* 2, 1, 77c; see *Bereshit Rabba* 1, 5, vol. 1, pp. 2–3. The correct version is *ki-mga'e* from the root *ge'e.* On the relation of this term to the *Merkaba* see Maimonides, *Guide,* sec. 1, chap. 70, pp. 120 (line 26)–21 (line 4). Cf. the rabbinic expression cited in *The World of the Sages,* 511, *ṣippita be-ga'ava.* On this theme see *Ḥagiga* 13b where the *ge'e* is associated with the semblance of man in the *Merkaba.*

169. *Yerushalmi Berakhot* 9, 1, 11d.

170. Maimonides, *Guide,* sec. 1, chap. 52, p. 79 (lines 21–22); see ibid., 79 (line 22)–80 (line 15).

171. Maimonides, *Guide,* sec. 1, chap. 59, p. 94 (lines 27–28); cf. ibid., 97 (lines 18–19), and end of 53.

172. See above pp. 37–38.

173. See Maimonides, *Guide,* sec. 1, chap. 54, p. 83 (line 27)–84 (line 20). On the sense of *tanzil* see the valuable comment of Solomon Munk in his translation, *Le Guide des Égarés,* 3 vols. (Paris: Editions G. P. Maisonneuve, 1960), 1:206 n. 1.

174. See Munk, *Le Guide des Égarés,* 1:188 n. 5.

175. Maimonides, *Guide,* sec. 1, chap. 51, p. 77 (lines 12–14).

176. A quotation from a lost rabbinic source, codified by Maimonides, *Mishne Tora, De'ot* 6:3, *Teshuba* 3:14.

177. *Yerushalmi Ḥagiga* 2, 1, 77c. See *Bereshit Rabba* 1, 5, vol. 1, pp. 2–3.

178. Maimonides, *Guide,* sec. 1, chap. 59, pp. 96 (lines 25)–97 (line 4).

179. *Ḥagiga* 16a.

180. See above, p. 205 n. 164.

181. *Shabbat* 33a.

182. Maimonides, *Guide,* sec. 3, chap. 8, p. 313 (lines 3–10). This coincides with the explanation given by Maimonides in his youth; see Maimonides, *Pirush ha-Mishnayot, Ḥagiga* 2:1, vol. 2, p. 378.

183. *Ḥagiga* 13a.

184. *Mo'ed Qaṭan* 5a; *Soṭa* 5b. See *Shemona Peraqim* 4, in Maimonides, *Pirush ha-Mishnayot*, vol. 4:387.

185. *Soṭa* 21a. Cf. below, p. 208 n. 206.

186. See p. 6 (lines 10–12); and sec. 1, chap. 35.

187. See ibid., sec. 3, Introduction, p. 298 (line 6).

188. Ibid., Introduction, p. 3 (lines 12–14).

189. Ibid., p. 9 (line 26)–10 (line 2).

190. My son, R. Abraham Faur, pointed out to me that the source for this idea is the story with Minyamin Sasqana'a in *Nidda* 65a.

191. Maimonides, *Guide*, Introduction, p. 10 (lines 2–4).

192. See above, pp. 25–26 n. 38.

193. The same technique was used by the rabbis; see Maimonides, *Guide*, sec. 2, chap. 29, p. 244 (lines 7–8).

194. *Oṣar ha-Ge'onim, Ḥagiga*, 23. See above, p. 196 n. 58; and Maimonides, *Guide*, sec. 2, chap. 29, p. 244 (lines 7–11).

195. On this fundamental concept see Faur, *Golden Doves*, xxvii–xxviii, 216.

196. The same technique was used by the rabbis; see above, n. 193.

197. See Faur, *Golden Doves*, 75–76.

198. See R. Nathan bar Yeḥiel, *'Arukh-Aruch Completum*, ed. Alexander Kohut, 8 vols. (Vienna: Menora, 1926), vol. 5, s.v. *miṭaṭor* p. 110 ff. For a discussion of this term see Saul Lieberman, "Metatron, the Meaning of His Name and His Functions," in *Apocalyptic and Medieval Mysticism* by I. Gruenwald (Leiden: Brill, 1980), 235–41.

199. See Faur, *Golden Doves*, xix, 72–73. Thus, God's light comes from His stole, which He uses to *cover* Himself; see *Bereshit Rabba* 3, 4, vol. 1, p. 20.

200. See below, p. 77.

201. *Sanhedrin* 38b. The first explanation reads *ke-farvanqa* 'as a letter carrier'; the second explanation reads *be-farvanqa* 'with an epistle', that is, with an official credential attesting to his mission. There is a fine discussion of this passage in Herford, *Christianity in Talmud and Midrash*, 285–90.

202. *Ḥagiga* 15a.

203. See ibid., 16a–b. For some valuable remarks on the Talmudic story of Elisha, see R. Travers Herford, "Elisha ben Abujah," In *Essays in Honour of the Very Rev. Dr. J. Hertz* (London: Edward Goldston, ca. 1942), 215–25.

204. *Berakhot* 58a. Concerning the "silent voice," R. Levi ben Gereshom (1288–1344) explained, "It is a voice composed of sound and silence." See his commentary ad loc., the Aramaic version of Jonathan ben 'Uzziel, and Jb 4:16. This is exactly how the rabbis interpreted the term *ḥashmal* (Ez 1:4); see *Ḥagiga* 13b; R. Ḥanan'el ad loc.; and Maimonides, *Guide*, sec. 3, chap. 7, p. 309 (lines 3–4).

205. *Ḥagiga* 16a. For an interpretation of this passage see Faur, *Golden Doves*, 83. R. Sheshat had access to the teachings of R. Johanan via R. Amme; see *Oṣar ha-Ge'onim, Ketubot, (Ha-Teshubot)*, 56.

206. *Berakhot* 28b. This story should be read in conjunction with the passage in *Soṭa* 21a stating that death itself is a crossroad. Cf. above, p. 206 n. 185.

207. Jorge Luis Borges, "Labyrinths," in *In Praise of Darkness,* trans. Norman di Giovanni (New York: Dutton, 1974), 39.

208. On this fundamental concept and the precise sense of *dalala* see Faur, *Golden Doves,* 74–76.

PART TWO: IMAGINATION

1. See Maimonides, *Mishne Tora, Yesode ha-Tora* 7:1; idem, *Guide,* sec. 2, chap. 32; sec. 3, chap. 45.

2. See Maimonides, *Guide,* sec. 3, chap. 9; cf. sec. 1, chap. 21, p. 33 (lines 7–8). Cf. Joseph ben Judah ibn 'Aqnin, *Hitgallut ha-Sodot,* ed. and trans. Abraham Halkin (Jerusalem: Mekize Nirdamim, 1964), 114–16, cf. 43, 94.

3. *Soṭa* 21a, see *Pesaḥim* 2b; *Ḥagiga* 12b; *Baba Meṣi'a* 83b; *Yerushalmi Ḥagiga* 2, 1.

4. See above, p. 197 n. 76.

5. *Ḥagiga* 12b–13a. Cf. Maimonides, *Guide,* sec. 3, chap. 9.

6. See commentary of R. Ḥanan'el on *Ḥagiga* 13b. This implies successive synthesis; see Faur, *Golden Doves,* 32–37.

7. Maimonides, *Guide,* Introduction, p. 3 (line 27)–4 (line 5).

8. See below, p. 74.

9. *Ḥagiga* 12a.

10. On the "mystical light" see Mircea Eliade, "Spirit, Light, and Seed," in *Occultism Witchcraft and Cultural Fashions,* by Mircea Eliade (Chicago: Univ. of Chicago Press, 1978), 93–119.

11. See Faur, *Golden Doves,* 23–24.

12. See Maimonides, *Guide,* sec. 1, chap. 19.

13. See ibid., sec. 2, chap. 12, pp. 194 (line 19)–95 (line 8). On the symbolism of "light," "cloud," and "dense fog" in the Scripture and their relation to the pillars of "cloud" and "fire" see the very valuable comments of R. Isaac Abarbanel, in *Pirush Nebi'im Rishonim* (Commentary to the early prophets) (Pesaro, 528011520) on 1 Kgs 8:65.

14. *Berakhot* 33a. Likewise the rabbis *(Vayyiqra Rabba,* 1, 6, vol. 1, pp. 18–19) taught, "If you had acquired intelligence, you are missing nothing; and if you are missing intelligence, you have acquired nothing." The source for this idea is Prv 20:15; see *Teshubot ha-Ge'onim ha-Ḥadashot,* no. 41, p. 42. On the designation *ot* 'sign'

for God see Faur, *Golden Doves,* 83. Cf. R. Joseph ben Judah ibn 'Aqnin, *Hitgallut ha-Sodot,* ed. and trans. Abraham Halkin (Jesusalem: Mekize Nirdamim, 1964). 10–12.

15. *Berakhot* 33a.

16. Ibid.

17. Cf. Faur, *Golden Doves,* xxiv–xxv.

18. Maimonides, *Guide,* sec. 3, chap. 51, p. 460 (lines 19–20).

19. Ibid., p. 456 (lines 24–27).

20. Ibid., p. 460 (lines 20–21).

21. Ibid., p. 461 (line 7).

22. Ibid., (lines 7–8).

23. Ibid., (lines 11–17). Hence the expression *al-maḥjubun 'an Alla* 'those who are fenced away from God' (ibid., sec. 3, chap. 8, p. 311 (line 19).

24. See below, pp. 128–29.

25. See Maimonides, *Guide,* sec. 1, chap. 60.

26. See ibid., chap. 58.

27. Maimonides, *Mishne Tora, Yesode ha-Tora* 7:1.

28. Maimonides, *Guide,* sec. 1, chap. 60, p. 99 (lines 25–28).

29. Ibid., p. 100 (lines 7–8).

30. Ibid., (lines 4–6).

31. Leone Ebreo, *Dialoghi d'amore* [1], 10. This subject was developed by Miguel de Cervantes, *Don Quijote,* ed. Fernandez de Avel (Madrid: Espasa-Calpe, 1984) 1, 7, one of many chapters with anti-Christian subtexts.

32. Maimonides, *Guide,* sec. 1, chap. 59, p. 97 (line 19); cf. chaps. 26, 51; and sources indicated above, p. 206 n. 171.

33. Maimonides, *Guide,* sec. 1, chap. 50.

34. Ibid., chap. 60, p. 99 (lines 10–12). As noted by Maimonides (ibid., lines 5–6), it would be improper "to refer to God with positive attributes, to exalt Him in your fancy."

35. See ibid., chap. 36, p. 57 (line 22); chap. 72, p. 134 (lines 16–20); sec. 3, chap. 51, p. 455 (lines 21–23).

36. On this phenomenon in human psychology see Silvano Arieti, *Creativity the Magic Synthesis* (New York: Basic Books, 1976), 107.

37. Maimonides, *Guide,* sec. 3, chap. 51, p. 456 (lines 19–24); cf. ibid., chap. 23, p. 357 (lines 5–19).

38. Ibid., sec. 1, chap. 26, p. 37 (line 24).

39. Ibid., p. 38 (lines 8–9); cf. ibid., Introduction, p. 12 (line 11).

40. Maimonides, *Guide,* sec. 1, chap. 17, p. 29 (lines 15–17).

41. This is the cause for the fifth type of contradictions; see *Guide,* Introduction, p. 11 (lines 19–26). Cf. above, p. 198 n. 95.

42. On the function of key-symbols see Faur, *Golden Doves,* 2–4.

43. Maimonides, *Guide,* Introduction, p. 4 (lines 9–12).

44. See below, p. 62ff.

45. The connection between "snake/ divination/ imagination" was made by the standard commentators in the Hebrew version of the *Guide, More ha-Nebukhim;* see Rabbis Shem Ṭob and Efodi on Maimonides, *Guide,* sec. 2, chap. 30.

46. Vico, *New Science,* no. 398, p. 125.

47. See J. S. Kasanin, "Disturbance of Conceptual Thinking in Schizophrenia," in *Language and Thought in Schizophrenia,* ed. J. S. Kasanin (Berkeley and Los Angeles: Univ. of California Press, 1944), 41–42.

48. See Eliade, *Myth and Reality,* 156. Accordingly, ugly and corpulent women are perceived by the travelers to "paradisical islands" as perfect beauties; see idem, *Images and Symbols,* 12.

49. See Lüdwig Wittgenstein, *Philosophical Investigations,* trans. G. E. M. Anscombe (New York: Macmillan, 1968), 2, xi, 193e–229e. There is a fine discussion of Wittgenstein's view by Mary Warnock, *Imagination* (Berkeley and Los Angeles: Univ. of California Press, 1976), 183–95; cf. ibid., 156–61. For a psychological analysis of this type of association see Silvano Arieti, *The Intrapsychic Self* (New York: Basic Books, 1976), 184–88. Conceptually, the as corresponds to the semantic context, which cannot be said but only indicated by words, discussed above, p. 6.

50. Before sinning Adam's language consisted of what Wittgenstein designates "elementary propositions," that is propositions that do not derive their sense from other propositions. Like names (see Gn 2:13), this type of proposition is absolutely simple and cannot be subjected to linguistic analysis. The different elements of the proposition are logically constructed and connected; see Gn 2:23–24.

51. The Hebrew particle *ve-khi* means 'since', thus inverting the relation between the two segments of the sentence.

52. See Vico, *New Science,* no. 398, p. 125.

53. Arieti, *Intrapsychic Self,* 121.

54. This expression brings to mind the rabbinic expression "delight his eyes," discussed above, pp. 37–38.

55. Maimonides, *Guide,* sec. 1, chap. 2, p. 17 (lines 11–20).

56. Maimonides, *Guide,* sec. 1, chap. 2, p. 16 (line 26). Cf. quotation below, p. 63.

57. For an in-depth analysis of this fundamental concept in Vico see John D. Schaeffer, *Sensus Communis* (Durham, N.C.: Duke Univ. Press, 1990). I have examined this concept Faur, "Basic Concepts in Rabbinic Hermeneutics," *Shofar* 16 (1997): 1–12. The binary system good/bad originated in a primary split of the *logos;* see Faur, "The Splitting of the *Logos,*" 85–103.

58. Maimonides, *Guide,* sec. 2, chap. 15, p. 202 (lines 21–23). Cf. Aristotle, *Analytica Posteriora,* 1, 6, 74b in *The Complete Works of Aristotle,* ed. Jonathan Barnes (Princeton, N.J.: Princeton Univ. Press), 1986. This underlies Sánchez's epistemology and his criticism of the scholastic concept of *authoritas;* see Faur, "Sánchez' Critique of *Authoritas*: *Converso* Skepticism and the Emergence of Radical Hermeneutics," in *The Return to Scripture in Judaism and Christianity,* ed. Peter Ochs, (Mahwah, N. Y.: Paulist Press, 1993), 256–76.

59. Baroja, *Camino de Perfección,* chap. 23, p. 100. See above, Introduction, p. 9.

60. Maimonides, *Guide,* sec. 2, chap. 30, p. 250 (lines 10–19); see the commentaries of Efodi, Shem Ṭob, and Crescas ad loc.

61. See ibid., sec. 3, chap. 22; and sec. 2, chap. 12, p. 195 (lines 15–17)]. Cf. above, pp. 11–12, and below, pp. 137–38.

62. Cf. Maimonides, *Guide,* sec. 3, chap. 8, p. 312 (line 3ff.).

63. Ibid., sec. 1, chap. 73, p. 146 (lines 28–29).

64. Ibid., pp. 146 (line 39)–47 (line 17).

65. On paleologic thinking see Arieti, *Creativity,* chap. 5; on the role of imagination see ibid., 75. For further material see his bibliographical note on p. 67.

66. Maimonides, *Guide,* sec. 1, chap. 2, pp. 17 (line 30)–18 (line 1).

67. Ibid., pp. 16 (line 26)–17 (line 7).

68. See Lucien Lévy-Bruhl, *The Notebooks on Primitive Mentality,* trans. Peter Riviere (New York: Harper and Row, 1978), 5, 6, 13. At this stage it is not possible to distinguish between semantic memory and experiential memory. On these two type of memories see Daniel L. Schacter, *Searching for Memory* (New York: Basic Books, 1996), 150–53.

69. *Guide,* 73, p. 144 (line 17). For a discussion of this theory see Harry A. Wolfson, *The Philosophy of the Kalam* (Cambridge, Mass.: 1976), 544–58.

70. See below, pp. 95–96.

71. See the brilliant remarks of the Hebrew grammarian R. Jonah ibn Jannaḥ, *Sefer ha-Riqma,* ed. M. Wilensky (Jerusalem: Ha-Aqademya lil-Shon ha-'Ibrit, 5724/1964), 22. This term is related to the Hebrew preposition *kan* 'here'.

72. Cf. Silvano Arieti, "Some Basic Problems Common to Anthropology and Modern Psychiatry," *American Anthropologist* 58 (1956): 27.

73. See Faur, *Golden Doves*, xxiv, 30–35.

74. Sylvano Arieti, "Primitive Intellectual Mechanisms in Psycho-Pathological Conditions," *American Journal of Psychotherapy* 4 (1950): 12.

75. Maimonides, *Guide*, sec. 1, chap. 73, p. 144 (line 4).

76. Ibid., p. 145 (lines 1–5).

77. Ibid., p. 144 (lines 8–12).

78. Ibid., (lines 15–23).

79. Ibid., (lines 5–7).

80. Ibid., sec. 1, chap. 2, p. 15 (lines 24–27).

81. See below, p. 215 n. 142. For a thorough discussion of this term see Umberto Cassuto, "The Episode of the Sons of God and the Daughters of Man," (in Hebrew) *Biblical and Canaanite Literatures*, vol. 1 (Jerusalem: Magness Univ. Press, 1972), 98–107. Cassuto believed that 'angels', 'divine beings', are correct, whereas the rabbinic rendition, 'judges', 'political leaders', was polemical, designed to rebuff Christological interpretations. This view overlooks the fact that in the ancient world kings and political leaders were gods; see below, n. 82. The Maimonidean / rabbinic interpretation reflects the early state of primitive humans when kings were gods.

82. On this theme see Henry Frankfort, *Kingship and the Gods* (Chicago: Univ. of Chicago Press, 1948).

83. Maimonides, *Guide*, sec. 1, chap. 73, p. 146 (line 14).

84. See ibid., sec. 2, chap. 36, pp. 260 (line 26)–61 (line 2), 263 (line 8); cf. chap. 32, p. 253 (line 25); sec. 3, chap. 49, p. 448 (lines 18–19).

85. Ibid., sec. 1, chap. 73, p. 146 (lines 12–14); sec. 2, Introduction, p. 168 (line 15).

86. Ibid., sec. 3, chap. 48, p. 440 (lines 15–17); cf. chap. 49, p. 448 (lines 20–28).

87. Ibid., sec. 2, chap. 36, p. 261 (lines 6–8).

88. Ibid., chap. 12, p. 195 (lines 8–9).

89. They are the constitutional laws of the state; see below, p. 165. On the political character of the *nomoi* see Maimonides, *Treatise on Logic*, ed. and trans. Israel Efros (New York: American Academy for Jewish Research, 1938), ibn Tibbon's version, 14, p. 63. The same term appears in the original Arabic, see Israel Efros, "Maimonides, Treatise on Logic," *Proceedings of American Academy for Jewish Research* 34 (1966): 14, 41.

90. Maimonides, *Guide*, sec. 2, chap. 37, p. 264 (lines 15–20). See below, p. 165. Concerning the dreamers of "accurate dreams," cf. Maimonides, *Guide*, sec. 2, chap. 45, p. 282 (lines 16–17). On the difference between "accurate dreams" and prophecy see ibid., pp. 284 (line 2)–85 (line 3), and below, p. 74ff.

91. Maimonides, *Guide*, sec. 2, chap. 40, p. 271 (lines 17–24).

92. See ibid., sec. 1, chap. 36, p. 57 (lines 21–22); sec. 3, chap. 29, p. 377 (lines 2–3); cf. sec. 1, chap. 36, p. 56 (lines 20–21); sec. 3, chap. 37, p. 397 (lines 4–7).

93. See above, pp. 63–65.

94. See Maimonides, *Guide*, sec. 2, chap. 59, p. 96 (lines 20–22); cf. sec. 3, chap. 8, p. 313 (lines 10–22); chap. 12, p. 318 (lines 9–12).

95. See Maimonides, *Sefer ha-Miṣvot*, 5. On the status of the *fuqaha* see idem, *Guide*, sec. 3, chap. 51, p. 455 (lines 21–23).

96. See *Teshubot ha-Rambam*, vol. 2, no. 180, p. 328; no. 207, pp. 365–66; no. 208, p. 369; no. 254, pp. 467–68.

97. See ibid., no. 261, pp. 490–91. The authority for this distinction is the Yerushalmi as cited and explained by R. Nissim Ga'on, *Sefer ha-Mafteaḥ* ed. J. Goldenthol (Vienna, 1947),on *Berakhot* 33b.

98. This means that Maimonides would have objected to some of the poetry current in the Sephardic liturgy, but not necessarily to the hymns in the Ashkenazic liturgy.

99. See Maimonides, *Guide*, sec. 1, chap. 74, p. 150 (lines 10–20). In this context, it is worth considering the fact that after 1916 Juan Ramón Jiménez, one of the most accomplished poets of modern times, went through a process of *depuración* (purification) and abandoned rhyme, fixed meter, and other poetic paraphernalia to write free verse. As with biblical poetry, the *piyuṭim*, and hymns in Ashkenazic liturgy.

100. See Ernst Cassirer, *The Philosophy of Symbolic Forms*, trans. Ralph Manheim, vol. 2, *Mythical Thought* (New Haven, Conn.: Yale Univ. Press, 1955); Georges Gudsorf, *Myth et métaphysique* (Paris: Flammarion, 1953).

101. E. Von Domarus, "The Specific Laws of Logic in Schizophrenia," in *Language and Thought in Schizophrenia*, ed. J. S. Kasanin (Berkeley and Los Angeles: Univ. of California Press, 1944), 110–111.

102. Arieti, *Creativity*, 70.

103. Ibid., 71.

104. Claude Lévi-Strauss, *The Savage Mind* (Chicago: Univ. of Chicago Press, 1970), 35.

105. Arieti, "Basic Problems" 27. Racism operates on the same principle

whereby identity is established on the basis of a predicate—skin pigmentation—rather than on the basis of subject or person.

106. See Faur, *Golden Doves,* 1–3, 27–29.

107. *Yerushalmi Bikkurim* 3, 3, 65d. The standard interpretation, that the judges in question had paid off the authorities to be appointed, misses the point. The purpose of this passage is to propose the principle that if someone had been appointed judge because of his wealth, that is, on the basis of pure semiotics, the appointment is invalid, regardless of his qualification. This coincides with another rabbinic principle establishing that if an animal exhibiting the signs of an impure animal were born from a pure animal, the animal would be pure (and vice versa); see Mishna *Bekhorot* 1:4. Similarly, a pure animal that had lost its split hoofs (e.g., the bases of its legs had been removed), is regarded as pure; see Maimonides, *Mishne Tora, Ma'akhalot Asurot* 1:3–7.

108. Maimonides, *Guide,* sec. 1, chap. 73. p. 146 (lines 14–15).

109. See Jean-Paul Sartre, *The Psychology of Imagination* (New York: Philosophical Library, 1948), 10.

110. Maimonides, *Guide,* sec. 1, chap. 71, p. 123 (lines 29–30). See below, p. 91ff. Cf. below, p. 80.

111. Maimonides, *Guide,* sec. 1, chap. 73, p. 146 (lines 15–16).

112. On the precise connotation of *ma'na, ma'ani* see Faur, *Golden Doves,* 69–76, 79–81.

113. Maimonides, *Guide,* sec. 1, chap. 73, p. 146 (lines 15–16).

114. See above, p. 66.

115. Maimonides, *Guide,* sec. 1, chap. 73, p. 146 (lines 15–26).

116. See ibid., chap. 68, p. 114 (line 20); cf. chap. 73, p. 147 (lines 27–30).

117. Ibid., sec. 2, chap. 32, p. 254 (lines 14–15); chap. 36, pp. 260 (line 22)–63 (line 6).

118. Cf. ibid., chap. 40, p. 272 (lines 1–15).

119. Ibid., sec. 1, chap. 34, p. 52 (lines 6–9); cf. sec. 2, chap. 36, p. 262 (lines 1–7). Cf. Maimonides, *Pirush ha-Mishnayot, Abot* 3:11, 4:432–33.

120. Maimonides, *Guide,* sec. 1, chap. 1, p. 14 (lines 20–23); chap. 2, p. 16 (lines 13–15); sec. 3, chap. 8, p. 311 (line 15).

121. Ibid., sec. 2, chap. 36, p. 260 (lines 20–23); cf. chap. 38, pp. 266 (line 25)–67 (line 11).

122. Ibid., chap. 34; cf. sec. 1, chap. 15; sec. 3, chap. 45, p. 423 (lines 3–6).

123. See ibid., sec. 1, chap. 49; sec. 2, chap. 42; cf. sec. 2, chap. 6, especially p. 184 (lines 15–18).

124. See Cassirer, *Philosophy of Symbolic Forms,* 2:139–40.

125. See *Shabbat* 10a, 119b.

126. See *Baba Batra* 10a; *Sanhedrin* 65b; *Midrash Tanḥuma,* ed. Solomon Buber, 2 vol. (Vilna, 5645/1885); *Tazria'* 7, 2:18. Cf. Faur, *Golden Doves,* xxii–xiv.

127. See Faur, *Golden Doves,* 28. Therefore the philosopher is an ineffectual leader; see below, p. 165.

128. The affinity between the phenomenology of creativity and the mystical experience was noted by Neumann, "Mystical Man," 377.

129. Cf. R. David Qamḥi's commentary *Nebi'im Aḥaronim* on Jer 23:28.

130. See Maimonides, *Guide,* sec. 2, chap. 37, p. 264 (lines 9–15). On the relation of imagination to *jibla* see ibid., chap. 32, p. 255 (lines 4–5); chap. 36, p. 263 (line 3); chap. 38, p. 266 (lines 2–3).

131. Ibid., chap. 38, p. 267 (line 8).

132. Ibid., p. 266 (lines 25–27).

133. Ibid., (lines 27–28).

134. See ibid., chap. 32.

135. Cf. ibid., chap. 11, p. 191 (lines 24–29).

136. Ibid., chap. 38, pp. 266 (line 28)–67 (line 4).

137. Ibid., p. 267 (lines 10–11).

138. See ibid., chap. 32; cf. chap. 36, pp. 262 (line 1)–63 (line 1); chap. 42, p. 277 (lines 3–11).

139. See above, p. 70.

140. See Maimonides, *Guide,* sec. 2, chap. 41, p. 275 (lines 2–10); cf. chap. 45, p. 283 (lines 25–26).

141. See ibid., 41, pp. 274 (line 10)–75 (line 2); cf. chap. 46, p. 289 (lines 19–23).

142. See ibid., sec. 2, chap. 42, pp. 276 (line 16)–77 (line 11); cf. sec. 1, chap. 2, p. 15 (lines 24–25); chap. 15, p. 28 (lines 3–4). The source is rabbinic; see *Midrash Tehillim,* ed. Salomon Buber (New York: Om Publishing, 1947), 103, 17, p. 438, and parallels indicated by editor.

143. See Maimonides, *Guide,* sec. 2, chap. 45, pp. 280 (line 26)–81 (line 15).

144. See ibid., pp. 281 (line 19)–82 (line 22), especially line 14.

145. See *Shemona Peraqim,* 7, in Maimonides, *Pirush ha-Mishnayot* 4:394.

146. See Maimonides, *Guide,* sec. 2, chap. 45, pp. 282 (line 25)–85 (line 3). See R. David Qamḥi, *Pirush Sefer Tehillim,* ed. A. Darom (Jerusalem: Mossad Harav Kook, n.d.), Introduction. Thus, the books contained in the Hagiographa are not canonically "read" in the liturgical services; see Faur, *Golden Doves,* 85.

147. Maimonides, *Guide,* Introduction, p. 4 (lines 4–5).

148. Ibid., sec. 2, chap. 45, pp. 285 (line 5)–86 (line 18).

149. *Sanhedrin* 94a. Accordingly, Raba declared that Daniel had erred in his computation of the rebuilding of the Temple; see *Megilla* 12a—prophets are not susceptible to error in their prophetic message; see *Shulḥan Kesef,* 145 ff. Jewish commentators in Christian lands dismissed rabbinic tradition and adopted the Christian doctrine that Daniel was indeed a prophet; see, for example, R. Isaac Abarbanel's commentary to the *Guide* ad loc.; and the discussion of R. Samuel Valero, *Ḥazon la-Mo'ed* (Venice, 5346/1586), Introduction, 2b–4b. The book of Daniel was extensively used by Christian exegetes for Christological purposes, and, therefore, it had to be regarded as prophetic. There was no such need in Judaism. Rather, this is another instance of Christian influence on medieval Jewish thought. On this type of influence see Faur, *In the Shadow of History,* chap. 1.

150. *Megilla* 15a. It meant that they "aspired to prophetize" but were not actual prophets; see below, p. 217, n. 176. The status of a prophet is higher than that of someone who is merely the recipient of prophecy; see Maimonides, *Mishne Tora, Yesode ha-Tora* 7:7. Occasionally, someone may be referred to as a "prophet" in a vernacular, casual sense; see Maimonides, *Guide,* sec. 2, chap. 32, p. 255 (lines 15–18).

151. See Maimonides, *Guide,* sec. 2, chap. 41, p. 272 (lines 21–24); chap. 42, p. 276 (lines 23–26); chap. 43, pp. 277 (lines 23–24), 278 (lines 1–4, 14–15); chap. 44, pp. 279 (line 23), 280 (line 1); Maimonides, *Mishne Tora, Yesode ha-Tora* 7:2.

152. Maimonides, *Guide,* sec. 1, chap. 3, pp. 17 (line 26)–18 (line 4). It pertains to the exteriority of a thing and is accidental to its inner structure. On the legal status of such a shape in rabbinic law,see *Baba Qamma* 96b.

153. Maimonides, *Guide,* sec. 1, chap. 3, p. 18 (lines 4–7).

154. Ibid., p. 18 (lines 4–7).

155. David Hume, *Enquiries Concerning Human Understanding* (Oxord: Clarendon Press, 1975); on his "Ideas" see sec. 2. On his "sensory perceptions" see ibid., 12, p. 18; 17, p. 20.

156. Maimonides, *Guide,* sec. 1, chap. 3, p. 18 (lines 7–10).

157. See above, p. 214 n. 109.

158. Maimonides, *Guide,* sec. 1, chap. 3, p. 18 (lines 10–12); cf. below, p. 217 n. 171.

159. Cf. Leone Ebreo, *Dialoghi d'amore* [I], 35.

160. *Yebamot* 49b. See Faur, *Golden Doves,* 127–29.

161. This motif appears also in Hermetic literature; see Gedaliahu G. Stroumsa, "Form(s) of God," *Harvard Theological Review* 76 (1983): 274–76.

162. Edited in Faur, *Rabbi Yiśrael Moshe Ḥazzan*, p. 145. Cf. below, p. 218 n. 191.

163. Faur, *Rabbi Yiśrael Moshe Ḥazzan*, p. 145.

164. See Maimonides, *Guide,* Introduction, pp. 6 (line 19)–7 (line 15).

165. Maimonides, *Mishne Tora, Yesode ha-Tora* 7:3. On the meaning of this term see Faur, *Golden Doves*, p. 28; it is synonymous with *pirush*. See ibid. 12, 111–13.

166. See Maimonides, *Guide,* sec. 2, chap. 43. On the precise definition and function of *sharaḥ* see Faur, *Golden Doves,* 72–76.

167. See Maimonides, *Guide,* sec. 2, chap. 43.

168. On this type of relationship see Faur, *Golden Doves*, pp. 111–12.

169. *Yebamot* 49b.

170. See above pp. 50–51.

171. See *Berakhot* 7a as paraphrased in Maimonides, *Guide,* sec. 1, chap. 5, pp. 19 (line 24)–20 (line 4). See above, p. 25ff.

172. Maimonides, *Guide,* sec. 2, chap. 38, p. 267 (lines 25–29); cf. chap. 32, pp. 254 (line 27)–55 (line 3). The term *lebab* 'heart', rather than the more common *leb,* is interpreted by the rabbis to include both the good and evil inclinations; see Mishna *Berakhot* 9:1, which for Maimonides stand for the intellect and imagination. Cf. Maimonides, *Guide,* sec. 1, chap. 39, p. 60 (lines 17–19). Maimonides treats *ve-nabi* as a homonym; its plain meaning, however, is "we shall bring." See the commentaries of R. Abraham ibn 'Ezra and Radaq ad loc.

173. Sartre, *Psychology of Imagination,* 3.

174. Maimonides, *Guide,* sec. 3, chap. 24, p. 364 (lines 13–15).

175. Sartre, *Psychology of Imagination,* 3–4.

176. See Maimonides, *Mishne Tora, Yesode ha-Tora* 7:5 where Maimonides defined *mitnabbe'im* not as those who actually prophetized but as those "who aspire to be prophets." See above, p. 216 n. 150.

177. See Maimonides, *Guide,* sec. 2, chap. 45, pp. 281 (line 19)–282 (line 22). On the early stage of Moses's prophecy see R. Joseph ibn Kaspi, *Meṣaref la-Kesef* (Krakow, 5666/1906), 125; R. Isaac Caro, *Derashot R. Yiṣḥaq Qaro,* ed. Shaul Regev (Ramat Gan: Bar Ilan Univ., 1995), 85; R. DeFijo, *Bina le-'Ittim,* 1:167–69.

178. See *Vayyiqra Rabba,* 1, 14, vol. 1, pp. 30–32.

179. See above, p. 74ff. The difference between him and David was that he had the divine spirit from the time that he reached manhood, whereas David

received it after he was anointed by Samuel. See Maimonides, *Guide,* sec. 2, chap. 45, p. 282 (lines 6–7, 11–12).

180. Maimonides, *Guide,* sec. 3, chap. 45, p. 422 (lines 19–21); cf. sec. 2, chap. 6, p. 184 (lines 17–24).

181. See ibid., sec. 1, chap. 4.

182. See ibid., sec. 2, chap. 35; idem, *Mishne Tora, Yesode ha-Tora* 7:6.

183. See *Shemona Peraqim,* 7, in *Pirush ha-Mishnayot,* 4,393.

184. Cf. Faur, *In the Shadow of History,* 4–8.

185. See *Pesaḥim* 54b.

186. Cassirer, *Philosophy of Symbolic Forms,* 2,1.

187. Borges, "La Rosa de Paracelso," in *Obras Completas* (Madrid: Ultramar, 1977), 390.

188. Arieti, "Primitive Intellectual Mechanisms," 14.

189. Maimonides, *Guide,* sec. 1, chap. 32, p. 47 (lines 8–9).

190. Ibid., chap. 5, p. 19 (lines 17–24). Cf. above, p. 211 n. 68.

191. Ibid., chap. 32, p. 46 (lines 13–17). The source is Geonic; see the citation from R. Ḥanan'el, above, p. 72.

192. Maimonides, *Guide,* sec. 1, chap. 5, p. 20 (lines 4–9).

193. See *Kuzari* 4, 3; and Moshe Idel, "The World of Angels in Human Form" (in Hebrew), in *Studies in Jewish Mysticism, Philosophy, and Ethical Literature Presented to Isaiah Tishby,* ed. J. Dan and J. Hacker (Jerusalem: Magnes Press, 1986), 15–19.

194. *Berakhot* 17a; cf. Maimonides, *Mishne Tora, Teshuba* 8:2. In *Vayyiqra Rabba,* 20, 10, vol. 2, pp. 464–65, it was explicitly said that "they delighted their eyes from the Shekhina." See above p. 203 n. 125.

195. See above, pp. 3–5.

196. Neumann, "Mystical Man," 411.

197. On this important subject see Idel, *Kabbalah,* chap. 4.

198. Johannes Eckhart, *Meister Eckhart,* trans. R. B. Blankey (New York: Harper Brothers, 1941), 181–82. See Faur, *In the Shadow of History,* 6–7.

199. See *Shabbat* 92a; *Nedarim* 38a.

200. Like the Romans, the rabbis identified *vigor* with *virtue.*

201. See *Shemona Peraqim* 7, in Maimonides, *Pirush ha-Mishnayot,* 4: 393–94.

202. *Sifre,* no. 13, p. 22; this is the plain meaning of Prv 14:24. Cf. ibid., v. 18: and Se'adya, *Commentary on Proverbs, Version Arabe de Proverbs,* ed. Joseph Derenbourg, (Paris: Librairie de la Société Asiatique de l'Ecole des Langues Orientales Vivant, 1894), ad loc. Hence, the rabbinic doctrine, "There is no

poverty except for [poverty] of mind" (*Berakhot* 33a); cf. *Midrash Rabba Qohelet* 6, 1 (b). For a full analysis of this subject see Faur, *Golden Doves*, 142–43.

203. Instead of trying to control the impulses through imagination, leading to neurotic deformations.

204. See Maimonides, *Guide*, sec. 1, chap. 5, p. 19 (lines 18–20), quoted above, p. 81, where Maimonides wrote that a man "should not initially charge onto this awesome and sublime subject with his initial impulse, [i] without [having] trained his soul in the sciences and knowledge, [ii] educated his mores as much as possible, [iii] and killed his desires and imaginary passions."

205. See above, p. 204 n. 134.

206. Maimonides, *Guide*, sec. 2, chap. 38, p. 266 (lines 25–26).

207. Ibid., p. 267 (lines 26–27).

208. Maimonides, *Mishne Tora, Yesode ha-Tora* 7:2. This could not apply to Moses; see ibid., 7:6; idem, *Guide*, sec. 2, chap. 35.

209. An allusion to *jahiliya;* cf. above, p. 204 n. 130.

210. That is, *Ma'aśe Bereshit* and *Ma'aśe Merkaba;* cf. Maimonides, *Mishne Tora, Yesode ha-Tora* 4:13.

211. *Comprehension* refers to the "head of chapters," and *realization* is the further development required of the proper student; see above, pp. 24–27.

212. The *Merkaba*; cf. *Kuzari* 4, 3; and Idel, *Kabbalah*, 335 n. 104. This state, however, is not attained upon *entering* the *pardes* but at a later phase; see the *Sifre* cited above, p. 39. Cf. however, Idel, *Kabbalah*, 125.

213. The source of this doctrine is *Sifre* no. 355, p. 422.

214. On these angels see Maimonides, *Mishne Tora, Yesode ha-Tora* 2:7. Cf. Joseph, *Hitgallut ha-Sodot*, 6, and editor's note on line 14.

215. See above, pp. 22–24.

216. *Shemot Rabba* 23, 15.

217. For a philological analysis of this pronoun and its legal connotation see Faur, "Ma Ben 'Ḥamor Ze' le-'Ḥamor ha-Hu'," *Sinai* 76 (1975): 189–92.

218. *Mekhilta de-R. Yishma'el*, ed. H. S. Horovitz and I. A. Rabin (Jerusalem: Wahrman Books, 1970), *Beshallaḥ*, 3, p. 126.

219. *Midrash Tehillim* 8, 5, p. 77. Maimonides accepted this view and maintained that certain experiences were phylogentically encoded in the collective memory of the people; see Faur, "Intuitive Knowledge of God in Medieval Jewish Theology," *Jewish Quarterly Review* 67 (1976–77), 100–110; idem, *In the Shadow of History*, 206; and below, pp. 139–42.

220. *Ta'aniyot* 31a.

221. *Yerushalmi Megilla* 2, 3, 73b; and *Mo'ed Qaṭan* 3, 7, 83b. Cf. *Hitgallut ha-Sodot,* 30; R. Baḥye bar Asher, *Bi'ur 'al ha-Tora,* 2:574, and below, n. 222.

222. See the brilliant note of Albert Hazan, *Le Cantique de cantiques enfin expliqué* (Paris: Librairie Lipschutz, 1936), 78–80. Because the biblical sense of *gyl/gwl* was no longer evident, the *Yerushalmi* (see above, n. 221), did not connect the notion of dance to the verse in Is 25:9 but to Ps 48:14 where the term *ḥw(y)la* appears.

223. See the commentary of R. Gereshom ad loc.

224. For a further analysis of the concepts involved in this perspective see Faur, *In the Shadow of History,* 273 n. 10; and idem, *Golden Doves,* 131.

225. See Faur, "Intuitive Knowledge of God," 100–4, 106–8; and below, pp. 140–42.

226. According to rabbinic tradition these liturgies were instituted by the Great Assembly, the rabbinic body governing the Jewish people during the Persian period (until Alexander's conquest of the Persian empire in the year 332 B.C.E.): see *Berakhot* 33a. The text of the *Shema'* is scriptural and, thus, is not included among these categories.

227. I have dealt extensively with this kind of words in "Delocutive Expressions in the Hebrew Liturgy," *The Journal of the Ancient Near Eastern Society* 16–17 (1984–85): 41–54.

228. Philo, *The Unchangableness of God,* in Philo, *Complete Works,* 10 vls. (Loeb Classical Editions), v, 19, vol. 3: 19–21.

229. See Maimonides, *Mishne Tora, Teshuba* 10:1.

PART 3: COSMOLOGY

1. Finklestein, *The Ox That Gored,* 10.

2. Ibid., 9.

3. Maimonides, *Treatise on Resurrection,* 30. On the reason that Creation is associated with Moses and Abraham in particular see below, p. 123, and the sources indicated below, p. 299 n. 172. On the reason that Moses is mentioned before Abraham, see Faur, *Studies in the Mishne Tora,* 13–14, 148–49, and below, pp. 146, 158.

4. See Maimonides, *Guide,* sec. 1, chaps. 55–58; cf. ibid., chap. 8.

5. Ibid., 52, pp. 79 (line 28)–80 (line 10). On the theoretical and Scriptural bases of this concept, see ibid., chap. 11. Although 'relation', 'relationship', would be a more accurate translation of *nisba,* the English 'analogy' better conveys the idiomatic sense of this term; cf. Wolfson, *The Philosophy of the Kalam,* 22.

6. *Guide,* chap. 58, p. 93 (lines 14–19). See Faur, *Golden Doves,* 80–83.

7. Maimonides, *Mishne Tora, Yesode ha-Tora* 2:10.

8. See Maimonides, *Guide,* sec. 1, chap. 72.

9. On water clocks in Medieval Arab countries see Ahmad Y. al-Hassan and Donald R. Hill, *Islamic Technology: An Illustrated History* (Cambridge: Cambridge Univ. Press, 1986); Donald R. Hill, "Mechanical Engineering in the Medieval Near East," *Scientific American* (May 1991): 100–105. A clock of al-Jazari was reconstructed for exhibition at the Science Museum, London.

10. Maimonides, *Guide,* sec. 3, chap. 21, p. 350 (line 14–28). The two categories of knowledge are implicit in the rabbinic distinction between the "golden doves" in the mind of the first person and the "silver dots" as processed in the mind of the second person; see Faur, *Golden Doves,* xvi–xviii, 114–16. Ideality is perceived simultaneously in the mind of the first person. To the second person the "silver dots"—in this case the unfolding of the created universe—appear invariably in successive terms; see ibid., xxii, 22. Because the "golden doves" are not reducible to the "silver dots," they result in countless variations; see ibid., xviii.

11. See Faur, "Francisco Sánchez' Theory of Cognition and Vico's *verum/factum," New Vico Studies* 5 (1987): 131–46.

12. Giambattista Vico, *On the Ancient Wisdom of the Italians,* in *Vico: Selected Writings,* ed. and trans. Leon Pompa (London: Cambridge Univ. Press, 1982), 1, 1, p. 51. See "Francisco Sánchez' Theory of Cognition," 131–46.

13. Rodolfo Mondolfo, *Il "Verum-Factum" prima di Vico* (Naples: Guida, 1969), 17.

14. Maimonides, *Guide,* sec. 3, chap. 21.

15. Ibid., chap. 20, p. 348 (line 30). The full passage is cited below, p. 121.

16. Maimonides, *Guide,* sec. 2, chap. 13, p. 199 (lines 4–8).

17. See *Pirush ha-Mishnayot, Sanhedrin* 10:1, vol. 4, pp. 210–12, doctrine 4, cited below, p. 125. Cf. Maimonides, *Mishne Tora, Teshuba* 3:7.

18. See Maimonides, *Mishne Tora, Teshuba* 5:5, cf. 6:5. On this problem in general philosophy see Nelson Pike, "Divine Omniscience and Voluntary Action," *Philosophical Review* 74 (1965): 27–46; Linda Trinkaus Zagzebski, *The Dilemma of Freedom and Foreknowledge* (London: Oxford Univ. Press, 1993).

19. Cf. Faur, *Golden Doves,* xiv–xv.

20. See Maimonides, *Mishne Tora, Teshuba* 5:5; cf. *Yesode ha-Tora* 1:9, 2:10.

21. Newton, *Principia,* 545.

22. *Mishne Tora, Yesode ha-Tora* 1:2–3. One can thus respond to Leibnitz famous paradox that if God were the perfect Clock Maker, as Robert Boyle

depicted Him, then one would have to admit that God no longer has a role in the universe, see Edwin Arthur Burtt, *The Metaphysical Foundations of Modern Physical Science* (London: Routledge and Kegan Paul, 1949), 288–93. Only a human clockmaker, who creates neither the parts of the clock ex nihilo nor the physical laws governing its mechanism, could be displaced by a perfect clock.

23. For a detailed study of this school see Wolfson's monumental work, *The Philosophy of the Kalam.*

24. *Guide,* sec. 2, chap. 27, p. 232 (lines 15–16).

25. Ibid., sec. 1, chap. 71, p. 123 (lines 4–5).

26. See Wolfson, *Philosophy of the Kalam,* 50–51.

27. See ibid., 43–56.

28. Maimonides, *Guide,* sec. 1, chap. 71, p. 125 (lines 11–13).

29. On the meaning of these terms see below, p. 102.

30. Maimonides, *Guide,* sec. 1, chap. 71, p. 123 (lines 10–18).

31. See above, p. 211 n. 70.

32. Maimonides, *Guide,* sec. 1, chap. 71, p. 124 (lines 2–5).

33. Ibid., (lines 5–16). For a definition of these three terms see Maimonides, *Treatise on Logic,* chap. 8.

34. See below, pp. 119–25.

35. Maimonides, *Guide,* sec. 1, chap. 71, p. 122 (lines 18–22). Except for a few departures the translation of this passage comes from Wolfson, *Philosophy of the Kalam,* 50.

36. Maimonides, *Guide,* sec. 1, chap. 71, p. 124 (lines 24–28).

37. Ibid., (line 10).

38. Ibid., p. 121 (lines 9–11, 25).

39. On the propensity of the persecuted to assimilate patterns of thought and feeling of the persecutor see Faur, *In the Shadow of History,* 9–10. This type of relationship was energetically pursued by anti-Maimonideans and other self-righteous Jews, past and present; see idem, *In the Shadow of History,* 11–12; and idem, "Two Forms of Jewish Spirituality," 5–46.

40. Maimonides, *Guide,* sec. 2, chap. 11, p. 192 (lines 21–25).

41. *Shemona Peraqim* 4, in Maimonides, *Pirush ha-Mishnayot,* vol. 4, p. 384. Pagan asceticism, too, is the sanction of violence against oneself.

42. Aristotle *Metaphysics* 12, 7, 1072a (lines 24–25). For a thorough discussion of this doctrine see Jaeger, *Aristotle,* chap. 14.

43. Jaeger, *Aristotle,* 345–46.

44. See Maimonides, *Guide*, sec. 2, chap. 25.

45. Ibid., p. 230 (lines 23–24).

46. Maimonides, *Letters and Essays of Moses Maimonides* (in Hebrew), ed. Isaac Shailat, 2 vols. (Maaleh Adumim: Maaliyot Press, 5748 [1988]), 2: 553. There are variants to this version; see Faur, *Studies in the Mishne Tora*, 7 n. 27.

47. See below, pp. 109–10. Cf. Kellner, *Maimonides on Human Perfection*, 30.

48. Hence, the antirationalistic movement common in the Christian and Jewish Middle Ages; see Faur, *In the Shadow of History*, 11–12.

49. Maimonides, *Guide*, sec. 1, chap. 71, pp. 125 (lines 18–21).

50. Maimonides, *Mishne Tora, Yesode ha-Tora* 1:1.

51. See Faur, *Golden Doves*, 36.

52. Spinoza further developed the logic of this principle, concluding that God and religion must be subordinated to the political sovereign; see Faur, *In the Shadow of History*, 172.

53. See ibid., 74. For Maimonides the essence of idolatry consists in positing a hierarchically superior entity through which humankind worships God; see Maimonides, *Pirush ha-Mishnayot, Sanhedrin* 10:1, vol. 4, p. 212; idem, *Mishne Tora, 'Aboda Zara* 1:1; idem, *Guide*, sec. 1, chap. 36.

54. Maimonides regarded Christianity as idolatry, see Faur, *Studies in the Mishne Tora*, 230–37. Essential to the Maimonidean juridical concept is the separation of power between the Temple (church), the Judiciary, and the political sovereign; see Faur, "Law and Hermeneutics in Rabbinic Jurisprudence," *Cardozo Law Review* 14 (May 1993), 1664–69. Sephardim maintained that religion is outside the perimeter of political authority. It is not incumbent upon the state to defend a particular religion but to protect the rights of the citizens to worship; see Faur, *In the Shadow of History*, 184–85.

55. Maimonides, *Guide*, sec. 1, chap. 71, pp. 125 (line 21)–126 (line 1).

56. See ibid., chap. 70.

57. Ibid., chap. 71, p. 126 (lines 1–3).

58. Aristotle *Metaphysics*, 12, 7, 1072b (lines 4–14), in *The Complete Works of Aristotle*.

59. According to Averroes, *Tahafut al-Tahafut*, ed. Simon Van den Bergh, 2 vols. (Oxford: Oxford Univ. Press, 1954), 1: 232, and the corresponding note in vol. 2, p. 132, in the realm of creation things do not exist necessarily: they merely "happen" to exist. Consequently, the essence of a thing does not coincide perfectly with its existence, hence, the fundamental difference

between the "essence" of something, and its actual "existence." In Maimonides, *Guide*, sec. 1, chap. 57, p. 90 (lines 4–9), one reads that "existence is an accident that happened to the existent. Therefore, it is an additional meaning to the existent's essence. This applies to everything whose existence is the effect of a cause—thus, its existence is appended to its essence. However, something whose existence is not the effect of a cause, and this is God alone, is of 'necessary existence'. His existence is His reality and verity, and His reality is His existence. It is not a reality which happened to exist, and His existence [is not] a meaning appended to [His essence]; since He always is of 'necessary existence'."

60. See Maimonides, *Guide*, sec. 2, Introduction, Axioms 19–20.

61. Ibid., chap. 1, p. 172 (lines 14–17). For a further analysis of this concept see R. Joseph b. Jehuda, *Drei Abhandlungen*, ed. Moritz Lowy, (Berlin, 1879). Cf. Harry A. Wolfson, *The Philosophy of Spinoza*, 2 vols. (Cambridge, Mass.: Harvard Univ. Press, 1934), 1: 67.

62. This parallels the Hebrew doctrine of Creation, discussed above, p. 89ff.

63. Maimonides, *Mishne Tora, Yesode ha-Tora* 1:2.

64. Ibid., 1:3.

65. Newton, *Principia*, 546.

66. Maimonides, *Guide*, sec. 1, chap. 19. Cf. ibid., sec. 2, chap. 17, p. 206 (line 24). See Faur, *Golden Doves*, 23–27.

67. For a thorough discussion of this doctrine see Jaeger, *Aristotle*, chap. 14.

68. See Maimonides, *Guide*, sec. 2, Introduction, pp. 168 (line 23)–69 (line 1); ibid., chaps. 15, 17–24.

69. Ibid., chap. 15, p. 202 (line 8).

70. Maimonides, *Treatise on Logic*, chap. 14, pp. 61–62.

71. See Averroes,' *Tahafut al-Tahafut*, 2: 179.

72. Maimonides, *Guide*, sec. 2, chap. 19, p. 211 (lines 20–21); cf. ibid., chap. 15, p. 203 (lines 5–10). See below, pp. 108–9. For a formal definition of *burhan* see Maimonides, *Treatise on Logic*, chap. 8.

73. See Faur, *Studies in the Mishne Tora*, 188–90; Maimonides, *Guide*, sec. 1, chap. 32, p. 46 (lines 6–17). Cf. ibid., chap. 31, p. 44 (lines 13–29); ibid., sec. 2, chap. 25, p. 230 (lines 2–5). On this fundamental distinction see Nachum L. Rabinovitch, *Probability and Statistical Inference in Ancient and Medieval Jewish Literature* (Toronto: Univ. of Toronto Press, 1973), 152–57; idem, "The Concept of Possibility in Maimonides" (in Hebrew), in *Studies in Maimonides*, ed. M. Idel, (Likkute Tarbiz V) (Jerusalem: Hebrew Univ. Press, 1985), 403–15.

74. See *Berakhot* 34b.

75. Maimonides, *Guide,* sec. 1, chaps. 31–32.

76. Ibid., sec. 2, chap. 24, p. 228 (lines 13–14).

77. Because mathematics is a human creation, it is perfectly known, in contradistinction to physics and other applied sciences that deal with elements not created by humans, and are, therefore deficient; see above, pp. 91–92. Vico, too, in *On the Wisdom of the Italians* (in *Vico: Selected Writings,* 68) writes:

> Thus, arithmetic and geometry and their offspring, mechanics, lie within human faculties, since in them we demonstrate the true because we make it. Physics, on the other hand, lies within a faculty of Almighty God, in whom alone the faculty is true, because it is in the highest degree easy and ready, so that what is a faculty in man is purest act in God.

78. Maimonides, *Guide,* sec. 1, chap. 31, pp. 43 (line 25)–44 (line 29).

79. Ibid., sec. 2, chap. 11, pp. 190 (line 24)–91 (line 9).

80. Ibid., chap. 24, p. 228 (lines 5–9). Maimonides held a formalistic view of nature whereby scientific models do not represent physical reality but are mere aids designed to help one conceptualize how certain physical phenomena unfold . For a discussion of this issue and the pertaining bibliography on the subject, see Menachem Kellner, "On the Status of the Astronomy and Physics in Maimonides's *Mishne Tora* and the *Guide of the Perplexed,*" *British Journal for the History of Science* 24 (1991): 453–63. Maimonides's formalism, however, is a function of the basic skepticism underlying his theory of science discussed in this section. This, too, was the position of R. David Nieto; see Faur, *Golden Doves,* 159 n. 4.

81. See Faur, "Sánchez' Critique of *Authoritas,*" 256–76.

82. Maimonides, *Guide,* sec. 1, chap. 71, p. 123 (lines 29–30).

83. See Faur, *Studies in the Mishne Tora,* 8 n. 38.

84. Maimonides, *Guide,* sec. 1, chap. 71, p. 126 (lines 5–6).

85. Maimonides, *Mishne Tora, Qiddush ha-Ḥodesh* 17:24. Cf. idem, *Guide,* sec. 2, chap.8; sec. 3, chap. 14, p. 331 (lines 15–22).

86. Maimonides, *Guide,* sec. 2, chap. 22, p. 223 (lines 8–9).

87. Ibid., chap. 4, pp. 178 (line 30)–79 (line 1).

88. Ibid., chap. 24, p. 228 (lines 12–14).

89. Ibid., chap. 15, p. 202 (lines 11–13).

90. Ibid., chap. 22, p. 223 (lines 14–24).

91. Ibid., chap. 24, p. 228 (lines 15–19).

92. See Jaeger, *Aristotle*, 380ff.

93. Maimonides, *Guide*, sec. 1, chap. 5, p. 19 (lines 12–17).

94. See Faur, *Studies in the Mishne Tora*, 7 n. 27.

95. See above, p. 65.

96. See Maimonides, *Guide*, sec. 2, chap. 40, p. 271 (lines 17, 22); sec. 1, chap. 31, p. 44 (line 30). For a description of *rayyis*, see R. Abraham Maimon, *Teshubot* (Jerusalem: Meoize Nirdamin, 1937), 19–20, 183. Maimonides himself was recognized as the *ra'is* (*rayyis*) of the Jews; see Shlomo D. Goiten, "Moses Maimonides, Man of Action," in *Homages à Georges Vajda*, ed. Gérard Nahon and Charles Touati, (Louvain: Editions Peeters, 1983), 161, 167.

97. See above, p. 66.

98. See above, pp. 80–82.

99. Maimonides, *Guide*, sec. 1, chap. 50, p. 75 (lines 12–13). Cf. above, p. 57.

100. Maimonides, *Guide*, sec. 1, chap. 5, pp. 19 (line 17)–20 (line 12).

101. See below, p. 122.

102. Maimonides, *Guide*, sec. 1, chap. 5, p. 20 (lines 12–13).

103. Maimonides does not use the first person plural indiscriminately; cf., for example, Maimonides, *Guide*, sec. 1, chap. 28, p. 41 (lines 2–3); sec. 3, Introduction, but only when speaking on behalf of Jewish tradition.

104. See above, n. 96, and below, p. 192.

105. Maimonides, *Guide*, sec. 2, chap. 36, p. 262 (lines 20–23).

106. See ibid., sec. 1, chap. 32.

107. Ibid., sec. 3, chap. 54, p. 470 (line 24). See below, p. 176.

108. *Ekha Rabba*, 2:13.

109. Cited above, p. 98.

110. See below, p. 169.

111. Maimonides, *Guide*, sec. 2, chap. 23, p. 225 (lines 6–7). The reference is to *Baba Batra* 116a.

112. It is connected to the expression *she-yesh sham* discussed above, p. 99. The final *mem* is not a sign of the plural or dual but an appendix designed to close an atonic final syllable as in *yeraḥim* (Dt 33:14), or *ṣahorayim* (Gn 43:16). In Maimonides, *Guide*, sec. 2, chap. 30, p. 245 (line 5), Maimonides translated *shamayim* 'the above'.

113. Note that unlike God, humans cannot ever know it "perfectly well"; see above, pp. 91–93.

114. Maimonides, *Guide,* sec. 2, chap. 24, p. 228 (lines 19–28).

115. See above, pp. 79–82.

116. Louis Vax, *La Séduction de l'étrange* (Paris: Presses Universitaires de France, 1965), 178. See above, pp. x–xi.

117. Joaquina Navarro, "Jorge Luis Borges, taumaturgo de la metáfora," *Revista Hispánica Moderna* 31 (1965): 339. The same occurs with physical laws when systems are thrust past their natural limit, see Ilya Prigogine and Isabelle Stengers, *Order out of Chaos* (New York: Bantam Books, 1984).

118. See above, p. 66.

119. See Faur, *Golden Doves,* xix. An absolute condition to discern the metaphoric passages in the Scripture is the rejection of the magical in nature. Otherwise, the reader is unable to realize that the text at hand is metaphoric.

120. See above, pp. 69–72.

121. See the article cited above, p. 221 n. 11.

122. The best book on the subject continues to be the pioneer work of Nachum L. Rabibnovitch, *Probability and Statistical Inference in Ancient and Medieval Jewish Literature* (Toronto: Univ. of Toronto Press, 1973).

123. On this expression see Maimonides, *Teshubot ha-Rambam,* no. 259, vol. 2, 460, cited in *Kesef Mishne, Ḥameṣ wu-Maṣṣa* 1:9. On its precise meaning see Faur, *Studies in the Mishne Tora,* 57 n. 75. For the distinction between rabbinic interpretation and the "Law" see Faur, "Law and Hermeneutics," 1674–76.

124. *On Rewards and Punishments,* 5, 28–29, vol. 8, p. 329.

125. *Sefer ha-Miṣvot,* Negative Commandment no. 290, p. 316.

126. *Radiya* is motivated, see Maimonides, *Guide,* sec. 2, chap. 18, p. 209 (line 20), whereas *sha'a* is a primary wish, which seeks "no goal and cannot be asked why?" Ibid., sec. 3, chap. 25, p. 366 (lines 12–13).

127. Ibid., sec. 2, chap. 18, p. 208 (lines 27–28).

128. See Faur, *Golden Doves,* 67–68.

129. Maimonides, *Guide,* sec. 2, 21.

130. See Faur, *Golden Doves,* xvi–xviii.

131. Maimonides, *Guide,* sec. 2, chap. 18, p. 210 (lines 18–21). Hence, the difference with *'ada,* cited above, p. 96. This leads to the Maimonidean concept of the "impossible"; see Maimonides, *Guide,* sec. 3, chap. 15.

132. See ibid., sec. 2, chap. 19, pp. 211 (line 15)–12 (line 1). The difference between this thesis and the *'ada* of the *Kalam* is that *takhṣiṣ* is not random; see ibid. and below, n. 139.

133. Maimonides, *Guide,* sec. 2, chap. 19, p. 219 (lines 8–9).

134. Ibid., chap. 20, pp. 218 (line 23)–19 (line 2).

135. See ibid., chap. 19, p. 211 (lines 15–18).

136. See ibid., sec. 3, chap. 13; and sec. 2, chap. 25, p. 230 (lines 5–17).

137. Ibid., sec. 2, chap. 18, p. 210 (lines 4–5).

138. Ibid., sec. 3, chap. 25, p. 367 (lines 6–7).

139. Cf. ibid., sec. 2, chap. 18, p. 210 (lines 18–21), and above, n. 132.

140. Maimonides, *Guide,* sec. 3, chap. 26, pp. 370 (line 26)–71 (line 2); cf. chap. 17, p. 342 (lines 16–22).

141. Ibid., chap. 20, p. 349 (lines 2–6).

142. Ibid., (lines 9–10).

143. On mental habits see Maimonides, *Guide,* Introduction, p. 3 (lines 25–26); sec. 1, chap. 31, p. 45 (line 12).

144. *Treatise on Logic,* chap. 11. The same expression *'ala al-akṭar* is used by Maimonides in the source cited in n. 145.

145. Maimonides, *Pirush ha-Mishnayot, 'Eduyot* 2:9, vol. 4, p. 299.

146. *Pirqe Abot* 5:5, Maimonides, *Pirush ha-Mishnayot,* 4: 456.

147. *Bereshit Rabba* 5, 5, vol. 1, p. 35. Maimonides, *Guide,* sec. 2, chap. 29, p. 242 (line 16), described this view as "strange" (*gariba*), a term not implying disapproval, but 'wonder', 'astonishment'. See, Introduction, p. 5 (lines 19–20); sec. 1, chap. 70, pp. 118 (line 27), 120 (lines 4, 8); sec. 2, chap. 19, pp. 213 (line 22), 215 (line 16); chap. 30, p. 250 (line 23); sec. 3, chap. 8, p. 313 (line 3); chap. 21, p. 351 (line 24); chap. 22, p. 351 (line 23); chap. 31, p. 383 (line 9); chap. 37, pp. 397 (line 9), 399 (line 2); chap. 45, p. 421 (line 28); chap. 46, pp. 431 (line 27), 433 (line 2); chap. 54, p. 467 (line 9), and so on.

148. See *Ḥagiga* 12a.

149. Maimonides, *Guide,* sec. 2, chap. 17, p. 207 (lines 18–19).

150. Ibid., chap. 30, pp. 244 (line 21)–45 (line 5).

151. Maimonides, *Guide,* sec. 2, chap. 30, pp. 245 (line 21)–46 (line 2). The rabbinic source is lost. See *Ḥagiga* 12a. On the variety of matter and its distribution throughout space see Maimonides, *Guide,* sec. 2, chap. 19.

152. Maimonides, *Guide,* sec. 2, chap. 30, p. 249 (line 24).

153. Ibid., (lines 13–14, 24). The Talmudic quotation is from *Rosh ha-Shana* 11a; *Ḥolin* 60a. Usually, this passage is interpreted as if it were written with

the preposition *be-* (with, in), meaning "fully finished and developed." Indeed, to support this view many manuscripts were doctored to read *be-*. The original text, however, reads *le-*, as it was quoted in the *Guide,* ibid., indicating 'direction', 'finality'. Cf. *Oṣar ha-Ge'onim,* vol. 5, *Rosh ha-Shana,* pp. 22–23.

154. Maimonides, *Guide,* sec. 2, chap. 17, p. 205 (line 10). See ibid., (line 15), p. 207 (line 21).

155. According to Maimonides, time was created, see ibid., chap. 13, pp. 196 (line 9)–97 (line 5); chap. 30, p. 245 (lines 3–21). See the incisive note of R. Joseph ibn Kaspi, *Shulḥan Kesef* (Jerusalem: Ben-Zvi Institute, 1996), 61. The source for Maimonides's thesis is rabbinic; see *Haggahot* of R. Z. H. Chajes, in *Talmud Babli* (Vilna: Re'em, 5668/1908), on *Megilla* 9a. This source and other basic concepts in rabbinic and Jewish thought were overlooked in the article by Sara Klein-Braslavy, "The Reality of Time and the Primordial Period in Mediaeval Jewish Philosophy" (in Hebrew), *Tarbiz* 45 (1976): 106–27.

156. See Maimonides, *Guide,* sec. 2, chap. 13, p. 196 (lines 14–15).

157. See Faur, *Golden Doves,* xxiii.

158. Maimonides, *Guide,* sec. 2, chap. 17, pp. 205 (line 14)–6 (line 5).

159. Ibid., p. 206 (lines 18–21).

160. See ibid., sec. 1, chap. 71, p. 124 (lines 19–21); sec. 2, Introduction, pp. 168 (line 23)–69 (line 1); 15.

161. See ibid., sec. 2, chap. 16.

162. See ibid., chaps. 13–24; on the *mutakallimun* see chap. 16.

163. See ibid., chap. 16, p. 204 (lines 12–27).

164. Ibid., sec. 2, Introduction, p. 168 (line 28); chap. 16, p. 204 (lines 27–28).

165. This argument was used by the Aristotelians to prove the eternity of the world; see Maimonides, *Guide,* sec. 2, chap. 14, p. 200 (lines 9–24).

166. Ibid., Introduction, axioms 24; cf. ibid., axiom 23; chap. 17, p. 207 (lines 11–14); chap. 18, pp. 208 (line 15)–9 (line 14).

167. See ibid., chap. 17, p. 208 (lines 1–9).

168. See ibid., sec. 3, chap. 15.

169. Ibid., p. 204 (line 24).

170. Ibid., chap. 16, pp. 204 (line 30)–5 (line 3); cf. ibid., chap. 25 p. 230 (line 3).

171. Ibid., chap. 16, p. 205 (line 1); cf. chap. 2, p. 175 (line 29). It is similar to *al-ra'i al-naḍri,* ibid., chap. 31, p. 253 (line 9). In opposition to *naḍr al-ṭab'i,* ibid., chap. 19, p. 213 (line 11).

172. Ibid., chap. 13, p. 197 (lines 8–10). Similarly, in *Mishne Tora, 'Aboda Zara* 1:3 (line 38) Abraham discovered that the world is created by means of *tebunato*

ha-nekhona (his proper intelligence). The authority for this tradition is *Bereshit Rabba*, 34, 12, i, vol. 1, p. 365, where Abraham is credited with the discovery that the world has a *manhig* (leader, guide); cf. Maimonides, *Guide*, sec. 2, chap. 18, p. 210 (line 28). The rabbis associated this discovery with wisdom; see ibid., chap. 3, p. 367. For a different version, closer to Maimonides's text, see *Midrash ha-Gadol, Bereshit*, ed. M. Marguilies (Jerusalem: Mossad Harav Kook, 5727/1967), 12, pp. 210–11.

173. Maimonides, *Guide*, sec. 1, chap. 32, p. 46 (lines 6–9).

174. Ibid., sec. 2, chap. 24, p. 228 (lines 26–28).

175. Ibid., p. 229 (lines 1–4).

176. See above, pp. 42–47.

177. Maimonides, *Guide*, sec. 2, chap. 23, p. 224 (lines 11–27).

178. Ibid., chap. 15, pp. 202 (lines 10–11), 204 (lines 5–6).

179. Ibid., chap. 23, p. 224 (line 30); see pt. 3, n. 180.

180. Ibid., chap. 16, p. 204 (lines 27–29).

181. See above, pp. 57–58.

182. See above, pp. 92–94.

183. See Maimonides, *Guide*, sec. 3, chaps. 19–21.

184. *Soṭa* 4b–5a; see Maimonides, *Mishne Tora, De'ot* 2:3.

185. *Baba Batra* 78b.

186. See *Berakhot* 58b; *Mishne Tora, Berakhot* 10:19.

187. Maimonides, *Guide*, sec. 3, chap. 20, pp. 348 (line 28)–49 (line 2). See ibid., (lines 15–27); chap. 19, p. 347 (line 8). According to this argument, the Aristotelians are blameworthy of confusing intentional with extentional semantics—a mistake characteristic of those who have yet to overcome omnipotence of thought; see above, Introduction, pp. 4–5.

188. Maimonides, *Guide*, sec. 3, chap.14, p. 330 (line 29).

189. Ibid., (lines 12–16).

190. Ibid., p. 331 (lines 3–4).

191. Ibid., sec. 2, chap. 23, p. 225 (lines 4–5).

192. See ibid., sec. 3, chap. 29; Maimonides, *Pirush ha-Mishnayot, 'Aboda Zara* 4:7, vol. 4, pp. 357–59. Cf. idem, *Guide*, sec. 1, chap. 70, p. 118 (lines 22–26).

193. Maimonides, *Guide*, sec. 2, chap. 23, p. 225 (lines 7–8).

194. On the function of such a Savior in mythological thought see Eliade, *Myth and Reality*, 39 ff, 90, 174–81. This term appears in rabbinic literature, and it was properly interpreted by R. Benjamin Musafia, *Musaf He-'Arukh*, s.v. *qozmiqon*, *Aruch Completum*, vol. 7, p. 76a.

195. Maimonides, *Guide*, sec. 2, chap. 23, pp. 224 (line 30)–25 (line 2).

196. Ibid., chap. 24, pp. 228 (line 28)–29 (line 1). Cf. sec. 3, chap. 21, p. 351 (lines 11–20).

197. Ibid., sec. 2, chap. 13, pp. 197 (line 10)–98 (line 8).

198. See, however, ibid., chap. 30, p. 245 (lines 18–20).

199. See ibid., chap. 26.

200. Ibid., chap. 25, pp. 229 (line 26)–30 (line 5).

201. Ibid., p. 230 (lines 2–5); cf. chap. 30, p. 252 (lines 4–5).

202. Ibid., chap. 23, p. 224 (lines 29–30).

203. Maimonides, *Guide,* sec. 2, chap. 25, p. 229 (lines 21–25).

204. See above, p. 121.

205. Maimonides, *Guide,* sec. 3, chap. 16, p. 333 (lines 3–5); see the continuation of the chapter; and ibid., chaps. 19–21.

206. See above, p. 119.

207. Cited above, p. 124.

208. Maimonides, *Guide,* sec. 2, chap. 30, p. 245 (lines 19–20).

209. Maimonides, *Pirush ha-Mishnayot, Sanhedrin* 10:1, doctrine 4, vol. 4, p. 212.

210. Maimonides, *Guide*, sec. 2, chap. 13, p. 199 (lines 6–9). Cf. ibid., chap. 17, p. 206 (lines 16–21); chap. 19, pp. 216 (line 26)–17 (line 1); chap. 22, p. 224 (lines 6–7).

211. J. M. Jauch, *Are Quanta Real?* (Bloomington: Indiana Univ. Press, 1989), 99 n. 3; see ibid., p.101 n. 13. For an in-depth analysis of this view see Ludwig von Bertalanffy, *General System Theory* (New York: George Braziller, 1993), chap. 10.

PART 4: ANTROPOLOGY

1. Maimonides, *Guide,* sec. 1, chap. 1, p. 14 (line 23), p. 15 (lines 6, 15). See ibid., chap. 72, p. 132 (lines 7–9).

2. Ibid., chap. 1, p. 15 (lines 15–16).

3. See above, pp. 53–55.

4. Maimonides, *Guide,* sec. 1, chap. 1, p. 15 (lines 18–19).

5. Ibid., sec. 3, chap. 18, p. 343 (lines 21–22).

6. Ibid., (lines 23–24). Cf. Dan 4:13, Ps 49:14, and *Bina le-'Ittim*, vol. 1, p. 140.

7. *R. Nissim Ga'on*, ed. Shraga Abramson (Jerusalem: Mekize Nirdamin, 1965), 112. The source is *Bereshit Rabba,* 22, vol. 1, p. 195. A similar tradition concerning the *shedim* is reported in an anonymous Arabic commentary to the *Guide, Ein Amonymer Arabischer Commentor aus dem XV. Jahrhunder See Maimonides Dalalat al-Ḥa'irin,*edited by R. Israel Horn (Breslau: H. Fleischmann, 1907), 7–8. See Faur, *Studies in the Mishne Tora,* 2.

8. Maimonides, *Guide*, sec. 1, chap. 7, pp. 21 (line 26)–22 (line 1).

9. Cf. *Bereshit Rabba* 16, 5, vol. 1, p. 149.

10. Maimonides, *Guide*, sec. 2, chap. 30, p. 251 (lines 12–14).

11. Ibid., sec. 1, chap. 7, p. 22 (lines 1–2). Accordingly, only in the genealogical list of Seth (Gn 5) it is written "and so and so *gave birth to him* (*holido*) to so and so" (vv. 4, 7, 10, etc.). Whereas in the genealogical list of Cain (Gn 4) it is written that "it was born to" (*va-yvaled le-*), or "she gave birth to" (*va-teled*), but never "he gave birth to" (*holido*). For an alternative explanation see R. Solomon ibn Adret, *She'elot wu-Tshubot*, vol. 4 (Salonika, 5563/1803), no. 30.

12. Maimonides, *Guide*, sec. 1, chap. 1.

13. Ibid., chap. 7, p. 22 (lines 2–8); cf. Maimonides, *Pirush ha-Mishnayot*, *Baba Qamma*, 4:3, vol. 4. p. 20. They are the protological men discussed above, pp. 65–69.

14. Maimonides, *Guide*, sec. 3, chap. 51, p. 455 (lines 7–8).

15. Ibid., (lines 10–12); cf. chap. 18, p. 34 (lines 11–27).

16. Mishna *Baba Meṣi'a* 2:11; cf. above, p. 8.

17. Maimonides, *Guide*, sec. 1, chap. 7, p. 21 (lines 21–23).

18. *Tosefta, Horayot* 2:7; see *Sanhedrin* 19a and ibid., 99b.

19. *Bereshit Rabba*, 84, 37, vol. 2, p. 1004; see *Targum Anqelos* ad loc.

20. *Tosefta, Horayot* 2:7. Cf. above, n. 18.

21. *Letters and Essays of Maimonides*, 1: 233–34. The source of this fundamental concept is scriptural. According to the Tora, a proselyte is duty bound to offer a Paschal sacrifice, exactly like a native citizen, see Nm 9:14; Ex 12:48–49; and Luzzato, *Commentary to the Pentateuch*, 453. This implies that he, too, is to celebrate the miracle of the Exodus that God made to *his* 'ancestors,' see Ex 12:26–27.

22. Maimonides, *Guide*, sec. 1, chap. 7, p. 21 (lines 18–21).

23. *Vayyiqra Rabba* 23, 2, vol. 3, p. 528. Cf. *Mekhilta de-R. Yishma'el*, *Beshallaḥ*, 6, pp. 111–12. See below, p. 151.

24. Maimonides, *Guide*, sec. 3, chap. 32, pp. 386 (line 24)–87 (line 4).

25. Cf. *Shemona Peraqim* 1, Maimonides, *Pirush ha-Mishnayot*, 4: 376.

26. On the relation of *habit* to *custom* see Maimonides, *Guide*, sec. 3, chap. 12, p. 321 (line 15).

27. See above, p. 228 n. 143.

28. See Maimonides, *Guide*, sec. 3, chap. 30, pp. 381 (line 10), 382 (lines 5–6); chap. 32, p. 384 (lines 18–19); chap. 46, pp. 429 (line 27), 430 (line 14), 431 (line 4).

29. See ibid., chap. 46, p. 430 (line 24).

30. See ibid., p. 431 (line 4).

31. See ibid., chap. 33.

32. Sigmund Freud, *Civilization and its Discontents*, 102.

33. Ibid., 103.

34. Maimonides, *Guide*, sec. 3, chap. 32, p. 384 (lines 24–25); cf. ibid., sec. 1, chap. 31, p. 45 (lines 4–16); sec. 3, chap. 32, p. 385 (line 26).

35. See ibid., sec. 3, chap. 32, p. 385 (lines 12–14).

36. Ibid., p. 384 (lines 11–13).

37. Maimonides, *Treatise on Resurrection*, 32–33; idem, *Guide*, sec. 3, chap. 24, pp. 362 (line 25)–63 (line 4). It is a rabbinic doctrine; see the sources cited in Judah Goldin, *Studies in Midrash and Related Literature* (Philadelphia: Jewish Publication Society, 5748/1988), 177 n. 14.

38. Maimonides, *Guide*, sec. 3, chap. 32, pp. 385 (line 25)–86 (line 4).

39. *Shemona Peraqim* 1, Maimonides, *Pirush ha-Mishnayot*, 4: 375.

40. Cf. Maimonides, *Guide*, sec. 3, chap. 31, p. 382 (lines 22–24); idem, *Pirush ha-Mishnayot, Ḥagiga* 2:1, vol. 2, p. 376.

41. By "opinions," psychic impulses and involuntary thoughts and ideas are meant.

42. Maimonides, *Guide*, sec. 2, chap. 38, p. 267 (lines 14–21).

43. *Pirqe Abot* 4:4, Maimonides, *Pirush ha-Mishnayot*, 4: 438.

44. See *Shemona Peraqim* 1, Maimonides, *Pirush ha-Mishnayot*, 4: 373 3–4,:378–87; 5: 390; idem, *Mishne Tora, De'ot* 2:1–2; idem, *Guide*, sec. 3, chap. 31, p. 382 (lines 22–23); chap. 32, p. 385 (line 19); chap. 46, p. 426 (lines 27–28). Cf. below, p. 239 nn. 143, 145.

45. *Shemona Peraqim* 2, Maimonides, *Pirush ha-Mishnayot*, 4:377.

46. Ibid., 3, p. 378. Cf. Maimonides, *Mishne Tora, De'ot* 2:1.

47. See *Shemona Peraqim* 6, Maimonides, *Pirush ha-Mishnayot*, 4: 391–93.

48. *Shemona Peraqim* 6, Maimonides, *Pirush ha-Mishnayot*, 4: 378–79.

49. See Maimonides, *Guide*, sec. 3, chap. 29, pp. 377 (line 12), 380 (line 28); chap. 30, p. 382 (line 18); chap. 32, p. 388 (line 4); chap. 37, p. 397 (lines 5–6).

50. See ibid., chap. 29, pp. 378 (line 8)–79 (line 26).

51. See *Kuzari* 4:11, 13. For the recurrence of this type of phenomena in the West, see Eliade, *Myth and Reality*, especially chap. 9. On their effect on modern intellectual trends, see idem, *Occultism, Witchcraft, and Cultural Fashions*, chap. 1.

52. Sigmund Freud, "Reflections upon War and Death," in *Character and Culture* (New York: Collier Books, 1963), 119.

53. *Images and Symbols*, 12.

54. George Deveraux, *Basic Problems of Ethnopsychiatry*, trans. Basia Miller

Gulati and George Deveraux (Chicago: Univ. of Chicago Press, 1980), 5.

55. C. G. Jung, "The Psychology of the Child Archetype," in *Essays on a Science of Mythology,* trans. R. F. C. Hull (Princeton, N.J.: Princeton Univ. Press, 1978), 72.

56. Ibid., 79.

57. Ibid., 72.

58. Ibid., 73.

59. Contrary to Mircea Eliade, *The Myth of the Eternal Return,* trans. Willard R. Trask (Princeton, N.J.: Princeton Univ. Press, 1965), 34.

60. Ibid.

61. Eliade, *Images and Symbols,* 25. Cf. idem, "Survivals and Camouflages of Myths," in ed. Diane Apostolos-Cappadona, *Symbolism, the Sacred, and the Arts* (New York: Continuum, 1992), 32–52.

62. *Shabbat* 146a.

63. Maimonides, *Guide,* sec. 2, chap. 30, pp. 250 (line 25)–51 (line 3).

64. Ibid., p. 250 (lines 10–19). The rabbinic reference is to *Pirqe de-R. Eli'ezer ha-Gadol* (New York: Om Publishing, 1946), 13, 31b; *Bereshit Rabba* 56, 4, vol. 2, p. 599.

65. Maimonides, *Guide,* sec. 2, chap. 12, p. 195 (lines 15–17); see above, p. 211 n. 61.

66. *Bereshit Rabba,* 15, 2, vol. 1, p. 141.

67. Maimonides, *Guide,* sec. 2, chap. 30, p. 251 (line 10).

68. See ibid., sec. 3, chap. 12, especially p. 322 (lines 1–4).

69. *Sanhedrin* 91b.

70. See Maimonides, *Guide,* sec. 3, chap. 22, pp. 354 (lines 4)–55 (line 13).

71. Ibid., sec. 2, chap. 30, p. 250 (lines 2–10).

72. See ibid., sec. 3, chap. 22, pp. 353 (line 28)–54 (line 4).

73. Ibid., sec. 2, chap. 30, p. 250 (lines 19–25). Note that the Hebrew *'aqeb* 'hill' can also apply to the tail of a snake; see Maimonides, *Pirush ha-Mishnayot, Berakhot* 5:1, vol. 1, p. 74 n. 3.

74. See Baḥye bar Asher, *Bi'ur 'al ha-Tora, 'Eqeb,* vol. 3, pp. 291–92.

75. See above, pp. 69–74.

76. Erich Neumann, *The Origins and History of Consciousness,* trans. R. F. C. Hull. (Princeton, N.J.: Princeton Univ. Press, 1993), 16.

77. Ibid.

78. Cf. Maimonides, *Guide,* sec. 1, chap. 10.

79. See Umberto Cassuto, *La Questione della Genesi* (Florence, 1934), 1–91; idem, *The Documentary Hypothesis* (in Hebrew) (Jerusalem: Magnes Press,

1953), 19–38; M. H. Segal, "The Names יי and א-להים in the Books of the Bible," (in Hebrew) *Tarbiz* 9 (1938): 123–62.

80. See Maimonides, *Guide,* sec. 3, chap. 23, p. 357 (lines 13–25). I have further developed this theme in Faur, "Reflections on Job and Situational Morality," *Judaism* 19 (1970): 219–25.

81. See Faur, *Golden Doves,* 130–31.

82. Maimonides, *Guide,* sec. 3, chap. 24, p. 363 (line 9).

83. *Horayot* 8a–b. Maimonides's decision is based on the fact that R. Simlai (third century) *darash* (publicly taught) this doctrine and it was further discussed by the Talmudic authorities in *Makkot* 23b–24a.

84. See above, pp. 69–74.

85. Maimonides, *Guide,* sec. 2, chap. 33, p. 256 (lines 18–27). On the distinction between "rational" and "conventional" commandments see idem, *Studies in the Mishne Tora,* 166–76.

86. Maimonides, *Guide,* sec. 2, chap. 33, pp. 256 (line 27)–57 (line 6).

87. See above, p. 4. This doctrine repudiates the basic premise of Elie Benamozegh, as presented in *Israel and Humanity,* trans. Maxwell Luria (New York: Paulist Press, 1995), 92–94. It should be emphasized, however, that the original French version of that work, *Israël et L'Humanité,* published posthumously (Paris: Ernest Leroux, 1914), seems to have been improperly edited and therefore may have distorted the author's view of this matter.

88. Cassirer, *Philosophy of Symbolic Forms,* 2:203–4.

89. See *Shabbat* 88b. The preceding rejects the view that monotheism and polytheism are somehow genetically connected either by maintaining with Wilhelm Schmidt that polytheism derives from some sort of primordial monotheism (Maimonides, *Mishne Tora, 'Aboda Zara,* chap. 1 refers to the children of Seth; cf. above, pp. 127–28) or with Renan that monotheism somehow evolves from polytheism. See R. Solomon ibn Verga, *Shebeṭ Yehuda,* ed. Azreil Schochet and Y. Beer (Jerusalem: Mossad Bialik, 5707/1947), 12, p. 58; and Faur, *In the Shadow of History,* 219 n. 8.

90. See Maimonides, *Guide,* sec. 2, chap. 33, p. 257 (lines 15–18).

91. This is based on a careful analysis of this term in Philo and Josephus that I developed in a forthcoming book, *Maimonides's Water-Clock: The Unfolding of a Metaphor.*

92. See Mircea Eliade, *Rites and Symbols of Initiation,* trans. William R. Trask (New York: Harpers and Row, 1975), index, under "Death and Resurrection."

93. See Maimonides, *Mishne Tora, 'Edut,* chap. 2.

94. See Faur, *Golden Doves,* 58. Hence the relevance of geography in scrip-

ture and rabbinic literature. For a brief survey of the subject see S. Klein, *History of Palestine Exploration* (in Hebrew) (Jerusalem: Bialik Foundation, 1937). In the archaic mind the desert is a godless place; see Mircea Eliade, *The Sacred and the Profane*, trans. williard R. Trask (New York: Harvest, 1959), 29–32; and idem, *Myth of the Eternal Return*, 9–10.

95. See *Mekhilta, Bo* 1–2, pp. 6–9; Maimonides, *Mishne Tora, Qiddush ha-Ḥodesh* 1:2.

96. *Rosh ha-Shana*, 25a; Maimonides, *Mishne Tora, Qiddush ha-Ḥodesh* 2:10. Cf. *Debarim Rabba, Va-'Etḥanan* 2:9, in *Midrash Rabba ['al ha-Tora ve-'al Ḥamesh Megillot]* (Venice, 5364/1604), 198a.

97. Eliade, *Sacred and the Profane*, p. 95; see idem, *Myth of the Eternal Return*, chap. 1.

98. See Faur, *Golden Doves*, 51–52; idem, *In the Shadow of History*, 188.

99. See R. Judah ha-Levi, *Kitab al-Radd wa-al-Dalil fi al-Dim al-Dhalil* [cited as Kuzari], edited by H. Baneth (Jesus alern: Magnes Press, 1977), 2: 20.

100. Cf. Faur, *Golden Doves*, xxiv. In contradistinction to the sacred calendars in pagan tradition where "one holy day is connected with another directly, without the intervention of profane days," see Mircea Eliade, *Autobiography*, vol. 2, 53.

101. Maimonides, *Guide*, sec. 2, chap. 33, p. 258 (line 4). Cf. ibid., chap. 34, p. 258 (lines 17–21). Eliade's interpretation of Is 11:15–16 and Jewish Messianism (*Myth of the Eternal Return*, 105–6) is not authentic to Judaism. Eliade had no direct access to the sources and could not know that his references came from Jewish circles whose fundamental concepts are rooted in Christian thought and ethos; see Faur, *In the Shadow of History*, chap. I.

102. Maimonides, *Guide*, sec. 2, chap. 33, p. 257 (line 11); cf. ibid., chap. 34, p. 258 (line 19); sec. 3, chap. 9, p. 315 (line 4); 24, p. 363 (lines 8–9); idem, *Iggeret Teman*, ed. A. S. Halkin (New York: Jewish Theological Seminary of America, 5712/1952), 26.

103. See Faur, *Golden Doves*, 30–35.

104. Eliade, *Sacred and the Profane*, 68.

105. See quotation above, p. 136. Hence the function of transmigration in pagan psychology and theosophy.

106. That is, *yaqin*; see above, p. 140.

107. *Mishne Tora, Yesode ha-Tora* 8:2.

108. See *Shabbat* 23a; *Megilla* 21b; *Mishne Tora, Megilla ve-Ḥanukka* 1:3; 3:4. Cf. *Berakhot* 54a; *Mishne Tora, Berakhot* 10:9; Maimonides, *Guide*, sec. 3, chap. 50, pp. 452 (line 16)–54 (line 11).

109. Eliade, *Myth of the Eternal Return,* 104. Eliade had no direct access to Jewish sources, and occasionally, gratuitous Christological remarks and innuendo—a fashionable must in certain 'intellectual' circles of the time—mar his writings. I was able to benefit from his brilliant insights by proceeding in the lines followed by Rabbi Me'ir with respect to Elisha; see *Ḥagiga* 15b.

110. See Faur, *In the Shadow of History,* chap. 9.

111. See Faur, *Studies in the Mishne Tora,* 13 n. 3, 5. For Maimonides this is a fundamental principle of the Jewish faith; see ibid., 148–50.

112.See Eliade, *Myth of the Eternal Return,* 42, 45.

113. See ibid., 46.

114. Ibid., 44. I was vividly reminded of this principle recently when visiting Agudat Dodim, a synagogue from Damascus, in my native Buenos Aires. A few members of the community asked me about the famous Blood Libel case that took place in Damascus in 1840. It was a *cause célèbre* of international proportions. The historical facts were documented and had been reported by all major Jewish historians of the period. The basic story had been transmitted orally until our own time. When I told them the story, some were surprised that I failed to mention a (new) version according to which the main hero was a rabbi who went to the place where the victim's body had been concealed (revealed to him in a vision) and pronouncing a cabalistic formula resurrected him. They then marched together to the French authorities. The victim identified himself and proceeded to give a full account of how and by whom he was murdered, exonerating the community from all charges. After the French authorities had the opportunity to question the victim and the real killer had confessed his crime, the rabbi pronounced another formula, and the victim died, returning presumably to his original sepulcher. (Knowing the attitude of the French authorities at the time toward anything Jewish, the fact that they did not charge the rabbi with homicide for returning the resurrected victim, a Christian monk and a French citizen, to death, should be counted as another miracle). When I told them that their hero had been neither the Chief rabbi nor a member of the court and, therefore, that he could not have spoken on behalf of the community, I was told that at the time there were *two* Chief rabbis, the minor rabbi being one of them. It was fully admitted that Jewish history counted no parallels to such a situation. Nonetheless, they insisted, this had been the case at the time. I pointed out to them that the said rabbi was not included in the special memorial services on the night of the Day of Atonement, when the community honors all of its spiritual leaders from the expulsion from Spain (1492) until modern

times. At the same time, the name of R. Ḥayyim Palaggi (1788–1869), the Chief rabbi of Izmir, was included in the memorial in gratitude for having brought the matter to the attention of Moses Montefiore (1784–1885). One of them, a professional who had completed his Univ. studies, replied that the historical evidence was irrelevant to our discussion and what was spiritually significant was the fact that the rabbi in question had resurrected the victim, and so on, thus, confirming the universality of the above.

115. See below, pp. 150–55.

116. See above, p. 134. Cf. *Shabbat* 156a–b.

117. *Sifra*, edited by Issac Hirsch Weiss (New York: Om Publishing, 1946), *Qedoshim*, 93d.

118. *Shemona Peraqim*, 6, Maimonides, *Pirush ha-Mishnayot*, 4:392–93.

119. Maimonides, *Guide*, sec. 2, chap. 33, p. 256 (lines 25–27).

120. Ibid., chap. 32, p. 255 (lines 23–27). Cf. ibid., chap. 33, p. 256 (lines 3–4); cf. Faur, *Golden Doves*, 11.

121. Maimonides, *Guide*, sec. 2, chap. 33, pp. 256 (line 13), 257 (lines 3–4). See the brilliant comment by R. Moses Alshekh, *Torat Moshe*, 5 vols. (Jerusalem: Makhon Leb Śameaḥ, 5750/1990), *Be-ha'alotekha*, 4:71.

122. Maimonides, *Guide*, sec. 2, chap. 33, p. 256 (lines 5–18).

123. See Faur, *Golden Doves*, 94.

124. See ibid., 42–44.

125. See *Guide* sec. 2, chap. 33, p. 256 (lines 10–14), where on the basis of this experience future "prophets" contradicting the Law of Moses will be rejected.

126. See Faur, *In the Shadow of History*, 205–6.

127. Jews of Damascus distinguish between *laṭafo kaf* (he slapped him kindly) when it is done with good intentions and *laṭasho kaf* (he smacked him) when it is done with the intention to inflict harm. Semantically, it parallels the Hebrew *tokheḥa*, a 'reprimand' to discipline a beloved one (see Prv 27:5), and *ge'ara* 'admonishment' (see Gn 37:10, Eccl 7:5). On the theological implications of this concept see Samuel de Usque, *Consolation for the Tribulations of Israel*, trans. Martin A. Cohen (Philadelphia: Jewish Publication Society, 1977), 229.

128. See Maimonides, *Guide*, sec. 3, chap. 54, pp. 466 (line 15)–67 (line 2). It is semantically included in the Hebrew *ḥokhma;* see ibid.

129. See ibid., chap. 32, p. 384 (lines 22–23); cf. sec. 2, chap. 24, p. 227 (line 16).

130. See ibid., sec. 3, chap. 32, pp. 383 (line 20)–84 (line 10).

131. Cf. Maimonides, *Treatise on Resurrection*, 32–33.

132. See Maimonides, *Guide,* sec. 3, chap. 27; Faur, ***Studies in the Mishne Tora***, 171–73.

133. Maimonides, *Guide,* sec. 3, chap. 31. The teachings of the Law are classified as "opinions" because generally they pertain to the realm of prophecy and cannot be demonstrated; see above pp. 109–15; cf., however, Maimonides, *Guide,* sec. 3, chap. 54, p. 467 (lines 2–27).

134. Maimonides, *Guide,* sec. 3, chap. 32, p. 384 (lines 13–14); chap. 51, p. 459 (lines 27–28).

135. Ibid., chap. 29, p. 381 (lines 5–7). The quote is from *Qiddushin* 40a.

136. See Maimonides, *Guide,* sec. 3, chap. 29, pp. 377 (line 25)–78 (line 10), 379 (line 12–13); chap. 32, p. 384 (lines 18–19); chap. 46, p. 430 (line 14). Cf above, p. 232 n. 23.

137. Ibid., chap. 29, p. 379 (line 12).

138. Ibid., chap. 29, p. 379 (lines 13–15), and above, p. 233 n. 51. On the contributions of Christianity and Islam to the advancement of pagan humanity see Maimonides, *Mishne Tora, Melakhim* 14:4 (uncensored editions).

139. Maimonides, *Guide,* sec. 3, chap. 32, p. 385 (lines 10–11).

140. See ibid., chap. 29, pp. 377 (lines 11–12), 380 (lines 25–29); chap. 30, p. 382 (lines 6–18); chap. 32, p. 388 (lines 4–5); chaps. 37, p. 397 (lines 5–6).

141. Ibid., chap. 29, p. 377 (lines 10–18); chap. 33, 37.

142. See ibid., chap. 32, pp. 384 (line 10)–86 (line 11), 388 (lines 3–4). The source for this idea is rabbinic; see the valuable note of R. Joseph Qafiḥ, *More,* ad loc., vol. 3, p. 575 n. 24*.

143. See Maimonides, *Guide,* sec. 3, chap. 46, pp. 426 (lines 27–28), 429 (line 28)–30 (line 30), 430 (line 21), 431 (line 8). On the sicknesses of the soul see above, pp. 134–36.

144. See Maimonides, *Guide,* sec. 3, chap. 46, p. 431 (lines 3–11).

145. Ibid., p. 426 (lines 26–28); cf. ibid., pp. 433 (line 19)–34 (line 12). On this type of harmful "opinions" see above, p. 233 n. 44. When referring to this type of atonement, Maimonides uses the Arabic verb *gafara*; see ibid. Maimonides, *Guide,* sec. 3, chap. 46, pp. 426 (line 27), 432 (lines 13, 28), 434 (lines 5, 6). To indicate atonement for a personal sin he uses the Hebrew *kappara;* see ibid., p. 428 (line 14). On the method of healing used by the Tora see ibid., p. 426 (lines 27–28); *Mishne Tora, De'ot* 2:2; *Shemona Peraqim* 4, Maimonides, *Pirush ha-Mishnayot*, 4:379–87. For kappara in the sense of 'cleansing' see *Baba Meṣi'a* 24a as quoted in *Oṣar ha- Ge'onim, Baba Meṣi'a, Ha-Pirushim*, 16 n. 4; *Ḥolin* 8b, and the comment of R. Moses Alshekh, *Torat Moshe,* vol. 3, *Emor,* 150b.

146. See Maimonides, *Guide*, sec. 3, chap. 46, pp. 432 (line 7)–33 (line 1).

147. See ibid., chap. 32, pp. 387 (line 5)–89 (line 4).

148. *Midrash Tanḥuma, Ḥuqqat*, 26 (260), 59b–60a. See *Mishne Tora, Miqva'ot* 11:12.

149. This doctrine coincides with the view expressed by Lüdwig Wittgenstein, "Lecture on Ethics," *Philosophical Review* 74 (1965): 15:

> Schick says that theological ethics contains two conceptions of the essence of the Good. According to the more superficial interpretation, the Good is good because God wills it; according to the deeper interpretation, God wills the Good because it is good.
>
> I think that the first conception is the deeper one: Good is what God orders. For this cuts off the path to any and every explanation 'why' it is good, while the second conception is precisely the superficial, the rationalistic one, which proceeds as if what is good could still be given some foundation.
>
> The first conception says clearly that the essence of the Good has nothing to do with facts and therefore cannot be explained by any proposition. If any proposition expresses just what I mean, it is: Good is what God orders.

See Maimonides *Mishne Tora, Miqva'ot* 11:12; and Faur, *Studies in the Mishne Tora*, 166–76.

150. See Faur, *Golden Doves*, xiv–xvi.

151. Maimonides, *Guide*, sec. 3, chap. 26, pp. 369 (line 18)–71 (line 4). Cf. above, pp. 74–79. The rabbinic source is in *Bereshit Rabba* 44, 15, vol. 1, pp. 424–25. Cf. *Shemona Peraqim* 6, Maimonides, *Pirush ha-Mishnayot*, 4:391–93. Obviously, the "details" here correspond to the "silver dots" of the "golden doves."

152. See Maimonides, *Guide*, sec. 3, chap. 32, pp. 385 (line 13)–89 (line 4). Cf. chap. 28, p. 374 (lines 15–21); chap. 46, p. 430 (lines 22–23).

153. *Mekhilta, Beshallaḥ* (*Masekhta de-Vayyisa'*), 158; see editors note on line 9, and *Mekhilta de-R. Shim'on bar Yoḥai, Beshallaḥ*, 105. Cf. *Pirqe Abot* 6:7. See *Qiddushin* 30b. In *Sifre* no. 37, pp. 70–71, *Baba Batra* 16a, the Tora is compared to *tablin* spices in the sense of having healing properties.

154. See Maimonides, *Guide* sec. 1, chap. 42. Cf. Fijo, *Bina le-'Ittim*, 2: 16–19.

155. See Faur, *Golden Doves*, 75–76.

156. Maimonides, *Guide*, sec. 3, chap. 32, p. 385 (line 23). In the *More, ha-*

Nebukhim, ed. R. Joseph Qafiḥ, 3: 576, the version *ḥayyad* is an emendation by someone who did not have sufficient *shaja'a* to understand the text. *Ḥayyad* is a negative 'departure,' without positive redeeming value; cf. Maimonides, *Guide,* Introduction, p. 9 (line 17); and Faur, *Golden Doves,* 173 n. 73.

157. *Midrash Tanḥuma, Mas'e,* 2, 2:81b. In this manner God will heal again Israel in the future; see Hos 2:16–17.

158. Maimonides, *Guide,* sec. 3, chap. 32, p. 386 (lines 4–9).

159. *Shemona Peraqim* 4, Maimonides, *Pirush ha-Mishnayot,* 4:380; cf. pp. 381, 382; 8, p. 396. On Maimonides attitude toward heroism see ibid., 4, p. 381, and "Two Models of Jewish Spirituality," 10–11.

160. Cf. *Pirqe Abot* 4:1. Otherwise, only anthropomorphic Jews could apply *gibbor, gebura* to God; cf. Dt 10:7; Jer 32:18; Neh 9:32; 1 Ch 29:11, 12; 2 Ch 20:6, and so on. Although it may occasionally be interpreted in terms of physical strength, see below, p. 176ff.

161. See n. 162 below.

162. Maimonides, *Guide,* sec. 3, chap. 24, pp. 361 (line 27)–62 (line 3).

163. *Pirqe Abot* 5:3.

164. *Midrash Tanḥuma* (Jerusalem: Merkaz ha-Sefer, 5747 / 1987), *Lekh Lekha* (3), p. 24. This is equivalent to *moneṭa* (coin) in *Bereshit Rabba, Lekh Lekha* 39, 12, vol. 1, pp. 374–75. For a further analysis of this term, see Faur, *Golden Doves,* 139–41.

165. Maimonides, *Guide,* sec. 1, chap. 16, p. 28 (lines 19–21).

166. See above, pp. 66–68.

167. Eliade, *Myth of the Eternal Return,* 5.

168. See Faur, *Golden Doves,* xvii, 52, 146.

169. See ibid., 54–58.

170. See Maimonides, *Guide,* sec. 3, chap. 24, p. 362 (lines 4–18). Cf. Is 16:19.

171. Maimonides, *Guide,* sec. 3, chap. 24, p. 363 (lines 8–9). This type of certainty is the effect of revelation; see ibid., p. 364 (lines 9–15). See above, pp. 140, 145–46.

172. Maimonides, *Guide,* sec. 3, chap. 24, p. 364 (line 22).

173. Ibid., pp. 362 (line 24)–63 (line 4). The source is the verse in Dt 32:10. The accurate translation is the Arabic rendition by Se'adya; *Version Arabe du Pentateuque,* edited by Joseph Derenbouy (Paris: Ernest Lenoex, 1893), 302. In English: "He [God] maintained him [Israel] in a desolated land; in a barren, despondent wasteland. He [God] made him [Israel] wander in circles, He [God] made him [Israel] thoughtful, He [God] guarded him [Israel] as the pupil of His eye," thus indicating the connection between Israel's wanderings

and the peculiar intelligence gained thereby while God was carefully protecting them as if they were the "pupil of His eye."

174. See *Berakhot* 5a.

175. See above, p. 237 n. 111.

176. See Maimonides, *Guide,* sec. 3, chap. 24, pp. 363 (line 14)–64 (line 27). Both these feelings are intimately related to one another: there could be no love of God without faith in the validity of prophecy and vice versa.

177. Eliade, *Myth of the Eternal Return,* 109–10.

178. *Yoma* 69b.

179. Maimonides, *Mishne Tora, Girushin* 2:20; cf. ibid., *Ḥames wu-Maṣṣa* 6:3. For some of the legal niceties of this concept see Faur, "Monolingualism and Judaism," 1724–29.

180. See Horst-Eberhard Richter, *All Mighty,* trans. Jan van Heurck (Claremont, California: Hunter House, 1984), chaps. 7–12.

181. Maimonides, *Guide,* sec. 3, chap. 23, p. 360 (lines 18–21).

182. See above, pp. 91–93.

183. Maimonides, *Guide,* sec. 3, chap. 23, p. 360 (lines 8–14).

184. Ibid., (lines 21–24).

185. Ibid., (lines 26–27).

186. See above, pp. 84–86.

187. Maimonides, *Guide,* sec. 3, chap. 23, p. 357 (lines 17–18). Cf. ibid., chap. 54, p. 468 (lines 1–13).

188. Ibid., chap. 23, p. 357 (line 14).

189. Ibid., (lines 18–19). On the relation between *ḥa'ira* and imagination see ibid., p. 360 (lines 19–20).

190. Ibid., p. 357 (lines 14–17).

191. Bertrand Russell, *Mysticism and Logic* (Garden City, N.Y.: Doubleday, 1957), 9.

192. Maimonides, *Guide,* sec. 3, chap. 23, p. 357 (line 14), p. 360 (lines 26–31).

193. Jorge Luis Borges, "The God's Script," in *Labyrinths,* trans. L. A. Murillo (New York: New Directions, 1964), 173.

194. Russell, *Mysticism and Logic,* 10.

195. Maimonides, *Guide,* sec. 3, chap. 23, p. 361 (lines 2–3). The quotation is from *Shabbat* 88b. Cf. *De'ot* 2:3, 5:13; Faur, *In the Shadow of History,* 191.

196. See above, pp. 57–67.

197. See Maimonides, *Guide,* sec. 3, chap. 29, pp. 375 (line 24), 377 (line 3); chap. 32, p. 385 (lines 1–2); chap. 37, p. 397 (line 6); chap. 46, pp. 429 (line 23), 431 (line 1).

198. See ibid., sec. 2, chaps. 37–38.

199. See ibid., sec. 1, chap. 14.

200. See ibid., sec. 3, chap. 27.

201. Ibid., sec. 2, chap. 40, p. 270 (lines 17–22).

202. See ibid., sec. 2, chap. 38, p. 267 (lines 12–14).

203. See ibid., sec. 2, chap. 38, p. 267 (lines 12–14).

204. See ibid., sec. 1, chap. 26, p. 38 (line 9); cf. ibid., chap. 49, p. 73 (line 23); sec. 3, chap 12, p. 318 (line 9).

205. See ibid., sec. 1, chap. 26, p. 38 (line 19). Cf. Faur, *Golden Doves*, 3.

206. See Maimonides, *Guide*, sec. 3, chap. 27, p. 371 (lines 19–20), cf. p. 372 (lines 6–7). A full quotation is below, p. 166. As one of his contemporaries, R. Joseph ibn 'Aqnin, *Hitgallut ha-Sodot*, 56, wrote, the esoteric meaning of the Tora, "can be only understood by individuals (*al-firad*)," that is, not as members of a crowd. Similarly, ibid., 410, he distinguished between *ta'lim jamhuri* 'public teaching', which must be at the exoteric level, and *ta'lim khasi* 'individual teaching', which is reserved for esoteric instruction; cf. ibid., 458. The source for this distinction is the Mishna *Ḥagiga* 2:1.

207. See Maimonides, *Guide*, sec. 2, chap. 36, p. 263 (lines 7–27).

208. See above, pp. 72–73.

209. Faur, *In the Shadow of History*, 216–17.

210. See Maimonides, *Guide*, sec. 2, chap. 40, p. 270 (lines 26, 27), p. 271 (lines 11, 13, 16, 22). Cf. above, p. 212 n. 89. On the specific character of these laws see Leo Strauss, *Persecution and the Art of Writing* (Glencoe, Ill.: Free Press, 1952), chap. 4.

211. Maimonides, *Guide*, sec. 2, chap. 37, p. 264 (lines 15–20).

212. Ibid., chap. 40, p. 271 (lines 17–24).

213. Cf. above, p. 116.

214. Maimonides, *Guide*, sec. 2, chap. 37, p. 264 (lines 13–15).

215. Hence, the title of Spinoza's famous *Tractatus*.

216. Maimonides, *Guide*, sec. 3, chap. 27, p. 371 (lines 17–30).

217. See ibid., sec. 2, chap. 40, p. 271 (line 10–29); sec. 3, chap. 27, pp. 371 (line 30)–73 (line 4).

218. Ibid., sec. 1, chap. 26, p. 38 (lines 8–9); see *Berakhot* 31b, Faur, *Golden Doves*, 151 n. 54.

219. Maimonides, *Guide*, sec. 2, chap. 29, p. 243 (lines 16–26). Cf. Faur, *Golden Doves*, xv, xvii, xix, xxv, 12–13, 69–76, 79–81.

220. Maimonides, *Guide*, Introduction, pp. 2 (lines 16–29), chap. 5 (lines 16–17).

221. Ibid., sec. 1, chap. 33, p. 48 (lines 1–9). Cf. chap. 35, p. 54 (lines 20–28).

222. Ibid., Introduction, p. 5 (lines 15–18); sec. 1, chap. 33, p. 48 (lines 9–12).

223. See ibid., sec. 2, chap. 47; cf. sec. 1, chap. 49; and above, pp. 69–74.

224. See Eliade, *Sacred and the Profane,* chap. 2; idem, *Myth and Reality,* chap. 5.

225. See above, pp. 94–98.

226. See Faur, *Golden Doves,* 74–76.

227. See Maimonides, *Guide,* sec. 2, chap. 39, pp. 269 (line 27)–70 (line 2).

228. Ibid., chap. 54, pp. 467 (line 28)–69 (line 13). Cf. below, pp. 173–78. The four types of perfection discussed by Maimonides in the name of the philosophers, parallel the four connotations of the term (ḥokhma) 'wisdom' discussed at the beginning of the chapter, pp. 466 (line 15)–67 (line 2). They also coincide with the three types of perfection attributed by the rabbis to the Patriarch Jacob; see *Shabbat* 33b. The last perfection *torato* (his Tora) includes both ethical and intellectual virtues, see ibid., p. 467 (lines 2–5). Both these virtues are intimately connected to each other, especially because the ethical virtues are a "precursory" (*tawṭiyat*) to the intellectual virtues; see ibid., p. 468 (line 25). Therefore, *torato* of the rabbis is equivalent to perfections three and four of the philosophers.

229. See Maimonides, *Guide,* sec. 1, chap. 26, p. 38 (lines 4, 20).

230. Ibid., sec. 3, chap. 54 p. 469 (lines 1–13). This is why someone reaching the full limits of her or his perfection must be a unique individual; cf. ibid., sec. 2, chap. 39, p. 269 (lines 6–10), and below, p. 245 n. 241.

231. See Maimonides, *Guide* Introduction, p. 4 (line 12); sec. 2, chap. 36, p. 263 (lines 1–6); sec. 3, chap. 51, pp. 455 (line 25), 456 (lines 4–5). See above, p. 22 n. 15.

232. See Maimonides, *Guide,* sec. 2, chap. 29, p. 243 (lines 28–29); chap. 36; chap. 38, p. 267 (lines 25–29).

233. Ibid., sec. 1, chap. 54, p. 86 (line 5); sec. 3, chap. 27, pp. 371 (lines 18, 20, 28), 372 (line 8); chap. 51, p. 457 (line 7); chap. 54, p. 471 (line 4). Similarly, see Maimonides, *Mishne Tora, Teshuba* 8:3, "the knowledge acquired by (the soul) according to her capacity"; and ibid., 10:6, "to understand and comprehend the sciences and knowledge which inform him about his Maker, according to the capacity that there is in man to understand and perceive." Cf. ibid., 5:2; *Melakhim* 12:4; *Shemona Peraqim,* 5, Maimonides, *Pirush ha-Mishnayot,* 4:387.

234. In general, to call attention to a key concept, Maimonides uses the same term a definite number of times (seven, ten, etc.). In this case it was repeated seven times; see Maimonides, *Guide,* sec. 3, chap. 27, p. 372 (lines 6, 9 [twice], 11, 15, 21, 25).

235. Ibid., pp. 371 (line 29)–73 (line 4). Cf. Maimonides, *Mishne Tora, Melakhim* 12:4–5.

236. See above, pp. 127–31.

237. Maimonides, *Guide,* sec. 3, chap. 51, p. 459 (lines 1–2).

238. Ibid., p. 454 (line 21).

239. For a detailed analysis of this parable see Kellner, *Maimonides on Human Perfection,* 15–39.

240. See Maimonides, *Guide,* sec. 3, chap. 51, p. 455 (lines 4–6), together with p. 46 (lines 5–8).

241. See ibid., p. 456 (lines 17–18).

242. See ibid., p. 457 (lines 1–2).

243. See ibid., p. 455 (lines 1–3, 26–28), together with p. 456 (lines 1–5).

244. See ibid., p. 456 (lines 24–25).

245. Ibid., chap. 54, p. 469 (lines 1–4).

246. It is not accidental that this chapter follows the chapter about the "secrets of the Tora," containing a long explanation about Israel's march through the Desert. Significantly, Maimonides opened the discussion with the Hebrew *massa'ot*—a term akin to Arabic *sa'y*; see ibid., chap. 50, p. 452 (line 24). Cf. *'Erubin* 54a.

247. Maimonides, *Guide,* sec. 3, chap. 51, p. 454 (lines 20–22). See below, n. 249.

248. Cf. below, n. 253.

249. Maimonides, *Guide,* sec. 3, chap. 51, p. 456 (lines 5–8), cf. p. 457 (line 6).

250. See ibid., pp. 456 (lines 20–25), 457 (lines 10–11), 459 (line 3); chap. 52, p. 464 (lines 3–4). On the phenomenology of God's "ways," see Faur, *Golden Doves,* xxiii.

251. See Maimonides, *Guide,* sec. 3, chap. 51, p. 457 (lines 1–10).

252. See ibid., chap. 28, p. 373 (lines 7–22); chap. 51, p. 457 (lines 1–12); chap. 52, pp. 464 (line 27)–65 (line 2).

253. Ibid., sec. 1, chap. 39, p. 60 (lines 18–20). Cf. ibid., sec. 3, chap. 51, pp. 456 (lines 5–9), p. 457 (lines 1–7); *Shemona Peraqim* 5, Maimonides, *Pirush ha-Mishnayot,* 4:390.

254. See Maimonides, *Guide,* sec. 3, chap. 27, p. 372 (lines 9–10).

255. See ibid., chap. 52.

256. Ibid., chap. 51, p. 465 (lines 2–4).

257. That is, God. Ibid., chap. 51, p. 457 (line 6). Concerning the designation of God as the "First Idea" cf. Munk, *Guide des Egarés,* 2: 438 n. 2. It is an allusion to Ps 111:10 and Prv 1:7 where the beginning of wisdom is identified with the fear of God.

258. Maimonides, *Guide,* sec. 3, chap. 51, p. 456 (line 25).

259. Ibid., p. 456 (lines 16–19). Cf. Maimonides, *Mishne Tora, Teshuba* 10:6.

260. Maimonides, *Guide,* sec. 3, chap. 51, p. 458 (lines 1–5).

261. Ibid., p. 457 (lines 5–6). See *Ta'aniyot* 2b and Maimonides, *Mishne Tora, Tefilla* 1:1.

262. Maimonides, *Guide,* sec. 3, chap. 51, p. 459 (lines 1–2); cf. ibid., pp. 454 (line 27), 456 (line 8).

263. Maimonides, *Mishne Tora, Tefilla* 4:16.

264. See ibid., 4:4.

265. Maimonides, *Guide* sec. 1, chap. 13.

266. Ibid., sec. 3, chap. 12, p. 322 (lines 4–9).

267. *Megilla* 15b.

268. See Maimonides, *Guide,* sec. 3, chap. 27, p. 373 (line 2).

269. Ibid., chap. 57, pp. 462 (line 17)–63 (line 10).

270. Ibid., p. 463 (lines 10–13).

271. Ibid., p. 456 (lines 26–27). These parallel the three aspects of intellectual worship cited above, pp. 169–70.

272. Maimonides, *Mishne Tora, Teshuba* 10:6.

273. Maimonides, *Guide,* sec. 3, chap. 51, p. 458 (line 15). Cf. idem, *Mishne Tora, Tefilla* 4:16.

274. *Mishna Berakhot* 5:1.

275. Maimonides, *Guide,* sec. 3, chap. 51, p. 458 (lines 15–16).

276. Ibid., pp. 458 (line 12)–59 (line 5).

277. See ibid., p. 456 (lines 13–15).

278. Ibid., p. 463 (line 15).

279. Ibid., p. 457 (lines 8–9).

280. Cited in Ibn 'Ezra's commentary to Gn 28:12.

281. *Nedarim* 20b.

282. See Maimonides, *Guide* sec. 1, chap. 15.

283. Ibid., sec. 2, chap. 37, p. 264 (lines 9–13). He belongs to the sixth group; see above, p. 169.

284. Maimonides, *Guide* sec. 3, chap. 54, p. 469 (line 4). It corresponds to the fourth class of perfection, which is achieved by the sixth group see above, p. 169.

285. See Maimonides, *Guide,* sec. 2, chap. 37, p. 264 (lines 3–9).

286. See *Ḥolin* 92a.

287. Maimonides, *Guide* sec. 1, chap. 15, p. 28 (lines 4–7).

288. R. Joseph b. Jehuda, "Un fragment d'un livre inconnu (Bustan al-Azhar) de Joseph ben Juda ibn Aknin," ed. Boaz Cohen, *Revue des Etudes Juive* 100 bis (1936), fragment 1, p. 54. On the different senses of this term see

Avempace (ibn Bajja), *Tadbir al-Mitwaḥḥed,* ed. and tran. Miguel Asín Palacios, *El Régimen del Solitario* (Madrid-Granada: Consejo Superior de Investigaciones Ciéntificas, 1946), especially pp. 3–12 of the original.

289. Cf. Maimonides, *Guide,* sec. 2, chap. 39, pp. 269 (line 26)–70 (line 2).

290. R. Joseph b. Jehuda, "Un fragment d'un livre inconnu," 54, fragment 2. From this point of view the role of Elijah in Jewish folklore, perennially involved in the aid of the people and the appointed herald of the future Messiah of Israel, is to compensate for his faulty ministry on earth.

291. See *Baba Meṣi'a* 99a; Maimonides, *Mishne Tora, She'ela wu-Piqadon* 3:1–2. Originally, a master was personally liable for the acts of his slave; see the episode related in *Sanhedrin* 19a. The change in the law was the result of a special legislation whereby a master was exempted from liability for the damages caused by a slave; see Mishna *Yadayim* 4:7; *Baba Qamma* 4a; Maimonides, *Mishne Tora, Geneba* 1:9. It follows that on this fundamental point there is agreement between the rabbinic and the English juridical systems about establishing liability of the employer for the damages caused by an employee. The difference is legislative, not juridical. This fundamental point was overlooked in the penetrating article by Haim S. Hefetz, "Vicarious Liability in Jewish Law," (in Hebrew) *Dine Israel* 6 (1975), 49–91. Cf. R. Moses Galante, *She'elot wu-Tshubot* (Venice, 5368/1608), no.14.

292. See *Shabbat* 92a; *Nedarim* 38a.

293. See Introduction to Maimonides, *Pirush ha-Mishnayot,* 1:7; *Shemona Peraqim,* 7, idem, *Pirush ha-Mishnayot,* 4:393; idem, *Mishne Tora, Yesode ha-Tora* 7:1–2; idem, *Guide* sec. 2, chap. 32, p. 254 (lines 15–16).

294. *Tamid* 32a.

295. Cf. Kellner, *Maimonides on Human Perfection,* 34.

296. This is a reference to the philosophers; see above, p.000.

297. Maimonides, *Guide,* sec. 3, chap. 54, pp. 470 (line 17)–71 (line 7). Cf. ibid., sec. 1, chap. 54; idem, *Mishne Tora, De'ot* 1:6–7.

298. See Maimonides, *Guide,* Introduction, p. 13 (lines 12–15; lines 8–9).

299. See above, pp. 194ff.

300. See Kellner, *Maimonides on Human Perfection,* 41–64.

301. See Faur, *In the Shadow of History,* 215–17.

302. See Maimonides, *Guide* sec. 3, chap. 54, p. 469 (lines 21–25). From this perspective the least important of the three is ethical virtue, whereas from the prophetic perspective, civic ethics, as practiced on the way down the ladder, is the highest form of perfection.

303. Rather than to create out of nothing, this verb means 'to do,' 'to compliment'; see Maimonides, *Guide,* sec. 3, chap. 30, pp. 251 (line 19)–52 (line 13). Cf. Faur, *Golden Doves,* 138. Hence *ma'aśe bereshit* and *ma'aśe merkaba*; cf. ibid., p. 249 (lines 3–16).

304. *Shabbat* 10a.

305. *Sanhedrin* 7a.

306. See above, pp. 18–19. Hence the superiority of the righteous functioning as as an *'ebed*, who has free access to God, over the righteous functioning as a "prince"; see *Berakhot* 34b.

307. Maimonides, *Guide,* sec. 2, chap. 48, p. 292 (lines 17–22).

308. Ibid. sec. 3, chap. 51, p. 463 (lines 14–17).

309. Issac Cordoso, *Philosophia Libera* (Venice, 1673), 750. Cf. David Nieto, *De la Divina Providencia* (London, 5476/1716), 141.

310. *Shabbat* 33b–34a. Cf. Faur, *Golden Doves,* 144–45.

311. See *Shabbat* 88b.

312. *Sanhedrin* 7a.

313. See above, pp. 35–38.

314. See Faur, *In the Shadow of History,* 193–202.

Bibliography

BIBLICAL AND RABBINIC SOURCES

Abot de-R. Natan. Edited by Salomon Schechter. Vienna, 5647/1887.

Bereshit Rabba. Edited by J. Theodor and C. Albeck. 3 vols. Jerusalem: Wahrmann Books, 1965.

Biblia Rabinica (Miqra'ot Gedolot). 4 vols. Venice, 5308/1548.

Diqduqe Soferim. Edited by Raphael N. N. Rabbinovicz. 15 vols. Jerusalem, 5720/1960.

Ekha Rabba. In *Midrash Rabba*.

Mekhilta de-R. Yishma'el. Edited by H. S. Horovitz and I. A. Rabin. Jerusalem: Wahrman Books, 1970.

Mekhilta de-R. Yoḥai. Edited by Y. N. Epstein and E. Z. Melamed. Jerusalem: Mekize Mirdamim, 1965.

Midrash ha-Gadol. Bereshit. Edited by M. Marguilies. Jerusalem: Mossad Harav Kook, 5727/1967.

Midrash ha-Gadol. Debarim. Edited by Solomon Fisch. Jerusalem: Mossad Harav Kook, 1972.

Midrash Rabba ('al ha-Tora ve-Ḥamesh Megillot). Venice, 5364/1604.

Midrash Rabba Qohelet. In *Midrash Rabba*.

Midrash Tanḥuma. Edited by Salomon Buber. 2 vols. Vilna, 5645/1885

Midrash Tanḥuma. Jerusalem: Merkaz ha-Sefer, 5747/1987.

Midrash Tehillim. Edited by Salomon Buber. New York: Om Publishing, 1947.

Mishna. Shishsha Sidre Mishna. 13 vols. Jerusalem: El-ha-Meqorot, 5715/1955.

Pesikta de-Rav Kahana. Edited by Bernard Mandelbaum. 2 vols. New York: Jewish Theological Seminary of America, 1962.

Pirqe de-R. Eli'ezer. New York: Om Publishing, 1946.

Sifra. Edited by Isaac Hirsch Weiss. New York: Om Publishing, 1946.

Sifre. Edited by Louis Finkelstein. New York: Jewish Theological Seminary of America, 1969.

Sifre (*Bamidbar*). Edited by M. Friedman. Vienna, 1864.

Talmud Babli. 24 vols. Venice, 5280–83/1520–23.

Talmud Yerushalmi (Palestinian Talmud). Venice, 5283/1523.

Targum Anqelos. In *Miqra'ot Gedolot.*

Tosefta. Edited by M. S. Zuckermandel. Jerusalem: Wahrman Books, 1970.

Vayyiqra Rabba. Edited by M. Margulies. 5 vols. Jerusalem: American Academy for Jewish Research, 1953.

JEWISH HELLENISTIC LITERATURE

Philo. *The Complete Works.* Translated by F. H. Colson and G. H. Whitaker. Loeb Classical Library. 10 vols.

GEONIC LITERATURE

Gaonic Responsa. Edited by Simcha Assaf. Jerusalem: Darom, 1928.

Ḥadashim Gam Yeshanim. Edited by Abraham E. Harkavi. Jerusalem: Carmiel, 5730/1970.

Ibn Shahin. See R. Nissim Ga'on.

R. Nissim Ga'on [ibn Shahin]. *An Elegant Composition Concerning Relief and Adversity.* Translated by William M. Brinner. New Haven, Conn.: Yale Univ. Press, 1977.

———. *Sefer ha-Mafteaḥ.* Edited by J. Goldenthal. Vienna, 1847.

Oṣar ha-Ge'onim. Edited by B. M. Lewin. 13 vols. Haifa and Jerusalem, 1928–43.

Se'adya Ga'on. *Version Arabe du Pentateuque.* Edited by Joseph Derenbourg. Paris: Ernest Leroux, 1893.

———. *Version Arabe de Proverbs.* Edited by Joseph Derenbourg. Paris: Librairie de la Société Asiatique de l'Ecole des Langues Orientales Vivant, 1894.

Teshubot ha-Ge'onim ha-Ḥadashot (Newly Discovered Geonic Responsa, in Hebrew). Edited by Simcha Emanuel. Jerusalem: Ofeq Institute, 5755/1995.

RABBINIC WRITERS

Abarbanel, R. Isaac. *Pirush 'al ha-Tora* (Commentary to the Pentateuch). Venice, 5339/1579.

———. *Pirush Nebi'im Rishonim* (Commentary to the early prophets). Pesaro, 5280/1520.

Abarbanel, R. Judah. See Leone Ebreo.

Alshekh, R. Moses. *Torat Moshe*. 5 vols. Jerusalem: Makhon Leb Śameaḥ, 5750/1990.

R. Baḥye bar Asher. *Bi'ur 'al ha-Tora*. Edited by Ch. D. Chavel. 3 vols. Jerusalem: Mossad Harav Kook, 1968.

Benamozegh, R. Elie. *Israël et L'Humanité*. Paris: Ernest Leroux, 1914. English translation, *Israel and Humanity*. by Maxwell Luria. New York: Paulist Press, 1995.

Cardoso, Isaac. *Philosophia Libera*. Venice, 1673.

Caro, R. Isaac. *Derashot R. Yiṣḥaq Qaro*. Edited by Shaul Regev. Ramat Gan: Bar Ilan Univ., 1995.

Caro, Maran Joseph. *Kesef Mishne*. In *Mishne Tora*. 4 vols. Venice, 5334–36/1574–76.

Chajes, R. Z. H. *Haggahot*. In *Talmud Babli*. Vilna: Re'em, 5668/1908.

Ein Anonymer Arabischer Commetar aus dem XV. Jahrhundert zu Maimonides's Dalalat al Ḥa'irin. Edited by R. Israel Horn. Breslau: H. Fleischmann, 1907.

Eisenshmat, R. Meir. *Panim Me'irot*. Vol. 1. Lemberg, 5649/1889.

Faur, José. *Rabbi Yiśrael Moshe Ḥazzan: The Man and His Works* (in Hebrew). Haifa: Academic Publishers, 1978.

———. "Signon ha-Mishna ve-ha-Shinnun be-'al-Pe." *Asupot* 4 (1990).

———. *Studies in the Mishne Tora* (in Hebrew). Jerusalem: Mossad Harav Kook, 5738/1978.

Fijo, R. 'Azarya de. *Bina le-'Ittim*. 2 vols. Jerusalem: Ch. Wagschel, 5749/1989.

Galante, R. Moses. *She'elot wu-Tshubot*. Venice, 5368/1608.

Ibn Adret. See R. Solomon ibn Adret.

Ibn 'Ezra, R. Abraham. *Pirush 'al ha-Tora*. In *Miqra'ot Gedolot*.

Ibn Jannaḥ, R. Jonah. *Sefer ha-Riqma*. Edited by M. Wilensky. Jerusalem: Ha-Aqademya lil-Shon ha-'Ibrit, 5724/1964.

Ibn Kaspi, R. Joseph. *Meṣaref la-Kesef*. Krakow, 5666/1906.

———. *Shulḥan Kesef*. Jerusalem: Ben-Zvi Institute, 1996.

Ibn Shahin. See R. Nissim Ga'on.

Ibn Verga, R. Solomon. *Shebeṭ Yehuda*. Edited by Azriel Schochet and Y. Beer. Jerusalem: Mossad Bialik, 5707/1947.

R. Joseph b. Jehuda. *Drei Abhandlungen*. Edited by Moritz Lowy. Berlin, 1879.

———. "Un fragment d'un livre inconnu (Bustan al-Azhar) de Joseph ben Juda ibn Aknin." Edited by Boaz Cohen. *Revue des Etudes Juive* 100 bis (1936).

R. Joseph ben Judah ibn 'Aqnin. *Hitgallut ha-Sodot*. Edited and translated by Abraham Halkin. Jerusalem: Mekize Nirdamim, 1964.

R. Judah ha-Levi. *Kitab al-Radd wa-al-Dalil fi al-Din al-Dhalil [Kuzari]*. Edited by H. Baneth. Jerusalem: Magnes Press, 1977.

Leone Ebreo [R. Judah Abarbanel]. *Dialoghi d'Amore*. English translation, *The Philosophy of Love*, by F. Friedberg-Seeley and Jean H. Barnes. London: Soncino Press, 1937.

R. Levi ben Gershom. *Pirush le-Sefer Melakhim*. In *Miqra'ot Gedolot*.

Lieberman, R. Saul. *Tosefta Ki-Fshuṭa, Mo'ed-Nashim-Neziqim*. New York: Jewish Theological Seminary of America, 1962–90.

Luzzato, D. S. *Commentary to the Pentateuch* (in Hebrew). Jerusalem: Horev, 1993.

Luzzato, R. Moshe Ḥayyim. *The Path of the Upright*. English translation by Mordcai M. Kaplan. Philadelphia: Jewish Publication Society, 1936.

Maimon, R. Abraham. *Teshubot*. Jerusalem: Mekize Nirdamim, 1937.

Maimonides, Moses. *Dalalat al-Ḥa'irin*. Edited by Isacchar Joel and Solomon Munk. Jerusalem: J. Junovitch, 5691/1931. Hebrew translation, *More ha-Nebukhim*, by R. Samuel ibn Tibbon. Venice, 5311/1551. *More ha-Nebukhim*, edited and translated by R. Joseph Qafiḥ. 3 vols. Jerusalem: Mossad Harav Kook, 1972. French translation, *Le Guide des Egarés*, by Solomon Munk. 3 vols. Paris: Editions G-P Maisonneuve, 1960.

———. *Iggeret Teman*. Ed. A. S. Halkin. New York: Jewish Theological Seminary of America, 5712/1952.

———. *Letters and Essays of Moses Maimonides*. (in Hebrew). Edited by Isaac Shailat. Maaleh Adumim. 2 vols. Maaliyot Press, 5748/1988.

———. "Maimonides, Treatise on Logic." Edited and translated by Israel Efros. *Proceedings of the American Academy for Jewish Research* 34 (1966).

———. *Mishne Tora*. 4 vols. Venice, 5334–36/1574–76.

———. *Sefer ha-Madda'*. Edited by R. Saul Lieberman and M. K. Katzenelebogen. Jerusalem: Mossad Harav Kook, 5724/1964.

———. *Pirush ha-Mishnayot*. Edited and translated by R. Joseph Qafiḥ. 7 vols. Jerusalem: Mossad Harav Kook, 1971.

———. *Qobeṣ Teshubot ha-Rambam*. Leipzig, 5619/1858.

———. *Sefer ha-Miṣvot*. Edited and translated by R. Joseph Qafiḥ. Jerusalem: Mossad Harav Kook, 1971.

———. *Teshubot ha-Rambam*. Edited and translated by J. Blau. 3 vols.

Jerusalem: Mekize Nirdamim, 1975.
———. *Treatise on Logic.* Edited and translated by Israel Efros. New York: American Academy for Jewish Research, 1938.
———. *Treatise on Resurrection.* Edited by Joshua Finkel. New York: American Academy for Jewish Research, 1939.
Me'iri, R. Menaḥem. *Pirush ha-Me'iri le-Sefer Mishle* (Commentary to Proverbs). Jerusalem: Hoṣa'at ha-Posqim, 5729/1969.
R. Moses bar Naḥman. *Pirush ha-Tora.* Edited by Ch. D. Chavel. 2 vols. Jerusalem: Mossad Harav Kook, 1963.
Musafia, R. Benjamin. *Musaf he-'Arukh.* Amsterdam, 5415/1655.
R. Nathan bar Yeḥiel. *'Arukh-Aruch Completum.* Edited by Alexander Kohut. 8 vols. Vienna and Berlin: Menora, 1926.
Nieto, David R. *De la Divina Providencia.* London, 5476/1716.
Qamḥi, R. David. *Pirush Nebi'im Aḥaronim.* In *Miqra'ot Gedolot.*
———. *Pirush Nebi'im Rishonim.* In *Miqra'ot Gedolot.*
———. *Pirush Sefer Tehillim.* Edited by A. Darom. Jerusalem: Mossad Harav Kook, n.d.
Rabinovitz, Z. W. *Sha'are Torath Eretz Israel.* Jerusalem: I. Rabinovitz, 5700/1940.
Ramban. See R. Moses bar Naḥman.
Rashi. *Commentary to the Pentateuch.* In *Miqra'ot Gedolot.*
R. Santob de Carrion. *Proverbios Morales.* Madison, Wisc.: Hispanic Seminary of Medieval Studies, 1986.
R. Solomon ibn Adret. *She'elot wu-Tshubot,* vol. 4. Salonika, 5563/1803.
Usque, Samuel de. *Consolation for the Tribulations of Israel.* Translated by Martin A. Cohen. Philadelphia: Jewish Publication Society, 1977.
'Uzziel, R. Ben-Ṣion. *Mishpeṭe 'Uzziel.* Vol. 1. Tel Aviv, 5695/1935.
Valero, R. Samuel. *Ḥazon la-Mo'ed.* Venice, 5346/1586.
Zrehen, R. Jacob Ḥai. *Bikkure Ya'aqob.* Tiberias, 5666/1906.

ARAB WRITERS

Avempace. *Tadbir al-Mitwaḥḥed.* Spanish translation, *El Regimen del solitario,* edited and translated by Miguel Asin Palacios. Madrid: Consejo Superior de Investigaciones Científicas, 1946.
Averroes. *Tahafut al-Tahafut.* Edited by Simon Van den Bergh. 2 vols. Oxford: Oxford Univ. Press, 1954.
Ibn Bajja. See Avempace.

WESTERN WRITERS

Abramson, Shraga, ed. *R. Nissim Ga'on*. Jerusalem: Mekize Nirdamin, 1965.

Albérès, R. M. *Histoire du roman modern*. Paris: Editions Albin Michel, 1962.

Arieti, Silvano. *Creativity: The Magic Synthesis*. New York: Basic Books, 1976.

———. *The Intrapsychic Self*. New York: Basic Books, 1976.

———. "Primitive Intellectual Mechanisms in Psycho-Pathological Conditions." *American Journal of Psychotherapy* 4 (1950).

———. "Some Basic Problems Common to Anthropology and Modern Psychiatry." *American Anthropologist* 58 (1956).

Aristotle. *Analytica Posteriora*. In *The Complete Works of Aristotle*. Edited by Jonathan Barnes. Princeton, N.J.: Princeton Univ. Press, 1984.

———. *De Caelo*. In *The Complete Works of Aristotle*. Edited by Jonathan Barnes. Princeton, N.J.: Princeton Univ. Press, 1984.

———. *Metaphysics*. In *The Complete Works of Aristotle*. Edited by Jonathan Barnes. Princeton, N.J.: Princeton Univ. Press, 1984.

Baroja, Pío. *Camino de Perfección*. New York: Las Américas Publishing Company, n. d.

Benveniste, Émile. *Indo-European Language and Society*. Translated by Elizabeth Palmer. Coral Gables, Fl.: Univ. of Miami Press, 1973.

Bertalanffy, Ludwig von. *General System Theory*. New York: George Braziller, 1993.

Blumenthal, David. "Maimonides: Prayer, Worship and Mysticism." In *Prière, Mystique et Judaisme*. Strasbourg: Collection Strasbourg, 1984.

———. "Maimonides's Intellectualist Mysticism and the Superiority of the Prophecy of Moses." *Medieval Culture* 10 (1978): 51–67.

Borges, Jorge Luis. "The Garden of Forking Paths." In *In Praise of Darkness*, translated by Norman di Giovanni. New York: Dutton, 1974.

———. "The Gods' Script." In *Labyrinths*, translated by L. A. Murillo. New York: New Directions, 1964.

———. "The Immortal." In *Labyrinths*, translated by L. A. Murillo. New York: New Directions, 1964.

———. "La Rosa de Paracelso." In *Obras Completas*. Madrid: Ultramar, 1977.

———. "Labyrinths." In *In Praise of Darkness*, translated by Norman di Giovanni. New York: Dutton, 1974.

———. *Prólogo*. In *Evaristo Carriego*, by Evaristo Carriego. Buenos Aires: Emecé Editores, 1955.

———. "The Zahir." In *Labyrinths,* translated by Dudley Fitts. New York: New Directions, 1964.

Breton, André. *Manifestation du surréalism.* Paris: J.-J. Pauvert, 1962.

Burtt, Edwin Arthur. *The Metaphysical Foundations of Modern Physical Science.* London: Routledge and Kegan Paul, 1949.

Caillois, Roger. *Anthologie du fantastique.* Paris: Editions Gallimard, 1955.

Cassirer, Ernst. *The Philosophy of Symbolic Forms.* Translated by Ralph Manheim. Vol. 2, *Mythical Thought.* New Haven: Yale Univ. Press, 1955.

Cassuto, Umberto. *The Documentary Hypothesis* (in Hebrew). Jerusalem: Magnes Press, 1953.

———. "The Episode of the Sons of God and the Daughters of Man" (in Hebrew). *Biblical and Canaanite Literatures.* Vol. 1. Jerusalem: Magnes Univ. Press, 1972.

———. *La Questione della Genesi.* Florence, 1934.

Cervantes, Miguel de. *Don Quijote.* Edited by Fernandez de Avel. Madrid: Espasa-Calpe, 1984.

Daub, David. "Ecstasy in a Statement by Rabbi Joshua ben Haninah." In *Collected Works of David Daube,* ed. Calum M. Carmichael. Vol. 1. Berkeley and Los Angeles: Univ. of California Press, 1992.

Deveraux, George. *Basic Problems of Ethnopsychiatry.* Translated by Basia Miller Gulati and George Deveraux. Chicago: Univ. of Chicago Press, 1980.

Eckhart, Johannes. *Meister Eckhart.* Translated by R. B. Blankey. New York: Harper Brothers, 1941.

Einstein, Albert. *Ideas and Opinions.* Translated by Sonja Bargmann. New York: Crown Trade Paperbacks, 1982.

Eliade, Mircea. *Autobiography.* Translated by Mac Linscott Ricketts. Vol. 2. Chicago: Univ. of Chicago Press, 1988.

———. *Images and Symbols.* Translated by Philip Mairet. Princeton, N.J.: Princeton Univ. Press, 1991.

———. *Myth and Reality.* Translated by Willard R. Trask. New York: Harper and Row, 1963.

———. *The Myth of the Eternal Return.* Translated by Willard R. Trask. Princeton, N.J.: Princeton Univ. Press, 1965.

———. *The Quest: History and Meaning in Religion.* Chicago: Univ. of Chicago Press, 1984.

———. *The Sacred and the Profane.* Translated by Willard R. Trask. New York: Harvest, 1959.

———. "Spirit, Light, and Seed." In *Occultism, Witchcraft, and Cultural Fashions.* Chicago: Univ. of Chicago Press, 1978.

———. "Survivals and Camouflages of Myths." In *Symbolism, The Sacred, and the Arts,* edited by Diane Apostolos-Cappadona. New York: Continuum, 1992.

Elior, Rachel. "From Earthly Temple to Heavenly Shrine" (in Hebrew). *Tarbiz* 64 (1995).

Evenshmuel, Yehudah. *More Nebukhim.* Pt. 2, vol. 1. Jerusalem: Mossad Harav Kook, 5718/1958.

Faur, José. "Basic Concepts in Rabbinic Hermeneutics." *Shofar* 16 (1997).

———. "The Biblical Idea of Idolatry." *Jewish Quarterly Review* 69 (1978).

———. "A Crisis of Categories: Kabbalah and the Rise of Apostasy in Spain." In *The Jews of Spain and the Expulsion of 1492,* edited by Moshe Lazar. Lancaster, Calif.: Labyrinthos, 1997.

———. "De-authorization of the Law: Paul and the Oedipal Model." In *Psychoanalysis and Religion,* edited by Joseph H. Smith and Susan A. Handelman. Baltimore, Md.: John Hopkins Univ. Press, 1990.

———. "Delocutive Expressions in the Hebrew Liturgy." *Journal of the Ancient Near Eastern Society* 16–17 (1984–85).

———. "Francisco Sanchez' Theory of Cognition and Vico's *verum/factum.*" *New Vico Studies* 5 (1987).

———. "God as a Writer: Omnipresence and the Art of Dissimulation." *Cross Currents: Religion and Intellectual Life* 6 (1989).

———. *Golden Doves with Silver Dots: Semiotics and Textuality in Rabbinic Tradition.* Bloomington: Indiana Univ. Press, 1986.

———. "Idolatry," *Encyclopaedia Judaica* 8 (1973). Reprint, *Jewish Values.* Israel Pocket Library, 1974.

———. *In the Shadow of History: Jews and Conversos at the Dawn of Modernity.* Albany: State Univ. of New York Press, 1992.

———. "Intuitive Knowledge of God in Medieval Jewish Theology." *Jewish Quarterly Review* 67 (1976–77).

———. "Law and Hermeneutics in Rabbinic Jurisprudence." *Cardozo Law Review* 14 (May 1993).

———. "Maimonides's Discovery of a Saboraitic Version of Tractate *Nidda*" (in Hebrew). *Tarbiz* 65 (1996).

———. "Monolingualism and Judaism." *Cardozo Law Review* 14 (May 1993).

———. "Newton, Maimonides and Esoteric Knowledge." *Cross Currents: Religion and Intellectual Life* 8 (1990).

———. "Reflections on Job and Situational Morality." *Judaism* 19 (1970).

———. "Sanchez' Critique of *Authoritas*: *Converso* Skepticism and the Emergence of Radical Hermeneutics." In *The Return to Scripture in Judaism and Christianity,* edited by Peter Ochs. Mahwah, N.Y.: Paulist Press, 1993.

———. "Some General Observations on the Character of Classical Jewish Literature." *Journal of Jewish Studies* 28 (1977).

———. "The Splitting of the *Logos*: Some Remarks on Vico and Rabbinic Tradition." *New Vico Studies* 3 (1985).

———. "Texte et societé: Histoire sociale du texte revelé." In *La Societé Juive a Travers les Ages.* Vol. 1. Edited by Shmuel Trigano. Paris: Librairie Fayard, 1992.

———. "The Third Person in Semitic Grammatical Theory and General Linguistics." *Linguistica Biblica Bonn* 46 (1929).

———. "Two Models of Jewish Spirituality." *Shofar* 10 (1992).

———. "Understanding the Covenant." *Tradition* 9 (1968).

Finkelstein, J. J. *The Ox That Gored*. Philadelphia: American Philosophical Society, 1981.

Frankfort, Henry. *Kingship and the Gods*. Chicago: Univ. of Chicago Press, 1948.

Freud, Sigmund. "An Autobiographical Study." In *The Standard Edition of the Complete Psychological Works of Sigmund Freud* (*S.E.*). Edited and translated by James Strachey. London: Hogarth Press, 1953–74.

———. *Civilization and Its Discontents.* Translated by Joan Riviere. New York: Doubleday Anchor Books, 1958.

———. *Group Psychology and the Analysis of the Ego.* Translated by James Strachey. New York: Bantam Books, 1965.

———. *The Future of an Illusion*. Translated by W. D. Robson-Scott. New York: Doubleday Anchor Books, 1957.

———. *New Introductory Lectures,* In *S.E.* Vol. 22.

———. "Reflections upon War and Death." In *Character and Culture.* New York: Collier Books, 1963.

———. *Moses and Monotheism*. In *S.E.* Vol. 23.

Goiten, Shlomo D. "Moses Maimonides, Man of Action." In *Homages à Georges Vajda,* edited by Gérard Nahon and Charles Touati. Louvain: Editions Peeters, 1983.

Goldin, Judah. *Studies in Midrash and Related Literature.* Philadelphia: Jewish Publication Society, 5748/1988.

Gudsorf, Georges. *Myth et métaphysique.* Paris: Flammarion, 1953.

al-Hassan, Ahmad Y., and Donald R. Hill. *Islamic Technology: An Illustrated History.* Cambridge: Cambridge Univ. Press, 1986.

Hawking, Stephen. *A Brief History of Time.* New York: Bantam Books, 1990.

Hazan, Albert. *Le Cantique de Cantiques enfin Expliqué.* Paris: Librairie Lipschutz, 1936.

Hefetz, Haim S. "Vicarious Liability in Jewish Law" (in Hebrew). *Dine Israel* 6 (1975).

Heller, Joseph. "Maimonides's Theory of Miracle." In *Between East and West,* edited by Alexander Altmann. London: East and West Library, 1958.

Herford, R. Travers. *Christianity in Talmud and Midrash.* London: William and Norgate, 1903.

———. "Elisha ben Abujah." In *Essays in Honour of the Very Rev. Dr. J. Hertz.* London: Edward Goldston (ca. 1942).

Hill, Donald R. "Mechanical Engineering in the Medieval Near East. "*Scientific American* (May 1991).

Hume, David. *Enquiries Concerning Human Understanding.* Oxford: Clarendon Press, 1975.

Idel, Moshe. *Kabbalah: New Perspectives.* New Haven, Conn.: Yale Univ. Press, 1988.

———. *Maimonide et la mystique juive.* Paris: Editions du Cerf, 1991.

———. "The World of Angels in Human Form" (in Hebrew). In *Studies in Jewish Mysticism, Philosophy, and Ethical Literature Presented to Isaiah Tishby,* edited by J. Dan and J. Hacker. Jerusalem: Magnes Press, 1986.

Jaeger, Werner. *Aristotle.* Oxford: Oxford Univ. Press, 1962.

Jammer, Max. *Concepts of Space.* New York: Dover, 1993.

Jauch, J. M. *Are Quanata Real?* Bloomington: Indiana Univ. Press, 1989.

Jiménez, Juan Ramón. "Intelligence." In *Segunda Antología Poética.* Madrid: Espasa Calpe, 1920.

Johnson, Robert A. *Inner Work.* San Francisco: Harper, 1986.

Jung, C. G. "Foreword" to *The Origins and History of Consciousness* by Erich Neumann. Translated by R. F. C. Hull. Princeton, N.J.: Princeton Univ. Press, 1993.

———. "The Psychology of the Child Archetype." In *Essays on a Science of*

Mythology, translated by R. F. C. Hull. Princeton, N.J.: Princeton Univ. Press, 1978.

Kaku, Michio. *Hyperspace*. New York: Anchor Books, 1994.

Kasanin, J. S. "Disturbance of Conceptual Thinking in Schizophrenia." In *Language and Thought in Schizophrenia*, edited by J. S. Kasanin. Berkeley and Los Angeles: Univ. of California Press, 1944.

Kellner, Menachem. *Maimonides on Human Perfection*. Atlanta: Scholars Press, 1989.

———. "On the status of Astronomy and Physics in Maimonides's *Mishne Tora* and the *Guide of the Perplexed*." *British Journal for the History of Science* 24 (1991).

Klein, S. *History of Palestine Exploration* (in Hebrew). Jerusalem: Bialik Foundation, 1937.

Klein-Braslavy, Sara. "The Reality of Time and the Primordial Period in Mediaeval Jewish Philosophy" (in Hebrew), *Tarbiz* 45 (1976).

Kristeva, Julia. *Powers of Horror*. Translated by Leon S. Roudiez. New York: Columbia Univ. Press, 1982.

Küng, Hans. *Freud and the Problem of God*. Translated by Edward Quinn. New Haven: Yale Univ. Press, 1990.

Lévi-Strauss, Claude. *The Savage Mind*. Chicago: Univ. of Chicago Press, 1970.

Levin, Michael David."The Loving Body of Tradition." *Religious Traditions* (Univ. of Sydney) 5 (1983).

Lévy-Bruhl, Lucien. *The Notebooks on Primitive Mentality*. Translated by Peter Riviere. New York: Harper and Row, 1978.

Lieberman, Saul.*Hellenism in Jewish Palestine*. New York: Jewish Theological Seminary of America, 1962.

———. "Metatron, the Meaning of His Name and His Functions." In *Apocalyptic and Medieval Mysticism*, by I. Gruenwald. Leiden: Brill, 1980.

———. *"Yaṣa le-'Olamo." Ginze Kedem* 5 (1934).

Liebes, Yehuda. *Ḥeṭ'o shel Elisha'*. Jerusalem: Academon, 1990.

Longhurst, C. A. "*Camino de perfección* and the Modernist Aesthetic." In *Hispanic Studies in Honour of Geffrey Ribbans*, edited by Ann L. Mackenzie and Dorothy S. Severin. Liverpool: Liverpool Univ. Press, 1992.

Mondolfo, Rodolfo. *Il "Verum-Factum" prima di Vico*. Naples: Guida, 1969.

Navarro, Joaquina. "Jorge Luis Borges, taumaturgo de la metáfora. "*Revista Hispánica Moderna* 31 (1965).

Nestor the Priest. In *The Polemic of Nestor the Priest,* edited by Daniel J. Lasker and Sarah Stroumsa. 2 vols. Jerusalem: Ben-Zvi Institute, 1996.

Newton, Isaac. *Principia.* 2 Vols. Berkeley and Los Angeles: Univ. of California Press, 1934.

Neumann, Erich. "Mystical Man."In *The Mystic Vision: Papers from the Eranos Yearbooks,* edited by Joseph Campbell. Princeton, N.J.: Princeton Univ. Press, 1982.

———. *The Origins and History of Consciousness.* Translated by R. F. C. Hull. Princeton, N.J.: Princeton Univ. Press, 1993.

Ortega y Gasset, José. *The Revolt of the Masses.* New York: W. W. Norton, 1957.

Pike, Nelson. "Divine Omniscience and Voluntary Action." *Philosophical Review* 74 (1965).

Prigogine, Ilya, and Isabelle Stengers. *Order Out of Chaos.* New York: Bantam Books, 1984.

Rabinovitch, Nachum L. "The Concept of Possibility in Maimonides." In *Studies in Maimonides* (Likkute Tarbiz V), ed. M. Idel. Jerusalem: Hebrew Univ. Press, 1985.

———. *Probability and Statistical Inference in Ancient and Medieval Jewish Literature.* Toronto: Univ. of Toronto Press, 1973.

Radin, Paul. *Primitive Religion.* New York: Dover Publications, 1957.

Ribi, Alfred. *Demons of the Inner World.* Translated by Michael H. Kohn. Boston: Shambala, 1990.

Richter, Horst-Eberhard. *All Mighty.* Translated by Jan van Heurck. Claremont, Calif.: Hunter House, 1984.

Russell, Bertrand. *Mysticism and Logic.* Garden City, N.Y.: Doubleday, 1957.

Sartre, Jean-Paul. *Anti-Semite and Jew.* Translated by George J. Becker. New York: Schocken Books, 1976

———. *The Psychology of Imagination.* New York: Philosophical Library.

Schacter, Daniel L. *Searching for Memory.* New York: Basic Books, 1996.

Schaeffer, John D. *Sensus Communis.* Durham, N.C.: Duke Univ. Press, 1990.

Schneider, Marcel.*La Littérature fantastique en France.* Paris: Librairie Arthème Fayard, 1964.

Scholem, Gershom.*Jewish Gnosticism, Merkabah Mysticism and Talmudic Tradition.* New York: Jewish Theological Seminary of America, 1960.

———. *Major Trends in Jewish Mysticism.* New York: Schocken, 1961.

Segal, M. H. "The Names יי and א-להים in the Books of the Bible" (in Hebrew). *Tarbiz* 9 (1938).

Smith, Morton. "Ascent to the Heavens and the Beginnings of Christianity." *Eranosjahrbuch* 50 (1981).

———. "The Reason for the Persecution of Paul and the Obscurity of Acts." In *Studies in Mysticism and Religion Presented in Honor of Gershom G. Scholem*. Jerusalem: Magnes Press, 1967.

Stengers, Isabelle. See Prigogine, Ilya.

Strauss, Leo. *Persecution and the Art of Writing.* Glencoe, Ill.: Free Press, 1952.

Stroumsa, Gedaliahu G. "Form(s) of God." *Harvard Theological Review* 76 (1983).

Trinkaus Zagzebski, Linda. *The Dilemma of Freedom and Foreknowledge.* London: Oxford Univ. Press, 1993.

Unamuno, Miguel de. *The Agony of Christianity.* Translated by Anthony Kerrigan. Princeton, N.J.: Princeton Univ. Press, 1974.

Urbach, Ephraim E. *The World of the Sages* (in Hebrew). Jerusalem: Magnes Press, 1988.

Vax, Louis. *La Séduction de l'étrange.* Paris: Presses Universitaires de France, 1995.

Vico, Giambattista. *New Science.* Translated by Thomas Goddard Bergin and Max Harold Fisch. Ithaca, N.Y.: Cornell Univ. Press, 1968.

———. *On the Ancient Wisdom of the Italians.* In *Vico: Selected Writings,* edited and translated by Leon Pompa. London: Cambridge Univ. Press, 1982.

Von Domarus, Eilhard. "The Specific Laws of Logic in Schizophrenia." In *Language and Thought in Schizophrenia,* edited by J. S. Kasanin. Berkeley and Los Angeles: Univ. of California Press, 1944.

Warnock, Mary. *Imagination.* Berkeley and Los Angeles: Univ. of California Press, 1976.

Wittgenstein, Lüdwig. "Lecture on Ethics." *The Philosophical Review* 74 (1965).

———. *Philosophical Investigations.* Translated by G. E. M. Anscombe. New York: Macmillan, 1968.

———. *Tractatus Logico-Philosophicus.* Tran. D. F. Pears and B. F. McGuinness. London: Routledge and Kegan Paul, 1961.

———. *Wörterbuch für Volkesschulen.* Vienna: Holder-Picher-Tempsky, 1977.

Wolfson, Harry A. *Cresca's Critique of Aristotle.* Cambridge, Mass.: Harvard Univ. Press, 1929.

———. *The Philosophy of Spinoza.* 2 vols. Cambridge, Mass.: Harvard Univ. Press, 1934.

———. *The Philosophy of the Kalam.* Cambridge, Mass.: Harvard Univ. Press, 1976.

Yates, Frances. *The Art of Memory.* Chicago: Univ. of Chicago Press.

Indexes

INDEX OF SOURCES

SCRIPTURE

Gn 1:1, 115; 1:2, 40, 127; 1:3, 54; 1:4, 40; 1:6–7, 39; 1:9, 247; 1:26, 4, 15, 18; 1:27, 127; 1:31, 138; 2:2–3, 18; 2:3, 178; 2:8, 9; 2:9, 137; 2:13, 210; 2:15, 128, 129; 2:20, 59; 2:23, 59; 2:23–24, 210; 3:5, 63, 65, 108, 128; 3:6, 60; 3:7, 60, 63; 3:8, 60; 3:10, 60; 3:12–13, 80; 3:15, 138; 3:22, 59; 3:24, 6, 23, 80; 4, 232; 5, 232; 5:1, 127; 5:3, 127; 6:4, 87; 8:6, 18; 10, 60; 12:5, 129; 18:8, 171; 18:19, 130; 18:22, 171; 25:30, 154; 26:24, 175; 28:12, 16, 173, 246; 28:13, 19; 32:27, 179; 37:10, 238; 41:2, 19; 41:46, 171; 43:16, 227; 50:71, 175

Ex 3:6, 50, 77; 9:29, 177; 12:2, 143; 12:12, 207; 12:14, 144; 12:26–27, 232; 12:48–49, 232; 13:3, 144; 13:17–18, 132; 14:3, 200; 14:5, 194; 14:27, 115; 15:2, 84; 15:20–21, 85; 19:1, 143; 19:6, 147, 151; 19:9, 146, 149; 19:11, 139; 19:19, 159; 20, 139; 20:2–3, 141; 20:7–10, 18; 20:10, 144; 20:19, 150; 20:20, 158; 21:1–5, 142; 24:1, 148; 24:2, 148; 24:7, 145; 24:10, 81, 108; 24:11, 82; 25:8, 8; 30:9, 10; 33:13, 176; 33:22, 202

Lv 10:1, 10; 25:42, 55, 175; 26:13, 175

Nm 9:14, 232; 9:23, 156; 12:7, 175; 12:8, 50, 75, 77, 79, 123; 15:39, 37; 16:9, 171; 19:2, 153; 24:16, 5

Dt 1:38, 171; 4:12, 149; 4:20, 142; 4:34, 142, 163; 4:35, 4; 5:5, 149; 5:8, 149; 5:20, 149; 6:5, 170; 6:13, 170; 8:2, 163; 8:16, 158; 10:7, 241; 10:8, 171; 16:3, 144; 17:3, 10; 18:7, 171; 31:17, 55; 31:18, 55; 32:10, 241; 32:39, 185; 33:14, 226; 33:26, 19; 33:27, 14; 34:5, 175

Jos 1:2, 175; 1:7, 175; 12:6, 175; 24:2, 131, 191; 24:29, 175

Jud 2:8, 175

1 Sam 10:6, 84; 17:8, 175; 18:23, 175; 18:30, 175; 25:10, 175; 25:20, 175; 25:40, 175

1 Kings 1:2, 171; 8:65, 208; 19:1, 202; 19:12, 51

2 Kings 2:3, 129; 2:10, 175; 9:7, 175; 10:23, 175; 17:3, 175; 17:9, 45

Is 2:6, 130; 6:3, 86; 11:15, 236; 16:19, 241; 25:9, 85, 220; 26:2, 195; 29:15, 55; 32:6, 45; 41:8–9, 175; 48:20, 175; 51:2, 157; 52:13, 175

Jer 2:2, 163; 7:25, 175; 9:22–23, 176; 23:28, 215; 26:55, 175; 32:18, 241; 44:4, 175

Ez 1:4, 207; 9:9, 177; 9:29, 177; 16:1–7, 131; 28:25, 175; 37:25, 175; 38:17, 175

Hos 2:16–17, 241; 12:11, 76

Hb 2:19–20, 68

Ps 1:2, 7; 3:18, x; 4:5, 23; 8:6, 65; 18:1, 175; 20:3, 201; 21, 175; 31:19, 44; 36:1, 175; 48:14, 220; 49:14, 231; 65:2, 23; 67:20, 14; 89:4, 175; 90:12, 77; 111:10, 99, 246; 115:16, 110

Prv 1:7, 99, 246; 14:24, 218; 15:25, 121; 20:15, 208; 26:16, 40; 27:5, 238; 28:18, 42

Jb 4:16, 207; 14:20, 60; 37:21, 58; 38:1, 162; 42:6, 162

Ecc 7:5, 238; 12:11, 35

Dan 1:19, 171; 2:2, 171; 4:13, 231

Neh 9:32, 241

1 Ch 2:6,13, 175; 12, 241; 18:2, 175; 23:30, 171; 29:11, 241

2 Ch 5:14, 171; 7:6, 171; 10:6, 171; 10:7, 175; 20:6, 241; 20:13, 171; 24:6, 175; 24:9, 175; 29:11, 171

RABBINIC SOURCES

Mishna
Berakhot 1:4, 214; 2:1, 200; 5:1, 246; 9:1, 217
Sheqalim 5:1, 195
Hagiga 2:1, 194, 197, 202, 206, 243
Baba Meṣi'a 2:11, 187, 232
Sanhedrin 4:5, 185
'Eduyot 2:9, 228
Pirqe Abot 1:14, 185; 4:1, 241; 4:3, 185; 4:4, 223; 4:8, 187; 4:18, 195; 4:21, 184, 197; 5:3, 241; 5:5, 228; 6:7, 240
Bekhorot 1:4, 214
Middot 4:5, 202
Ohalot 13:4, 203
Yadayim 4:7, 247

Tosefta
Megilla 3(4):28, 197
Ḥagiga 2:1, 194, 206; 2:2, 196, 199; 2:3, 195, 199, 204; 2:4, 203; 2:5, 204; 2:6, 200, 204; 2:7, 202
Yebamot 8:7, 195
Soṭa 7:11, 199
Qiddushin 1:13, 185
Baba Batra 1:4, 202; 1:5, 202
Horayot 2:7, 232
Ohelot 14:4, 203

Talmud Yerushalmi
Berakhot 2, 1, 4b, 200; 9, 1, 11d, 206
Bikkurim 3, 3, 65d, 214
Shabbat 13, 3, 14a, 188
Megilla 2, 3, 73b, 220
Ḥagiga 2, 1, 76a, 196; 2, 1, 77a, 195; 2, 1, 77b, 195, 196, 203; 2, 1, 77b–c, 205; 2, 1, 77c, 196, 197, 204, 206
Sanhedrin x, 8, 30c, 197

Talmud Babli
Berakhot 5a, 242; 7a, 186, 200, 217; 12b, 203; 17a, 218; 27b, 200; 28b, 208; 31b, 243; 33a, 208, 209, 219, 220; 33b, 213; 34b, 184, 225, 248; 54a, 236; 55a, 33, 191; 58a, 207; 58b, 230
Shabbat 10a, 215, 248; 15a–b, 238; 23a, 236; 33a, 206; 33b, 202, 244; 33b–34a, 248; 64a–b, 203; 88b, 235, 242, 248; 92a, 218, 247; 119b, 215; 146a, 234
'Erubin 53b, 195; 54a, 245
Pesaḥim 2b, 208; 54a, 202; 54b, 218; 67a, 191
Yoma 69b, 242
Sukka 45b, 196, 197, 201
Rosh ha-Shana 11a, 228; 25a, 236; pp. 22–23, 229
Ta'aniyot 2b, 246; 10a, 204; 29a, 184
Megilla 9a, 229; 9b, 188; 10b, 190; 12a, 216; 13a, 189; 15a, 216; 15b, 246; 21b, 236; 24b, 200
Ḥagiga 3b, 193, 199; 12a, 208, 228; 12b, 196, 208; 12b–13a, 208; 13a, 194, 196, 206; 13b, 206, 207, 208; 14a, 198; 14b, 196, 199, 203, 204; 15a, 195, 204, 205, 207; 15a–b, 205; 15b, 194, 237; 15b–16a, 204; 16a, 206, 207
Yebamot 49b, 217; 61a, 203; 63b, 195
Ketubot 21b, 195; 66b, 184
Nedarim 20b, 203, 246; 25a, 190; 31a, 191; 38a, 218, 247
Soṭa 4b–5a, 230; 5b, 206; 21a, 206, 208
Qiddushin 30b, 240; 33b, 187; 40a, 189, 239; 40a–b, 185; 66b, 195
Baba Qamma 4a, 247; 9b, 194; 59b, 187; 96b, 216
Baba Meṣi'a 24a, 239; 83b, 208; 85a, 196; 99a, 247
Baba Batra: 3a, 202; 4a, 204; 10a, 215; 16a, 240; 78b, 230; 116a, 226
Sanhedrin 7a, 248; 17b, 199; 19a, 232, 247; 38b, 207; 65b, 215; 89a, 203; 91b, 234; 94a, 216; 98a, 202; 102a, 203; 107b, 203
Makkot 22b, 187; 23b–24a, 235
Horayot 2b, 199; 8a–b, 189, 235
Ḥolin 8b, 239; 60a, 228; 92a, 247
Tamid 32a, 247
Nidda 65a, 207
Mekhilta de-R. Yishma'el 6–9, 236; 111, 232; 158, 219
Mekhilta de-R. Shim'on bar Yoḥai 105, 240
Sifra 93d, 238
Sifre (Bamidbar) no. 115, 203
Sifre no. 13, 218; no. 33, 190; no. 37, 240; no. 49, 190; no. 355, 190, 204, 219; no. 356, 184, 192
Abot de-R. Natan 24, 194; 33, 204
Bereshit Rabba 1, 5, 206; 3, 4, 207; 4, 204; 5, 228; 15, 234; 16, 232; 22, 231; 34, 230; 39, 241; 44, 240; 56, 234; 68, 190, 191; 69, 192; 82, 192; 84, 232
Shemot Rabba 23, 219;
Vayyiqra Rabba 1, 208; 20, 218; 23, 203, 204, 232; 31, 201
Debarim Rabba 2, 236
Midrash Tanhuma: Lekh Lekha, 241; *Tazria'*, 215; *Ḥuqqat*, 240; *Mas'e*, 241
Ekha Rabba I, 20, 203

Maimonides's Works
Pirush ha-Mishnayot
Introduction 7, 247; 35, 197; 35–36, 196; 41–42, 191; 42, 191; 43, 192; 45, 199
Berakhot 5:1, 234
Ḥagiga 2:1, 194, 205, 206, 233
Baba Qamma 4:3, 232

Sanhedrin 10:1, 205, 221, 223, 231
'Eduyot 2:9, 228
'Aboda Zara 4:7, 230
Abot, Shemona Peraqim 1, 232, 233; 2, 233; 3–4, 233; 4, 206, 222, 239, 241; 5, 244, 245; 6, 233, 238, 240; 7, 215, 218, 247; 8, 241; 3:11, 214; 4:4, 233; 4:8, 187; 5:5, 228
Sefer ha-Miṣvot Introduction, 213; positive commandment no. 3, 190; negative commandment no. 290, 227
Mishne Tora
Yesode ha-Tora 1:1, 190; 1:2–3, 221; 1:9, 198, 221; 2:7, 219; 2:10, 221; 2:12, 194; 3:14, 219; 4:13, 200, 219; 7:1, 82, 200, 201, 208, 209; 7:1–2, 247; 7:2, 219; 7:3, 217; 7:5, 217; 7:6, 218; 7:7, 216; 8:2, 236
De'ot 1:6–7, 247; 2:1, 233; 2:1–2, 233; 2:2, 239; 2:3, 230; 4:14, 203; 6:3, 206; 7:1, 203
'Aboda Zara 1:1, 223; 1:3, 229; 2:1, 188
Teshuba 3:7, 221; 3:14, 206; 5:2, 185; 5:5, 221; 6:5, 221; 8:2, 218; 8:3, 244; 8:7, 184; 10:1, 220; 10:6, 246
Tefilla 1:1, 246; 4:16, 246
Tefillin 1:2, 187
Berakhot 10:9, 236; 10:19, 230
Ḥameṣ wu-Maṣṣa 6:3, 242
Qiddush ha-Ḥodesh 1:2, 236; 2:10, 236; 17:24, 225
Megilla ve-Ḥanukka 1:3, 236; 3:4, 236
Girushin 2:20, 242
Ma'akhalot Asurot 1:3–7, 214
Nedarim 9:20–21, 191
Bi'at ha-Miqdash 3:4, 191
Geneba 1:9, 247
Gezela 14:13, 196
She'ela wu-Piqadon 3:1–2, 247
Melakhim 12: 4–5, 245; 14:4, 239
Teshubot no. 180, 213; no. 207, 213; no. 254, 213; no. 261, 213
Treatise on Logic 8, 222, 224; 11, 228; 14, 212, 224
Treatise on Resurrection 4, 205; 30, 220; 32–33, 233, 238
Iggeret Teman 26, 236
Letters and Essays of Moses Maimonides 1:233–34, 232
Guide for the Perplexed
Introductory Epistle, 193
Introduction 192, 193, 194, 197, 198, 205, 207, 208, 209, 210, 216, 217, 226, 228, 229, 230, 235, 241, 243, 244, 247
Sec. 1 chap. 1, 211, 214, 231, 232; chap. 2, 203, 210, 211, 212, 214, 215; chap. 3, 214, 216; chap. 4, 218; chap.5, 188, 217, 218, 219, 226; chap. 7, 232; chap. 8, 190, 210, 220 chap. 10, 230, 234; chap. 13, 246; chap. 15, 214, 215, 246, 247; chap. 16, 241; chap. 17, 209; chap. 19, 208, 224; chap. 21, 202; chap. 26, 184, 209, 243, 244; chap. 28, 226; chap. 31, 192, 224, 225, 226, 228, 233; chap. 32, 192, 202, 203, 204, 206, 218, 224, 225, 226, 230; chap. 33, 194, 195, 198, 243; chap. 34, 204, 214; chap. 35, 192, 205, 243; chap. 36, 188, 213, 223; chap. 39, 217; chap. 42, 240; chap. 49, 214; chap. 50, 209, 226; chap. 51, 206, 209; chap. 52, 206; chap. 54, 206, 244, 247; chap. 55–58, 220; chap. 57, 224; chap. 58, 186; chap. 59, 193, 206, 209, 213; chap. 60, 209; chap. 70, 191, 192, 205, 206, 228, 230; chap. 71, 196, 197, 198, 205, 214, 222, 223, 225, 229; chap. 72, 221; chap. 73, 211, 212, 214; chap. 74, 213;
Sec. 2 Introduction, 224, 229; chap. 2, 243, 129; chap. 6, 214, 218, 243; chap. 8, 225, 227; chap. 11, 222, 225; chap. 12, 187, 208, 234; chap. 13, 221, 229, 231; chap. 14, 229; chap. 15, 211, 224; chap. 16, 229; chap. 17, 224, 228, 229, 231; chap. 18, 227, 230; chap. 19, 224, 228, 231; chap. 21, 227; chap. 22, 225, 231; chap. 23, 226, 230; chap. 24, 225, 227; chap. 25, 223, 224, 231; chap. 27, 222; chap. 29, 190, 195, 196, 205, 207, 228, 243, 244; chap. 30, 204, 210, 211, 227, 228, 231, 232, 233, 234, 248; chap. 32, 208, 212, 214, 215, 216, 217, 247; chap. 33, 235, 236, 238; chap. 34, 236; chap. 35, 218, 219; chap. 36, 212, 214, 215, 226, 243, 244; chap. 37, 213, 215, 243, 246; chap. 37–38, 242; chap. 38, 217, 219, 233, 244; chap. 39, 194, 244, 247; chap. 40, 203, 213, 214, 226, 243; chap. 41,

215, 216; chap. 42, 214, 215, 216; chap. 43, 216, 217; chap. 44, 216; chap. 45, 213, 215, 216, 217, 218; chap. 48, 248
Sec. 3 Introduction, 196, 197, 198, 206, 209, 226, 231; chap. 7, 195, 207; chap. 8, 203, 206, 209, 211, 213, 214, 228; chap. 9, 208, 236; chap. 12, 187, 213, 232, 234, 246; chap. 13, 228; chap. 14, 225, 230; chap. 15, 227, 229; chap. 16, 231; chap. 17, 215, 228; chap. 18, 231; chap. 19–21, 230; chap. 20, 230; chap. 21, 221, 228; chap. 22, 188, 209, 228, 234; chap. 23, 230, 235, 242; chap. 24, 217, 233, 235, 236, 241, 242; chap. 25, 227; chap. 26, 228, 240; chap. 27, 239, 243, 244, 245, 246; chap. 29, 213, 231, 233, 239, 242; chap. 30, 232, 233; chap. 31, 228, 233, 239; chap. 32, 232, 233, 238, 239, 240, 241, 242; chap. 37, 213, 228, 233, 242; chap. 45, 208, 214, 218, 228; chap. 46, 228, 232, 233, 239, 240, 242; chap. 48, 212; chap. 49, 212; chap. 50, 236; chap. 51, 197, 200, 204, 209, 213, 232, 239, 244, 245, 246; chap. 54, 187, 226, 228, 238, 239, 242, 244, 246, 247, 248

INDEX OF NAMES

Aaron, 143, 148
Abarbanel, Isaac, R., 59
Abarbanel, Judah, 2, 6, 57
Abihu, 38, 148
Abraham (Patriarch), 17, 26, 30, 89, 93, 119, 123, 125, 129, 130, 151, 157, 158, 159, 175
Adam, 9, 15, 59, 60, 61, 62, 65, 69, 70, 71, 80, 110, 127, 128, 130, 137, 138, 144
Ahab, 175
Alexander, 176
Amme, R., 54
Arieti, Silvano, 67
'Aqiba, R., 38, 40
Aristotle, 93, 98, 99, 100, 102, 103, 105, 106, 107, 108, 109, 112, 113, 114, 117, 118, 120, 122
Aybu, R., 153, 154
Azai, ben, 3, 39

Balaam, 5
Baroja, Pío, 9, 61
Bergson, H., 160
Borges, Jorge Luis, 2, 3, 16, 32, 33, 50, 52, 76, 80, 111, 127, 162
Bezalel, 14
Daniel, 74, 75
David, King, 74, 78, 175
Descartes, René, 78

Eckhart, Johannes, 82
Einstein, Albert, 18
Eleazar, R., 54, 85
Eleazar b. 'Arakh, R., 25, 26, 27, 44
Eliade, Mircea, 10, 24, 59, 136, 145, 146, 158
Elijah, 51, 175
Elisha, 37, 43, 51, 76, 81, 109, 175
Elisha ben Abuya, 40, 44, 51
Enoch, 30
Essau, 139, 179
Eve, 9, 60, 62, 80, 137, 138

Faur, Abraham, ix, 196, 207
Faur, Joseph, ix
Finkelstein, J. J., 89
Freud, S., 11, 12, 13, 16, 18, 135

Gabirol, R. Solomon ibn, 49, 174
Ge'onim, 29, 86
Gibbs, Yoshiah Willard, 115
Ger, Rabbi of, 2
Goliath, 78
Gorgias, ix

Ḥanan'el, R., 75, 76
Hayye Ga'on, 28, 30, 39, 49
Hille, 12
Hume, David, 75

Isaac (Patriarch), 158, 159
Isaiah, 85, 157
Ismael ben Elisha, R. 37

Jacob (Patriarch), 16, 17, 19, 139, 154, 173, 177, 179, 180
Jeremiah, 163, 176, 178
Jesus, 67
Jiménez, Juan Ramón, x, 213
Job, 138, 140, 160, 161, 162, 163
Johanan, R., 19, 51
Johanan ben Zakkai, Rabban, 25, 26, 51, 152, 153
Joseph b. Jehuda, R., 208, 247
Joseph ibn Abitur (ibn Śatnaś), R., 14
Joseph ibn Judah, R., 174
Joshua, 175
Joshua, R., 36, 37, 40
Jove, 60
Judah bar Il'ai, R., 78
Judah ha-Levi, R., 49, 78, 135, 151, 166
Jung, C. G., 6, 16, 135, 136

Kant, I., 49
Kepler, Johann, 71
Kierkergaard, S. A., 8

Kung, Hans, 12

Lessing, G. E., 34
Lévi-Strauss, Claude, 67
Levin, Michael David, 7
Lieberman, Saul, 29

Me'ir, R., 13, 190, 237
Mondolfo, Rodolfo, 92
Montefiore, Moses, 238
Moses, 2, 21, 30, 38, 50, 69, 74, 75, 77, 78, 79, 89, 93, 109, 114, 123, 125, 141, 143, 145, 147, 148, 149, 150, 155, 156, 165, 166, 175, 176, 179, 184, 189, 190, 202, 217, 219, 220, 223, 226, 232, 238, 239, 247
Munk, Solomon, ix

Nadab, 38, 148
Neḥunya ben Ha-Qana, R., 30
Neumann, Erich, 1, 32
Newton, Isaac, 5, 14, 18, 93, 101
Nieto, R. David, 225
Nissim Ga'on, R., 213

Obadiah (the Proselyte), 129
Ortega y Gasset, José, ix
Ossorio, 9, 61

Palaggi, Ḥayyim, R., 238
Paracelso, 32, 33, 80
Pascal, B., 8
Patrizzi, Francesco, 71
Peirce, Charles, 61
Pharaoh, 19
Philo, 54, 87, 112

Rab, 44, 82, 85
Raba, 7
Russell, Bertrand, 161

Samuel, 98, 238, 218
Sánchez, Francisco, 92
Santob de Carrion, R., ix
Sarah, 129
Sartre, J. P., 12, 68, 75, 77, 78
Scholem, Gershom, 29, 30, 31, 32, 33
Se'adya Ga'on, 49, 154
Seth, 15, 127, 128, 129
Sherira Ga'on, 127
Sheshat, R., 51
Simon bar Yoḥai, R., 18, 30, 179
Samuel ibn Tibbon, R., 98
Socrates, ix
Solomon, King, 21, 74

Themistius, 105
Tzinican, 162

Unamuno, Miguel, 8

Vax, Luis, 111
Vico, x, 61, 66, 92, 127
Von Domarus, Eilhard, 66
Wolfson, Harry A., 95
Wittgenstein, Ludwig, 6, 59, 60

Yophiel, 30
Yose bar Ḥanina, R., 45

Zoma, ben, 37, 39, 40

INDEX OF PRINCIPAL CONCEPTS AND TERMS

'Aboda, 175. *See also 'Amida*, Worship
'Aboda Zara, 10, 11, 13, 188. *See also* Idolatry
Aduma, 154
'Aliya, 39. *See also* Upper chamber
'Amida, 54, 87, 144, 171–72. *See also 'Aboda*, Worship
Angel, 10, 50, 51, 65, 74, 79, 82, 84, 88, 131, 139, 173, 174, 179, 219; ministering, 293
Anthropocentric, 3, 71, 80, 83, 86, 90, 161, 172, 177; theology, 79, 82; universe, 2, 5, 13, 14, 15, 44, 54, 84, 87, 89, 91, 93, 94, 95, 101, 103, 111, 112, 113, 115, 116, 117, 118, 121, 123, 190
Anthropocentrism, 4, 90, 121, 170
Anthropology, 15, 128, 131
Apophasis, 5, 9, 22, 46, 56, 76, 83
Apophatic knowledge, 6, 16, 20–22, 58
'Aqeb, 234
Archaic humanity, 9
Archaic thought, 67
Archetypes, 16, 32, 136, 155; of Israel, 155–56; of pagan humanity, 156–57
Aristotelian: astronomy, 103, 105–7; cosmology, 117; logic, 99, 102, 111; physics, 105–6; rationality, 13, 16, 102, 118. *See also* Logic
Arrogance, 121, 134
Aṣile, 108, 109
Assimilation, mental, 97, 130, 186, 188
Astronomy, 103–6; Ptolomean, 71. *See also* Aristotelian astronomy
Atonement, 80, 152, 154, 237
Attributes, 20
Authoritas, 99–100, 105–6, 108–9, 120

Berit, 11, 142–45
Blood label, 237

Book, x
Bricolage, 67

Calendar, Jewish, 105, 143, 144. *See also* Moses
Captivity, mental, 130
Causality, 98, 102, 112–15, 119
Cherub, Cherubim. *See* *Kerub*
Chorus and Dance, 82
Christian culture, 12, 188
Christianity, 3, 10, 12, 94, 95, 97, 100, 135, 151
Church Fathers, 94
Clock: Arab, 221; cosmic, 91
Coercion, 96, 97, 159, 160
Collective thinking,16, 164
Commandment(s), 11, 147–52, 159, 170, 171–72; ceremonial, 148, 154–55; conventional, 140, 147, 148; first two, 140–42, 159; second, 141; ten, 140
Consciousness, 1, 9, 16, 32, 33, 62, 70, 85, 86, 139, 142, 146, 155, 162, 163, 168; collective, 136–37, 154, 160; historical, 158; imaginative, 80; prophetic, 83; rational, 80, 83; reflective, 74, 75–78; reflexive, 59, 76
Conventional, conventionalities, 61, 62, 65; rationality, 84; thinking, 115
Cosmic: force, 4; mechanism, 144; perspective, 111; religion, 3; sacrality, 3, 10; seeds, 116, 117. *See also* Clock
Cosmocrator, 123, 126
Cosmology, 13, 18, 116–19, 125. *See also Ma'ase Bereshit*
Cosmos, 2, 14, 19, 137
Creation, ix, 2, 5, 20, 80, 99, 101, 107, 116, 119, 122, 144, 178, 190, 220, 223; acausal, 112–15; cannot be demonstrated, 14, 117–20; ex nihilo 3, 89, 94, 97, 100, 118, 120, 121, 123, 124, 125; Hebrew, 123
Creator, 3, 4, 5, 10, 11, 15, 43, 84, 86, 89, 91, 93, 94, 113, 114, 118, 119, 121, 126, 147, 153, 190
Crowd, 164, 243
Custom, 131, 158

Dabar, x
Dalala, 50, 52, 102, 168, 208
Dalil, 96, 99, 102, 118, 119
Dance-chorus, cosmic, 86–88
Daniel, book of, 74–75
Demarcation of cultures, 163
Derasha, xi, 24, 25, 26
Derekh, 45, 46, 112
Desert, 132, 143, 155–56, 158, 160, 163
Deus absconditus, 43, 53, 55, 60
Divination, 59
Divine, light, 54, 83; names, 30, 49; Presence, 37, 38, 39, 75, 78, 129, 130; Providence, 19, 74, 161, 171, 178, 179. *See also Shekhina*
Don Quijote, 209
Doresh, 26, 44
Dumya Tehilla, 23, 84

'Ebed, 175, 178, 248. *See also* Moses
Eden, Garden of, 6, 23, 34, 35, 51, 60, 76, 85, 86, 128, 144
Education, 15, 36, 47, 120, 128
Elohenu, 85, 86
Elohim, 63, 65, 77, 85, 86, 108, 139, 140. *See also* YHWH
Empirical phenomena, 100
Esoteric, esoterics, x, 3, 37, 83, 108, 167; discourse, 41; dissemination, 27–28, 31; dissertation, 26; experience, 33–35, 50, 83; insight, 33, 34, 35, 41, 46, 47; instruction, 6, 24–27, 46, 49; knowledge, 6, 9, 11, 24, 26–29, 33, 34, 51, 120; material, 42, 49, 97; rabbinic, 18, 19, 24, 28, 29, 31, 33, 41, 42, 120, 125, 180; teachings, 28, 29, 31, 35, 49; texts, 25, 27, 29, 30, 31, 34; tradition, 34, 43; vision, 40, 51
Eternity of the World, 110
Ethics, 11, 70, 153; civic, 248; theological, 240

First Idea, 170
Flashes (of light), 17, 193
Freedom of choice, 93
Fuqaha'a, 66, 213

Gabra rabba, 7, 187
Galut, 156
Gebura, 156, 158, 160, 161, 163
Geography, 146
Gnosticism, Gnostic, 30, 31, 32, 33, 34, 43, 50, 51, 76, 79, 178; Jewish, 29, 201. *See also* Kabbalah
God: absolutely different, 90; affronting, 124–25; assault upon, 9–10, 118; attributes, 21, 43–46; cannot be discovered, 4; as Clockmaker, 91; communicates with man, 4, 55, 83; corporeal vision of, 81–82; faith in, 1; heralds of, 53; human projections on, 161–62; image of, 8, 15, 18, 70, 127–28, 138;

knowing the mind of, 5, 121; necessary existence, 98–101; perfect knowledge, 92–94, 110, 114; revelation of, 4, 53; of Scripture, 13, 89, 98; as Supreme reality, 3, 101, 139; *temuna* of, 75–79; transcendence, 20, 23, 56, 90, 142; ways of, 160–62, 170. *See also* *Deus absconditus*, *Elohim*, YHWH
Golden calf, 152, 154
Good and evil, 63, 65, 138
Grossi bestioni, 127

Habdala, 144, 191
Ḥakham , 8, 24, 25, 26, 27, 47, 176, 178
Halakha, 10, 11, 29, 30, 31
Ḥashmal, 207
Hasidism, German 30, 32
Haughty spirit, 121, 124
Ḥayyad, 240, 241
Hekhalot: literature, 24, 25, 26, 29, 30, 31, 35, 38, 40, 42, 45, 50, 54, 66, 72, 122, 15, 176
Heresy, heretics, 32, 38, 43, 203
Hermeneutics: creative, xi; Platonic, 5
Hero, 29, 30, 136, 144, 156
Ḥeṭ, 12, 62
Hibbiṭ, 79
Hierarchical relationships, 5, 35, 61, 109, 123, 167
Higgid, 149
Ḥijaj, 102, 117
Hirṣa, 25, 26, 27, 36
Hiskim, 27
Historiography, German, 183
History, historical: 5, 18, 32, 34, 86, 89, 103, 135, 139, 140, 145, 147, 153, 156, 157; begins at Sinai, 158; characters, 146; event, 142; facts, 146; pre-Sinaitic, 146, 158; rationality, 146; sacred 2, 10, 11, 24, 143, 144, 159
Ḥokhma, 7, 8, 77, 176
Holy of Holies, 10, 90. *See* Temple
Homo absconditus, 53, 55, 60, 80
Homo mysticus, 1, 2
Human, humans, 1, 2, 15, 16, 76, 160; projections, 9, 44, 63, 80, 108; nature, 16, 131, 132, 164, 165
Humanity, 9, 10, 13, 16, 17, 18, 59, 72, 98, 105, 109, 111, 121, 122, 125, 128, 129, 131, 132, 135, 137, 139, 142, 147, 148, 151, 155, 157, 163, 166, 169
Hyperspace, 7

Id, 131, 132, 160
Idolatry, 4, 10, 60, 94, 121, 129, 135, 151, 152, 155, 159, 223; by uneducated masses, 188. *See also* *'Aboda Zara*
Imagination, 11, 13, 16, 17, 37, 77, 79, 85, 86, 94, 98, 99, 109, 110, 111, 116, 119, 125, 142, 159, 170, 173, 174; anthropocentric, 121–23; and apophasis, 56; deceiving, 44, 56–57, 61, 62–64, 76, 80–82; epistemology of, 68–69; and human misery, 9; and human projections, 57, 108, 118; and human traces, 133–34; and *Kalam*, 95–96; level of consciousness, 62; and mythical thinking, 9, 66–67, 161–62; paleologic, 70–74; popular, 58; and prophecy, 70–74; and reason, 65–68, 70–72, 77, 83–84, 138; and Satan, 137–39; and semiotics, 67–68; and sensory perception, 70–72, 83–84, 138; source of heathenism, 9, 18, 58–59, 66, 163–65, 167–68
Imaginative faculty, 59, 62, 65, 66, 70, 72, 73, 133, 137, 165
Individuation, 2, 17, 148, 165
Intentionality, 98, 112, 113, 114
Interpreted system, 76, 77
Islam, 10, 94, 95, 97, 135, 151
Israel, Israelites, 5, 10, 11, 16, 19, 26, 28, 35, 45, 51, 68, 81, 84–86, 97, 108, 109, 131, 132, 137–43, 145–52, 155–56, 158–61, 163, 174–75, 178, 179
I'tiqad, 57, 58, 107, 108

Jacob's Ladder, 17, 173, 177, 180
Jamhur, xi, 16, 58, 163, 164, 175, 178
Jibla, 73, 165
Judaism, 2, 10–13, 30, 32, 43, 94, 97, 100, 125, 129, 130, 142, 148, 180, 188, 192, 203, 216, 236

Kabbalah, 3, 32, 82. *See also* Gnosticism
Kalam, 63, 94, 95, 96, 97, 99. *See also* Mutakallimun
Kappara, 203, 239
Karaites, 97, 140
Kerub, Kerubim, 10, 19, 38, 178
Key-symbols, 16, 17, 18, 58, 61, 164
Kitab al-Muṭabaqat, 42
Kitab al-Nabu'a, 42
Knowledge: contemplative, 72, 91, 93, 121, 178; critical, 12, 47, 83; intuitive,

140, 158, 161; perfect, 30, 91, 92, 93, 103, 111, 124, 160; scientific, 103, 110, 120; theory, x, xi
Language, 6, 59, 90, 160; linguistic subjectivity, 4; of Tora 167; syntax, 3, 6, 7, 14
Lapis philosophorum, 53
Law, Oral, 28, 37, 186
Laws of physics, 115. *See also* Nature
Lazun, 37, 39, 202
Leviathan, 160, 161
Light, primeval, 54
Liturgy, 86, 213
Logic, 15; Aristotelian, 13, 102, 111; totemic, 67
Logos, ix, x, 54
Lul, 37, 202
Luṭf, 150–55, 163, 168

Maḥol, 85, 173
March, 38, 55, 157, 169, 173, 245
Ma'aśe Bereshit, 18, 25, 44, 115, 116, 118
Ma'aśe Merkaba, 25, 125
Mamṣi/nimṣa, 190
Maskim, 27, 195
Masses, 14, 15, 16, 188
Mathematics, 104
Matter, primeval 124
Memra, 54. *See also* Logos
Meqayyem, 26, 27
Merkaba, 18, 19, 25, 31, 38, 125, 178, 199, 201, 205, 206, 219. *See also* *Ma'aśe Merkaba*
Metamorphosis, 7, 16, 19, 84, 147
Metaphor, 111
Metaphysics, 103, 105, 106, 107
Meṭaṭron, 48, 50, 51
Middat ha-din, 86
Middat ha-raḥamim, 86
Miracles 13, 115, 124, 131
Mirror, 75, 76, 78, 80
Miṣva, miṣvot, 11, 154
Mithappekhet, 193
Modus sciendi, 92
Monolatry, 11, 188
Monotheism, 8, 11, 17, 18, 20, 89, 93, 141, 151
Moses, 2, 21, 30, 114, 125, 141, 145, 147, 155, 156, 166, 179; articulates commandments, 149, 150; delighting in Divine vision, 38; establishes calendar, 143; glancing at the Divine, 50, 77; inspired to save Hebrew slave, 79; and prophecy, 69, 74, 75; represents human perfection, 165; as servant of God, 175; *sid* of sages, 109; Sinaitic experience, 148, 150; speaks with God, 123; and *speclaria*, 75
Mutakallimun, 63, 64, 66, 71, 94, 98, 100, 117, 119; Jewish, 97. *See also* Kalam
Mysticism, mystical, 5, 6, 18, 24, 29, 30, 31, 32, 33, 34, 82, 141, 174, 184, 196; Hebrew, 1, 4; illumination, 2, 17, 160, 161, 162; light, 54
Myth, myths, mythical: man, 139, 157; thinking, 9, 15, 66, 80, 98, 138, 141, 165, 168; time, 145
Mythology, mythological, 1, 4, 13, 14, 63, 122, 125, 135, 142, 143, 147, 150, 154, 156, 157, 158; deities, 12, 13, 89, 141, 146; discourse, 59; society, 145, 167

Naḥash, 59
Nature, 5, 80, 91, 92, 95, 101–2, 113, 116, 172; random, 63–64; statistical character of, 115
Necessary, 112
Neurosis, 18, 132, 219
New Moon, 143
Nissayon, 156, 157, 158, 161
Nomos, 66
Now, 2, 25
Numinous, 4, 14, 38, 94
Neurosis, 18, 132

Objectivity, 1, 14, 28, 33, 35, 41, 100, 110, 111
Oedipal: relations, 5; scholarship, x; structure 185
Oedipus complex, 189
Omnipotence of thought, 5, 82
Ontology, ix, 137, 146
Opinion, 21, 45, 58, 96, 97, 98, 100, 102, 103, 106, 110, 113, 117, 122, 124, 178, 179
Orchard, 35, 36, 37, 38, 39, 41. *See also* Pardes

Pagan civilization, 9, 16, 18, 66. *See also* Imagination, Pagan humanity
Pagan humanity, 10, 16, 59, 72, 98, 105, 122, 125, 131, 139, 142, 147, 151, 155, 163, 239. *See also* Imagination, Pagan civilization
Paleologic man, 62
Paleologic thought, 64, 67, 80, 211
Palingenesis, 137, 142
Parade, mental, 203
Paradise, 5, 38, 60, 80
Paradox, 6, 22, 23, 46, 177, 178
Parashat Derakhim, 46
Pardes, 35, 82, 83, 84, 180. *See also* Orchard
Parergon, 49, 51, 68
Pathological retrogression, 59
Perfection, 76, 168, 169, 175; Hebrew, 17. *See also* Moses

Person, 4, 5, 7, 16, 46, 50, 69, 76, 106, 133, 134, 148, 150, 160, 166, 176
Petiha, patah, 25, 26, 36, 37
Philosophers, 17, 23, 42, 66, 73, 92, 95, 102, 105, 106, 107, 109, 118, 122, 124, 165, 177, 178
Phylogenetic experience, 150, 219
Physics, 103, 104, 105, 106, 107, 115, 117, 118, 120; laws, 115; physical phenomena, 62, 95, 105, 116, 117
Piyuṭ, 66
Poetry, 66, 111
Political leadership, 65, 66, 108, 164
Political organization, 174
Political system, 66
Polytheism, 4, 89, 141, 165
Possible, 112
Prayer, 4, 26, 33, 54, 86, 130, 144, 171, 172
Pre-Seth humanoids, 129
Prime mover, 98, 99, 101, 112, 113, 114, 118, 119, 121
Primeval substance, 120, 123–25
Probability, 112, 113, 114, 115, 118, 154
Progress, 2, 5, 35, 126, 151
Prophecy, prophets, 4, 5, 16, 17, 20, 22, 34, 38, 42, 43, 56, 69, 70, 72, 73, 74, 75, 76, 78, 79, 82, 83, 94, 98, 99, 105, 109, 110, 111, 119, 121, 125, 126, 138, 139, 145, 147, 148, 149, 150, 165, 167, 168, 173, 174, 176, 177; and love of God 13, 158, 170, 242; authority, 120; false 133
Protological projections, 4, 121, 163
Psyche, collective, 16, 18, 134; Jewish 159
Psychological suppression, 133
Public, general, 166–67

Qabbala, 28
Qaddish, 114
Qadosh, 87
Qedusha, 86, 87
Qiddush, 144
Qiyas, 107, 123
Qodesh, 37, 87

Rabbani, 42, 43, 97
Rabbinic: dissertations, 25; doctrine, 13, 38, 46, 58, 124, 128, 129, 147, 151, 154, 156, 179, 188, 218, 233; initiation, 24; literature, 24, 25, 26, 31, 35, 38, 40, 42, 45, 50, 54, 72, 155, 176, 193, 197, 235; period, 3, 159; system, 111, 112; tradition, 6, 11, 27, 40, 86, 115, 143, 144, 157, 176, 179, 196, 216, 220. *See also* Esoteric
Rabrebaya, 108
Rashe peraqim, 6, 7, 24
Rational, 1, 15, 16, 48, 61, 62, 69, 72, 73, 75, 77, 80, 81, 82, 83, 85, 94, 98, 102, 111, 112, 123, 138, 139, 140, 153, 159, 164, 165, 167, 169
Rayyis, 107, 108, 109, 122, 123, 126
Red heifer, 152, 153, 154
Reflexive condition, 76
Religion, 9, 10, 11, 12, 14, 15, 58, 59, 66, 94, 95, 96, 97, 98, 99, 100, 122, 142, 151, 157; cosmic 3, 4
Revelation, 4, 5, 13, 14, 31, 50, 51, 53, 55, 76, 86, 99, 122, 133, 139, 140, 161, 162; pagan, 143
Rituals, 7, 10, 11, 46, 66, 142, 147, 148, 152, 163, 171
Rosh maḥol, 85, 173
Ruwaḥ ha-Qodesh, 74, 82, 84

Sabbath, Jewish, 144
Sabeans, 122, 123, 168
Sacramental sacrifices, 152
Ṣafra, 154
Sage, sages, 8, 25, 26, 27, 47, 56, 83
Salvation, 167, 168
Sanctuary, 35, 37, 38, 39, 55, 74, 82. *See also* Temple
Satan, 62, 137, 138, 202
Savior, 230
'Seeing as', 59, 60. *See also* Transferance
Scientific, 4, 13, 14, 15, 64, 65, 68, 71, 92, 101, 102, 104, 105, 106, 126; knowledge, 103, 110, 120
Semiological entity, 101
Semiological system, 61, 62, 67
Sensus communis, 61
Sex, 16, 67, 203
Shabbat Bereshit, 144
Shamayim, 110, 111, 227
Shedim, 127, 128, 129, 132, 151
Shekhina, 38, 54, 129, 171, 203, 218
Shi'ur Qoma, 29
Sid, 109
Silence, 6, 14, 22, 23, 44, 45, 46, 51, 52, 84, 177, 193, 198, 199, 207
Silent voice, 207
Sinai, 4, 11, 16, 131, 137, 139, 140, 141, 142, 143, 145, 146, 147, 148, 149, 150, 158, 159, 161
Sinaitic experience, 144, 148, 150
Sinaitic theophany, 131, 137, 139, 140, 142, 143, 145, 146, 147, 149, 158
Skepticism, 25, 103, 105, 146
Snake, 59, 65, 80, 137, 138, 147; slime of primeval, 16, 142
Sod, Sodot, 43, 87, 167
Space-time continuum, 142, 143

Speclaria, 75
Statistics, 112, 113, 115, 116, 118
Subjectivity, 1, 4, 5, 33, 34, 35, 38, 41, 47, 52, 84, 120
Substance, primeval, 120, 123, 125
Suffering, 160, 161, 162. *See also* Imagination
Supreme reality, 3, 5, 139
Synthetic unit, 68, 75

Tabernacle, 8, 14, 201, 202, 216, 223. *See also* Temple
Talmid ḥakhamim, 24, 46
Talmid vatiq, 27
Talqin, 6
Taqlid, 57, 120, 123, 140
Tarjiḥ, 118, 120, 122, 123, 125
Tawṭiyat, 244
Ṭayyel, 37, 38
Tefillin, 187
Temple, 10, 31, 37, 38, 39, 40, 54, 121, 152
Temuna, 75, 76, 77, 78, 79
Ṭeraqlin, 197
Teshuba, 80, 168
Theocentric, theocentricism, 3, 5, 121, 161, 172
Theologians, 14, 15, 63, 94, 95, 96, 98. *See also* Mutakallimun
Theology 4, 5, 20, 43, 44, 79, 80, 82, 83, 95, 103
Time: chronological, 143; created 229; cyclical 143, 167; extratemporal 143, 145; linear 144, 157, 168
Tora, 3, 7, 9, 10, 13, 16, 17, 28, 29, 30, 33, 35, 36, 40, 41, 42, 43, 45, 47, 51, 54, 55, 58, 109, 110, 122, 125, 130, 137, 147, 149, 156, 157, 158, 159, 167, 168, 171, 172, 173, 179, 180; aims of, 28, 104, 155, 166; strategy of, 8, 98, 99, 150, 151, 153, 164, 165, 166, 205
Traces, 13, 14, 16, 131, 132, 133, 134, 135, 137, 139, 147, 151, 154, 156, 159, 163; of pagan past, 152, 155
Tradition, authentic, 108. *See also* Taqlid
Transference, 58, 59, 60, 66, 194
Tree of knowledge, 137, 138
Tree of life, 137, 138
Troglodytes, 16, 127

Unconscious, 133, 135, 136, 137, 139
Universe, vastness, 122
Upper chamber, 31, 37, 38, 39, 41, 201, 202, 203

Verisimilitude, 102
Verum/factum, 92
Vestigium pedi, 14
Via negativa, 5, 20, 82, 83
Violence, 61, 62, 94, 96, 97, 99, 128, 167, 222
Volition, 13, 98, 112, 113

Water, 40, 64, 91, 152, 153
Will, 2, 3, 6, 7, 8, 13, 14, 15, 17, 18, 19, 21, 23, 24, 32, 33, 34
Wissenschaft des Judentums, x
Worship, intellectual, 169, 170, 171, 172, 173, 175

Yalad, 129
YHWH, 4, 85, 86, 140, 141, 149. *See also* Elohim
Yeser ha-ra', 9, 62, 137, 138,159
Yeser ha-tob, 138

Ze, 84, 85, 86

www.ingramcontent.com/pod-product-compliance
Lightning Source LLC
Chambersburg PA
CBHW011950150426
43195CB00018B/2877
* 9 7 8 0 8 1 5 6 2 7 8 1 4 *